CRITICAL SURVEY OF LONG FICTION

French Novelists

Editor

Carl Rollyson
Baruch College, City University of New York

SALEM PRESS
Ipswich, Massachusetts • Hackensack, New Jersey

Cover photo:
Simone de Beauvoir (© Eric Preau/Corbis)

Copyright © 2012, by Salem Press, A Division of EBSCO Publishing, Inc.
All rights in this book are reserved. No part of this work may be used or reproduced in any manner whatsoever or transmitted in any form or by any means, electronic or mechanical, including photocopy, recording, or any information storage and retrieval system, without written permission from the copyright owner. For information, contact the publisher, EBSCO Publishing, 10 Estes Street, Ipswich, MA 01938.

978-1-4298-3690-6

CONTENTS

Contributors iv

French Long Fiction to the 1850's. 1
French Long Fiction Since the 1850's 21

Honoré de Balzac. 41
Simone de Beauvoir 56
Albert Camus. 66
Jean Cocteau 82
Cyrano de Bergerac 92
Alexandre Dumas, *père* 104
Anatole France 119
Julien Green 131
Victor Hugo 142
Marcel Proust 157
François Rabelais 185
Jean-Jacques Rousseau 194
George Sand. 203
Jean-Paul Sartre 217
Jules Verne 228
Voltaire 242

Bibliography 259
Glossary of Literary Terms 262
Guide to Online Resources 274
Category Index 279
Subject Index 281

CONTRIBUTORS

Cynthia A. Bily
Adrian, Michigan

Edmund J. Campion
University of Tennessee

J. Madison Davis
Original Contributor

Lillian Doherty
Original Contributor

Irma M. Kashuba
Original Contributor

Rebecca Kuzins
Pasadena, California

Avril S. Lewis
Original Contributor

Charles E. May
California State University, Long Beach

Laurence W. Mazzeno
Alvernia College

John C. O'Neal
Original Contributor

David B. Parsell
Furman University

Carole Deering Paul
Original Contributor

Murray Sachs
Original Contributor

Jan St. Martin
Original Contributor

John K. Saunders
Original Contributor

Lucy M. Schwartz
Original Contributor

Brian Stableford
Reading, England

Sonja G. Stary
Original Contributor

James A. Winders
Appalachian State University

French Long Fiction to the 1850's

The roots of French fiction run deep in France's history, from the medieval epic *chansons de geste* and *romans*, or "romances," of the late medieval period to the Renaissance and early modern periods, when the novel in its modern form began to emerge. Storytelling is fundamental to human life, and certainly the French are no exception to this rule. Stories can be told in verse, as in French epic poems and great tragedies and comedies for the stage; prose chronicles and histories also share a storytelling function, but they promise their readers "truth," not fiction, even when employing the technical devices of prose fiction writing. Long fiction in France, as in other Western societies, found its métier in the novel, and it is the story of the novel's rise to prominence and popularity among critics and the reading public alike that necessarily forms the central focus of this survey. While to modern readers the novel's place in literature is beyond dispute, the reasons for its emergence, development, and survival are varied and complex.

In English, the distinction between novel and novella is easier to grasp than in French; short fiction means the short story, and a novella represents some sort of halfway mark between a story and a full-fledged novel. The French word *roman* means simply "novel" to the modern reader, but its original usage conveyed instead the sense of "romance," a literary genre lacking what are now taken to be some of the novel's central features, even if certain conventions can be said to have survived. In the eighteenth century, when the novel was coming increasingly into its own, the philosophe Denis Diderot (1713-1784), in a glowing appreciation of the novels of Samuel Richardson, complained of the unfortunate connotations of *roman* and argued that a different word needed to be found for Richardson's novels.

As for "novella," the French *nouvelle*, which serves today as that word's equivalent, originally meant something other than a short novel. In the sixteenth and seventeenth centuries, *nouvelles* were more akin to short factual reports and were linked to what is now thought of as historical writing. This, in turn, points to a state of confusion concerning the relationship between novels and histories—*chroniques* or *histories*—confusion that occasionally resurfaces when contemporary historians debate the merits of employing novelistic techniques in their writing or perhaps express grudging envy for a best-selling "popular" historian whose books "read like novels."

In addition, both the English "novel" and the French *nouvelle* convey an obvious sense of something new—that is, novel. To eighteenth century French anglophiles, such as Diderot, who no doubt believed that they were witnessing the development of a unique new genre, the English word must have seemed more propitious than the French *roman*.

The novel, then, has evolved in France and elsewhere into a genre marked by certain conventions and formal characteristics. Yet even while pointing to the distinctiveness of the novel, one cannot lose sight of its kinship with earlier forms of storytelling and fictional narrative.

From *Chansons de Geste* to *Romans Comiques*

Today, fiction is associated with prose, but the earliest French tales appeared in verse, often in rhyming couplets. One notable thirteenth century exception to this rule was the anonymous *chante-fable* (song-fable) *Aucassin et Nicolette* (c. 1200; *Aucassin and Nicolette*, 1880), with its mixed prose and verse form. The earliest examples of the French verse epics were the tales of the great deeds of warriors and heroes known as the *chansons de geste*; the word *chansons* (songs) is a reminder of their beginnings in the oral tradition. The most famous of them, the *Chanson de Roland* (c. 1100; *The Song of Roland*, 1880), was set down by an anonymous author during the twelfth century, but it recounts deeds of the great French hero Roland from around the year 800. Despite its poetic form and its pretensions to historical accuracy, *The Song of Roland* established the idealized theme of the noble hero that would dominate French fiction until at least the seventeenth century.

The twelfth century was the period of high feudalism in France, characterized by the dominant role of the landholding aristocracy and the central importance of the Roman Catholic faith. The first works to be called *romans* were the *romans courtois* (courtly romances) of the twelfth century. The best-known author of such works was Chrétien de Troyes (c. 1135-c. 1183). His *romans courtois* featured idealized knights and aristocratic figures of court society, much like the personae of Arthurian legend. Similar to the songs of the Provençal troubadours, the *romans courtois* were composed of octosyllabic lines and rhyming couplets.

The most important romance of the thirteenth century was *Le Roman de la rose* (thirteenth century; *The Romance of the Rose*, 1846) of Guillaume de Lorris (c. 1215-c. 1278) and Jean de Meung (c. 1240-1305), a long epic poem that extolled modes of feminine conduct befitting the Cult of the Virgin, the increased preoccupation with the legend of the Virgin Mary in the popular religion of the day, a concern that complemented some of the themes of courtly love. As latter-day feminist scholars and others have been able to appreciate acutely, these idealized literary treatments of women not only masked the reality of their oppression but also participated directly in that oppression.

The late Middle Ages also saw the rise in importance of urban commercial centers on a limited scale. A bourgeois, or merchant, class played a vital cultural role in the towns and served as the audience for a newer form of literature, known as bourgeois or "realistic." *Fabliaux* (the word is of Breton or Norman origin), or "fables," were the chosen form of this new literature in the thirteenth and fourteenth centuries and, by featuring nonaristocratic characters, served to broaden the representational scope of French fiction. If the connotations of words such as "bourgeois" or "realistic" were far from positive, they nevertheless prefigured the later sense of those terms as applied to the novelistic treatment of recognizable figures placed within a familiar social landscape, even if such characters in the *fabliaux* are more often to be found in improbable situations.

Despite the popular trend, there was in the late Middle Ages at least one important aristocratic use of prose in the official chronicles of such beneficiaries of royal patronage as

Jean Froissart (c. 1337-c. 1404), remembered for his *Chroniques de France, d'Engleterre, d'Éscose, de Bretaigne, d'Espaigne, d'Italie, de Flandres et d'Alemaigne* (1373-1410; *Chronicles*, 1523-1525) of the Hundred Years' War. This work serves as a reminder that, as far as the upper classes were concerned, the function of prose narrative was to supply historical chronicles, recording the deeds of actual historical personages in a favorable light. For many centuries to come, notions of "great literature" required the use of verse, as in the more valued genres of epic poetry and drama.

In the fifteenth and sixteenth centuries, French artistic and cultural life shared in the world of the Renaissance, deriving originally from the Humanism of Florence in the age of the Medicis. The aged Leonardo da Vinci spent his last years as the guest of the French king Francis I at the latter's château at Amboise, and this act of hospitality is symbolic of the interest taken in Italian Humanism by the arbiters of French cultural taste. The Renaissance in France was a great age for poetry and for both Neoplatonic and Neo-Aristotelian philosophy. Prose fiction realized a much smaller output. For that matter, the first of the two important French authors of fiction during this period derived her style and subject matter almost exclusively from Italian sources. That author was Marguerite d'Angoulême de Navarre (1492-1549), or Marguerite de Navarre, whose collection of seventy-two stories, known as *L'Heptaméron* (1559; *The Heptameron*, 1959), was heavily modeled on Giovanni Boccaccio's *Decameron: O, Prencipe Galetto* (1349-1351; *The Decameron*, 1620) and shared that work's tendencies toward the ribald. This similarity is worth mentioning, especially as a reminder that for centuries, salacious and erotic details and themes were thought to be the unavoidable tendencies of prose fiction, which thus by definition could never rise to the heights of eloquence and moral example to be gained from the more idealized genres of poetry and drama, especially great tragedy. The mimetic tendency of fiction to represent realities that aristocratic culture depended on literature to obscure was thus suspected early in the history of the novel, although it was not until the nineteenth century that this lifelikeness was to be celebrated as the ultimate goal of fiction.

This observation provides a fitting point at which to take up the achievement and significance of the second great French Renaissance author of fiction, one of the world's most entertaining and outrageous storytellers: François Rabelais (1490-1553). While the original sense of Humanism derived from the effort pioneered in Florence to cull from ancient writings exemplary models of moral and civic conduct to be applied to contemporary life, Rabelais represents the later expanded sense of Humanism as the appreciation of and even delight in all things human, including the coarsest details of bodily activity. It is this latter tendency by which most readers have known Rabelais over the centuries. In 1532, Rabelais, a Benedictine monk and physician, published *Pantagruel* (English translation 1653), following it two years later with *Gargantua* (English translation 1653). It was not until after Rabelais's death that the two were published together as *Gargantua et Pantagruel* (1532-1564; *Gargantua and Pantagruel*, 1653-1694, 1929). Ever since, Rabelais's masterwork has stood as one of the most ambitious, sprawling, and encyclopedic tales in Western literature, rivaling Dante's *La divina commedia* (c. 1320; *The Divine Comedy*, 1802) and James Joyce's *Ulysses* (1922) in its will to comprehensiveness. Fusing epochal synthesis with humor, *Gargantua and Pantagruel*, like Dante's and Joyce's works, encapsulates much of the cultural activity and controversy of its age.

"Tall tale" best captures for an American reader the sense of the surface narrative found in this book. Gargantua and Pantagruel are portrayed as giants, with character traits writ equally large. Indeed, the adjective "gargantuan" enshrines the Rabelaisian penchant for exaggeration. The giants, father and son respectively, are given grandiose characteristics, qualities, and appetites. Accordingly, they find themselves in outlandish situations that allow Rabelais to exploit their inherent excessiveness to rich comic effect. The result, for generations of critical readers, has been to rule this book out of bounds in discussions of the novel, one of whose chief characteristics is assumed to be believable characters of everyday proportions. Alternately, the book has been interpreted as a rich expression of the "carnivalesque" spirit of the folk culture of Rabelais's time. Erich Auerbach, author of perhaps the most authoritative study on the representation of reality in Western literature, treats *Gargantua and Pantagruel* in a manner more typical of a critical reading of a realist novel. In *Mimesis: The Representation of Reality in Western Literature* (1953), Auerbach focuses upon descriptive passages in which Rabelais presents a clearly recognizable world, once the fantastic premises introducing such episodes have been accepted by the reader. Such a reading differs from those that treat *Gargantua and Pantagruel* as an aberration in the French literary canon and places it instead more squarely in the novelistic tradition.

An important common characteristic of the texts mentioned thus far is that these works were not written in the modern French language, whose spelling and punctuation were not standardized until the seventeenth century. That was the achievement of the Académie Française, or French Academy, founded in 1635 by the powerful Cardinal Richelieu and charged with the immediate task of compiling a dictionary of the French language. Today, the French Academy functions more as a national honorary society for distinguished writers, yet it nevertheless retains something of its role as chief guardian of the treasure that is the national language. Its very existence might be taken as a symptom of the French compulsion toward centralization, a trend whose origins are located in the early seventeenth century period, during which the foundations of monarchical absolutism, of which Richelieu was a principal architect, were erected. Richelieu, regent to the boy king Louis XIII, undertook the establishment of more centralizing political and cultural policies. Analogous to the later national mercantilist projects of Louis XIV's finance minister, Jean-Baptiste Colbert, Richelieu's aim was not only to establish language itself, in an age in which "French" was still unknown in some regions of France, but also to establish a literary use of language on a truly national basis. For that, a learned body, or *académie*, was needed. By the end of the century—by which time Louis XIV had withdrawn, in the Revocation of the Edict of Nantes in 1685, royal toleration of religions other than Roman

Catholicism—a parallel standardization that rigidly proscribed linguistic and aesthetic activity had been imposed.

If absolutism meant the vigorous assertion of hereditary monarchy and the imposition of rigid models of linguistic and literary expression, then it is not difficult to understand that the aristocracy would be in a position to dictate rules of literary composition, theme, and style. In Richelieu's day, "preciosity" held sway as the dominant literary aesthetic. Taking shape in the fashionable salons of upper-class aficionados, preciosity complemented the baroque spirit of the early seventeenth century in its emphasis on idealized love and heroism in literature, as well as in its affection for prolixity and highly embellished language. In prose, the most memorable example of a work embracing the aesthetic code of preciosity was the enormously long novel *L'Astrée* (1607-1628; *Astrea*, 1657-1658), written by Honoré d'Urfé (1568-1625).

Astrea was a tour de force within the novelistic genre of its day, but it was a genre for which even the French authors who worked within it felt the need to apologize; after all, "novels" were not really French but were instead derived from the literary traditions of Spain. French readers had been most impressed with Miguel de Cervantes' *Don Quixote de la Mancha* (1605, 1615)) and had developed some appreciation for the picaresque tradition in Spanish fiction; many of the French *romans* that followed in the decades after *Astrea* were based heavily on this imported style. They were adventure stories, often wildly comic and improbable—*romans comiques*, as they came to be known in France. Like the picaresque heroes of the Spanish novels from which they derived, such novels featured roguelike protagonists whose misadventures perhaps best qualified them as antiheroes. Leading examples include *Histoire comique de Francion* (1623, 1632; *The Comical History of Francion*, 1655), by Charles Sorel (1597-1674), and *Roman comique* (1651, 1657; English translation, 1651, 1657; also known as *The Comical Romance*, 1665), by Paul Scarron (1610-1660). Members of the French reading public, quite small and by definition elitist in this age, enjoyed these stories but were at the same time almost embarrassed to admit it. If one considers the apologies that intellectuals of today routinely offer for watching television, one can gain some sense of the mixture of bemusement and discomfort with which readers of the seventeenth century confronted this output that they were not quite willing to call "literary."

The legacy of this more or less imported tradition was that the word *roman*, like the word "bourgeois" in this aristocratic age, came to convey a sense of something low or debased, so that when Antoine Furetière (1619-1688) published his somewhat Swiftian parody of the heroic novel called *Le Roman bourgeois* (1666; *City Romance*, 1671), the title must have seemed redundant to his contemporaries. Those who clung to an older notion of *roman* as heroic romance, on the other hand, must have regarded the title as an oxymoron, by definition a contradiction in terms. In a country less prone to elevate questions of literary style and taste to a national focus, these trends might scarcely have been heeded. Yet this was France, and under Louis XIV, its most successful absolute monarch, leading cultural figures could flourish and influence the national aesthetic life only to the degree that the royal sun beamed down upon them.

By appointing the great tragedian Jean Racine (1639-1699) and the poet-critic Nicolas Boileau-Despréaux (1636-1711) to the newly created post of royal historiographer, Louis XIV vigorously reasserted the dominant positions of classical tragedy and poetry as the genres most capable of lending radiance to his royal splendor. Just as Jacques-Bénigne Bossuet (1627-1704), one of the leading prelates of the French Church, used his sermons and theological writings to unify the nation around its king and chief defender of the faith, so Boileau, steeped in the aesthetics of neoclassicism, joined forces with the French Academy to clearly spell out the acceptable forms and styles of literary creation, most vividly in his *L'Art poétique* of 1674. Prose fiction was banished from the fold; this cultural policy had the unintended effect, while codifying rules and criteria for the use of verse, of freeing the novel and other prose fiction for experimentation and innovation, constrained only by the threat, applied intermittently, of royal censorship.

The French novel in the twilight years of the ancien régime

During the hundred years or so that transpired before the great revolution of 1789, France experienced profound cultural, social, economic, and demographic changes. The realities of these changes can be obscured by excessive emphasis on narrowly defined political history or by a tendency to assume from the shock waves of 1789 that France was a dormant country prior to that time. From the artificially sheltered, and therefore distorted, point of view of the absolutist Bourbon monarchs, the social fabric lay largely undisturbed. This was the Age of Enlightenment, the *Siècle des lumières*, when a new class of writers and social critics called philosophes advanced progressive ideas to a rapidly expanding bourgeois readership critical of the Crown and anxious to be rid of the feudal obligations and restrictions that undergirded the edifice of French absolutism. Such philosophes as Voltaire (1694-1778), Charles de Montesquieu (1689-1755), and Denis Diderot also lashed out at the Roman Catholic Church for its legacy in France of persecution and bigotry. Here, too, they found ready assent from the middle-class readers to whom they appealed.

The philosophes could count on a burgeoning readership for their tracts and treatises and for the massive multivolume *Encyclopédie: Ou, Dictionnaire raisonné des sciences, des arts, et des métiers* (1751-1772; partial translation *Selected Essays from the Encyclopedy*, 1772; complete translation *Encyclopedia*, 1965) edited by Diderot and Jean le Rond d'Alembert (1717-1783); a steadily increasing literacy rate, an increasing number of outlets and vehicles for literary activity, and a general and dramatic population increase resulting largely from the growth of a middle, or bourgeois, class were perhaps the most significant trends shaping the literary culture of this period. Population growth was itself linked to a significant decline in pestilence and other natural disasters and to an impressive expansion of the food supply. Indeed, economic growth was steady throughout the eighteenth century, although England was as yet the only country in which manufacture rather than agriculture largely set the pace.

It is estimated that the percentage of literate (defined as those who could sign their names) French people at the end of the seventeenth century was 21 percent, increasing by the end of the eighteenth century to 37 percent. Unlike England, France had to wait until the revolution to experience a real proliferation in newspapers, but they were increasing, as were broadsides and pamphlets of various kinds. By the mid-eighteenth century, the institution of the café, modeled on the British coffeehouse, had taken hold as the social setting for reading and discussing new books, periodicals, and newspapers. Voltaire and the other philosophes all experienced censorship at one time or another, and several of them, including Voltaire, knew imprisonment and exile, yet they lived to see the ban lifted and experience the sense that their ideas circulated ever more widely. The growing body of readers to whom they appealed, however, were interested in more than political treatises and satires. They read novels eagerly, and occasionally the philosophes themselves accommodated them with *contes philosophiques* (philosophical tales) and didactic novels.

Though it would occupy a more central role in the publishing world of the nineteenth century, the novel's popularity was increasingly noted by French publishers of the ancien régime. On the face of it, the "frivolous" novel would seem to have been a safer venture for a publisher than the more overtly political writings of a Voltaire, but the latter were not always more vulnerable to censorship. The world of French publishing was far from standardized in the eighteenth century, and this lack of predictability and routine provided headaches for publisher and author alike. Surely one of the publisher's major headaches was the uneven and unpredictable exercise of royal censorship. In order to operate, a publisher needed a royal license, or *privilège*, which granted him, in some cases, a monopoly in certain types of publishing, but this could easily be withdrawn on a royal whim. Apart from that major uncertainty, publishers could not be sure when they might face censorship. By definition, broad powers of censorship were in the hands of royally sanctioned provincial courts called *parlements*, of which the most important and most active was the Parlement de Paris. The institution of *parlements* reflected the increasing tendency since the age of Louis XIV for publishing to be concentrated in and around Paris itself, whereas regional centers such as Rouen and Lyons had been prominent in earlier centuries. Even the Parlement de Paris, Voltaire's great nemesis, occasionally let a "scandalous" book pass. When censorship came, however, punishment was often harsh. This fact, coupled with the pessimistic tendencies of some publishers to expect the worst from the *parlements*, led to the creation of a thriving underground publishing industry. Diderot is the best-known name associated with this illegal publishing activity.

Authors, too, faced an uncertain existence—and not merely because of the more serious threats of censorship and imprisonment. Authors' relationships with their publishers were often severely strained. To begin with, nothing resembling a modern copyright law existed in the eighteenth century. An author's name would not necessarily appear on the book, and payment was not always guaranteed. Piracy was a common problem; unscrupulous publishers were known to seize manuscripts of authors whose names could be counted upon to sell copies. Royalties were unknown. Today, an author commonly receives a fixed percentage of the price of each copy that is sold. This practice was not, however, adopted until the nineteenth century.

In the age of the philosophes, it was possible for an author to enter into an agreement whereby he would receive a fixed sum for a certain number of copies to be printed, regardless of whether they were actually sold. If the book proved popular and additional printings were run, the author received nothing. Not until nearly the end of the eighteenth century was this practice modified so that the author was paid a fixed amount on a certain quantity of copies that were actually sold, and it was well into the nineteenth century before the per-copy royalty practice was adopted. As a result of these many uncertainties, most eighteenth century authors were forced to rely on some sort of patronage from wealthy admirers and benefactors. Diderot was one of the few examples of a truly professional writer who attempted to earn a living, albeit a modest one, by his pen, and even he benefited, at least temporarily, from the royal patronage of the Russian empress Catherine the Great.

Most critics and historians of French literature reserve the adjective "great" for the novels of the nineteenth century, but within the changing eighteenth century milieu, the French novel began to come into its own. To a great extent, this can be attributed to the very exclusion pronounced by Boileau and other guardians of tradition in the preceding century. Not that the sense of shame and apology held toward the novel, even by novelists themselves, was completely dispelled in the eighteenth century, but the novel and other fictional genres were free, in a sense, to develop in an undefined new literary space: a terra incognita unglimpsed by *académiciens* and other traditionalists. The novel's proven popularity with a steadily expanding readership further undermined whatever reservations authors might have.

It has become commonplace in French literary history to assign *La Princesse de Clèves* (1678; *The Princess of Clèves*, 1679), by Madame de La Fayette (1634-1693), the position of "first" in the development of the modern French *roman*, using the argument that it embodies the essential characteristics of the genre in its modern form: recognizable, believable characters; ordinary settings; and attention to the feelings, motivations, and psychological states of the principal characters. Set in the period of the French Renaissance, La Fayette's novel nevertheless offers descriptions of scenes much more recognizable to her late seventeenth century readers. In portraying privileged court society, she adhered to the aesthetic of the more established genres but broke radically with literary tradition by translating this milieu into the novelistic realm.

Much of the interest this novel has held for readers past and present has been its presentation of a woman as the central tragic figure, coupled with the fact of its feminine authorship. The Princess is a woman caught in an intolerable situation, for she is married to a man she does not love. Though she is pursued by a would-be lover, she resists temptation as she remembers the counsel of her beloved mother with regard to the crucial importance of wifely virtue. Even her virtue goes unrecognized and unacknowledged by her husband, who torments and eventually destroys himself through suspicious jealousy. At the end of the novel, the Princess has become widowed, and, shunning the attentions of the man she would then be free to marry, she retires to a convent, remaining true to the memory of the husband she never loved.

Certainly, in one sense, *The Princess of Clèves* reaffirmed the carefully circumscribed social role available to women, even women of the privileged class. Ending her days in the convent, the Princess recalls the much earlier, prototypically tragic, figure of Héloïse. Yet La Fayette was able to portray her protagonist in such a way as to encourage empathy with her on the part of readers both male and female. As an author herself, like her aristocratic predecessor, Marguerite d'Angoulême de Navarre, La Fayette provides a case study of the relatively greater degree of freedom enjoyed by an admittedly small group of women of her era. Not merely literate but an accomplished prose stylist, La Fayette has served to illustrate Virginia Woolf's well-known claim that, if women had been permitted incomes and "rooms of their own," they would have been the ones producing the world's literature. Still, the association between a well-to-do woman and a marginally acceptable literary genre would scarcely have posed a threat to the social and sexual order of the French classical age.

While few novels of the eighteenth century in France matched *The Princess of Clèves* in attention to human psychology, most continued to examine central themes of social life, often exposing the contradictions and injustices of the social sphere to the harsh light of irony. This accords well with the project of the philosophes, and, not surprisingly, most leading philosophes tried their hand at the novel. More often, they showed little interest in extensive plot or character development, preferring to exploit the genre for didactic purposes. The typical novel or novella of the philosophes was what the French call a *roman à thèse*, or "thesis novel," like the *contes philosophiques* of Voltaire, of which *Candide* (1759; English translation, 1759) is the best-known example. In many such novels, the characters are extremely one-dimensional, mere mannequins over which the author has draped the extravagant clothing of his or her political opinions.

Occasionally, however, the philosophes made real contributions to the evolution of the novel as a genre. *Les Lettres persanes* (1721; *Persian Letters*, 1722), by Charles de Montesquieu (1689-1755), better known for his legal and juridical writings, was one such example. As a specious travel narrative, it was certainly typical of the writings of the philosophes. The text purports to be the discovered letters of a Persian sheikh, written to his homeland during a sojourn in France. He relentlessly dissects the baffling mores of the French people, much as an anthropologist might report on the customs of an isolated tribe. Naturally, this affords Montesquieu the opportunity to unleash his barbed criticism on his own society, under the ruse of claiming that this text is but a translation from the Persian.

Suffice it to say that Montesquieu could avoid censorship best and perhaps register his criticism of France most effectively by these indirect means.

Philosophes occasionally availed themselves of the time-honored devices of adventure novels, with their improbable occurrences and their cliff-hanger episodes. It became clear that such novels could accomplish their goals of social criticism more effectively by including entertainment. Voltaire's *Candide* is once again the best-known such example. The earlier picaresque form remained somewhat in vogue during the eighteenth century and was recast most memorably in the novel *Histoire de Gil Blas de Santillane* (1715-1735; *The History of Gil Blas of Santillane*, 1716, 1735, better known as *Gil Blas*, 1749, 1962), by Alain-René Lesage (1668-1747), whose reputation in his own time was established more by his plays. Lesage's debt to Cervantes and the Spanish picaresque tradition was clear. Even though the adventures of Gil Blas might strain the reader's credulity, the settings had become recognizably French. Along with *The Princess of Clèves*, *The History of Gil Blas of Santillane* helped establish the novelistic practice of constructing the plot against a more recognizable backdrop.

Another playwright who, like Lesage, tried his hand at the writing of novels was Pierre Carlet de Chamblain de Marivaux (1688-1763). Despite the fact that he never completed his *La Vie de Marianne* (1731-1741; *The Life of Marianne*, 1736-1742; also known as *The Virtuous Orphan: Or, The Life of Marianne*, 1979) or *Le Paysan parvenu* (1734-1735; *The Fortunate Peasant*, 1735), these novels have not lacked for readers, as they provide rich and complex insights into the shifting, sometimes contradictory psychological states of their introspective characters. Marivaux's characters are continually expressing confusion and indecision, prompting some contemporary critics and literary historians to cite Marivaux as an example of the kind of eighteenth century novelist who, in this embryonic period of the novel's formation, prefigures the more difficult and ambiguous texts of literary modernism.

A particularly rich evocation of psychological torment is provided by *Histoire du chevalier des Grieux et de Manon Lescaut* (1731, 1733, 1753; *Manon Lescaut*, 1734, 1786), by the Abbé Prévost (1697-1763). *Manon Lescaut* is the story of the doomed love of des Grieux for the young Manon Lescaut, who, unlike the Princess of Clèves, is the embodiment of confusion and contradiction where sexual morality is concerned. Prévost depicts his characters' emotions more vividly and with much less ambiguity than does Marivaux.

Prévost also played a central role in discussions of novelistic form based on the examples being established in England. "Anglomania" was rife in French intellectual life in the eighteenth century. The English were admired for their freedom of the press and much greater religious and social toleration. For that matter, the expression of admiration for England was developed by the philosophes into an effective indirect means of criticizing France. The eighteenth century was the age of great achievement in the English novel; the names of Jonathan Swift, Daniel Defoe, Samuel Richardson, Henry Fielding, and Laurence Sterne spring immediately to mind. Prévost championed Richardson, one of the more complex, even daunting, English novelists, and translated his *Pamela* (1740-1741) in 1742, *Clarissa* (1747-1748) in 1751, and *Sir Charles Grandison* (1753-1754) between 1755 and 1758.

Prévost opened up a debate over the place of the novel in French letters, a debate joined by a novelist named Claude Crébillon (or Crébillon, *fils*, 1707-1777), who argued for an experimental approach as the one most befitting the genre itself, developing as it was in a sort of aesthetic limbo. Societies have a way of imposing limits on experimentation, however, and Crébillon, by publishing such novels as *Le Sopha* (1740; *The Sofa*, 1742) and *Les Égarements du cœur et de l'esprit* (1736; *The Wanderings of the Heart and Mind*, 1751), was judged by his society to have overstepped those boundaries. His books were condemned, and he served a sentence in that infamous prison of the ancien régime known as the Bastille. Crébillon was a member of the scandalous group of writers and wits known as "libertines." These libertines argued for the removal of all restrictions on the enjoyment of sexual pleasure, which they saw as indispensable to intellectual freedom. This "forbidden" tradition in French intellectual life resurfaced from time to time during the eighteenth century, most notably in the notorious Marquis de Sade (1740-1814) in the years of the great French Revolution.

The philosophe who contributed most to the ongoing discussion of the novel's aesthetic was Denis Diderot, the great encyclopedist who was himself the author of several works of fiction, including the novel *La Religieuse* (1796; *The Nun*, 1797) and the novella *Le Neveu de Rameau* (1821, 1891; *Rameau's Nephew*, 1897). The latter is thought to have been written around 1773 even though it was not published until 1821. With its frank discussion of sexual morality, including equality of the sexes and the toleration of homosexuality, Diderot judged it unsuitable for publication in his lifetime. Diderot's major intervention in the critical debate over the novel came in the form of a gushing expression of admiration for the novels of the English writer Samuel Richardson. This "Éloge de Richardson" (1762) was symptomatic of the anglomania to which many French writers were prey, yet Diderot went so far as to argue that Richardson's achievement constituted a radical break with earlier traditions in prose fiction. Richardson had ennobled the new genre, Diderot argued, but the connotations of the French word *roman* prevented people from realizing it. Diderot called for a search for a new word in the French language to designate the new "novel." Given Diderot's stature, this essay has had an unfortunate impact on later French criticism and literary history, creating a serious, though recently somewhat corrected, undervaluation of earlier works such as *The Princess of Clèves*.

If Diderot was perhaps the most representative of the philosophes, his contemporary Jean-Jacques Rousseau (1712-1778) was far less typical. While Rousseau joined with other philosophes in criticizing the monarchy and the injustices of the ancien régime and, like Diderot and Voltaire, produced a large body of writings of various types and genres, he sharply condemned the artificiality and aridity of the intellectual climate of his day. His one great novel, *Julie: Ou, La Nouvelle Héloïse* (1761; *Eloise: Or, A Series of Original*

Letters, 1761; also known as *Julie: Or, The New Eloise*, 1968; better known as *The New Héloïse*), exemplified his project of exhorting his contemporaries to abandon "polite" society to find true meaning and redemption in the natural world. *The New Héloïse* is suitably steeped in what would come to be called the Romantic attitude toward nature, and the story of Julie is extravagantly sentimental. Julie is presented to the reader as the paragon of feminine virtue, a "new Héloïse," recalling the devotion of Héloïse to Abélard. The source of her virtue, glimpsed through her unaffected personality, is her contact with nature. This heroine's "nature," however, turns out to be most typically expressed in her subservience toward her husband and serves as a reminder that Rousseau, who was widely and enthusiastically read by women as well as men, helped influence the strong reassertion of the patriarchal family put firmly in place by the later revolutionary and Napoleonic eras. It is one of the tragic ironies of this complicated genius that Rousseau, the "apostle of liberty," should have contributed so substantially to the tradition of modern misogyny.

Rousseau was a celebrated iconoclast, but other contemporary writers shared affinities with him, though his reputation has tended to relegate them to the shadows. One writer who should be mentioned in any survey of eighteenth century French fiction is Jacques-Henri Bernardin de Saint-Pierre (1737-1814). He was the author of a long and little-read work called *Études de la nature* (1784; *Studies of Nature*, 1796), which nevertheless contained the influential novella *Paul et Virginie* (1787; *Paul and Mary*, 1789; also known as *Paul and Virginia*, 1795). Rousseauesque in its natural settings and extreme sentimentality, *Paul and Virginia* became an important part of the stream of exoticism in modern French culture. One of the defining characteristics of Romanticism, this taste for the exotic was also manifested in the late nineteenth century novels of Pierre Loti (1850-1923) and paintings by Paul Gauguin (1848-1903) and Henri Rousseau (1844-1910).

The suppressed current of "libertinism" was to surface again in French fiction in the last years of the Bourbon monarchy and the heady early days of the French Revolution, before the austere Maximilien de Robespierre (1758-1794) imposed a Cromwellian "republic of virtue" on the infant French Republic in 1793. Thus, it is perhaps not surprising that one of the most notorious of the libertines, Nicolas Restif de la Bretonne (1734-1806), wrote both borderline pornographic novels and utopian political tracts. Restif de la Bretonne was a salacious fetishist whose most memorable novel is *Le Paysan perverti* (1776; *The Corrupted Ones*, 1967) and who, like the great utopian socialist Charles Fourier (1772-1837) whom he somewhat resembles, called for the establishment of a utopian community featuring, among other things, gratification of the most minutely specific forms of sexual pleasure.

Restif de la Bretonne's works are seldom read today, but one of the most famous libertine novels, *Les Liaisons dangereuses* (1782; *Dangerous Acquaintances*, 1784; also known as *Dangerous Liaisons*, 1962), by Pierre Choderlos de Laclos (1741-1803), has gained more and more readers in subsequent centuries. Laclos was a well-known libertine who later served under Napoleon Bonaparte. His contemporaries thought the book pornographic, but *Dangerous Liaisons* has been interpreted according to other criteria by later critics. An important example of the epistolary tradition in French fiction, *Dangerous Liaisons* consists entirely of letters circulated among four principal characters. Like Lovelace in Richardson's *Clarissa* (which may have served as a model for Laclos), the fictional authors of these letters attempt, successfully, to use them as vehicles for actual seduction. With a mixture of candor and dissimulation, they probe their shifting psychological states, attempting to register love's complicated emotional impact. The achievement of Laclos has been likened in this regard to the much later poems of Charles Baudelaire (1821-1867) and the great novel of Marcel Proust (1871-1922) in its contribution to the psychology of love. The aspects of *Dangerous Liaisons* that scandalized the late eighteenth century public would today be far from shocking.

The same cannot be said for the brutally sordid novels of the Marquis de Sade (1740-1814), whose books retain the ability to offend the modern reader. This author, who spent a significant portion of his life as a prisoner of King Louis XVI in the Bastille and, after the destruction of that hated symbol of royal oppression, in the asylum at Charenton (where he died), adhered to a philosophical outlook dominated by the central concept of evil. In such books as *Justine* (1791; English translation, 1889) and *Les 120 Journées de Sodome* (1904; *The 120 Days of Sodom*, 1954), he relentlessly and dispassionately cataloged the varieties of the human capacity for evil, including bestiality and the "sadism" that serves as a constant reminder of Sade's name. Perhaps these preoccupations can be likened to the taxonomic effort of eighteenth century biologists or, as Roland Barthes (1915-1980) suggested, to the massive effort evident in the theological writings of Saint Ignatius Loyola or the utopian writings of Fourier; less justifiable is the facile equation of some sort of Sadean "sexual revolution" with the political and social upheaval of the French Revolution.

Likewise, the relationship between Romanticism and the political events from 1789 through Napoleon's rule (1799-1814) has been exaggerated, at least with regard to French Romantic literature. This error is somewhat akin to the overestimation of the role played by the ideas of the philosophes in the revolutionary era. This is not to say that no link may be demonstrated. Certainly the spirit of Voltaire, Rousseau, and others was invoked by the revolutionaries themselves. Just as certainly, significant Romantic poets, composers, and artists celebrated the coming of the revolution, even if its excesses later prompted some of them to repudiate it. At the time most of the events of the period from 1789 to 1814 took place, however, the Romantics who commented on them were for the most part not French. Romanticism in literature, music, and the visual arts was late in coming to France, partly because of the heroic classicism embraced by the Napoleonic regime and partly because the French identified Romanticism with Germany and England. Only after nearly running its course in those countries did Romanticism enter the main currents of French literature; once Romanticism arrived in France, however, it put down very deep roots.

Romanticism and Early Nineteenth Century French Novels

The seeds of Romanticism were sown to a great extent within the Enlightenment period that preceded the Romantic age, most obviously in the writings of Rousseau. Rousseau's influence on English and German Romantics was considerable, but the full-blown Romanticism that developed in those traditions reentered France by a circuitous route. Matters were complicated by the political and military upheaval of the quarter of a century, roughly, that transpired from the advent of the French Revolution to the defeat of Napoleon. European Romantics had been divided in their support for the French Revolution and likewise divided into groups expressing either admiration or contempt for Napoleon Bonaparte. Occasionally, this division became manifest within the same person, as in the example of the composer Ludwig van Beethoven (1770-1827), who moved sharply from adoration to hatred for the man he came to see as a tyrant. The story of the growing Romanticism in French literature during the last years of Napoleon's rule is further complicated by its mediation by writers such as Chateaubriand (1768-1848), who enjoyed official approval, as well as by Madame de Staël (1766-1817), denounced by the Bonapartist regime.

Be that as it may, clear distinctions can be made between Romanticism and the Enlightenment outlook that preceded it. The philosophes had stressed universal attributes and qualities, whereas Romantics savored the unique and the particular. Philosophes had championed the rational mind's capabilities, but Romantics asserted the claims of the heart and such alternatives to rational consciousness as dreams and the mysterious processes of the creative imagination. Romantics elevated the role of the suffering creative genius marked by his alienation from others—something of a repudiation of the philosophe's self-appointed role as crusader on behalf of his fellow human beings. The Enlightenment interpretation of history, inseparable from an ongoing propaganda war against the claims of the Church, had demanded the total discrediting of the Middle Ages as a backward age of superstition and hysteria, but many leading Romantics rehabilitated Christianity and celebrated the medieval period as a rich and poetic age of faith and imagination.

The lonely, questing spirit of the troubled Romantic protagonist emerges from the pages of two of the earliest French Romantic novels: *Obermann* (1804; English translation, 1910-1914), by Étienne de Senancour (1770-1846), and *Adolphe* (1816; English translation, 1816), by Benjamin Constant (1767-1830). Indeed, the title *Obermann* is certain to evoke for readers of today the "overman" (*Übermensch*) of Friedrich Nietzsche (1884-1900), a philosopher sometimes viewed as one whose work represents a late nineteenth century revival of Romantic themes. Senancour's novel seems more akin to an early, somewhat pre-Romantic style of German literature known as Sturm und Drang (storm and stress). The great Johann Wolfgang von Goethe (1749-1832) and Friedrich Schiller (1759-1805) had been the leading writers of this movement, and *Obermann* is strikingly similar to Goethe's *Die Leiden des jungen Werthers* (1774; *The Sorrows of Young Werther*, 1779).

Both *Obermann* and *The Sorrows of Young Werther* are notable examples of the epistolary novel. Senancour's work is a compilation of eighty-nine letters that, like the letters of Werther, portray their fictional author's turbulent emotional life. Like Goethe, Senancour presents a protagonist suffering from Romantic *Weltschmerz* combined with a sense of being isolated and overwhelmed by life; *mal du siècle* is the French phrase that was eventually adopted to denote this state of the soul. Constant's *Adolphe* continues this theme as well, and Adolphe's life unfolds in the novel along the lines of what Goethe and others have called a bildungsroman (a development novel, the story of the successive stages of a character's life through childhood, education, adolescence, and the entry into the adult world).

While these novelists made no particular issue of their debt to German literature, the French writer who campaigned most tirelessly on behalf of the examples set by German Romantics was perhaps the most famous European woman of the Napoleonic age: Madame de Staël (1766-1817). Acquainted with most of the leading writers of Continental Europe and especially partial to German writers (which is notable for the usually ethnocentric world of French letters), Madame de Staël became deeply interested in differences among national literatures. She avoided, however, the growing tendency in early nineteenth century culture to imagine some separate realm called "literature," divorced from specific historical and social contexts. Her great critical work, *De la littérature considérée dans ses rapports avec les institutions sociales* (1800; *A Treatise on Ancient and Modern Literature*, 1803; also known as *The Influence of Literature upon Society*, 1813), anticipated the day when twentieth century critics such as Lucien Goldmann (1913-1970) would call for the establishment of a sociology of literature. De Staël also argued vigorously for drastic improvement in the status of women, a stance that earned her the detestation of Napoleon Bonaparte, whose repressive *Code Napoléon* (1804) had legitimated a reactionary patriarchal sexual hierarchy. Her novels *Delphine* (1802; English translation, 1803) and *Corinne: Ou, L'Italie* (1807; *Corinne: Or, Italy*, 1807) feature strong, superior women who encounter the idiotic obstacles of sexual discrimination; the autobiographical element in them is pronounced.

If de Staël was the thorn in Bonaparte's side, Chateaubriand (1768-1848), devoutly Roman Catholic and Bonapartist, was almost the empire's poet laureate. Nobly handsome in a manner reminiscent of the English Romantic poet Lord Byron, with an ego of equally Byronic proportions, François-René de Chateaubriand nevertheless irked Bonaparte as something of a rival claimant to his mystique, or charisma. Chateaubriand made his mark with *Le Génie du Christianisme* (1799, 1800, 1802; *The Genius of Christianity*, 1802), the most substantial contribution to the Romantic project of restoring Christianity to its central cultural role. Themes of Christian faith and inspiration continued throughout Chateaubriand's long literary career, from *Les Martyres* (1809; *The Martyrs*, 1812) to *La Vie de Rancé* (1844; the life of Rancé). At the same time, the religious emphasis was worked in with the standard Romantic theme of the isolated creative genius who, by definition, cannot thrive in conventional human society. For example, *La Vie de Rancé* glorifies the extreme solitude of monastic life.

French Romanticism found one of its greatest champions in its most acclaimed writer of the nineteenth century, Victor Hugo (1802-1885), whose early plays and poetry exemplified the more dominant role Romanticism came to play in the years from 1815 to 1848. His celebrated novel *Notre-Dame de Paris* (1831; *The Hunchback of Notre Dame*, 1833) provides perhaps the best example outside the English novels of Sir Walter Scott of the Romantic fascination with the Middle Ages. However, Hugo was to live and write well beyond the limits of Romanticism in France, and his later novels owe more to realism and the increased stature realized by the French novel in the first half of the nineteenth century. Romantic attitudes continued to play a role in French literature but lost ground as the novel came more and more to eclipse other literary genres for the French reading public.

The golden age of the French novel: Balzac to Flaubert, 1829-1857

After the downfall of Napoleon, France attempted to reenter the ancien régime for a time. The Bourbon monarchy was revived, with Louis XVIII occupying the throne from 1814 to 1824 and Charles X, the last Bourbon king, reigning thereafter until 1830. Prerevolutionary France was a lost world that could not genuinely be revived. The bourgeoisie continued to expand and longed to reclaim the promise of property rights affirmed by the French Republic. France lagged behind England in the Industrial Revolution, but industrialization was under way, adding impetus to the bourgeois drive for recognition and enfranchisement. In 1830, the rebellion in Paris forced Charles X into exile, and Louis-Philippe, the Duc d'Orléans, formed a government that came to be known as the July Monarchy, in honor of the revolutionary events that ended the Bourbon monarchy.

Louis-Philippe originally enjoyed the support of the middle class but continually postponed real reforms and frustrated bourgeois hopes. A more decisive uprising followed in 1848, precipitating a general European rebellion in major capitals that Karl Marx (1818-1883) and Friedrich Engels (1820-1895) were briefly tempted to interpret as the opening chapter of the universal proletarian revolution they envisioned. France became a republic once again, but, after an interlude marked by constitutional wrangling and class division leading at one point to massacres in working-class neighborhoods of Paris, Louis Bonaparte, recapitulating his celebrated uncle's coup of 1799, seized control of the government in December, 1851. Not long afterward, he proclaimed the Second Empire, which lasted until 1870.

France thus experienced, during the first half of the nineteenth century, major episodes of revolution and rebellion, as well as the first wave of changes wrought by industrialization. These memorable and traumatic events, the stuff of heroic paintings by such artists as Eugène Delacroix (1798-1863), awakened the French people to an acute sense of history. Perhaps more than any other European nation, France entered into consciousness of what was to become one of the central preoccupations of nineteenth century culture: historical time and its transformations. The modern study of history was in fact a nineteenth century invention, and among its greatest practitioners was the great French historian Jules Michelet (1798-1874).

Novels, like works of history, depend on the accumulation of successive stages and episodes in the lives of their characters. Narrative has traditionally been seen as indispensable respectively to long fiction and historical writing. As far back as the seventeenth century, when it was possible for a poet to occupy the post of royal historiographer, confusion had been registered over the possible distinction between a *roman* and an *histoire*. The nineteenth century novel proved to be the literary genre most capable of nurturing, in the century of geology, morphology, and Darwinian evolution, this new consciousness of chronology, bringing to its readers the dramatic sweep of historical transformations.

The transformations visited upon French society by an emergent industrial capitalist economy, if not yet of the magnitude of those transformations observed in Britain in the same period, nevertheless increasingly became the focus of critical social commentary. As in England, the novel came to be regarded as the genre best suited to the demanding task of representing the complexities and contradictions of the society as a whole. The novel's mimetic capabilities were therefore assumed, and the longer the novel, the more comprehensive and supposedly more successful was the feat of representation. Readers demanded long novels, easily assimilable in their customary serialized form. The growth of a literate reading public favored the proliferation of a variety of newspapers (a variety that would astound a reader of today), and, through the practice of serialization, the novel's growth in popularity kept pace with expanded newspaper circulation. Because newspapers were usually willing to pay more for fiction than book publishers were, authors profited from this practice, as long as they were prolific.

Such a novelist was Honoré de Balzac (1799-1850), considered by many to have been the greatest realist of the nineteenth century (realism being defined as the literary or artistic effort to capture in detail the essence of everyday life). Balzac was an indefatigable writer, capable of writing for fifteen hours at a stretch. The demands of his publishers, to whom he continued to promise new books, kept him almost continually at his task. In all, he produced ninety-one novels and novellas. His first novel was a historical treatment of a chapter in the French Revolution. Then, in 1833, he conceived a plan for a comprehensive series of novels with the collective title *La Comédie humaine* (1829-1848; *The Comedy of Human Life*, 1885-1893, 1896; better known as *The Human Comedy*, 1895-1896, 1911).The echoes of Dante in this title were assuredly deliberate.

Balzac portrayed life as it was in postrevolutionary French society, particularly under the Bourbon Restoration. Out of sympathy with the spirit of the 1830 revolution, he preferred returning to the past in celebrating the promise of the future. In order to, in a sense, "repopulate" this lost world, he hoped to create ten thousand characters, a veritable universe. As it turned out, he managed to create "only" two thousand or so. These novels typically feature ambitious, often unscrupulous arrivistes, characters determined to take advantage of the new world of expanding opportunities afforded by nineteenth century Paris. The novels *Le Père Goriot* (1834-1835; *Daddy Goriot*, 1860; also known as *Père Goriot*, 1902) and *Illusions perdues* (1837-1843; *Lost Illusions*, 1893) provide especially memorable examples in the characters of Eugène de Rastignac and Lucien de Rubempré, respectively. The dialectic of the individual in society was thus central to Balzac's fictional project.

A monarchist at heart, Balzac was nevertheless able to portray peasants and urban laborers in a sympathetic light. Because his stated goal was to interject himself as little as possible into his narrative, for which he fashioned a neutral language that allowed him to hold a mirror up to the society of his day, he took pride in his ability to report dispassionately on the facts of life among the social orders he personally did not prefer. Many readers have argued that Balzac portrays the lower classes both more realistically and more sympathetically than those authors who profess much more egalitarian views. As for the other Balzacian boast, close reading of the novels will show that Balzac failed to live up to his credo of impersonal detachment from his narrative. Indeed, he intervenes vigorously and frequently with various rhetorical asides and digressions. Modern critics of fictional realism have grown increasingly distrustful of such claims.

Contemporary critical opinion assigns Marie-Henri Beyle, who is better known as Stendhal (1783-1842), a nearly equally distinguished position alongside Balzac in the history of the early nineteenth century novel. Yet, as Stendhal himself gloomily predicted, he was largely unnoticed and unread during his own time. In part, this fact may have resulted from the greater ambiguity of Stendhal's writing, particularly with regard to his characters' roles and motivations, though he shared with Balzac a fascination for the drama of the individual finding his way within a complex and often corrupt society. Stendhal painted, so to speak, with a softer brush, so that his novelistic canvases appear perhaps less vivid than those of Balzac. Moderately liberal, he was less pronounced in his political opinions and less imbued than the almost messianic Balzac with a grandiose sense of his artistic career. In his greatest novels, *Le Rouge et le noir* (1830; *The Red and the Black*, 1898) and *La Chartreuse de Parme* (1839; *The Charterhouse of Parma*, 1895), however, Stendhal was certainly capable of touching upon the conflicting and often confusing array of political, philosophical, and social trends at work in his time. The shadow of Napoleon haunts Stendhal's work, as does the legacy of the revolution. The novels of both Balzac and Stendhal illustrate the claim frequently made by literary historians that the novel flourishes during times of social or political turmoil.

The long literary career of Amandine-Aurore-Lucile Dupin, or George Sand (1804-1876), unfolded in such times. Known chiefly as a novelist, she moved from an early Romanticism to, after 1848, an increasingly pronounced avowal of a somewhat revolutionary socialism. Having taken by necessity a masculine nom de plume in order to publish her books, she organized her keen political sensibilities around the central theme of the oppression of women. This theme dominates such early novels as *Indiana* (1832; English translation, 1833) and *Lélia* (1833, 1839; English translation, 1978), while later novels, perhaps most notably *François le champi* (1850; *Francis the Waif*, 1889), embody themes of socialism and compassion for the lower classes. In enunciating humanitarian themes, Sand played a role similar to that of Victor Hugo in nineteenth century French culture. In her day, Sand's works were widely read in France and abroad. Even if she attracted more attention in her early years as the lover of Alfred de Musset (1810-1857) and Frédéric Chopin (1810-1849) and as one contemptuous of the opinions of conventional society than as a novelist, she came to be considered one of the most illustrious of French writers, and she received glowing tributes from foreign novelists. From her death until the resurgence of feminist literary scholarship, however, she was consigned to literary oblivion.

Prosper Mérimée (1803-1870) was one of the many fellow writers Sand befriended, and, like her, Mérimée cultivated his own circle of friends among foreign writers. Like Madame de Staël in her endorsement of German literature, Mérimée broke new ground in introducing nineteenth century French readers to the works of some of the greatest names in Russian literature. He befriended Nikolai Gogol and Leo Tolstoy and translated some of their writings. Mérimée was the author of a historical novel, *Chronique du règne de Charles IX* (1829; *A Chronicle of the Times of Charles the Ninth*, 1830; also known as *A Chronicle of the Reign of Charles IX*), and, in *Colomba* (1841; English translation, 1853), produced one of the notable examples in the novella genre.

James A. Winders

BIBLIOGRAPHY

DeJean, Joan. *Tender Geographies: Women and the Origins of the Novel in France*. New York: Columbia University Press, 1991. Witty, highly readable study of the role of women in the development of the French novel includes analyses of salon life, social class, and the relationship between gender and authorship. Supplemented with a rich bibliography.

Gaunt, Simon, and Sarah Kay, eds. *The Cambridge Companion to Medieval French Literature*. New York: Cambridge University Press, 2008. Collection of seventeen critical essays includes several that analyze works of long fiction, including *Le Roman de la rose* and *Chanson de Roland*. Includes an essay by Keith Busby titled "Narrative Genres" and a bibliography.

Hollier, Denis, ed. *A New History of French Literature*. Cambridge, Mass.: Harvard University Press, 1989. Comprehensive and accessible history of French literature is arranged in a somewhat unusual fashion, approaching French literary history through selected landmark dates. Includes several valuable essays on the history of French fiction.

Jensen, Katherine Ann. *Writing Love: Letters, Women, and the Novel in France, 1605-1776*. Carbondale: Southern Illinois University Press, 1995. Examines the works of women novelists who used the epistolary tradition as a strategy for constructing novels and shows how men adopted this technique, often using female pseudonyms to take advantage of the popularity of this genre.

Kay, Sarah, Terence Cave, and Malcolm Bowie. *A Short History of French Literature.* New York: Oxford University Press, 2003. Discussion of French literature is divided into sections chronologically, with the first of three parts covering the earliest works through the Middle Ages, the second discussing the period 1470 to 1789, and the third addressing the period 1789 to 2000. Includes an informative introduction, illustrations, an extensive bibliography, and an index.

Showalter, English, Jr. *The Evolution of the French Novel, 1641-1782.* Princeton, N.J.: Princeton University Press, 1972. Classic work, with ambitious scope and clarity of presentation, is still a valuable source of information. Few critics cover such a wide range of novels, novelists, and themes.

Thiher, Allen. *Fiction Rivals Science: The French Novel from Balzac to Proust.* Columbia: University of Missouri Press, 2001. Presents analyses of the works of four important French novelists of the nineteenth century: Honoré de Balzac, Gustave Flaubert, Émile Zola, and Marcel Proust.

Unwin, Timothy, ed. *The Cambridge Companion to the French Novel: From 1800 to the Present.* New York: Cambridge University Press, 1997. Collection of critical essays provides an overview of the French novel of the nineteenth and twentieth centuries. Topics addressed include women and fiction, Romantic and realist fiction, and popular fiction of the nineteenth century.

Wolfgang, Aurora. *Gender and Voice in the French Novel, 1730-1782.* Burlington, Vt.: Ashgate, 2004. Analyzes four novels, including Marivaux's *The Life of Marianne* and Laclos's *Dangerous Liaisons*, and two lesser-known works by other authors, *Letters Written by a Peruvian Princess* and *Lettres de Mistriss Fanni Butlerd*.

FRENCH LONG FICTION SINCE THE 1850'S

The ascendancy of the novel as the prime literary genre in France was established, by no means accidentally, during the reign of the so-called Bourgeois King, Louis-Philippe (r. 1830-1848). The shifting patterns of population and of economic status had made the middle class dominant, especially in that cradle of culture, Paris; it was perhaps no more than normal that the kind of reading the bourgeoisie preferred—the novel—should in that era have become what the nation as a whole preferred. The key factor in the novel's development to ascendancy, during the years 1830 to 1850, was that Honoré de Balzac, with his visionary ideal of the novel as society's true reflection and record, had imposed on the reading public, by his creative energy and example, his private conception of what a good novel should be: an accurate portrayal of some aspect of the contemporary world. By the start of Napoleon III's Second Empire in 1851, it could be said that, from an exercise in imagination, the serious French novel had become an exercise in observation. The novel had turned decisively realistic. Unhappily, however, the Second Empire, which owed its existence to the violent repression of revolt, was a sternly restrictive regime that alienated writers by its policy of censorship. After Napoleon seized dictatorial powers in the coup d'état of 1851, artists and intellectuals tended to withdraw into silence, concerning themselves with abstract theory rather than with the concrete, observable world around them.

Not surprisingly, the span of the Second Empire (1842-1870) was not a richly productive period for the French novel, or indeed for any of the literary arts. Accurate observation of reality was a risky business under such a regime, unless the reality being observed was inconsequential. On the basis of such reasoning, a literary school took shape in the 1850's that called itself Le Réalisme, publishing its own journal and offering readers novels exemplifying the aesthetic. Writers of this school avoided the attention of the state censor simply by defining realism as the art of depicting the ordinary, everyday life of humble citizens, arguing that literature had too long neglected the commonplace activities that were reality for the greatest number of French citizens. The novels produced by this school were, by and large, flat and pedestrian and did not sell; their authors had misunderstood the nature and purpose of Honoré de Balzac's insistence on the principle of realism in the novel.

Only one writer of that period really understood what Balzac meant—Gustave Flaubert (1821-1880), a brilliant recluse and a great admirer of Balzac's work, who managed to revolutionize the course of the modern novel with his first publication, the celebrated *Madame Bovary* (1857; English translation, 1886). Flaubert recognized that Balzac's ingenious notion of the novel as a record of what exists was focused on the need to be accurate, to avoid distorting reality, rather than on a specific definition of which aspect of reality merited attention from the novelist. Balzac was interested not only in the common person but also in all of society, which is why his novel *Le Père Goriot* (1834-

1835; *Daddy Goriot*, 1860; also known as *Père Goriot*) offered a microcosm of Parisian society, from top to bottom, in the cast of characters associated with Madame Vauquer's boardinghouse. Flaubert's dismissive comment on the theories of the *réalistes* of the 1850's (Jules Champfleury, Louis-Émile-Edmond Duranty, and Ernest-Aimé Feydeau were the best known) was to note, dryly, that "Henri Monnier [author of a comic novel about a bourgeois who thinks and speaks in clichés] is not more real than Racine."

For Flaubert, the term "realism" as used by his contemporaries had no valid literary meaning, since it was restricted to but one corner of the observable world. Accordingly, he always rejected the label of "realist" whenever it was applied to him. Yet Flaubert fully embraced Balzac's insistence on fidelity to the real, for that was a matter of being true to the facts, which to Flaubert was not only a writer's obligation but also an aesthetic necessity; Flaubert was a firm believer in Plato's conception of beauty, according to which the preconditions for any object to be beautiful were that the object be true and good. Since the only worthy objective for a writer, Flaubert thought, was to create something beautiful, he argued that the writer's first task is to render the truth—*faire vrai* was his expression. If the writer's words faithfully render the truth, they will necessarily be morally good, for the truth cannot be evil, and if the words are both true and good, they meet the Platonic standard of beauty. From that reasoning, Flaubert derived the logic of his own practice as a novelist: Research the facts meticulously to be sure that what was written was true. Since the aesthetic value of what he produced depended wholly, according to his theory, on his fidelity to the truth, he took elaborate pains to get everything correct. Documentary research and recorded observations were indeed part of his method, as he readily acknowledged, but he refused to call that effort "realism," for that word distorted his literary purpose. The problem he saw with "reality" was that it can be whatever anyone decides it to be, whereas the truth is never merely a matter of opinion.

There was a good deal more to truth, as Flaubert saw it, than merely rendering the facts. To convey truth, words must be chosen and arranged properly, providing all the necessary nuances and distinctions and bearing the imprint of natural human speech. The mode of expression—which is to say, the style—is an implicit element in the truth of any assertion. A sentence or paragraph that is unnatural or artificial in its rhythm, sound, or vocabulary, Flaubert believed, was ipso facto false. For that reason, Flaubert devoted much of his time to rewriting, recasting his sentences over and over again, in search of the perfect arrangement that would "ring true" and pass the test of being read aloud. A sentence that could not be read aloud comfortably, without forcing the reader to breathe abnormally, was to Flaubert unacceptable and in need of revision. That kind of truth, both factual and stylistic, is a difficult standard to meet and explains why Flaubert took so long to complete each of his compositions and why his correspondence is filled with epic lamentations about the suffering he endured for the sake of his art—what he called *les affres du style*, or the tortures of style. There can indeed have been few writers for whom writing was a slower or more painful process than it was for Flaubert. Yet this strangely excruciating torture to which he subjected himself had a coherent rationale that points clearly to the nature of the revolution that Flaubert effected in the modern novel and that constitutes his most important contribution to its development.

While still an unpublished aspirant to the literary life, Flaubert meditated often on the art of composition and exchanged thoughts on the subject through letters with his friends. In response to a correspondent's question about his addiction to novel writing and his lack of interest in writing verse, Flaubert remarked that the art of poetry had been practiced for so long that every secret of meter, rhyme, rhythm, and sonority was known, and there were consequently no new discoveries to be made in that medium. The great attraction of novel writing for him, he declared, was that the art of prose was still relatively new and unstudied, and the most important discoveries about what makes a sentence artistic were yet to be made. From that observation, Flaubert elaborated a personal conception of the art of the novel that would make the novel as exacting to write as a poem, with each word weighed and selected for its perfect fit in its context, each sentence the perfect expression of its intended thought, and all parts of the novel carefully integrated into a harmonious and coherent whole. It became his ambition to raise the artistic level of the novel in his own lifetime and make it the equal of poetry in every respect. Much as he admired Balzac, he was pained by Balzac's frequent lapses of style and taste—which Flaubert knew to be the product of haste and a lack of concern for beauty. He set out to make his own first publication, *Madame Bovary*, a model of what a novel should be if it is an accomplished work of art. He succeeded, and the novel has never been the same since, anywhere in the Western world. Readers of *Madame Bovary* are still discovering new ways in which Flaubert's fanatic attention to detail gave that novel such a subtle, fine texture. Like a carefully wrought poem, *Madame Bovary* conceals its art beneath a seamless surface and gives up its secrets grudgingly.

It was not, however, *Madame Bovary*'s delicate art that attracted attention when the novel was published but rather what was perceived by the government censor to be its offenses against public morality. It was, after all, the story of sordid bourgeois adultery in a dull provincial town—shocking for the times. Because it did not concern heroic or noble people but rather scrutinized in minute detail the tawdry doings of commonplace characters, *Madame Bovary* was hailed—or denounced—for its daring realism, much to Flaubert's dismay. In spite of his many disclaimers, Flaubert was forced to watch helplessly as his suddenly notorious novel was avidly bought and read for what he considered to be the wrong reasons. His lovingly created masterpiece gave added impetus to the determinedly realist direction the French novel had taken since Balzac—an irony that Flaubert himself appreciated. Realism was what the age seemed to demand—or at least what the readers of novels in that age wanted—and Flaubert has been classified ever since as one of the masters of realism. Almost a generation passed before it was realized that the abiding importance of *Madame Bovary* was not that it was an example of realism but that it had transformed the novel, raising it to a high literary art and setting a new standard of excellence for the genre.

While the novel continued to be a popular form, published in profusion during the 1850's and 1860's, Flaubert now stands out as the only novelist of his generation to have made a lasting contribution to the genre. Only after the Franco-Prussian War did a new generation of young novelists begin to attract attention. The best of the new generation, it soon became apparent, were admirers and even disciples of Flaubert, who understood his artistic principles well enough to apply them to their own work and who had a clearly realistic bent. What set them apart was that their realism seemed more reasoned and more thoroughly grounded in theory and a sense of system. These novelists saw storytelling as both an art and a badly needed instrument of information gathering and analysis for a world grown too complex for the individual to grasp unaided. The special gift, and responsibility, of the artist, as they conceived it, was a superior sensibility that allowed a more profound perception of reality than most people commanded, as well as the ability to transmit that perception effectively through the power and attraction of art. Such ideas were repeatedly articulated by novelists in prefaces, manifestos, and journal articles during the 1870's and 1880's, presenting a concept of the novel's function that honored Flaubert's artistic idealism while simultaneously accepting a utilitarian role that served deeply felt public needs.

Authors in this new generation seemed to write not out of pure instinct or desire but rather as the result of a process of reasoning that justified their calling in practical terms; they were clearly influenced by their times, for it was an age of growing faith in the inevitability of progress based on the seemingly unlimited power of human reason to penetrate the secrets of nature and to understand—and therefore eventually control—the evolution of humanity's social institutions. It was an age that tended to place its hope for the future on the newly developed fields of sociology, psychology, and science. Science especially, with its well-advertised methods of investigation that guaranteed objectivity, had attained enormous public prestige by 1870, and writers found an irresistible logic in assimilating their own enterprise to that of the experimental scientists, seeing themselves as equally objective observers and investigators of the human animal.

The novelist who emerged as the clear leader of this new generation, Émile Zola (1840-1902), was also the one who undertook to codify and publicize its new artistic principles. The resulting action in the novel is not the product of the novelist's imagination, he argued, but the carefully observed consequence of the newly discovered laws of heredity, environment, and human physiology and psychology. In other words, Zola agreed with Balzac that the novel records and interprets social reality as it exists, but Zola insisted that the novel was able to be scientifically accurate and objective about many things not known in Balzac's day fifty years before. To underline the close relationship of the novelist's methods to those of the natural sciences, Zola gave the new form of realism the name "naturalism," and in a series of theoretical essays to which he did not hesitate to give the title *Le Roman expérimental* (1880; *The Experimental Novel*, 1894), he suggested that the novelist who chooses a milieu and a set of characters for a novel is actually setting up an experiment in much the same way as the laboratory scientist.

Whether Zola fully believed his published theories—and there is evidence that he did not, but was rather exercising his considerable gifts as a publicist—the concept proved popular and influential, and the great majority of the novels published in the 1880's were unmistakably in the naturalist vein. To be sure, not even Zola's own novels could be plausibly compared to a laboratory experiment in any literal sense, but the naturalist vein was readily identifiable by the tendency to write about a specific milieu, to provide the kind of detailed information about that milieu that could come only from direct observation or experience, and to govern all action in the novel by a consistently deterministic view of human nature.

In the heyday of naturalism, running from the mid-1870's to the mid-1880's, the major contributors, in addition to Zola himself, were Edmond de Goncourt and Jules de Goncourt, Joris-Karl Huysmans, Alphonse Daudet, and Guy de Maupassant, all of whom produced work of distinction that was widely read at the time. The novel was naturalism's ideal vehicle, but the movement extended, to an important degree, to the short story as well, and with less, but by no means negligible, impact on drama and even on poetry. Probably in no period in French cultural history has literature been more in consonance with the mood of the surrounding society than was the case during naturalism's hour of triumph, and for that reason, the greatest achievement of the naturalistic novel was that it provided for posterity an extensive, detailed, and quite reliable portrait of French society of the 1870's and 1880's. Zola alone delved into an impressive array of French social and economic institutions, each of which constituted a unique milieu: the world of banking, the atmosphere of the department store, the demimonde, squalid urban tenements, a coal-mining community, the artist's life, the railroad industry, and so on. One must add that, because the best of the naturalist novelists also wrote with skill and grace and imagination, striving to live up to the standards of form and style set by Flaubert, their works remain readable and worthy of study today, being both informative and aesthetically satisfying.

It was perhaps the very success of the movement, and the exceptional productivity of its members, that caused naturalism's dominance of the novel to wane toward the end of the nineteenth century. By 1890, the public seemed surfeited with solemnly presented information about themselves, and plainly longed for more inspiring—or more frivolous—fare. A journalistic survey of 1891 confirmed that writers and readers agreed that naturalism's moment had passed. With historical hindsight, one can even recognize the telling symptoms of disaffection that had already appeared during the 1880's among some of naturalism's strongest partisans: the publication in 1884 of Huysmans's strange antinaturalist novel À rebours (*Against the Grain*, 1922); the violent antinaturalist manifesto of 1887 signed by five of Zola's young disciples; and the success of Paul Bourget's disturbing antirationalist novel *Le Disciple*, published in 1889 (*The Disciple*, 1898). Whatever the causes, there was no mistaking the fact that, in 1890, the French novel, its genius for realistic representation of society confirmed by a half century of outstanding achievement, had grown tired and was earnestly groping for new directions to take and new worlds to conquer.

NEW REALITIES, NEW TECHNIQUES: 1890-1940

If naturalism in literature had indeed run its course by 1890, it was surely because faith in science's role as the savior of French society had proved illusory. As it became clearer in the 1880's that there were many questions science could not answer, a wave of skepticism, sometimes turning to darkest pessimism, swept over intellectual circles, and it became fashionable to point to those phenomena of the natural order—including human nature—which the rationalism of the scientific method could never hope to explain. The irrational, the supernatural, the metaphysical, in all their variety of forms, once again fascinated those who had been most devastated by the discovery of the limits of science. By the 1890's, a religious revival and an intense curiosity about the human subconscious were in full bloom in France, and no time was lost in incorporating these new interests into the flow of fiction that continued unabated, inundating the reading public with what writers believed the public wanted to read.

Weary of the analysis of the observable data of their society, writers and readers now directed their attention to what was not observable, though just as real: the mysteries of belief and desire; the power over humans of the will to live and the consciousness of mortality; the exact nature of existence, time, and change—all the intangibles that define and distinguish the human spirit beyond its purely mechanistic components. Novelists began to pursue realities that were, by definition, missing in the naturalistic novel. Yet such is the power of custom that the analytical method, which had served the purposes of naturalism so effectively, continued to be the basic approach employed by the novelists of the 1890's and beyond. Though these were quite different realities with which they were now concerned, novelists instinctively recognized that the great strength of the novel was its representational or mimetic power, and they were content to use its analytical process to render these nonphysical realities as well.

A typical expression of this new mood among novelists can be found in the opening chapter of a novel about Satanism, *Là-bas* (1891; *Down There*, 1924; better known as *Là-Bas*, 1972), by Joris-Karl Huysmans (1848-1907), one of the original naturalist group. The protagonist is—what else?—a novelist who has been a practicing naturalist and an admirer of Zola. As the novel opens, the protagonist is discussing naturalism as a literary theory with a physician friend. They agree that Zola and company have served literature well but believe that the theory is now producing dull repetitions of its best work, because there is nowhere else for it to go, given the strict limits of material reality—the only reality naturalism recognizes. After the discussion, the protagonist (whose name is Durtal and who is clearly a surrogate for Huysmans himself) meditates regarding his next work and decides the naturalistic method itself must be adapted to the task of writing, not about the body exclusively but about the body and the soul, a duality that is far truer to the reality of human nature.

It is necessary, he said to himself, to retain the veracity of the document, the precision of the detail, the substance and vitality of language in realism—but we must at the same time trace out a parallel path, another road, in order to get at what lies above and beyond the material realm, in a word, a spiritual naturalism.

With such arguments—or rationalizations, as some might say—Huysmans tried to bridge the gap between his past and present outlooks and to apply the methods of naturalism to the evocation of religious ideas, one of the new realities that naturalism had so far not touched.

Huysmans was articulating more than a private, personal mood with *Là-Bas*. By using a writer as a protagonist and by stressing the moral and spiritual realm as subject matter, he was forecasting the basic characteristics of the novel as it developed among the two generations of novelists whose work appeared between 1890 and World War II. The use of writers and other artists as fictional protagonists was a tradition that had begun with the Romantics and had been memorably represented in the work of Balzac, Flaubert, and Zola, to name only the most important French practitioners. In the original tradition, the focus of attention was on the troubled and often misunderstood personality of the artist, whereas after 1890 the focus tended to be much more on the nature of the art and of the creative process.

It should be noted that the novel about artists was not exclusively French; rather, it was European in scope, and because some of the earliest examples were in German, this type of novel has acquired the name *Künstlerroman*. What one may say of the European *Künstlerroman* generally—and it is entirely valid for the French tradition in particular—is that in the nineteenth century, its theme tended to be the sufferings of the artist as a human type. In the twentieth century, its theme shifted to the legitimacy of the art itself and the theoretical basis on which the art could claim to have a valid function in the world. Huysmans's novel *Là-Bas* was thus an early instance of what became a hallmark of twentieth century fiction: self-consciousness about the novel itself and a restless, self-scrutinizing investigation into its right to exist as an art. *Là-Bas* was equally the herald of a second hallmark of twentieth century fiction in France, the impulse to analyze and to probe into new realities not only more immaterial and more elusive than the realities that had preoccupied the naturalists but also more compelling and more urgent as topics of concern: the role of ideas in human conduct and the struggle with the moral and spiritual issues of existence. The twentieth century novel became, in short, a literature of thought and of moral anguish, characteristically centered on the dual themes of the legitimacy of art and of traditional values.

Nothing comparable to the naturalist movement took shape among French novelists as the nineteenth century turned into the twentieth century; no one theory or approach won enough adherents to become the focal center of a school or a movement. Novelists went their separate ways, each anxiously seeking new ground on which to stand as a replacement for the outworn naturalism. Between 1890 and 1914, the only coherent trends discernible in the torrent of novels being published were those suggested by *Là-Bas*: constant self-questioning about the nature of the novel and anxious exploration of ideas and moral problems. These two trends found a wide variety of modes of expression, however, leaving little in common to connect one novelist with another. Huysmans, for example, after *Là-Bas*, seemed to abandon the novel of invention, writing three barely disguised autobiographical narratives in which his novelist-character, Durtal, traverses the stages of Huysmans's own conversion to orthodox Catholicism and to acceptance of the monastic life. These narratives, though published as novels, have neither plot nor cast of characters nor structure; they simply record a writer's inward journey to salvation.

Meanwhile, Huysmans's contemporary, Anatole France (1844-1924), also wrote a novel with a writer as a protagonist, *Le Lys rouge* (1894; *The Red Lily*, 1898), but this novel treated the themes of love and jealousy and offered the ruefully ironic spectacle of a worldly and sensitive writer who could not understand a woman's desire for independence—in that way making an indirect comment on the limitations of the naturalistic novel. Thereafter, France turned to the theme of the past and tended to emphasize the inability of the historian to recover the past with any accuracy, suggesting the folly of claiming to represent reality exactly with the written word. Others of that same generation, such as Paul Bourget and Maurice Barrès, wrote in an increasingly dogmatic vein about moral and political ideas, to overcome the impasse into which they felt the naturalist novel had fallen by its presumed objectivity and determinism.

As for the younger generation of that period—those born around 1870, who began publishing in the 1890's and the early 1900's—they showed by their experiments with form and style, their introspective focus on artistic or intellectual protagonists, and their irresistible gravitation toward the world of ideas and of moral dilemmas that they, too, belonged fully to the postnaturalistic world. They worked in very different ways and had no discernible influence on one another. Among these distinctive voices were those of André Gide, Marcel Proust, Romain Rolland, and Colette. The period that the French call *la belle époque* (1890-1914) was, in the novel, a time of ferment, experimentation, and an uneasy search for new, viable directions, ways to renew and revitalize an art that had known great achievement but had lost its way when it narrowed its sights to the mere reporting of what can be readily observed.

Gide (1869-1951) and Proust (1871-1922), unquestionably the finest and most original novelists of their generation, succeeded in giving the novel new direction and new principles during the transitional era which preceded World War I, influencing profoundly not their own contemporaries but the next generation, those who came to prominence in the 1920's and 1930's. Nothing illustrates better, perhaps, the kind of privacy and isolation in which writers of that era seemed to work than the fact that these two innovators, although born only two years apart and schooled in the same Parisian literary milieu, should have had so little contact with each other and so little apparent appreciation for each other's work. It is even true that in 1913, Gide, acting as editor of *La Nouvelle Revue française*, the journal he helped to found, turned down for publication an early segment of Proust's great novel, *À la recherche du temps perdu* (1913-1927; *Remembrance of Things Past*, 1922-1931, 1981), because he failed to recognize its originality. It is also true, however, that Gide made a full and honorable admission of his error in judgment after World War I, when Proust was awarded the prestigious Prix Goncourt. The principal works of both authors were completed before the war, but it was only after the war that each became famous and truly influential, when a younger generation could appreciate the novelty of their separate yet similar concepts of what fiction could accomplish.

For Gide, fiction was always a personal, if not literally autobiographical, vehicle for expressing both the moral conflicts of private existence and the dilemmas of the novelist's craft. In two early specimens of the first-person confessional novel, *L'Immoraliste* (1902; *The Immoralist*, 1930) and *La Porte étroite* (1909; *Strait Is the Gate*, 1924), Gide examined both sides of the ethical problem created by the coexistence within the same individual of a reasoned rejection of traditional morality and a deeply ingrained puritan outlook. At the same time, both novels demonstrated, in a brilliant display of technique, the dangers of the first-person narrative style by presenting a text whose surface assures the narrator's absolute sincerity but whose subtle undercurrents alert the attentive reader to the narrator's bad faith. The two works, taken together, shake the reader's confidence both in the moral coherence of human behavior and in the truth of narrative discourse.

A few years later, Gide turned to the comic vein with *Les Caves du Vatican* (1914; *The Vatican Swindle*, 1925; better known as *Lafcadio's Adventures*, 1927) to tell a willfully improbable and convoluted story, featuring wildly unrealistic characters set in very real and carefully described surroundings. The central event of the novel brings together on a train, by pure chance, two of the main characters, who are strangers to each other; one character throws the other out a window of the speeding train, purely for the pleasure of performing a motiveless crime and observing the confusion of the authorities who try to decipher its meaning afterward. By such devices, Gide contrived to make his comic novel a disturbing challenge both to the reader's preconceptions about the rational basis of human conduct and, even more, to standard notions about order and coherence in the form and structure of novels. Life is never neat or orderly, Gide seems to be saying, and the traditional modes of fiction actually falsify reality, rather than represent it, by imposing an artificial order on events and presenting them as clear instances of cause and effect.

Gide's most daring and innovative challenge to the novel, however, came in 1925, with the publication of his longest and most complex narrative, *Les Faux-monnayeurs* (*The Counterfeiters*, 1927), the only one he chose to identify with the label "novel." There can be no doubt that *The Counterfeiters* is intended as a critique of the novel itself, since its central figure is a novelist who happens to be writing a novel called *The Counterfeiters* and who keeps a diary of his artistic dilemmas and decisions as he writes. The title ostensibly refers to the activities of a band of teenagers who defy society by making counterfeit coins and passing them off as real, but Gide is explicit about the title's more important symbolic value, suggesting not only that most individuals are "moral counterfeiters," passing themselves off as other than who they really are, but also that novelists are unwittingly the greatest counterfeiters of all, passing off as the true image of reality the sadly distorted products of their imaginations. What Gide did for the novel was to undermine previous assumptions about reality and about the fictional techniques appropriate for the rendering of that reality, and to offer models of narrative that could deal with the stubborn ambiguity and irrationality of the human world. Gide simply shattered the foundation upon which the naturalist novel of his predecessors had been constructed.

Proust chose a different approach, but he had approximately the same objective: to refute the validity of the traditional novel of realism and to demonstrate the techniques and concepts by which a novel can engage with a comprehensive view of reality and still be a work of art. These ideas he embodied in a single monumental novel, in excess of three thousand pages in length, composed over a period of more than a decade and bearing the evocative title *À la recherche du temps perdu*, rendered felicitously into English by C. K. Scott Moncrief with a phrase from Shakespeare as *Remembrance of Things Past*. The novel was so long that it had to be published in separate volumes, in spite of Proust's reluctance to distort his design in that way. Indeed, the first volume had to be published at the author's own expense in 1913, because no publisher would undertake the complete work, and its continuation was delayed until after the war. The final volumes appeared posthumously, for although Proust raced against a debilitating illness to complete his novel in 1922, he did not live to see all of it published.

Proust's one great novel may stand as the greatest single achievement of the twentieth century in the French novel and one of the most revolutionary works of fiction in the French canon. At the heart of the novel is a philosophical concept, the notion that time has a major role in shaping one's perception of reality and that traditional narrative modes have never given that role its due. Above all, Proust wanted to deal with the problem of the rapid passage of time and the consequent obliteration of the past, unless the memory of that past can somehow be recovered and preserved. Those ideas are implicit in his title. Two thematic strands make up the armature of that search for lost time that the title promises: One strand is the first-person account that the narrator, Marcel, is able to give of his own growing up, thanks to his involuntary memory, which brings back the past so vividly; the other strand is the careful dissection of the society in which Marcel grew up and the changes in it that he witnessed and finally learned to understand, as memory overcame the effects of time and enabled him to see the truth. When these two strands fuse at the end of the novel, Marcel realizes why he wants to be a writer: If the effects of involuntary memory can suddenly conjure up his own past so completely and in such exact detail, only the power of the written word can fix that past permanently and preserve it for future generations. For that reason, the calling of novelist seems to him both noble and worthy, and, having thus confirmed his vocation, Marcel decides to write the novel that the reader has just finished reading—a novel that demonstrates how art can recapture lost time.

As long, meandering, and formless as the novel can seem to readers making their way through it for the first time, there is a firm guiding hand in control at all times, for Proust planned his novel meticulously, like a piece of architecture, as he was fond of saying. Some have suggested that symphonic form is a better analogy for the way the novel is composed, because of Proust's use of themes that are stated, developed, interwoven with other themes, and returned to in a kind of grand recapitulation at the end. Characters appear and reappear, always as seen by Marcel at the different stages of his own development, so that they seem to have changed, sometimes startlingly. In this way, Proust is able to make readers aware of time and allows them to experience the effects of time's passing in the same way they experience it in real life. This was one of the ingenious devices Proust invented to make time a tangible presence in his novel and to convey the quality of one's encounter with it. Perhaps the novel's greatest success is that it really does recapture lost time for the reader: The world in which Proust grew up, and which he frequented during his formative years, springs to life in the witty and brilliant pages of the novel, and the reader comes away grateful that one corner of the past, at least, has been saved from oblivion. It is a pleasant paradox of Proust's work that, while the world he describes is, for the most part, snobbish and petty, utterly deserving of the scathing satire he heaps upon it, the reader is nevertheless gladdened by its resuscitation. Even a distasteful image can please when it represents, as does Proust's novel, human victory over time.

Proust's great masterpiece, which combines the values of the *Künstlerroman* with the grand-scale re-creative power of the naturalist novel at its best, proposes a new way to look at reality by adding the dimension of time, and demonstrates a new range of possibilities for giving a novel freedom to grow without losing the sense of form. These are capital enrichments of the novel's potential, but Proust's greatest contribution to the genre's development was surely the exalted function he imagined for the art of fiction: to reclaim the past for posterity from the dead hand of time. Proust's vision helped to give new dignity and prestige to the calling of novelist in the twentieth century.

Proust and Gide were not alone in laying the groundwork for influential new directions in the novel during the period before World War I. A significant, though lesser, role was also played by their contemporary Romain Rolland (1866-1944), who published a novel cycle almost as massive as Proust's masterpiece well before the first volume of *Remembrance of Things Past* appeared. This novel was a ten-volume saga of a musician's life called *Jean-Christophe* (*John-Christopher*, 1910-1913; better known as *Jean-Christophe*, 1913), published between 1904 and 1912. While there is no evidence that Rolland's multivolume novel had any direct influence on Proust's, the surface similarities at least are striking, since both works have an artist's consciousness at their center and both exhibit a looseness of structure aimed at breaking free of the nineteenth century tradition of the well-made novel. Rolland made no original contribution to the definition of reality or to the discovery of new novelistic techniques for the rendering of reality; he was, in fact, taking Balzac's novel sequence *La Comédie humaine* (1829-1848; *The Comedy of Human Life*, 1885-1893, 1896; also known as *The Human Comedy*, 1895-1896, 1911) and Zola's *Les Rougon-Macquart* (1871-1893, 20 volumes; *The Rougon-Macquarts*, 1896-1900) and modernizing the idea by giving it more unity.

Jean-Christophe is organized around a single central character rather than a family of characters or a society, and in relaxing the inclusive realism that would depict a milieu in depth (in order to concentrate on the psychological and moral development of the protagonist), Rolland can be credited with having renewed and modernized the concept of the novel cycle as developed by Balzac and Zola. That his creation proved a fruitful example for others can be seen in the successful cycles published in the 1920's and 1930's by Roger Martin du Gard, Georges Duhamel, and Jules Romains, to say nothing of the 1920's success of Proust's cyclic novel, which probably owed something, at least, to the fact that Rolland had created an audience willing to give its attention to a multivolume composition.

The period between World War I and World War II was dominated, in the novel, by the influences of Gide and Proust and, to a degree, by that of Rolland. Insofar as that period produced fiction that broke with nineteenth century practices and pursued new forms and new themes, it was a vigorous continuation of the trends established during the belle époque. It cannot be said, however, that the interwar era changed the direction or the concept of the novel in any fundamental way, as Gide and Proust had done earlier.

Several writers carved out unique niches for themselves through their work in this period, mainly because of highly individual personal traits rather than because of new ideas about the genre. As a result, those authors generally had no influence on posterity. Each was one of a kind. Typical of the leading novelists of the between-wars generation was Colette (1873-1954), who perfected the small but delicate art of the novel of female sensuality. In her many novels, she made the depiction of all the pleasures of the senses her personal domain, evoking the sensations of smell and touch and taste as successfully in prose as Charles Baudelaire (1821-1867) had done in verse in the previous century. Wildly controversial and popular (as much for her open lesbian relationships and her three marriages as for her work), Colette became in 1945 the first woman admitted to the Académie Goncourt, and in 1948 she became its president. Her most popular novel, *Gigi* (1944; English translation, 1952), was made into a motion-picture musical, released in 1958, and subsequently was adapted as a Broadway musical. Colette was considered France's greatest writer during her lifetime, and she received a state funeral when she died in 1954.

The Catholic novelist François Mauriac (1885-1970) analyzed the sinful compulsions of the newly enriched provincial bourgeoisie with fine psychological insight and a remarkable flair for the dramas of the soul. Although he was also named a member of the Académie Goncourt and was awarded the Nobel Prize in Literature in 1952, his art and subject matter were too private to have inspired a trend.

The two outstanding novelists of the 1930's, Antoine de Saint-Exupéry (1900-1944) and André Malraux (1901-1976), are often compared because they are both associated with the novel of adventure and with writing about aviation as a new frontier. On inspection, however, their work, too, can be seen as highly individualized and only superficially similar. Saint-Exupéry romanticizes flying, presenting aviators most engagingly as the heroic pioneers of a new industry, venturing bravely and alone into an alien environment. Malraux, in contrast, writes obsessively about the adventurer as tragic hero, conscious of his doomed destiny as a mortal and determined to achieve some kind of dignity in his fated encounter with death. Malraux may be credited with inventing a modern technique of narration, eliminating the nineteenth century dependence on passages of physical description to set scenes and on sequential narrative to effect transitions from scene to scene. Instead, he plunges the reader abruptly and without preliminaries into each new scene, doing nothing to connect the scenes in terms of time or even cause and effect. The method forces the reader to participate in the "creation" of the novel as a coherent tale and, at the same time, imparts an extraordinary feeling of rapid action and high tension to the novel. In that technical aspect of his work, Malraux was an innovator and has apparently had some influence on subsequent generations, being one of the likely sources, for example, of the nervous, cinematographic style of rapid scene shifts employed in the novels of Alain Robbe-Grillet (1922-2008) and Michel Butor (born 1926) in the 1950's and 1960's. Malraux, however, is a solitary exception in his generation.

The conception of what a novel should be and how it should be composed, as exemplified by the novels published in France in the half-century from 1890 to 1940, was essentially the creation of Gide, Proust, and Rolland, insofar as that conception differed in significant degree from nineteenth century practices in the genre. The outbreak of World War II wrote a forcible end to that era, and what emerged after the war, in the domain of fiction, ushered in a new phase in the history of the novel in France.

The Age of Anxious Experiment: After 1940

Symptoms of the new phase could have been spotted by discerning readers even before the outbreak of war, in 1938, when Jean-Paul Sartre (1905-1980) published his first novel, *La Nausée* (*Nausea*, 1949), and in 1939, when Nathalie Sarraute (1900-1999) brought out her first work of fiction, *Tropismes* (*Tropisms*, 1963)—both works now recognized as belonging in spirit to the postwar era. In the late 1930's, however, those works passed almost unnoticed; they were not accorded serious attention until a decade later. The war years, mostly years of the Nazi Occupation in France, did not encourage much literary activity, and the production of novels slowed considerably, though one may note that the celebrated novel *L'Étranger* (*The Stranger*, 1946), by Albert Camus (1913-1960), also now associated with the postwar atmosphere, was published in 1942 without causing any stir.

With the bitter experience of World War II and the Occupation behind them, the French were suddenly receptive to philosophies of despair, because what they had witnessed of human nature and the value of life during the war proved to be profoundly demoralizing. The existentialist movement, led by Sartre, the Theater of the Absurd, which dominated the postwar Paris stage, and the first eyewitness accounts of the Holocaust, which began to find their way into print after 1945, all confirmed the postwar French public in their mood of pessimism, for all those phenomena proclaimed the same fundamental perception of life—namely, that it was random and meaningless, the product of pure chance and ungoverned instinct, and that such human-made concepts as virtue, morality, conscience, and belief in a just God had been revealed to be grotesque fantasies by the events the world had recently witnessed. In such an atmosphere, it was obviously difficult for both writers and readers to take the novel, as it had existed before the war, with any degree of seriousness or to believe very readily in the Proustian vision of the novel as the human instrument of victory over time. The urgently felt need in the late 1940's, and indeed throughout the 1950's and 1960's as well, was to devise a new kind of novel capable of giving adequate and truthful expression to this mood of despair and nihilistic outlook.

During the first postwar decade, it was chiefly those novels that reflected the philosophies of despair in their content that seemed to meet the public need best, while beginning in the late 1950's, public success went especially to those novels that dramatically shattered tradition in their form and technique. Both kinds of novel, however, were self-consciously experimental, for their authors were plainly responding to the anxious fear that the novel was a dying genre; they were motivated by the desperate hope that, with the right formula, the novel could be brought back to life and made relevant again. Indeed, since 1940, the French novel can be said to have been passing through an age of anxious experimentation, with both form and content, which has been giving to the genre a hesitant and tentative character suggestive of a period of transition, the outcome of which remains in doubt. Moreover, no durable trends have yet appeared, and few novels or novelists of this period seem likely candidates for lasting fame. There are, however, concepts and innovations associated with the philosophical novels of the 1940's and 1950's and with the New Novel group of the 1950's and 1960's that promise to have an ongoing influence on the way novels will be conceived and written in the future.

The leading innovators of the philosophical novel were Sartre and Camus, both of whom were trained in philosophy and could deal competently and naturally with philosophical ideas in their writing. Sartre's most important novel, *Nausea*, takes the form of an intellectual's diary and is therefore a novel of ideas—at the opposite extreme from a novel of action or adventure. Indeed, nothing happens in *Nausea* except that the diarist, Roquentin, who has been writing a biography of a minor historical figure, decides to abandon his project as pointless. The novel's focus is on the thought process by which Roquentin reaches his decision: He comes to realize that the past has no existence and that it is therefore an act of futility to try to recover it. Moreover, in a kind of strange, visionary experience, he discovers that the mere sight of what does exist, including himself, fills him with the sensation of nausea. His nausea is a symbolic reaction to his discovery that all existence is without inherent value and that no person or object has any significance beyond itself, even though people are constantly contriving specious arguments that would invest the world with transcendent meaning.

Although the novel offers a variety of examples of this incorrigible human need to find meaning in life—a philosophical idea that Sartre adapted from German philosopher Martin Heidegger (1889-1976)—the real originality of the book lies in the way that philosophical idea is communicated. Rendering the discovery of meaninglessness as a physical sensation, nausea, was a stroke of imaginative genius on Sartre's part. Moreover, he describes the sensation in elaborate clinical detail, including the stomach-turning alien ugliness that familiar objects such as a newspaper page, a tree's roots, or his own hand suddenly take on for Roquentin. The descriptions are as precise and as vivid as any to be found in a realistic novel of the nineteenth century, even though what is being described is an idea in Roquentin's mind rather than a tangible object. Sartre, in other words, had contrived a metaphoric means of rendering a new reality, the "feel" of an idea, thus fusing literature and philosophical thought. It was a device that Sartre himself would use again, effectively, in his plays, and that other writers of his generation would adapt to their own needs. The device added significantly to the expressive capabilities of the novel, once it was fully understood. Paradoxically enough, however, the philosophical idea that Sartre had discovered how to render in literature implied the pointlessness of all literature. It is perhaps because of that underlying contradiction that Sartre's fiction writing reached an impasse soon after the appearance of *Nausea*. During the 1940's he attempted a cyclic novel in four volumes as a portrait of his times, abandoning it after completing three undistinguished volumes.

The innovative contribution to the philosophical novel made by Camus was, like Sartre's, embedded in the first novel he published, *The Stranger*; it was also, as it happens, related to the same philosophical idea of the radical meaninglessness, or absurdity, of life. Camus invented not a metaphor but a character as the means of translating the idea into fictional terms. *The Stranger* is a monologue in written form, the account by a man named Meursault of his chance involvement in a crime and his subsequent trial and conviction. What fascinates the reader is that Meursault, by the indirect evidence of his own choice of words, has a disconcertingly detached and unemotional perception of the events he describes, not because he is pathological but because he is, in the most profound sense, a stranger to the beliefs and values of his society, as though he were a creature from another planet. Meursault's flat, matter-of-fact narrative style dramatizes for the reader the consequences of a confrontation between the philosophical idea that life has no meaning and a social order that attributes significance to life by all its laws, institutions, and customs. The confrontation shocks the reader into recognizing that it is Meursault who sees the world as it really is, while everyone around him invents fictions that give the illusion of meaning to their actions. Camus thus imagines an idea as a person in order to explore the full consequences of that idea when loosed upon the real world. It was a device he found fruitful, refining it with even more impressive results in his next two novels, *La Peste* (1947; *The Plague*, 1948) and *La Chute* (1956; *The Fall*, 1957). All three works constitute a major contribution to the novel of ideas, marrying the discipline of philosophy with the art of the novel.

The phenomenon known as *le nouveau roman* (the New Novel) can best be understood not as something really new in itself but as a systematic assault on the old. No two of the practitioners of that kind of novel actually apply the same principles in their work, so it is hardly accurate to speak of it as a coherent movement or school. Rather, it is a case of a generation of writers who concluded, each independently, that the novel was an outworn form whose conventional devices of plot, characterization, point of view, and time representation distorted the reality of the twentieth century world. Their analyses of the inadequacies of the conventional novel led them to experiment with novels that did without one or more of the devices they found to be so unsatisfactory.

Nathalie Sarraute, suspicious of the neat logic of human psychology as portrayed in the nineteenth century novel, depicted characters whose behavior is enigmatic, erratic, springing from inner impulses—and therefore more authentically human, from her point of view. Marguerite Duras (1914-1996) rejects both plot and psychological coherence in favor of depicting the effects of mood, atmosphere, and chance on events and of showing that people often tend to live their lives vicariously, in fantasy, rather than in coherently motivated actions. Her best-selling novel is the autobiographical *L'Amant* (1984; *The Lover*, 1985). Samuel Beckett (1906-1989) reduces plot, character, and time to the most primitive and elemental level conceivable, depicting derelicts who are little more than passive consciousnesses undergoing the brief but meaningless experience of existing in the mud and slime of the material world.

The most abstractly theoretical of the New Novelists, Alain Robbe-Grillet (1922-2008), conducted a series of novelistic experiments in which he gradually eliminated all the conventional devices of nineteenth century fiction, leaving only an incoherent sequence of images whose meaning never becomes certain for the reader. His best-known work, *La Jalousie* (1957; *Jealousy* 1959), evokes a suspected love triangle without employing any elements of plot or characterization and without supplying any clarifying circumstantial details of time or place. The narrator remains unidentified, unmotivated, and uninvolved, recording in cameralike fashion only what can be seen at a given time and from a given vantage point. So far as the reader can tell, the drama of the love triangle may be real or only imagined, a fact or the fevered fantasy of a jealous husband. The reader is deliberately given no way of knowing the truth. By implication, Robbe-Grillet has composed a scathing critique of a thousand conventional novels of jealousy, which analyze in subtle detail the motives of all the characters, describe intimately the actions of sin or folly committed, and so contrive to create the illusion of an eyewitness account of events that no person could know about or understand so completely. *Jealousy* illuminates brilliantly the artificialities of the conventional novel, but whether it succeeds as a novel as well as it succeeds as criticism is open to serious question.

In 2001, after twenty years without a new novel (having published only works of autobiographical fiction since 1981), Robbe-Grillet published the spy thriller *La Reprise* (*Repetition*, 2003). In this work, the protagonist, Henri Robin, is a spy who finds that his memory is unreliable and his account of a murder is contradictory and suspicious. As in *Jealousy*, the eyewitness account cannot be trusted, and the reader is tossed about between memory and the subconscious.

The most significant French novelists of the second half of the twentieth century are generally considered to be Marguerite Yourcenar (1903-1987), Michel Butor, and Claude Simon (1913-2005). They explored in highly creative ways the human effort to deal with the heavy weight of past events on present lives. Claude Simon received the Nobel Prize in Literature in 1985, and Yourcenar became, in 1981, the first woman elected to the French Academy since its creation in 1635. Although these novelists are highly original, their careers have been very different. Yourcenar was born into a wealthy French family. She emigrated to the United States in 1938 and became a U.S. citizen in 1947. Butor was born in France and taught literature for many years at the University of Geneva. Simon was born on Madagascar, an island off the southeastern coast of Africa, which was then a French colony. He was educated in France. During World War II he was a prisoner of war, and as a result of this traumatic experience he developed a tragic view of the world and came to understand the fragility of human life.

Yourcenar is especially famous for her historical novels, which frequently deal with classical antiquity. Her 1951 book, *Mémoires d'Hadrien* (*Memoirs of Hadrian*, 1954; also known as *Hadrian's Memoirs*), is her masterpiece. She presents this novel as autobiographical fiction written by the aging Roman emperor Hadrian to his friend Marcus. Yourcenar carefully re-creates court intrigue and power struggles in Rome: Hadrian reflects on his long reign and his successful efforts to expand the boundaries of the Roman Empire. Although Hadrian considers himself a tolerant and peaceful emperor in comparison with such violent tyrants as Nero and Caligula, it soon becomes clear to the reader that the Roman peace of which Hadrian is so proud was achieved at a terrible human cost. Fear, terror, and exploitation were the foundations of Roman domination in its extensive colonies. Readers come to distrust the first-person narrator in this fictional autobiography. Hadrian is oblivious to the true suffering of the vast majority of his subjects, and he compliments himself on the many beautiful monuments that he constructed throughout the Roman Empire. Hadrian's love for the young man Antinous brought him a great deal of pleasure, but Hadrian fell into profound depression after the death of his lover. In his grief, Hadrian ordered coins, monuments, and statues to honor the memory of Antinous. His obsession with death makes it abundantly clear to readers that Hadrian is a self-centered individual who is indifferent to the real needs of his subjects.

Claude Simon also explores classical antiquity in his 1969 novel *La Bataille de Pharsale* (*The Battle of Pharsalus*, 1971). The Battle of Pharsalus was the decisive battle in the Roman civil war. After the defeat of the republican forces, Julius Caesar succeeded in destroying the Roman Republic, and he established a dictatorship ruled by omnipotent emperors. As the narrator reflects on Caesar's description of this battle, he remembers his own difficulty in translating Caesar's Latin sentences into French and decides to visit the historical site where the battle took place. As he approaches Pharsalus, the narrator comes to realize that the use of military force by Caesar to overthrow an established and relatively democratic government is disturbingly reminiscent of the Nazis' use of military force to occupy countries and enslave citizens. This historical novel includes numerous references to the horrendous crimes against humanity committed by the Nazis and their collaborators. Memories of these traumatic events continue to haunt the narrator long after the liberation of Europe from Nazi domination. Both Simon and Yourcenar show in their novels that thinking about the past can enable people to understand more deeply the meaning of contemporary events.

Simon is known not just for his themes of war, history, time, and visual perception but also for his experimental style. His novels, which have been compared to those of Proust and of William Faulkner (1897-1962), frequently alternate passages of narration with passages of stream of consciousness, and it is not unusual for single sentences to run three pages or more. Punctuation is used rarely, with the exception of parentheses. Despite these manipulations, Simon's prose is readable and has attracted a large audience, although he once commented, "I am a difficult, boring, unreadable, confused writer." His autobiographical novel *Le Tramway* (2001; *The Trolley*, 2002) is representative: It is a collection of memories and anecdotes loosely connected through image or stream of consciousness, not chronologically arranged. Individual scenes focus on the visual but hint at the themes of aging (Simon was in his eighties when he wrote this work), the experience of war, and the pleasures of youth.

Michel Butor also eloquently described how the past continues to influence people; his finest novel is generally considered *La Modification* (1957; *Second Thoughts*, 1958; better known as *A Change of Heart*). In this second-person narrative, the narrator is speaking to a French businessman named Léon Delmont, who is traveling by train from Paris to Rome to join his mistress Cécile. For years Léon traveled regularly between these two cities; while in Paris, he stayed with his wife Henriette, and when in Rome he stayed with his mistress. He has a guilty conscience, and as the train slowly moves toward Rome, Léon thinks about his previous train trips between the French and Italian capitals. Readers come to understand Léon's hypocrisy and selfishness. By the end of the novel, readers no longer care whether Léon decides to live with Cécile or Henriette; just as in Yourcenar's *Memoirs of Hadrian*, readers of *A Change of Heart* are profoundly alienated from the major character.

New voices

At the close of the twentieth century and the beginning of the twenty-first, France, no less than other European countries, embraced the new voices that came with the era of globalization. After Simon won the Nobel Prize in 1985, the next French writer to win it was Gao Xingjian (born 1940), an immigrant from China, who won in 2000 for his novels and absurdist plays. Gao, who majored in French in college, writes in Chinese and has produced Chinese translations of the works of English and French absurdist playwrights. He settled near Paris in 1987 and became a French citizen in 1997. Gao's best-known novel is *Ling shan* (1990; *Soul Mountain*, 2000). The story, based on a trip the author took through rural China after he received a misdiagnosis of terminal cancer, is about a man's search for a mythical mountain and his exploration of what it means to be an individual self and a member of the human community.

Other important writers who illustrate the diversity of French novelists in this period include Christine Angot (born 1959), best known for her autobiographical and metafictional novel, *L'Inceste* (1999), about an incestuous affair with her father; Virginie Despentes (born 1969), whose novel and film, *Baise-moi* (1999), which is explicitly violent and sexual, has been referred to as an example of the "New French Extremity"; postmodernist Simonetta Greggio (born 1961 in Italy), whose first novel, *La Douceur des hommes* (2005; the softness of men), made her a critical and popular success; and Michel Houellebecq (born 1958), controversial for his explorations of the interchange between economics and sexuality, whose *La Possibilité d'une île* (2005; *The Possibility of an Island*, 2005) is set within a cloning cult. Other contemporary French writers have explored the experience of North African immigrants in France; novelists in this group include Nina Bouraoui (born 1967) and Farida Belghoul (born 1958).

In 2008, the Nobel Prize in Literature went to J. M. G. Le Clézio, author of novels as well as short stories, travel diaries, essays, and books for children. Over a long career, Le Clézio has worked in a variety of novel forms. His first novel, *Le Procès-Verbal* (1963; *The Interrogation*, 1964), is an experimental work exploring insanity and language. Later, he turned from experimentalism and began to write realist fiction about travel and the environment, and about childhood. By the time he won the Nobel Prize, he had become one of the most popular writers in France, although rather few Americans had heard of him. Among his best-known works are *Désert* (1980; *Desert*, 2009), about the conflict between desert tribes and the French colonialists in Morocco in the period 1910-1912; *Le Chercheur d'or* (1985; *The Prospector*, 1993), set on the island of Mauritius; and *Onitsha* (1991; English translation, 1997), about a European boy traveling through colonial Nigeria in the 1940's. By the end of the twentieth century, the French novel had moved beyond France's cities and countryside, and beyond the lives of the French middle class, to embrace the wider world.

Murray Sachs; Edmund J. Campion
Updated by Cynthia A. Bily

BIBLIOGRAPHY

Baguley, David. *Naturalist Fiction*. New York: Cambridge University Press, 1990. Contains a thoughtful analysis of French naturalist novels written in the late nineteenth century and explains clearly the originality of Émile Zola as a novelist.

Best, Victoria. *An Introduction to Twentieth-Century French Literature*. London: Duckworth, 2002. Provides an overview of French literary movements and the major writers of the period, including Marcel Proust and Marguerite Duras.

Cardy, Michael, George Evans, and Gabriel Jacobs, eds. *Narrative Voices in Modern French Fiction*. Cardiff: University of Wales Press, 1997. Collection of essays includes excellent studies on important French novelists, including Nathalie Sarraute, Gustave Flaubert, and Albert Camus.

Fallaize, Elizabeth. *French Women's Writing: Recent Fiction*. New York: Macmillan, 1993. Presents insightful analyses of many important French women writers who were active in the second half of the twentieth century.

Frackman Becker, Lucille. *Twentieth-Century French Women Novelists*. Boston: Twayne, 1989. Provides good analyses of the contributions of several major twentieth century French women novelists. Includes a solid bibliography of primary and secondary works.

Kay, Sarah, Terence Cave, and Malcolm Bowie. *A Short History of French Literature*. New York: Oxford University Press, 2003. Discussion of French literature is divided into sections chronologically, with the first of three parts covering the earliest works through the Middle Ages, the second discussing the period 1470 to 1789, and the third addressing the period 1789 to 2000. Includes an informative introduction, illustrations, an extensive bibliography, and an index.

Motte, Warren. *Fables of the Novel: French Fiction Since 1990*. Normal, Ill.: Dalkey Archive Press, 2003. Focuses on the works of French avant-garde novelists since 1990. Includes a bibliography and an index.

Pasco, Allan H. *Novel Configurations: A Study of French Fiction*. Birmingham, Ala.: Summa, 1987. Good introduction to the French novel includes a series of well-written studies on such major novelists as Émile Zola, Marcel Proust, and Joris-Karl Huysmans.

Worth-Stylianou, Valerie, ed. *Cassell Guide to French Literature*. London: Cassell, 1996. Includes excellent studies on the general development in French novels. Each essay is supplemented with a solid bibliography.

HONORÉ DE BALZAC

Born: Tours, France; May 20, 1799
Died: Paris, France; August 18, 1850
Also known as: Honoré Balzac; Lord R'Hoone; Horace de Saint Aubin

PRINCIPAL LONG FICTION
 La Comédie humaine, 1829-1848 (17 volumes; *The Comedy of Human Life*, 1885-1893, 1896 [40 volumes]; also known as *The Human Comedy*, 1895-1896, 1911 [53 volumes]; includes all titles listed below)
 Les Chouans, 1829 (*The Chouans*)
 Physiologie du mariage, 1829 (*The Physiology of Marriage*)
 Gobseck, 1830 (English translation)
 La Maison du chat-qui-pelote, 1830, 1869 (*At the Sign of the Cat and Racket*)
 Le Chef-d'œuvre inconnu, 1831 (*The Unknown Masterpiece*)
 La Peau de chagrin, 1831 (*The Wild Ass's Skin*; also known as *The Magic Skin* and *The Fatal Skin*)
 Sarrasine, 1831 (English translation)
 Le Curé de Tours, 1832 (*The Vicar of Tours*)
 Louis Lambert, 1832 (English translation)
 Maître Cornélius, 1832 (English translation)
 La Femme de trente ans, 1832-1842 (includes *Premières fautes*, 1832, 1842; *Souffrances inconnues*, 1834-1835; *À trente ans*, 1832, 1842; *Le Doigt de Dieu*, 1832, 1834-1835, 1842; *Les Deux Rencontres*, 1832, 1834-1835, 1842; and *La Vieillesse d'une mère coupable*, 1832, 1842)
 Eugénie Grandet, 1833 (English translation, 1859)
 Le Médecin de campagne, 1833 (*The Country Doctor*)
 La Recherche de l'absolu, 1834 (*Balthazar: Or, Science and Love*, 1859; also known as *The Quest of the Absolute*)
 Histoire des treize, 1834-1835 (*History of the Thirteen*; also known as *The Thirteen*; includes *Ferragus, chef des dévorants*, 1834 [*Ferragus, Chief of the Devorants*; also known as *The Mystery of the Rue Solymane*]; *La Duchesse de Langeais*, 1834 [*The Duchesse de Langeais*]; and *La Fille aus yeux d'or*, 1834-1835 [*The Girl with the Golden Eyes*])
 Le Père Goriot, 1834-1835 (*Daddy Goriot*, 1860; also known as *Père Goriot*)
 Melmoth réconcilié, 1835 (*Melmoth Converted*)
 Le Lys dans la vallée, 1836 (*The Lily in the Valley*)
 Histoire de la grandeur et de la décadence de César Birotteau, 1837 (*History of the Grandeur and Downfall of César Birotteau*, 1860; also known as *The Rise and Fall of César Birotteau*)

Illusions perdues, 1837-1843 (*Lost Illusions*)
Splendeurs et misères des courtisanes, 1838-1847, 1869 (*The Splendors and Miseries of Courtesans*; includes *Comment aiment les filles*, 1838, 1844 [*The Way That Girls Love*]; *À combien l'amour revient aux vieillards*, 1844 [*How Much Love Costs Old Men*;] *Où mènent les mauvais chemins*, 1846 [*The End of Bad Roads*]; and *La Dernière Incarnation de Vautrin*, 1847 [*The Last Incarnation of Vautrin*])
Pierrette, 1840 (English translation)
Le Curé de village, 1841 (*The Country Parson*)
Mémoires de deux jeunes mariées, 1842 (*The Two Young Brides*)
Une Ténébreuse Affaire, 1842 (*The Gondreville Mystery*)
Ursule Mirouët, 1842 (English translation)
La Cousine Bette, 1846 (*Cousin Bette*)
Le Cousin Pons, 1847 (*Cousin Pons*, 1880)

Other literary forms

In addition to his fiction, Honoré de Balzac (BAHL-zak) wrote several plays, including *Cromwell* (wr. 1819-1820, pb. 1925), *Vautrin* (pr., pb. 1840; English translation, 1901), and *Le Faiseur*, also known as *Mercadet* (pr. 1849; English translation, 1901), but he was not a playwright and generally devoted time to the theater only when he felt that there was a good profit to be made with little effort. Likewise, many of the articles and essays that Balzac wrote between 1825 and 1834, published in such journals as *Le Voleur, La Mode, La Caricature, La Silhouette*, and *La Revue de Paris*, were composed to enable the author to acquire ready money. Balzac's letters to the Polish baroness Evelina Hanska, to his family, and to Madame Zulma Carraud were published after the novelist's death.

Achievements

The Human Comedy, Honoré de Balzac's masterwork, is one of the greatest literary achievements of all time. It contains many novels beyond those listed above, the bulk of which were written between 1830 and 1847. Before 1829, Balzac wrote under various pseudonyms—notably "Lord R'Hoone" and "Horace de Saint Aubin"—and frequently composed novels in collaboration with other writers. These twenty or so early volumes, which include *Sténie: Ou, Les Erreurs philosophiques* (1936; *Sténie: or, philosophical errors*), *Falturne* (1950), *Le Centenaire: Ou, Les Deux Beringheld* (1822; *The Centenarian: Or, The Two Beringhelds*, 1976), and *La Dernière Fée* (1823; the last fairy), were later renounced by Balzac, and rightly so, for they were written in haste and were obvious attempts to exploit the current taste for gothic melodrama and romantic adventures.

Honoré de Balzac
(Library of Congress)

BIOGRAPHY

Honoré Balzac was born in Tours, France, on May 20, 1799, of bourgeois parents. He was to acquire the predicate of nobility—the name by which he is known today—when, in 1831, in tribute to his official commitment to embark on the writing of *The Human Comedy*, he dubbed himself Honoré *de* Balzac. This change of name is symptomatic of Balzac's lifelong craving to be an aristocrat and to enjoy the deep respect and the want-for-nothing lifestyle that accompanied that status.

The eldest of four children, Balzac was treated very coldly by his parents, who entrusted him to the care of a wet nurse for four years, then sent him to board with a family of strangers for two years, and finally had him attend for seven years a boarding school in Vendôme. Balzac's childhood years were loveless and painful, which probably encouraged him to turn inward toward dreams and fantasies. By 1816, Balzac had finished his studies in Vendôme, albeit with far less than a brilliant record, and was sent off to Paris to study jurisprudence, his mother ordering him to "shape up" and work very hard. At the age of twenty, however, Balzac declared to his family his surprising intention to become a writer, not a lawyer. When his parents skeptically agreed to his wishes, Balzac was permitted to live in Paris for two years, where he was set up in a poorly furnished apartment and was given a deliberately insufficient allowance, which was intended to demonstrate to this wayward son the harsh economic facts of life.

Between 1819 and 1829, Balzac was forced to earn a living from writing, a situation that led him to compromise his literary genius for money; when this endeavor proved inadequate, he was not too proud to undertake other occupations. In an effort to ensure his freedom to write, Balzac became a bookseller, then a printer, then a journalist. All of these enterprises, however, ultimately failed. His most notorious business venture occurred in 1838, when he speculated on Sardinian silver mines. Everything Balzac tried to do as a businessman only drove him deeper into debt, a state of affairs that he often transposed to the realm of his fiction; yet even when Balzac was at the mercy of creditors and in danger of being arrested, he remained, at bottom, optimistic. His new novel would rescue him, at least temporarily, from financial embarrassment, or his current business venture would surely make him wealthy, or, best of all, an aristocratic lady—and there was nearly always a prospect—would soon become his wife and give him not only her love but also her fortune. Nearly all of the women who mattered to Balzac were, in fact, noble, from Madame Laure de Berny, who sacrificed both her morals and her money to help the budding genius to survive, to Madame Evelina Hanska, the Polish baroness who began by writing anonymous letters of admiration to the well-known author and eventually, after her husband's death and her daughter's marriage, consented to become Balzac's wife.

It is an irony that suitably parallels that of the fictional world portrayed in *The Human Comedy* that Balzac's marriage to this woman of his dreams occurred only five months before his death. Balzac died from what one may term outright exhaustion on August 18, 1850.

Analysis

At the age of thirty, Honoré de Balzac resolved to become a great French writer. At first, he believed that he could accomplish this goal by emulating the Scottish writer Sir Walter Scott, whose historical novels were highly esteemed in France during the first half of the nineteenth century. Like Scott, Balzac would be a historian of social, psychological, and political life. Later, however, as Balzac explains in his preface to *The Human Comedy*, this idea was modified. Balzac finally saw his true and original role to be that of "the secretary of society" rather than that of a social historian; that is, instead of bringing the past to life, as Scott had done, Balzac chose to transcribe the life around him into fiction. In many ways, the author of *The Human Comedy* is faithful to this role, drawing a picture of French society at all levels from roughly 1815 until the end of Balzac's writing career in 1848.

The Human Comedy

In his novels, Balzac reveals the driving passions and needs of a wide range of individuals in various social positions: noblemen and aristocratic ladies; politicians, bankers, businessmen, and moneylenders; scientists, doctors, and priests; lawyers, policemen, and criminals; musicians, painters, sculptors, and writers. This picture of society delineates not only ambitious members of the bourgeoisie and proud aristocrats but also the environments in which they live and work, including the luxurious, exhilarating, and cutthroat life of Paris and the comparatively dull and inactive existence of small provincial French towns. The two thousand characters whom Balzac depicts in *The Human Comedy* are not, however, mere social types. On the contrary, Balzac's protagonists are, in general, strongly individualistic, some of them to the point of eccentricity.

Each novel of *The Human Comedy* contains a single story that may be read and appreciated for itself; at the same time, each story is linked to the whole. A protagonist encountered in one novel might very well appear again, like an old acquaintance, within the context of another novel and possibly a very different plot. The small number of characters who travel from one novel to another give unity to Balzac's works and at the same time convey the impression that the fictional world described in *The Human Comedy* is alive and infinite in scope.

With regard to tone, Balzac's plots embrace a wide range of attitudes: tragically sad or comically ironic, highly idealistic, fantastic, or romantic. The novelist, however, is judged to have excelled particularly as a realist in his candid portrayal of the tremendous will to power of human nature and of the influence of money on social behavior.

In Balzac's works, many of the characteristic impulses of the nineteenth century coincided and reinforced one another. Balzac's legendary energy, his enormous, hubristic ambition, his tireless interest in the world, and his sheer appetite for experience—all these elements worked together to produce a massive tapestry of an entire society, unmatched in scope and detail before or since the author's time.

Three themes in Balzac's fiction can be seen as reflections of the novelist's personality: The first of these is the theme of madness or monomania, the second is the large role given to money, and the third is the recurrent search of Balzac's characters for love and success. The madmen of *The Human Comedy* include some of Balzac's most original and memorable characters. These figures are generally obsessed by ideas that they try to make into reality and for which they sacrifice everything. Although the individual obsessions of these protagonists vary, Frenhofer, the painter in *The Unknown Masterpiece*, Grandet, the miser in *Eugénie Grandet*, and Claes, the scientist in *The Quest of the Absolute*, are nevertheless shadows of Balzac, the author, who expresses through them his own obsession: the painstaking composition of *The Human Comedy*. Balzac wrote for hours, weeks, and months on end to prove his genius to the world. Everything was sacrificed for his literary task, including comfortable lodging, clothes, and the most insignificant of worldly amusements.

The monomaniacs of Balzac's creation are particularly interesting figures. They are intelligent and possess glorious ideas that, if they initially seem eccentric, at the same time denote genius. Their bold determination to accomplish all they have set out to do is admirable only to a point, however. Balzac always shows that the obsessions of his monomaniacs dehumanize them. When, for example, Claes in *The Quest of the Absolute* sacrifices the sustenance of his family in order to continue financing his experiments, Balzac pushes his protagonist's passion to an extreme. The manias of Balzac's characters slowly annihilate everything around them until, in the end, these figures appear so blinded by their passion that they are completely enslaved by it. The tragic depiction of Balzac's monomaniacs is undoubtedly one of the cornerstones of *The Human Comedy*. These characters, who first command one's admiration, then appeal to one's sympathy, and finally elicit one's scorn, cause one to ponder with Balzac the force of human thought and willpower. Moreover, by means of his monomaniacs, Balzac expresses his own obsession and his fear of it.

Another important theme of *The Human Comedy* is money, which, in Balzac's fictional world, dominates all other values. In a sense, Balzac's attitude toward money is ambivalent. On one hand, he often shows nostalgia for the neoclassic age, when, under the monarchy, a member of the nobility was assured a life of ease and intellectual grandeur. On the other hand, however, Balzac accepts and objectively portrays the bourgeois society of his day. It is a society whose wheels are oiled by money, but many of Balzac's heroes feel optimistically that, by means of their intelligence, they can succeed in conquering the cycle. Apparently, Balzac himself believed that the appearance of having money was enough to command respect and social acceptance. Sometimes when his characters wear expensive-looking clothes and ride about in fancy carriages, they are, in fact, engaged in a carefully calculated masquerade to fool society by using its own superficial code against it. Of course, some of Balzac's protagonists succeed in this way, but most of them fail—paralleling the novelist's career, in which successes were few and financial failures many. Balzac's most pointed criticism of the role of money in society is not, however, that it is the entry ticket to social success. In such novels as *Père Goriot* and *Eugénie Grandet*, Balzac portrays money in its most diabolical role, as a corrupter of the noblest of human feelings, love.

Balzac depicts two kinds of love in his novels. Ideal love is the quest of many protagonists of *The Human Comedy*, who suffer in its absence and fail to realize its glorious promise. Desirable women in Balzac's fiction are often much older than their aspiring lovers, leading biographers to speculate about Balzac's own mother's indifference toward him and about the novelist's first amorous adventure with Madame de Berny, who—when Balzac met her at the age of twenty-two—was twenty-two years older than he. Aristocratic and maternal women such as Madame de Mortsauf in *The Lily in the Valley* represent a supreme love the likes of which cannot be matched. The very ideal quality of this love, however, is perhaps what leads to its impossibility. Although Balzac's characters glimpse the perfect love object time and time again, the latter generally remains out of reach because of societal or financial constraints. In contrast, love, as Balzac portrays it in his fictional society, is a dangerous counterfeit. Coquettish females of *The Human Com-*

edy, such as Antoinette de Langeais in *The Duchess de Langeais* (a part of *The Thirteen*), provoke innocent gentlemen to fall in love with them only to cultivate their own egos. For the boldest male protagonists of *The Human Comedy*, love is like money, something to be used to advance oneself in society. Rastignac in *Père Goriot* and Raphaël de Valentin in *The Wild Ass's Skin*, for example, make the calculated decision to fall in love, one with a wealthy banker's wife and the other with an aristocratic lady. Family love and devotion are also shams, falling into insignificance when confronted by personal ambition and money.

THE WILD ASS'S SKIN

Balzac classified the novels of *The Human Comedy* into three large areas: "Studies of Social Manners," "Philosophical Studies," and "Analytical Studies." *The Wild Ass's Skin*, published in 1831, was placed into the category "Philosophical Studies," probably because of its fantastic theme, the possession of a magic skin. Like many of Balzac's best novels, however, *The Wild Ass's Skin* is actually a mixture of cold reality and fantastic illusion. The hero of the novel, Raphaël de Valentin, a downtrodden genius whom society persistently ignores, is clearly a figure with whom the novelist could identify. Balzac's protagonist has written a philosophical treatise titled "Théorie de la volonté" ("Theory of the Will"), a work whose exact contents are never revealed but whose significance for Balzac and for *The Human Comedy* is evident. Like his hero, Valentin, Balzac is engaged in an analysis of man's will. Valentin may appear to be more theoretical than the novelist, but both Balzac and his protagonist find the power of ideas at work in the mind to be a fascinating and dangerous study. One suspects that Valentin is actually an image of Balzac's own projected success as well as the foreboding prototype of his failure.

The destiny of Raphaël de Valentin follows a curve from failure to success and back to failure again. At the beginning of the book, Valentin thinks seriously about committing suicide for two reasons. First, he has suffered very deeply in his love for a beautiful but heartless coquette named Foedora. Second, he is destitute. Even though his "Theory" has finally been completed—a lifework that ought to be acknowledged as striking proof of his genius—societal acclaim is still denied him. When Balzac later explains in his epilogue to the novel that Foedora is actually a symbol of society, one understands that her indifference to Valentin includes not only a condemnation of a would-be lover but also a cruel underestimation of his intelligence, the hero's very raison d'être. The initial tragedy of Valentin is realistically portrayed as a battle between a sensitive romantic young man and Parisian society.

In the next phase of Valentin's destiny, however, one sees an abrupt transformation that at first appears to project Balzac's hero to the heights of success. Valentin acquires from a mysterious antiquarian a wild ass's skin. Because, as in a fairy tale, the magic skin grants its owner's every wish, Valentin need no longer be poor. Indeed, it is society's turn to court him! Now the Parisian society that Valentin previously hoped to please is depicted as thoroughly repulsive and morally corrupt. As a sign of Valentin's rejection of it, one of his wishes is that he may forget Foedora, the novel's symbol of society. One may find in Valentin's change of attitude toward society the novelist's own admission to himself that what he ultimately seeks—general recognition of his genius as a writer—simply does not exist in a world ruled by personal vanity and money. Now that Foedora has been forgotten, she is replaced in Valentin's heart by Pauline, a poor, innocent young girl who has always shown him true love and devotion.

This "happy ending" is short-lived, however. In the final phase of Valentin's destiny, Balzac returns to the philosophical theme of the human will. The wild ass's skin that Valentin possesses is not a blessing after all, but a curse. After each wish that it grants to its owner, the skin shrinks in dimension, its dwindling size quickly becoming a horrifying picture of the diminishing length of Valentin's life.

It is interesting to correlate this tragic depiction of Balzac's hero with the situation of the novelist himself. When Balzac wrote *The Wild Ass's Skin* in 1831, he was already aware that his enormous writing task would take him away from the world of reality and cause him to become a more firmly established inhabitant of his fictional world. After the protagonist of *The Wild Ass's Skin* has unmasked society, he attempts to withdraw from it. Perhaps, pen in hand, wearing his monk's cloak, Balzac, too, may have thought that he could escape to the fictional realm of his imagination. Eventually, however, reality always intervened and subjugated the writer to its practical demands. Hence, Balzac gives that part of himself that repudiates money and all those who worship it a kind of allowance analogous to money. Valentin must make fewer and fewer wishes and finally tries not to express any desires at all, simply in order to continue living.

In this complex novel, Balzac transposes into fiction his own misery, his maddening drive to succeed, his dreams and love for life, while giving the reader a survey of the themes that will permeate many novels of *The Human Comedy*: money, unrealized love, the drive to succeed, and madness.

THE VICAR OF TOURS

Balzac finished writing *The Vicar of Tours* in April, 1832. In this short novel, Balzac, like Gustave Flaubert in his famous short story "Un Cœur simple" ("A Simple Heart"), relates a story that superficially seems unworthy of mention. Balzac's hero, Birotteau, like Flaubert's heroine, Félicité, is rather simpleminded and lives an uneventful life. True to the nature of Balzac's most memorable heroes, however, Birotteau is quite different from Félicité in that, despite his lack of intelligence, he is ambitious. Furthermore, he is naïvely happy. Balzac alternately pities and ridicules his provincial priest, whose passion it is to possess the beautiful apartment of his colleague, Chapeloud. While pointing out that a desire for material wealth is not seemly for a priest, Balzac ironically pardons his hero, who is, after all, only human and whose ambition, as ambitions go, can only be termed petty.

When Birotteau's ambition is fulfilled upon the death of Chapeloud, the apartment becomes the subject of a war of wills involving not only Birotteau's spinster landlady, Mademoiselle Gamard, but eventually the whole town of Tours. Indeed, a political career in the highest echelons of the French government and the important advancement of a priest within the Catholic Church both end up having, in some way, a relationship to what begins as Birotteau's "insignificant" passion.

In some ways, Birotteau is the opposite of the typical Balzacian monomaniac. Happy to let everything be handled by his friends and incapable of understanding what is going on, he watches the battle rage around him. Birotteau would not purposely hurt a fly, and he does not have an inkling of why he is being attacked.

As in many novels of *The Human Comedy*, an important turn in the plot of *The Vicar of Tours* hinges on a legal document, in this case the apartment lease. Balzac's years as a law student often served him well, as he used his knowledge of the law in composing many of his plots. Essentially missing from this novel is one of Balzac's major themes, money. Nevertheless, the vanity of the characters in *The Vicar of Tours* and their drive for personal success and power are keenly developed subjects of satire and, at the same time, very realistic studies of human psychology and social behavior. Balzac classed *The Vicar of Tours* under the heading "Scenes of Provincial Life," a subcategory of "Studies of Social Manners"—where the largest number of novels in *The Human Comedy* can be found.

LOUIS LAMBERT

Approximately three months after completing *The Vicar of Tours*, in July, 1832, Balzac finished *Louis Lambert*. This novel was eventually included with *The Wild Ass's Skin* and eighteen other novels in the category "Philosophical Studies," but its relationship to Balzac's "Studies of Social Manners" is strengthened through the device of recurring characters. One of the minor figures of *The Vicar of Tours* is an old woman, Mademoiselle Salomon de Villenoix, who befriends Birotteau and shows him a great deal of compassion. In *Louis Lambert*, the same woman plays a more important role, as Balzac describes Mademoiselle de Villenoix in her youth, when she was the ideal love object of Louis Lambert, the principal character of the novel.

The parallels between *The Wild Ass's Skin* and *Louis Lambert* are quite interesting. Like Raphaël de Valentin, Louis Lambert is a genius who composes a philosophical work on the will; the title of his work, "Traité de la volonté" ("Treatise on the Will"), is virtually identical to the title of Valentin's. Each of the two characters succeeds in finding an ideal woman whose name is Pauline: Pauline de Villenoix in *Louis Lambert* and Pauline de Witschnau in *The Wild Ass's Skin*. Finally, the tragedy of each of the genius heroes lies in the fact that he goes mad. The Paulines of the two novels react to the inexplicable madness of the men they love by devoting themselves totally to them, somewhat like nurses or angels of mercy.

The similarities between *Louis Lambert* and *The Wild Ass's Skin* give one a fairly clear idea of what must have been Balzac's attitude toward himself. The novelist instills in his heroes two great passions that are undoubtedly reflections of his own drives: to become a recognized genius and to be loved. In these two novels, Balzac appears to demonstrate his belief that love and genius cannot coexist and that when one attempts to blend them, they annihilate each other. In this sense, the madness that overcomes Balzac's protagonists represents a double failure. Both Lambert and Valentin fall short of attaining ideal love and also fail to develop the potential of their genius.

It is nevertheless true that Balzac shows the passions of Louis Lambert for love and for recognition of his genius somewhat differently from the way he portrays these passions in his earlier novel. In *Louis Lambert*, the novelist seems to indicate a preference for one of the two goals when he emphasizes Lambert's genius. From the beginning of the novel, Lambert is seen through the eyes of an admiring narrator who relates in retrospect the bitter experiences of school days shared with Balzac's genius hero. In detailing these experiences, Balzac transposes into fiction many of his own memories of the lonely years he spent as a boarder at the Collège de Vendôme. Both the narrator and Lambert are neglected by their parents, ostracized by their peers, punished by their teachers, and forbidden—as in a prison—to enjoy even the slightest amusement. The narrator admits to being inferior to Lambert, whose genius he sensed when they were in school together and whose insights, although they are now only half-remembered, had the power of truth.

At the end of the novel, Balzac intensifies sympathy for the plight of his genius hero gone mad by reproducing a series of philosophical fragments that, because they are written down by Lambert's loving companion, Pauline, are only sketchy transcriptions of his actual thoughts. It is not important that these fragments appear puzzling and in some cases absurd: Like the incomplete recollections of the narrator, they are powerfully evocative *because* they are fragmentary, tantalizingly so, suggestive of what the world lost when it lost the genius of Louis Lambert.

EUGÉNIE GRANDET

Before the publication of *Eugénie Grandet* in 1833, Balzac had continued to experiment in his novels with the theme of madness. In addition to *Louis Lambert*, Balzac had written other "Philosophical Studies" in the period 1830-1832 that expand on this theme, including *The Unknown Masterpiece* and *Maître Cornélius*. In *The Unknown Masterpiece*, Balzac portrays a painter, Frenhofer, whose madness manifests itself in his increasing inability to transpose the idealized feminine figure he imagines to a canvas. The hero of *Maître Cornélius* suffers from an insidious malady: When he sleepwalks, his unconscious self steals the money that, in reality, he is supposed to guard.

In *Eugénie Grandet*, however, the theme of madness reaches a turning point. Balzac's protagonist, Old Grandet, like Maître Cornélius, is a miser, but what distinguishes him from the latter is that his mania does not indicate total sickness or madness. Grandet's passion does not seem to debilitate him in any way. On the contrary, it is his raison d'être and is willfully and, one may even say, intellectually directed. Grandet, one of the most fascinating characters of *The Human Comedy*, is a full-blown monomaniac. What makes him so interesting is that he is not one-dimensional. Although Grandet's obsessive drive for money remains constant throughout the novel, he is not always seen in the same light. In relations with his wife, his cook, his small-town neighbors, and especially his daughter, Eugénie, Grandet sparks off a variety of reactions to his miserly behavior. At times he is admired and feared for his sharp intelligence; at other times he is condemned for his lack of understanding and unyielding ruthlessness.

Yet manifestations of Grandet's monomania do not, by themselves, dominate the novel. Rather, Grandet's avarice competes for importance with another, complementary plot: the awakening of Grandet's daughter to love. Indeed, in *Eugénie Grandet*, the three subjects that have been identified as key themes in Balzac's fiction—madness, money, and the search for love—converge. Grandet's obsession with money comes into conflict with Eugénie's equally strong impulse to love. While her father's nature is to hoard money even if it means that his family must be destitute, Eugénie finds in giving away all of her money to her beloved cousin, Charles, a supreme expression of love.

Balzac pits his young heroine against other adversaries as well: provincial opportunism, social morality, and Charles's ambitions. Using his innocent and naïve heroine as a foil, Balzac reveals the crass motives of provincial society, contrasting Eugénie's exceptional, giving nature with the self-interest of others who, like Eugénie's father, are motivated primarily by money. Balzac placed *Eugénie Grandet* into the subcategory of *The Human Comedy* titled "Scenes of Provincial Life."

PÈRE GORIOT

Published in 1835, *Père Goriot*, given its Parisian locale, could easily have been placed into the category of *The Human Comedy* called "Scenes of Parisian Life." Balzac finally classified it, however, among his "Scenes of Private Life," which is an equally suitable designation for the novel. *Père Goriot* is a pivotal novel of *The Human Comedy* in several ways. First, with respect to Balzac's trademark, the use of recurring characters, nearly all the characters in this novel, whether their roles are large or small, can be found somewhere else in Balzac's opus, with the exception of Goriot himself. Some characters were already seen in works published before 1835; others would be developed in subsequent novels. Eugène de Rastignac, the young hero of *Père Goriot*, for example, appeared briefly as a friend of Raphaël de Valentin in *The Wild Ass's Skin*. Similarly, Goriot's older daughter, Anasthasie, was already portrayed in a short novel, *Gobseck*, published in 1830. The criminal Jacques Collin, alias Vautrin, who makes his debut in *Père Goriot*, would be given prominent roles in such later works as *Lost Illusions* and *The Splendors and Miseries of Courtesans*.

Balzac successfully interweaves three different plots in *Père Goriot*, their relationship being that the principal protagonists of all three live in the same Parisian boardinghouse, La Maison Vauquer. Eugène de Rastignac is an innocent provincial young man, new to Parisian manners but eager to learn. In a sense, Rastignac takes up the same crusade as does Raphaël de Valentin in *The Wild Ass's Skin*, in that he directs all his efforts toward "conquering" society—which means that, like Valentin, he strives to earn social acceptance and esteem. One notes, however, that Balzac does not make Rastignac a writer, like Valentin. Rather, shadowing another part of Balzac's own past, the young hero of *Père Goriot* is a poor law student.

Old Goriot himself is another inhabitant of La Maison Vauquer. He is a Balzacian monomaniac, a hero whose "madness" is self-willed and consciously directed. Goriot is not, however, another copy of Balzac's miser, Grandet; rather, Balzac opposes these two figures. Goriot is not a miser; he does not hoard money. On the contrary, he spends it on his two daughters, Anasthasie and Delphine. Whereas Grandet causes his family to live like paupers in order to continue amassing money, Goriot willingly strips himself of his means of sustenance in order to continue giving money to his daughters. Balzac's intent in portraying Goriot may have been to examine the power of money in a situation that contrasts directly with that of his miser, Grandet. Certainly, Balzac never found a more intense formula for tragedy than when he created his monomaniac Goriot, who attempts to link money and love.

The third major plot of *Père Goriot* centers on another inhabitant of La Maison Vauquer, Vautrin, who—unbeknown to the other boarders of Madame Vauquer's establishment—is an escaped convict wanted by the police. Vautrin's view of society is in absolute opposition to that of Rastignac; whereas the young man attempts to court social favor, Vautrin denounces everything to do with the social order, calling it a *bourbier*, or mud hole. Intelligent and cynical, Vautrin advocates a different sort of social conquest, namely, bold defiance and outright rebellion.

Unlike most of the preceding novels in *The Human Comedy*, *Père Goriot* is a novel with multiple heroes and multiple plots. Balzac offers the reader a fresco of social manners through characters who represent very different classes of society, from the aristocrat and the bourgeois to the criminal *révolté*. Balzac uses his technique of portraying protagonists from various contrasting angles—seen in *The Vicar of Tours* and in *Eugénie Grandet*—much more extensively in *Père Goriot*. Goriot, Goriot's daughters, Rastignac, Vautrin, and other characters as well are alternately judged to be admirable, honest, and powerful, and to be imperfect, deceitful, and helpless. Goriot, in particular, is delineated by means of a kaleidoscope of contrary impressions. He loves his daughters, but he also hates them. His love is fatherly and not so fatherly. He is both self-sacrificing and self-interested. In death, he curses his daughters and pardons them in the same breath. Clearly, in *Père Goriot*, Balzac reached maturity as a novelist.

Cousin Bette

Cousin Bette was published rather late in Balzac's career, in 1846, and was placed, along with a complementary work titled *Cousin Pons*, among the "Scenes of Parisian Life." In the ten years between the publication of *Père Goriot* and that of *Cousin Bette*,

Balzac wrote approximately forty-five other novels, many of which continued to develop the three major themes in his fiction—madness, money, and the search for love and success.

It is interesting to see all three themes once again interwoven in *Cousin Bette*, albeit in a strikingly different manner. In one of the novel's subplots, a new type of monomania is depicted in Baron Hulot d'Evry, who is driven repeatedly to commit adultery although his actions are an embarrassment to himself, his wife, and his family. Balzac hints at Hulot's hidden motivation when he describes his protagonist's wife, Adeline, as a martyr figure, a religious zealot, and a model of propriety.

Elisabeth Fischer—called Cousin Bette—is aware that the Hulot family, headed by Adeline, receives her only out of family duty and that, as a poor relation, she is neither loved nor esteemed by them. Even though she realizes that the apparent good fortune and happiness of the Hulot family are a carefully contrived sham, Bette is jealous of her cousin Adeline for having always been prettier, wealthier, and more successful than she. Cousin Bette's vengeance against the Hulot family, which is the principal plot of the novel, incorporates all three of the major themes of Balzac's fiction. Because Cousin Bette has no money, no success, and no love, her maddened drive for vengeance is unleashed. Her desire for revenge becomes a mania, and she is soon driven to the point where there is absolutely no limit to what she will do to ruin her cousin's life, including finding new females to entice both the Baron and Adeline's proposed son-in-law, Steinbock.

As though to intensify the diabolical power of Cousin Bette, Balzac adds to it the equally unscrupulous machinations of his heroine's pretty neighbor, Valérie Marneffe. Valérie helps Bette carry out her revenge against the Hulot family, and Bette, in return, aids her neighbor in an enterprise to extract money from her many male admirers. Valérie, a beautiful and ambitious middle-class woman, discovers that she can find financial success by seducing men and making them pay for her love. It is interesting that when Valérie is given the chance to run away to South America with an exotic Brazilian nobleman who loves her sincerely, she refuses in order to continue the business of her lucrative and ego-building seductions. In *Cousin Bette*, the achievement of an ideal love, like that glimpsed in earlier novels such as *The Wild Ass's Skin* and *Louis Lambert*, is seen as utterly impossible.

In *Cousin Bette*, Balzac makes a mockery not only of love but also of monomania. Through a gross exaggeration, this eccentric passion no longer characterizes a single figure of the novel, as in *Eugénie Grandet* or *Père Goriot*. Rather, no fewer than three characters of the novel can be called monomaniacs: Cousin Bette, Valérie Marneffe, and Baron Hulot. It is true, however, that the two females are far more developed than Hulot. These two female protagonists, as they strengthen and complement each other, offer a hyperbolic image of monomania, parodying one of the trademarks of Balzac's fiction. By means of this parody, Balzac plainly shows that he has dissociated himself from his characters' plight. Perhaps he was able to satirize monomania because his career as a novelist was unquestionably successful, and he was beginning to receive some of the recognition he had always sought. Nevertheless, his own "mania" persisted: Until he simply became too sick to write, he continued to work on yet another novel in *The Human Comedy*, with ten more volumes projected and endless bills to pay.

Sonja G. Stary

OTHER MAJOR WORKS

SHORT FICTION: *Les Contes drolatiques*, 1832-1837 (*Droll Stories*, 1874, 1891).

PLAYS: *Vautrin*, pr., pb. 1840 (English translation, 1901); *La Marâtre*, pr., pb. 1848 (*The Stepmother*, 1901, 1958); *Le Faiseur*, pr. 1849 (also known as *Mercadet*; English translation, 1901); *The Dramatic Works*, 1901 (2 volumes; includes *Vautrin*, *The Stepmother*, *Mercadet*, *Quinola's Resources*, and *Pamela Giraud*); *Cromwell*, pb. 1925 (wr. 1819-1820).

NONFICTION: *Correspondance*, 1819-1850, 1876 (*The Correspondence*, 1878); *Lettres à l'étrangère*, 1899-1950; *Letters to Madame Hanska*, 1900 (translation of volume 1 of *Lettres à l'étrangère*).

BIBLIOGRAPHY

Beizer, Janet L. *Family Plots: Balzac's Narrative Generations*. New Haven, Conn.: Yale University Press, 1986. A careful study of the family and other hierarchies in Balzac's novels. Argues that the structure of the family itself is an ordering principle of the fiction. Introduction clearly situates this work in the tradition of Balzac criticism while making clear how it differs from earlier studies.

Bell, David F. *Real Time: Accelerating Narrative from Balzac to Zola*. Urbana: University of Illinois Press, 2004. Cites examples from novels and short stories to explore how the accelerated movement of people and information in the nineteenth century was a crucial element in the work of Balzac and three other French authors.

Bloom, Harold, ed. *Honoré de Balzac*. Philadelphia: Chelsea House, 2003. One in a series of books designed to introduce readers to the works of significant authors. In addition to Bloom's introductory overview, features essays analyzing *The Wild Ass's Skin*, *Cousin Pons, Eugénie Grandet, Père Goriot*, and *Cousin Bette*.

Festa-McCormick, Diana. *Honoré de Balzac*. Boston: Twayne, 1979. Provides an excellent introduction to the works of Balzac. Describes with much subtlety Balzac's evolution as a novelist and offers insightful comments on his representations of women. Contains a very well annotated bibliography.

Garval, Michael D. "Honoré de Balzac: Writing the Monument." In *"A Dream of Stone": Fame, Vision, and Monumentality in Nineteenth-Century French Literary Culture*. Newark: University of Delaware Press, 2004. Chapter on Balzac is part of a volume that describes how France in the nineteenth century developed an ideal image of "great" writers, viewing these authors' work as immortal and portraying their literary successes in monumental terms. The work as a whole traces the rise and fall of this literary development by focusing on Balzac, George Sand, and Victor Hugo.

Madden, James. *Weaving Balzac's Web: Spinning Tales and Creating the Whole of "La Comédie humaine."* Birmingham, Ala.: Summa, 2003. Explores how Balzac structured his vast series of novels to create continuity both within and between the individual books. Describes how internal narration, in which characters tell each other stories about other characters, enables the recurring characters to provide layers of meaning that are evident throughout the series.

Maurois, André. *Prometheus: The Life of Balzac.* Translated by Norman Denny. New York: Harper & Row, 1965. The standard biography of Balzac analyzes the author's formative years, his place in the Parisian literary circles of the 1830's and 1840's, and his long relationship with Evelina Hanska. Makes judicious use of Balzac's extant letters in order to give readers a sense of Balzac's personality.

Pritchett, V. S. *Balzac.* New York: Alfred A. Knopf, 1973. Beautifully illustrated book by an eminent writer and literary critic enables readers to understand the milieu in which Balzac wrote. Presents interpretations of Balzac's short stories and his novel *The Wild Ass's Skin* that are especially thought-provoking. Includes a good bibliography of critical studies on Balzac.

Robb, Graham. *Balzac: A Life.* New York: W. W. Norton, 1994. Detailed biographical account of the life and work of Balzac focuses on his philosophical perspectives as well as on his fiction. Speculates on the psychological motivations underlying his work.

Rogers, Samuel. *Balzac and the Novel.* Madison: University of Wisconsin Press, 1953. Thoughtful study of Balzac's narrative techniques and his use of recurring characters in *The Human Comedy.* Also describes Balzac's portrayal of different social classes in his novels.

Thomas, Gwen. "The Case of the Missing Detective: Balzac's *Une Ténébreuse Affaire.*" *French Studies* 48 (July, 1994): 285-298. Discusses how Balzac, in his novel *The Gondreville Mystery,* anticipates a number of the conventions that would come to be associated with the detective story. Argues that Balzac retains gaps and indeterminacies in his work and that his final revelation is a literary device rather than a logical conclusion.

Zweig, Stefan. *Balzac.* Translated by William Rose and Dorothy Rose, edited by Richard Friedenthal. New York: Viking Press, 1946. After Maurois, Zweig is the best biographer of Balzac. This fascinating book reads almost like a novel about the author's life. Zweig's tendency to offer his own interpretations of events makes his work more subjective than Maurois's, and perhaps less reliable in some particulars, but it remains an excellent introduction for the nonspecialist.

SIMONE DE BEAUVOIR

Born: Paris, France; January 9, 1908
Died: Paris, France; April 14, 1986
Also known as: Simone Lucie-Ernestine-Marie-Bertrand de Beauvoir

PRINCIPAL LONG FICTION
L'Invitée, 1943 (*She Came to Stay*, 1949)
Le Sang des autres, 1945 (*The Blood of Others*, 1948)
Tous les hommes sont mortels, 1946 (*All Men Are Mortal*, 1955)
Les Mandarins, 1954 (*The Mandarins*, 1956)
Les Belles Images, 1966 (English translation, 1968)

OTHER LITERARY FORMS

Simone de Beauvoir (duh boh-VWAHR) is best known for her social and political philosophy, especially her contributions to feminism. Foremost among her nonfiction works is her four-volume autobiography, *Mémoires d'une jeune fille rangée* (1958; *Memoirs of a Dutiful Daughter*, 1959), *La Force de l'âge* (1960; *The Prime of Life*, 1962), *La Force des choses* (1963; *Force of Circumstance*, 1964), and *Tout compte fait* (1972; *All Said and Done*, 1974). Equally important is her monumental sociological study on women, *Le Deuxième Sexe* (1949; *The Second Sex*, 1953). Two other sociological works follow *The Second Sex*, the first on China, *La Longue Marche* (1957; *The Long March*, 1958), and the second on the aged, *La Vieillesse* (1970; *The Coming of Age*, 1972). *Les Bouches inutiles* (1945), her only play, has not been translated into English. She also published two collections of short stories, *La Femme rompue* (1967; *The Woman Destroyed*, 1968) and *Quand prime le spirituel* (1979; *When Things of the Spirit Come First: Five Early Tales*, 1982). Her most important philosophical essays include *Pyrrhus et Cinéas* (1944), *Pour une morale de l'ambiguïté* (1947; *The Ethics of Ambiguity*, 1948), *L'Existentialisme et la sagesse des nations* (1948), and *Privilèges* (1955; partial translation "Must We Burn Sade?," 1953). A number of her other essays appeared in newspapers and journals. She also wrote a chronicle of her travels in the United States, *L'Amérique au jour le jour* (1948; *America Day by Day*, 1953); a powerful account of her mother's illness and death, *Une Mort très douce* (1964; *A Very Easy Death*, 1966); and a tribute to Jean-Paul Sartre, *La Cérémonie des adieux* (1981; *Adieux: A Farewell to Sartre*, 1984).

ACHIEVEMENTS

Simon de Beauvoir was a presence in French intellectual life during the second half of the twentieth century. She is one of the foremost examples of existentialist *engagement* and its most respected moral voice; the breadth of her writing alone secures de Beauvoir a prominent position in twentieth century letters. Her novels, especially *She Came to Stay*,

The Blood of Others, and *The Mandarins* (for which she won the Prix Goncourt in 1954), pose some of the central philosophical and ethical questions of our time, exploring the problems of social morality, political commitment, and human responsibility. Along with her autobiography, her novels chronicle the time before and after World War II and the experiences that made her one of the most influential writers of the twentieth century.

De Beauvoir wrote numerous articles for *Les Temps modernes*, a periodical founded and directed by Sartre, and she was a member of its editorial board. In 1973, she became the editor of the journal's feminist column. *The Second Sex*, her carefully documented study of the situation of women, became one of the major theoretical texts of the women's movement. Always an activist for women's rights and social justice, she demonstrated against France's restrictive abortion laws and signed the "Manifeste des 343," a document listing women who admitted having had abortions. She was president of Choisir (1971) and of the Ligue des Droits des Femmes (1974), an organization devoted to fighting sex discrimination. De Beauvoir was also one of the founders of the feminist journal *Questions féministes*. Her indictment of social injustice is evidenced by *The Coming of Age*, her defense of a free press (the Maoist underground newspaper *La Cause du peuple*), and her political actions.

Biography

Simone Lucie-Ernestine-Marie-Bertrand de Beauvoir was born in Paris on January 9, 1908. Her father, Georges de Beauvoir, came from a wealthy family and was a lawyer by profession. A religious skeptic, he was openly contemptuous of the bourgeoisie and encouraged his daughter in intellectual pursuits. In contrast, her mother, Françoise, came from a provincial town, received her education in convents, and was a devout Catholic. Under her mother's supervision, the young de Beauvoir was educated at a conservative Catholic school for girls, the Cours Désir.

In *Memoirs of a Dutiful Daughter*—which covers the years from 1908 to 1929—de Beauvoir describes her early piety, her subsequent disenchantment with Catholicism, and the beginning of her rebellion against her middle-class background. Influenced by early readings of Louisa May Alcott and George Eliot, she decided at age fifteen that she wanted to be a writer. After leaving the Cours Désir, she pursued the study of literature at the Institut Catholique in Paris. In 1926, she attended the Sorbonne and studied philosophy, Greek, and philology. Three years later, after a year at the prestigious École Normale Supérieure, she passed the examination for the *agrégation de philosophie*, the highest academic degree conferred in France.

In 1929, de Beauvoir met the writer-philosopher Jean-Paul Sartre and began an association with him that lasted until his death in April, 1980. The years from 1929 to 1944 are chronicled in the second volume of her autobiography, *The Prime of Life*. Having completed her academic degrees, she was assigned a series of teaching positions, first in Marseilles and later in Rouen and Paris. Her first novel, *She Came to Stay*, appeared in 1943; it established her as a writer, and she stopped teaching. During the war years, she became interested in political action. By the end of World War II, de Beauvoir and Sartre were labeled "existentialists," and their success and celebrity were assured. In 1947, de Beauvoir was invited on a lecture tour of the United States (described in *America Day by Day*) and began a four-year affair with American writer Nelson Algren.

During the postwar years, de Beauvoir became increasingly preoccupied with the problems of the intellectual in society, and she continued to examine the relationship between freedom and social commitment. In *Force of Circumstance* (which spans the years 1944 to 1962), the third volume of her autobiography, political events such as the Korean War and the Algerian crisis occupy progressively more space. She saw Sartre destroy his health to work on *Critique de la raison dialectique, I: Théorie des ensembles pratiques* (1960; *Critique of Dialectical Reason, I: Theory of Practical Ensembles*, 1976) and became painfully aware of human mortality and solitude. Old age and death are themes that run through de Beauvoir's work from this period, such as *The Woman Destroyed*, *The Coming of Age*, and the last volume of her autobiography, *All Said and Done*. In spite of this, the general tone of *All Said and Done*—as well as of the frequent interviews de Beauvoir gave—is one of a woman content to have achieved her existentialist project before her death in 1986.

Analysis

Simone de Beauvoir's novels are grounded in her training as a philosopher and in her sociological and feminist concerns. *She Came to Stay*, *The Blood of Others*, *All Men Are Mortal*, and *The Mandarins* all revolve around the questions of freedom and responsibility and try to define the proper relationship between the individual and society. Her characters search for authenticity as they attempt to shape the world around them. Their education is sentimental as well as intellectual and political. While most of her heroes accommodate themselves successfully to reality, the same may not be said of her heroines. In the later novels, *The Mandarins* and *Les Belles Images*, her female characters, who are successful by worldly standards, suffer a series of psychological crises. As they undertake what the feminist critic Carol Christ has called spiritual quests, they often face suicide and madness. The existentialist enterprise of *engagement*, or commitment with a view of defining the self through action, seems more possible for the men in her novels than for the women. Jean Leighton has observed the absence of positive heroines in de Beauvoir's work: Woman seems condemned to passivity while man's fate is one of transcendence. Arguments from *The Second Sex* and from de Beauvoir's philosophical essays echo in the novels. The tension between the author's philosophical ideas and their potential realization by the women characters is clearly visible in her fiction.

She Came to Stay

De Beauvoir's first novel, *She Came to Stay*, is an imaginative transposition of her relationship with Olga Kosakiewicz. In 1933, de Beauvoir and Sartre had befriended

Kosakiewicz, one of de Beauvoir's students. They had attempted a ménage à trois; *She Came to Stay* is the story of its failure.

The heroine of the novel, Françoise Miquel, is a young writer who has lived with Pierre Labrousse, a talented actor and director, for eight years. They feel that their relationship is ideal because it allows them both a great deal of freedom. Françoise befriends Xavière, a young woman disenchanted with provincial life, and invites her to Paris, where she will help Xavière find work. Once in Paris, Xavière makes demands on the couple and is openly contemptuous of their values. Pierre becomes obsessed with Xavière; Françoise, trying to rise above the jealousy and insecurity she feels, struggles to keep the trio together. Out of resentment, Françoise has an affaire with Gerbert, Xavière's suitor. The novel ends as Xavière recognizes Françoise's duplicity; Xavière has now become the critical Other. Unable to live in her presence, Françoise turns on the gas and murders her.

She Came to Stay is a meditation on the Hegelian problem of the existence of the Other. The novel plays out the psychological effects of jealousy and questions the extent to which coexistence is possible. Critics such as Hazel Barnes and Carol Ascher have noted the close ties between de Beauvoir's first novel and Sartre's *L'Être et le néant* (1943; *Being and Nothingness*, 1956), published in the same year. Both texts deal with the central existentialist theme of letting others absorb one's freedom.

Despite Françoise's apparent independence, she needs Pierre to approve her actions and give them direction. Françoise's self-deception and the inauthenticity of her life anticipate de Beauvoir's analysis of *l'amoureuse*, the woman in love, in *The Second Sex*. Confronted with a rival, Françoise becomes aware that her self-assurance and detachment are illusory. Her growth as a character occurs as she sheds the unexamined rational premises she holds about herself and her relationship with Pierre. The gap between the intellect and the emotions continues to widen until it reaches a crisis in the murder of Xavière. Françoise is finally forced to confront her long-concealed hatred. In spite of its often stylized dialogue, *She Came to Stay* is a lucid, finely executed study of love and jealousy and one of de Beauvoir's finest novels.

THE BLOOD OF OTHERS

Although de Beauvoir was later to consider her second novel overly didactic, *The Blood of Others* is one of the best novels written about the French Resistance. The book opens with the thoughts of Jean Blomart as he keeps vigil over his mistress Hélène, who is dying from a wound received during a mission. The novel proceeds by flashback and alternates between the stories of Jean, a Resistance hero, and his companion Hélène. The son of a wealthy bourgeois family, Jean is plagued by feelings of guilt over his comfortable situation. He takes a job as a worker and tries to lead a life of uninvolvement. His attempted detachment is based on his belief that he can thus avoid contributing to the unhappiness of others. Passive at the outbreak of the war, he is finally drafted. Upon his return to Paris, he realizes that his detachment is actually a form of irresponsibility. He organizes a resistance group and becomes its leader. As he watches the dying Hélène, he questions whether he has the right to control the lives of his comrades. Although he is doomed to act in ignorance of the consequences of his decisions, he decides that he nevertheless has an obligation to act. The novel ends with Hélène's death and Jean's renewed commitment to the Resistance.

If *The Blood of Others* is the story of Jean's *engagement*, it is also the story of Hélène's political awakening. Like him, she is politically indifferent until a young Jewish friend is in danger of deportation. She then turns to Jean and becomes an active member of his group. In contrast with most of de Beauvoir's women, Hélène is one who, in her political commitment, manages to define herself through her actions rather than through her emotional attachments.

The Blood of Others presages the discussion of individual freedom in *The Ethics of Ambiguity*. In both the novel and the philosophical essay, the problem of the Other is interfaced with the question of social responsibility. With its emphasis on the denial of freedom during the Nazi occupation of France, the novel underscores the necessity of political action to ensure individual freedoms. The closed space of the love triangle in *She Came to Stay* is replaced by the larger obligations of the individual to a historical moment. *The Blood of Others* conveys the problematic quality of ethical decisions; as Robert Cottrell has noted, it evokes "the sense of being entrapped, of submitting to existence rather than fashioning it." Nevertheless, *The Blood of Others* is a more optimistic book than *She Came to Stay* in its portrayal of the individual working toward a larger social good.

All Men Are Mortal

Individual actions are seen against a series of historical backdrops in *All Men Are Mortal*. The novel traces the life of Count Fosca, an Italian nobleman who is endowed with immortality. At the request of Régine, a successful young actress, he recounts his varied careers through seven centuries. A counselor to Maximilian of Germany and then to Charles V of Spain, he discovers the Mississippi, founds the first French university, and becomes an activist in the French Revolution. Like other existentialist heroes, Fosca paradoxically admits that only death gives life meaning. His goal of building an ideal, unified humanity remains unrealized as violence and useless destruction prevail.

Fosca's story is framed by that of Régine, who is embittered by her life and haunted by death. When she learns of Fosca's immortality, she thinks that she can transcend death by living forever in his memory. Like the women in love in de Beauvoir's preceding novels, Régine depends on others to give her life meaning. The story ends with Régine's cry of despair as she understands the futility and vanity of human action.

All Men Are Mortal takes up the theme of the uncertain outcome of individual actions and gives it a more decidedly pessimistic turn. This theme is modified somewhat by the more optimistic section on the French Revolution. Here, Fosca follows the career of one of his descendants, Armand. Armand's zeal in fighting for the Republican cause leads Fosca to modify his skepticism about human progress and to take comfort in the solidarity he experiences with Armand and his friends.

Fosca's discovery of the rewards of comradeship is very similar to that of Jean Blomart. Although Fosca's individual actions are either undercut by the presence of others or lost in history, actions taken by the group seem to have a more powerful impact on reality. Like *The Blood of Others*, *All Men Are Mortal* predicts de Beauvoir's later Marxist sympathies and reflects her growing politicization. Both Jean and Fosca tend to break with the solipsistic tendencies of the characters in *She Came to Stay* and move in the direction of greater social commitment. The context of the action in *All Men Are Mortal* is wider than in the preceding novels from a narrative and political point of view. It is perhaps its vast historical scope that makes *All Men Are Mortal* the least satisfying of de Beauvoir's novels. Philosophical speculations on love, history, and death dominate the narrative; the characters are lifeless and seem caught in a series of historical still lifes.

THE MANDARINS

The Mandarins, de Beauvoir's finest novel, covers the period from 1944 to the early 1950's and focuses on the relationship between political commitment and literature. The narrative voice shifts between Henri Perron, a novelist, journalist, and Resistance hero, and Anne Dubreuilh, a respected psychiatrist and the wife of Robert Dubreuilh, a prominent writer.

Robert, initiated into political activism during his years in the Resistance, believes that literature must now take second place to political concerns. He engages himself wholeheartedly in founding the S.R.L., an independent leftist political party. The problems that Robert confronts as a political figure point to the painful reality of making decisions that are not always satisfactory. He draws Henri into politics by convincing him that his newspaper, *L'Espoir*, should be the voice of the S.R.L. When they receive news of Soviet labor camps, they try to decide if they should publish the information. Knowing that they will play into Gaullist hands and alienate the Communists to whom they are sympathetic, they reluctantly decide to print the story.

For Henri, questions of political commitment after the war are more problematic. He would like *L'Espoir* to remain apolitical and is nostalgic for the prewar years, when literature and politics appeared to be mutually exclusive interests. Henri tries to act in good faith, but because of his sensitivity to others, he often opts for the less idealistically pure solution. He is reluctant to break with Paule, his mistress of ten years, and he protects acquaintances who collaborated with the Germans because he fears that, like Paule, they could not survive without his help. Throughout the novel, he is torn between politics and a desire to return to literature. He gradually faces the impossibility of "pure" literature. At the end of the novel, having lost *L'Espoir*, he and Robert decide to found a new journal of the Left.

The questions that de Beauvoir examines through Robert and Henri have a striking immediacy that captures the problem of the intellectual in the modern world. Much of the action in *The Mandarins* is a fictionalized account of her experiences as a member of the intellectual Left during the postwar years. Critics have sought to identify Sartre with Robert, Albert Camus with Henri, and de Beauvoir herself with Anne. In *Simone de Beauvoir and the Limits of Commitment* (1981), Anne Whitmarsh notes that there is much of Sartre's experiences with the Rassemblement Démocratique Révolutionnaire in Robert's ties with the S.R.L. and that some of the early problems facing *Les Temps modernes* are reflected in the debates on the political role of *L'Espoir*.

The problems faced by the male characters are less pressing for Anne. Married to a man twenty years older, she seems out of touch with herself and her surroundings. Her work as a psychiatrist fails to occupy her fully, and her relationship with her unhappy daughter, Nadine, gives Anne little satisfaction. Encouraged by Robert, she accepts an invitation to lecture in the United States. In Chicago, she experiences an emotional awakening when she falls in love with Lewis Brogan, an up-and-coming writer. Her visits to Brogan are described in a highly lyric style full of images of country life and nature. The physical and affective aspects of her life with Brogan form an effective counterpoint to the intellectual character of her relationship with her husband. The shifting loyalties she experiences for both men give Anne's narrative a schizophrenic quality.

Back in Paris, Anne tries to help Paule, who has suffered a nervous breakdown. Paule rarely leaves her apartment and is unable to function without Henri. Anne sends her to a psychiatrist, who "cures" her by having her forget the past. Like Françoise and Régine, Paule represents the temptation of living through others. In Paule's case, however, the dependence reaches an existential crisis from which she never fully recovers. Paule's illness is mirrored in Anne as the psychiatrist herself plunges into a long depression. When Brogan ends their relationship, she contemplates suicide. Thinking of the pain her death would cause Robert and Nadine, she decides to live. Despite this decision, Anne's alienation from her family and indeed from her own being is more acute than ever.

Anne's emotional awakening and Paule's mental breakdown leave them both as only marginal participants in life. Neither woman achieves the transcendence that characterizes the life of her male counterpart. As Robert and Henri accommodate themselves to political realities, they become more integrated into society. The female quest for self-knowledge acts as a negative counterpoint to the male quest. The final scene is not unlike a collage in which the two parts of the composition are radically divided. The enthusiasm of Henri and Robert as they search for an appropriate title for their journal is juxtaposed to Anne's stillness; she sits off to the side, withdrawn, and hopes that her life may still contain some happiness.

LES BELLES IMAGES

Les Belles Images is one of de Beauvoir's most technically innovative novels. Laurence, the main character, is a young woman who writes slogans for a French advertising agency. She is married to a successful young architect and has two daughters. Catherine, her eldest daughter, is beginning to question social values. Laurence comes from the same mold as de Beauvoir's other heroines. She is, for all appearances, a confident young woman, but her facade of well-being dissolves to reveal an individual profoundly alienated from herself and her society. *Les Belles Images* is the story of Laurence's progressive withdrawal from society. Her interior journey ends in a mental and physical breakdown.

The novel is set in Paris during the 1960's. Some friends have gathered at the fashionable home of Dominique, Laurence's mother. Laurence, uninterested in the group, leafs through a number of magazines containing the *belles images*, or beautiful pictures, she is paid to create. The dialogue among the guests is filtered through Laurence, who then adds her own reflections. The conversations are trite and filled with clichés; like the slogans Laurence invents, they conceal the real problems of war, poverty, and unhappiness. The discrepancy between the advertisements and the things they represent precipitates Laurence's budding consciousness of herself as yet another *belle image*. Laurence's perception of the inauthenticity of her own life and of the lives of the people around her results in illness. Having already suffered a nervous breakdown five years before, she becomes anorexic and unable to relate to the artificial world around her.

Through her daughter Catherine, Laurence faces her unresolved feelings toward her childhood. She recalls the lack of emotional contact with her mother in a series of flashbacks in which she appears dressed as a child in a publicity snapshot. At the insistence of Laurence's husband, Catherine has been sent to a psychiatrist because she is overly sensitive to social injustices. Laurence sees the treatment that Catherine receives as an attempt to integrate her daughter into the artificial bourgeois world. At the novel's end, Laurence emerges from her illness to save her daughter from a fate similar to hers. Like other de Beauvoir heroines, Laurence chooses her illness as a means of escaping certain destructive social myths. Her breakdown, rather than the result of an original flaw discovered within herself, is an indication of the failure of society as a whole. Against the inauthentic world of the other characters, Laurence's illness appears as a victory and an occasion for emotional growth. Much like Anne in *The Mandarins*, Laurence is a voice from the outside who sees the social games and reveals them for what they are.

All of de Beauvoir's novels examine the relationship between the self and the Other that is at the heart of existentialist philosophy. In her early novels—*She Came to Stay, The Blood of Others*, and *All Men Are Mortal*—there is often an explicit existentialist premise underlying the action. In her later works, *The Mandarins* and *Les Belles Images*, the philosophical message, although still present, is clearly subordinated to the narrative. De Beauvoir's conclusions in *The Second Sex* appear to have led her to a closer examination of the lives of her female characters. Her later fiction adds another dimension to the quests for authenticity that mark her early production. For her heroes, the quest usually ends in some type of existentialist commitment; for her heroines, the quest seems to involve a withdrawal from harmful social myths. If at times the quests border on madness or isolation, they do so without losing their striking immediacy or their profound sense of reality. Like other great twentieth century quests, de Beauvoir's novels chart a journey into the heart of contemporary alienation.

Carole Deering Paul

OTHER MAJOR WORKS

SHORT FICTION: *La Femme rompue*, 1967 (*The Woman Destroyed*, 1968); *Quand prime le spirituel*, 1979 (*When Things of the Spirit Come First: Five Early Tales*, 1982).

PLAY: *Les Bouches inutiles*, pb. 1945.

NONFICTION: *Pyrrhus et Cinéas*, 1944; *Pour une morale de l'ambiguïté*, 1947 (*The Ethics of Ambiguity*, 1948); *L'Amérique au jour le jour*, 1948 (travel sketch; *America Day by Day*, 1953); *L'Existentialisme et la sagesse des nations*, 1948; *Le Deuxième Sexe*, 1949 (*The Second Sex*, 1953); *Privilèges*, 1955 (partial translation "Must We Burn Sade?," 1953); *La Longue Marche*, 1957 (travel sketch; *The Long March*, 1958); *Mémoires d'une jeune fille rangée*, 1958 (4 volumes; *Memoirs of a Dutiful Daughter*, 1959); *La Force de l'âge*, 1960 (memoir; *The Prime of Life*, 1962); *La Force des choses*, 1963 (memoir; *Force of Circumstance*, 1964); *Une Mort très douce*, 1964 (*A Very Easy Death*, 1966); *La Vieillesse*, 1970 (*The Coming of Age*, 1972); *Tout compte fait*, 1972 (memoir; *All Said and Done*, 1974); *La Cérémonie des adieux*, 1981 (*Adieux: A Farewell to Sartre*, 1984); *Lettres à Sartre*, 1990 (2 volumes; Sylvie Le Bon de Beauvoir, editor; *Letters to Sartre*, 1992); *Lettres à Nelson Algren: Un Amour transatlantique, 1947-1964*, 1997 (Sylvie Le Bon de Beauvoir, editor; *A Transatlantic Love Affair*, 1998; also known as *Beloved Chicago Man: Letters to Nelson Algren, 1947-1964*, 1999); *Philosophical Writings*, 2004 (Margaret A. Simons, editor).

EDITED TEXTS: *Lettres au Castor et à quelques autres*, 1983 (2 volumes; volume 1, *Witness to My Life: The Letters of Jean-Paul Sartre to Simone de Beauvoir, 1926-1939*, 1992; volume 2, *Quiet Moments in a War: The Letters of Jean-Paul Sartre to Simone de Beauvoir, 1940-1963*, 1993).

BIBLIOGRAPHY

Appignansei, Lisa. *Simone de Beauvoir*. London: Penguin Books, 1988. Provides a significant appraisal of de Beauvoir's concept of the independent woman. Aptly explicates de Beauvoir's existentialist ethics and her suppositions of woman's subjectivity.

Bair, Deirdre. *Simone de Beauvoir: A Biography*. New York: Summit Books, 1990. This work, which some critics have termed the definitive study of de Beauvoir, covers her philosophical life and her inquiry into the nature of woman. It also focuses on her relationship with John-Paul Sartre.

Brown, Catherine Savage. *Simone de Beauvoir Revisited*. Boston: G. K. Hall, 1991. Contains chapters on de Beauvoir's life, on her role as a woman writer, and on her early fiction and drama, later fiction, philosophical and political studies, and memoirs. Aims to present a focused study and criticizes the emphasis on anecdotal reports and biography in other works on de Beauvoir.

Card, Claudia, ed. *The Cambridge Companion to Simone de Beauvoir.* New York: Cambridge University Press, 2003. Collection of essays focuses on de Beauvior's philosophy, including an analysis of the philosophy in her fiction. Includes a chronology, introductory overview, bibliography, and index.

Fallaize, Elizabeth. *The Novels of Simone de Beauvoir.* New York: Routledge, 1988. Contains separate chapters on *She Came to Stay, The Blood of Others, All Men Are Mortal, The Mandarins,* and *Les Belles Images.* Includes an introduction, biographical notes, and a bibliography.

Moi, Toril. *Simone de Beauvoir: The Making of an Intellectual Woman.* Cambridge, Mass.: Blackwell, 1997. Two chapters in this study are of particular interest regarding de Beauvoir's fiction. Chapter 3 recounts the hostile reception of de Beauvoir's work by those in France and elsewhere who did not believe that de Beauvoir, as a woman, had the intellectual strength and integrity of male philosophers, and chapter 4 examines *She Came to Stay.*

Rowley, Hazel. *Tête-à-Tête: Simone de Beauvoir and Jean-Paul Sartre.* New York: HarperCollins, 2005. Chronicles the relationship between de Beauvoir and Sartre, offering insights into their commitment to each other, their writing, their politics, and their philosophical legacy.

Sandford, Stella. *How to Read Beauvoir.* New York: W. W. Norton, 2007. Provides an introductory overview to de Beauvior's philosophy. Cites excerpts from de Beauvoir's books to explain her examination of identity, gender, sexuality, old age, and other topics.

Simons, Margaret A., ed. *Feminist Interpretations of Simone de Beauvoir.* University Park: Pennsylvania State University Press, 1995. Collection contains essays on *The Second Sex,* de Beauvoir's relationship with Sartre, *The Mandarins,* and the author's views on the Algerian war. Includes bibliography and index.

Whitmarsh, Anne. *Simone de Beauvoir and the Limits of Commitment.* New York: Cambridge University Press, 1981. Contains succinct discussions of de Beauvoir's long fiction, including a section summarizing her fictional works. Biographical notes and bibliography add to this volume's usefulness.

ALBERT CAMUS

Born: Mondovi, Algeria; November 7, 1913
Died: Near Sens, France; January 4, 1960

PRINCIPAL LONG FICTION
L'Étranger, 1942 (*The Stranger*, 1946)
La Peste, 1947 (*The Plague*, 1948)
La Chute, 1956 (*The Fall*, 1957)
La Mort heureuse, 1971 (wr. 1936-1938; *A Happy Death*, 1972)
Le Premier Homme, 1994 (*The First Man*, 1995)

OTHER LITERARY FORMS

Albert Camus (kah-MEW) considered his vocation to be that of novelist, but the artist in him was always at the service of his dominant passion, moral philosophy. As a result, Camus was led to cultivate several other literary forms that could express his central concerns as a moralist: the short story, drama, and nonfiction forms such as the philosophical essay and political journalism, all of which he practiced with enough distinction to be influential among his contemporaries. Moreover, these works were generally written side by side with his novels; it was Camus's customary procedure, throughout his brief writing career, always to be working on two or more compositions simultaneously, each expressing a different facet of the same philosophical issue. Thus, within a year of the publication of his most celebrated novel, *The Stranger*, there appeared a long essay titled *Le Mythe de Sisyphe* (1942; *The Myth of Sisyphus*, 1955), a meditation on the meaning of life in an irrational universe that begins with the assertion that the only serious question confronting modern man is the question of suicide and concludes with a daring argument that finds in the legend of Sisyphus a strangely comforting allegory of the human condition. Sisyphus, who becomes in Camus's hands an exemplary existentialist, spent his days in the endlessly futile task of pushing a boulder to the top of a hill from which it always rolled down again. Every human life is expended as meaninglessly as that of Sisyphus, Camus argues, yet one must conceive of Sisyphus as happy, because he was totally absorbed by his assigned task and found sufficient satisfaction in its daily accomplishment, without requiring that it also have some enduring significance. There are close links between such reasoning and the ideas that inform *The Stranger*, but it is erroneous to argue, as some have, that *The Myth of Sisyphus* is an "explanation" of *The Stranger*. The former work is, rather, a discussion of similar themes in a different form and from a different perspective, in accordance with Camus's unique way of working as a writer.

That unique way of working produced another long philosophical essay, *L'Homme révolté* (1951; *The Rebel*, 1956), which has affinities with the novel *The Plague* as well as with four of Camus's plays written and produced in the 1940's: *Caligula* (pb. 1944; Eng-

Albert Camus
(The Nobel Foundation)

lish translation, 1948); *Le Malentendu* (pr., pb. 1944; *The Misunderstanding*, 1948); *L'État de siège* (pr., pb. 1948; *State of Siege*, 1958), and *Les Justes* (pr. 1949; *The Just Assassins*, 1958). Each of these plays is also related by certain thematic elements to the two novels that Camus published in the same period.

Camus's earliest political journalism, written before 1940 and dealing with the problems of his native Algeria, attracted little attention, but his work for the underground newspaper *Combat* during and after World War II achieved considerable celebrity, and the best articles he wrote for *Combat* were later collected in a volume that was widely read and admired. During the civil war in Algeria, in the 1950's, Camus again entered the lists as a political journalist, and because he was by then indisputably Algeria's most famous man of letters, his articles were of major importance at the time, though highly controversial and much less widely approved than the wartime pieces from *Combat*.

Camus produced only one collection of short stories, *L'Exil et le royaume* (1957; *Exile and the Kingdom*, 1958), composed during the same years as the novel *The Fall*, but those stories have been very popular and are regarded by many as among the finest short stories published in France in the twentieth century. The volume is particularly noteworthy because it offers the only examples Camus ever published of fiction composed in the third-person mode of the omniscient narrator. The first three of his published novels are variations of the limited-perspective first-person narrative.

Deeply involved in the theater throughout his career, both as writer and director, Camus adapted for the French stage the work of foreign novelists Fyodor Dostoevski and William Faulkner, and of playwrights of Spain's Golden Age, including Pedro Calderón de la Barca and Lope de Vega Carpio. These adaptations have all been published and form part of Camus's contribution to the theater.

Achievements

To the immediate postwar public, not only in France but also throughout Europe, Albert Camus seemed a writer of unassailable stature. Although Camus himself repudiated the designation, he was regarded worldwide as one of the two principal exponents of existentialism (the other was Jean-Paul Sartre), the single most influential philosophical movement of the twentieth century. Indeed, the existentialist worldview—according to which the individual human being "must assume ultimate responsibility for his acts of free will without any certain knowledge of what is right or wrong or good or bad"—has profoundly shaped the values of countless people who have never read Camus or Sartre.

In the 1950's, Camus was widely admired not only as a writer but also as a hero of the war against fascism, a spokesman for the younger generation, and a guardian of the moral conscience of Europe. That reputation was consecrated in 1957 with the award to Camus of the Nobel Prize in Literature, at the remarkably young age of forty-four. Yet, as has happened to many other recipients of the Nobel Prize, the award seemed almost a signal of the rapid deflation of his renown. Camus suddenly came under severe criticism for his stand on the Algerian Civil War, was attacked as self-righteous and artistically sterile, and was finally denounced as irrelevant by the new literary generation then coming to prominence, who were weary of moral issues and more concerned with aesthetic questions of form and language. Camus's fame and influence appeared to many to have suffered an irreversible decline by the end of the decade, at least in France. (In the United States, the case was different: Made more accessible by the "paperback revolution," Camus's works were enormously influential among American college students in the 1960's.) There were those who suggested that the automobile accident that took his life in January of 1960 was a disguised blessing, sparing him the pain of having to witness the collapse of his career.

It is true that, in the late twentieth century, generations after the height of Camus's fame, French writers and intellectuals showed no influence of Camus in their writings and scant critical interest in his works. Still, his works have enjoyed steady sales among the French public, and outside France, especially in the United States, interest in Camus has remained strong. There has been an inevitable sifting of values, a crystallization of what it is, in Camus's work, that still has the power to survive and what no longer speaks to successive generations. It has become clear, for example, that his philosophical essays are too closely tied to the special circumstances that occasioned them; in spite of a few brilliant passages, those essays now seem rambling and poorly argued as well as irrelevant to the concerns of modern readers. Camus's works for the theater, too, have held up poorly, being too abstract and inhuman to engage the emotions of audiences. Although his plays have continued to be performed on both sides of the Atlantic, interest in them has steadily declined over the years. It is his fiction that still seems most alive, both in characters and ideas, and that still presents to the reader endlessly fascinating enigmas that delight the imagination and invite repeated readings.

Although the total number of Camus's fictional works is small, those works are, in both form and content, among the most brilliantly original contributions to the art of fiction produced anywhere in the twentieth century. In particular, Camus expressed through fiction, more powerfully and more memorably than anyone else in his time, the painful moral and spiritual dilemmas of modern man: evil, alienation, meaninglessness, and death. He invented techniques and created characters by which he was able to make manifest, in unforgettable terms, the eternal struggle of Everyman for some shred of dignity and happiness. His stories have accordingly taken on some of the haunting quality, and the prestige, of myths. For that reason, it seems safe to predict that it is his fiction that represents Camus's greatest achievement—an achievement that will endure long after his philosophical musings and political arguments have been forgotten.

BIOGRAPHY

Although he was born in the interior village of Mondovi, near Constantine, Algeria, Albert Camus was actually brought up in the big city, in a working-class suburb of Algiers. His widowed mother, who was from Algiers, took her two sons back there to live after her husband was killed early in World War I. Albert, the younger of the two sons, was not yet a year old when his father died, and he was to grow up with a need for relationships with older men, apparently to replace the father he never had. It was important to Camus that his father's forebears had immigrated *by choice* to Algeria from France in the nineteenth century, since it made him feel that his roots were authentically both French and Algerian. Because his mother was of Spanish extraction, Camus felt himself to be even more authentically Algerian, for Spanish blood gave him his share of that passionate Mediterranean temperament that he felt made French Algeria distinctive and unique. It comes as no surprise, therefore, that the great bulk of Camus's writing is set in Algeria or relates directly to that country. Being Algerian was the central fact of Camus's consciousness.

In his early twenties, Camus began to write essays for a leftist political journal published in Algiers; his subject was the political and economic plight of Algeria in its role as a colony of France. During those same years, he helped to found a theater group, for which he acted, directed, and did some writing, and he was a candidate for an advanced degree in philosophy at the University of Algiers. At times, he had to interrupt his studies because of ill health; he had contracted tuberculosis in 1930, at the age of seventeen, and was subject to periodic attacks from it for the rest of his life. When only twenty-one, he made a rather impulsive marriage that ended in separation within a year and eventual divorce. He worked at a number of odd jobs before becoming a full-time journalist, and he was active enough in politics in the 1930's to have become, for a few months, a member of the Algerian Communist Party. Altogether, his Algerian youth had been a difficult and turbulent experience, yet it had also been a time of growth and self-discovery, and he looked back on those years ever after with a special nostalgia for the sun, sand, sea, and simplicity of life that he felt had formed him and made him what he had become.

Early in 1940, with a war in progress and the newspaper for which he worked closed down, Camus found himself forced to leave Algeria in order to make a living. He went to Paris to work for a Paris newspaper—a job procured for him by his older friend Pascal Pia, with whom he had worked on the Algiers newspaper before it folded. Within a year, the Paris job ended, and Camus, who had married again, returned to Algeria with his wife. They lived in Oran, his wife's hometown, and while she worked as a teacher, Camus worked at his writing projects, completing both the novel *The Stranger* and the essay *The Myth of Sisyphus* and arranging for their publication in Paris by Gallimard.

By late 1942, Camus was so ill with tuberculosis that his wife persuaded him to seek a more favorable climate in the mountainous area of central France, which was then unoccupied territory. He went there alone, to continue writing, and found himself cut off from all contact with his family when the Allies invaded North Africa and the Germans occupied the rest of France as a defensive measure. During this period of isolation, Camus began to sketch out his next novel, *The Plague*. He also began to make frequent trips to Paris to see literary friends. His publisher, Gallimard, not only sent him royalties for *The Stranger*, which sold quite well, but also helped Camus by putting him on the Gallimard payroll as a reader—a position he enjoyed so much that he continued to fulfill it for the rest of his life.

Late in 1943, Camus moved to Paris to be where the literary action was, increasingly associating with those friends who were in the Resistance movement, with which Camus was strongly sympathetic. Before long, Camus joined the Resistance and was assigned the task of writing for the Resistance newspaper *Combat*. After the liberation of Paris in 1944, *Combat* went aboveground as a daily newspaper, and Camus was for a time its editor. He had become part of the Paris literary world, had met its best-known figures—Sartre, André Malraux, and many others—and had achieved a certain fame. By that time, it was clear that he would never go back to Algeria to live. As soon as it was possible for her to do so, Camus's wife joined him in Paris, and in September of 1945 she gave birth to twins, a boy and a girl. By war's end, Camus was not only a confirmed Parisian but also a domesticated one, with a family to support.

In the postwar years, Camus's fame quickly began to spread outside France—*The Stranger* appeared in English translation in 1946 and was an immediate sensation—and Camus took up the life of a lionized man of letters, dropping all employment except for his work with Gallimard and making lecture tours to foreign countries, including the United States. The publication of *The Plague* in 1947 was hailed by critics as the fulfillment of his great promise as a writer, and that book became one of the best sellers of the postwar era, making Camus economically secure for the first time. Success and fame seemed to make him artistically insecure, however—there were suddenly too many demands from admirers, too many intrusions into his privacy and working time, and, above all, too much self-doubt about his own powers for him to be able to live up to his public's expectations of him. Camus soon began to experience a crisis of literary sterility. It took him until 1951 to complete the essay *The Rebel*, begun nearly ten years earlier, and throughout the first half of the decade of the 1950's he published nothing and was rumored to have a permanent case of writer's block. The outbreak of violence in Algeria and the campaign for independence, which began in 1952, added severely to Camus's troubled state, and the controversial articles he wrote in that period on the Algerian question certainly lost him many friends and much support. His unhappy attempt to be the voice of reason and conciliation at a time in the dispute when opinions had already become hopelessly polarized ("If you are not with us, you are against us") is poignantly described in the powerful tale "The Guest," one of the best stories in the collection *Exile and the Kingdom*.

Camus emerged from this period of intense personal suffering and frustration by venting his feelings in the short, bitterly satiric novel *The Fall*, published in 1956—his first work of fiction in nearly ten years, as his detractors were quick to point out. Nevertheless, the comic verve of the work attracted many readers, even though its intended meanings often seemed obscure to them. The book sold well, and Camus's reputation rebounded somewhat, especially outside France. The publication of the volume of short stories *Exile and the Kingdom* the following year earned for him additional respect as a writer who still had something to say. Internationally, his reputation peaked with the award of the Nobel Prize later that same year.

Reinvigorated by the successes of 1956 and 1957, Camus was, as the decade ended, once again confidently and productively at work, with the usual three or four projects going simultaneously, one of which was an autobiographical novel about his youth in Algeria, to be called "Le Premier Homme" (the first man). His "block" seemed to be definitively overcome, and friends and family who spent Christmas of 1959 with him at the country retreat he had purchased in southern France recalled that he was in a generally optimistic frame of mind about his career. Fate, however, abruptly shattered that optimism. Camus's career came to a premature—and, he would have said, absurd—end only a few days after that happy Christmas. On January 4, 1960, Michel Gallimard, nephew of Camus's publisher, lost control of his car, in which Camus was riding as a passenger, just outside the tiny village of Villeblevin, and crashed into a tree. Camus, who had passed his forty-sixth birthday only two months before, died instantly. The evolution of the author's work strongly suggests that a banal motor accident cut him off when he seemed, finally, to have mastered his craft and to be entering his prime creative years.

ANALYSIS

Two persistent themes animate all of Albert Camus's writing and underlie his artistic vision: One is the enigma of the universe, which is breathtakingly beautiful yet indifferent to life; the other is the enigma of man, whose craving for happiness and meaning in life remains unextinguished by his full awareness of his own mortality and of the sovereign indifference of his environment. At the root of every novel, every play, every essay, even every entry in his notebooks can be found Camus's incessant need to probe and puzzle over the ironic double bind that he perceived to be the essence of the human condition: Man is endowed with the imagination to conceive an ideal existence, but neither his circumstances nor his own powers permit its attainment. The perception of this hopeless double bind made inescapable for Camus the obligation to face up to an overriding moral issue for man: Given man's circumscribed condition, are there honorable terms on which his life can be lived?

A HAPPY DEATH

In his earliest attempt at casting these themes in fictional form, Camus made use of the traditional novel of personal development, or bildungsroman, to describe one young man's encounters with life, love, and death. The result was an episodic novel, obviously based on his own experiences but composed in the third person and so lacking in unity and coherence as to betray the central idea on which he wished to focus: the problem of accepting death. He called the novel *A Happy Death* and showed his hero resolutely fixing his consciousness on the inanimate world around him, striving to become one with the stones and achieve a happy death by blending gently and painlessly into the silent harmony of the universe while retaining his lucidity until his last breath. The book's last sentence strives to convince the reader by rhetoric that the hero has indeed achieved the happy death he sought: "And stone among the stones, he returned in the joy of his heart to the truth of motionless worlds."

Camus seems to have sensed, however, that the rhetoric was unconvincing and that the ideal of a happy death was an illusion. Perhaps he even recognized that his hero's struggle to remain conscious of life until his last breath was, in reality, a protest against death and a contradiction of his desire to make the transition to death serene and imperceptible. It was doubtless some such sense of the book's failure that convinced Camus not to publish this work, composed when he was not yet twenty-five. Its posthumous publication has given scholars the opportunity to see Camus's first halting steps in trying to formulate the subtle and complex themes of the novels that were to make him great.

THE STRANGER

The Stranger, Camus's second attempt at writing a novel, includes a number of the scenes, characters, and situations found in *A Happy Death* (Mersault, the hero of *A Happy Death*, becomes Meursault in *The Stranger*). A detailed comparison of the two novels, however, makes it clear that *The Stranger*, which appeared in 1942, four years and many events after Camus abandoned *A Happy Death*, is a wholly different work in both conception and theme. No longer preoccupied with happiness in death, Camus turned his attention in *The Stranger* to the problem of happiness in life, to man's irrational and desperate need to find meaning in existence. His protagonist, Meursault, is not the frail, sophisticated, death-haunted figure of the earlier novel, but rather a robust primitive who seems eerily devoid of the normal attitudes, values, and culturally induced feelings of his society, as though he had been brought up on some other planet—a "stranger" in the fullest sense of the word. Moreover, Camus hit upon the device of first-person narration as the most effective and dramatic means of confronting his readers with his disturbing protagonist, so alien to his environment. The famous opening words shock the reader into an awareness of the disquieting strangeness of the narrator:

> Mama died today. Or perhaps yesterday, I don't know. I received a telegram from the home: "Mother passed away. Funeral tomorrow. Yours truly." That doesn't mean anything. Perhaps it was yesterday.

Shrewdly focusing on a mother's death as a revealing touchstone of humankind's most deeply ingrained social attitudes, these words achieve a double effect: They tell the reader that the son of the deceased mother can speak of her death without any of the expected symptoms of grief, but, at the same time, they remind the reader that the rest of society, having no familial ties with the deceased, habitually masks its indifference under empty rhetorical formulas such as the telegraphic announcement.

This dual perspective is fully developed in subsequent chapters as the basic theme of the book: While Meursault shows by his own forthright account of his life that he does not share his society's conventional notions about death, religion, family, friendship, love, marriage, and ambition, he also manages to reveal—often without realizing it—that those conventional notions are often shallow, hypocritical, or delusory and constitute the pathetic inventions of a society desperate to invest its existence with a meaning it does not have. Thus, when Meursault, asked by his boss whether he would be interested in an assignment to establish a Paris office for his boss's business, says that he has no interest in living in Paris, the reader recognizes that Meursault simply does not believe that material surroundings can make his life any different. At the same time, the boss's dismayed reaction to Meursault's indifference to opportunity subtly disturbs the reader with the suspicion that, after all, the boss may have a touching but misplaced faith in the value of ambition. A similar moment occurs when Meursault and his girlfriend, Marie, discuss love and marriage. The reader is surely made uncomfortable by Meursault's casualness in saying that he does not know what love is, but that he is willing to marry Marie if she wants it. It is, however, a different order of discomfort that overcomes the reader when Marie insists that marriage is a very serious matter and Meursault calmly replies that it is not.

All of part 2 of the novel, devoted to Meursault's trial after he has killed an Arab, brings additional and even more disturbing changes on the same dual perspective, with Meursault showing no awareness or acceptance of conventional beliefs about justice, murder, legal procedures, and the nature of evidence, while all the "normal" people involved show unexamined or self-deceiving convictions about all such matters. The ironic meaning that emerges from the novel is that although Meursault is guilty of taking a life, society sentences him to death not for his crime, with which it seems incapable of dealing, but for his refusal to live by society's values, for not "playing the game." As Camus himself laconically remarked, his novel means that any man who does not weep at his mother's funeral risks being condemned to death.

Critics have regularly protested that, in *The Stranger*, Camus manipulates his readers' emotions, inducing sympathy for Meursault even though he is a moral monster and ridiculing everyone else as representative of a society afraid to face reality, hence threatened by Meursault's clear-eyed and unsentimental acceptance of the world. Such protests are justified, however, only if one assumes that Camus intended *The Stranger* to be a realistic representation of the world, holding the mirror up to nature. In fact, Meursault is not a believable human figure, the events of the novel are but dimly evoked and unconvincingly motivated, and the very existence of the text itself, as Meursault's first-person account of events, is never explained. In *The Stranger*, Camus makes almost no concessions to the conventional procedures of realism, constructing instead a kind of mythic tale of philosophical intent to dramatize an imaginary confrontation between man's basic nature as a simple, sensual being and his grandly narcissistic self-image as an intelligent being whose every gesture has transcendent significance. Read as a kind of poetic allegory rather than as an exemplary tale of human conduct, *The Stranger* is seen as a powerful depiction of man's painfully divided soul, at once joyous for the gift of life and miserable at the absence of any discernible purpose in that life and at the indifference of the surrounding universe. Viewed that way, *The Stranger* deserves its reputation as one of the great works of art of the first half of the twentieth century.

THE PLAGUE

The allegorical mode is given a much more detailed and realistically human foundation in Camus's next novel, *The Plague*, regarded by many critics as his masterpiece. This time, Camus makes a concerted effort to create a strong sense of place in a real setting and to depict fully rounded and believable characters. With the vividness of concrete details and actual place-names, Camus takes the reader to the city of Oran, in Algeria—a city of which he had intimate personal knowledge, having lived there for an extended period— and describes the impact on that real place of an imaginary outbreak of bubonic plague.

The reader shares the first frightening discovery of rats dying in the streets and apartment house hallways and experiences the spread of terror and panic as the first human victims of the plague appear in random locations around the city. Soon, the city is ordered closed, quarantined from the rest of the world, and the authorities try to mobilize the trapped population and lay down strict sanitation rules to try to limit the impact of a disease they know they cannot cure.

The heart of the novel is the depiction of the various ways in which individuals react to the fear and isolation imposed by this sudden state of siege, in which the invading army is invisible. To convey the variety of responses to such an extreme and concentrated crisis in human affairs, Camus deliberately eschews the convenient device of the omniscient narrator, making the depiction of every event and scene an eyewitness account in some form: the spoken words of reports or dialogues, the written words of letters or private diaries, and, as the main device, the written record of the daily observations of the novel's main character, Dr. Rieux. Whereas in *The Stranger* first-person narration is primarily a device of characterization, used to portray an alien figure's disconcertingly remote and hollow personality, in *The Plague* it is a device of narrative realism, used to reduce devastatingly incomprehensible events to a human, hence believable, scale by portraying the way these events are seen by a representative group of ordinary citizens.

The Plague differs from its predecessor not only technically but also thematically. Camus's inspiration for *The Plague* was no philosophical abstraction but a specific event of his own life: the frustration and despair he experienced during the war, when the aftermath of the Allied invasion of North Africa trapped his wife in Oran (while he was in the Resistance organization in the Massif Central) and cut off all communication between them. That experience started the fictional idea germinating in his mind, and a literary model—Daniel Defoe's *A Journal of the Plague Year* (1722)—gave the idea more concrete form.

Central to the idea of *The Plague*, certainly, is the theme of man's encounter with death rather than the theme of man's interpretation of life, which dominates *The Stranger*. Indeed, with *The Plague*, Camus was returning to the preoccupation of his earliest work of fiction, *A Happy Death*, but with a major new emphasis. *The Plague* concerns not an individual's quest in relation to death but a collectivity's involuntary confrontation with it. In *The Plague*, death is depicted as a chance outgrowth of an indifferent nature that suddenly, and for no apparent reason, becomes an evil threat to humankind. Death in the form of a plague is unexpected, irrational—a manifestation of that absurdity, that radical absence of meaning in life that is a major underlying theme of *The Stranger*. In *The Plague*, however, Camus proposes the paradox that when death is a manifestation of the absurd, it galvanizes something in a person's spirit that enables the individual to join with others to fight against death and thus give meaning and purpose to life. From evil may come happiness, this novel seems to suggest: It is a painful irony of the human condition that individuals often discover their own capacities for courage and for fraternal affection—

that is, for happiness—only if they are forced by the threat of evil to make the discovery.

The hint of optimism in this paradoxical theme—happiness is, after all, possible for some if the circumstances are dire enough—is, however, insufficient to offset the fundamental pessimism of *The Plague*. A glance at the fates of the main characters will make the basic bleakness of this work manifest. At the center of the action is Bernard Rieux, a doctor who risks his life every day to lead the fight against the plague and who, more than anyone else in the novel, experiences the satisfaction and the joy of finding himself equal to a heroic task and feeling with others a fraternal bond engendered by their common struggle. His satisfaction is brief and his joys few, however. He knows that he cannot cure victims of the plague and must suppress his sympathy for them if he is to be effective in palliating their suffering and in keeping them from infecting others. The result of this bind is that Rieux strikes his patients and their families as cold and indifferent; he ends up being hated by those he is trying to help. The fraternal bond with others who are trying to help develops in only a few instances, since most of his fellow citizens are too frightened or egocentric to join him in the effort. Moreover, where the bond does develop, it proves too tenuous to penetrate his natural isolation.

The limits of the fraternal bond are most graphically expressed by the moment in the novel when Rieux and Jean Tarrou (a traveler through whose journal part of the novel is related), seeing the first signs that the plague is receding, decide to go for a swim together, in celebration. The point is carefully made that, while each feels a sense of fraternity with the other as they swim in the same water, each is also conscious of being ultimately quite alone in the joy and freedom of moving serenely through the water and forgetting the plague for a short while. In spite of the shared emotion that unites them, each feels the swim to be predominantly a solitary experience. Finally, when the plague does end, Rieux finds himself strangely empty and alienated from the joyous crowds now once more filling the streets of Oran; the urgency of his task no longer exists to summon forth his courage. Indeed, because he has lost those dearest to him—his wife and Tarrou—he feels more alone than ever after the plague has gone.

The other important characters fare no better than Rieux: Tarrou is killed by the plague; Joseph Grand suffers from it but recovers and resumes his self-imposed task of writing a novel, of which he has yet to complete the first sentence, because he has endlessly revised and recast it in a fruitless search for perfection; Rembart, a journalist who is trapped in Oran by the plague, leaves when it is over, but without having written anything about it, having found his profession inadequate to such an awesome task; and Cottard, who engages in black-market profiteering during the plague, goes crazy when the plague ends, shooting citizens at random until he is caught and killed by the police. There is little in this novel to nourish an optimistic outlook, except for the hesitant and tentative statement of Rieux, at the end of his chronicle, that amid the ravages of pestilence, one learns that "there are, in men, more things to admire than to despise."

The Plague is the longest, the most realistic, and artistically the most impressive of

Camus's novels, offering a richly varied cast of characters and a coherent and riveting plot, bringing an integrated world memorably to life while stimulating the reader's capacity for moral reflection. In spite of its vivid realism, *The Plague* is no less mythical and allegorical in its impact than is *The Stranger*. When first published, *The Plague* was widely interpreted as a novel about the German Occupation and the French Resistance, with the plague symbolizing the evil presence of the Nazis. Since the 1940's, however, more universal themes and symbols have been discovered in the book, including the frighteningly random nature of evil and the perception that humankind's conquest of evil is never more than provisional, that the struggle will always have to be renewed. It has also been widely recognized that *The Plague* is, in significant degree, a profound meditation on the frustrating limits of human language both as a means of communication and as a means of representing the truth about human existence. The discovery of that theme has made *The Plague* the most modern of Camus's novels, the one with the most to say to future generations of Camus's readers.

For nearly a decade after the publication of *The Plague*, impeded by the consequences of fame, Camus struggled to find enough time and privacy to compose a new work of fiction and to complete philosophical and theatrical writings begun before he wrote *The Plague*. In the mid-1950's, he began to compose a group of short stories with the common theme of the condition of the exile, and it was one of those stories that he was suddenly inspired to expand into a short novel written in the form of a monologue and published in 1956 as *The Fall*.

THE FALL

The product of a troubled time in Camus's life, *The Fall* is a troubling work, full of brilliant invention, dazzling wordplay, and devastating satire, but so profoundly ironic and marked by so many abrupt shifts in tone as to leave the reader constantly off balance and uncertain of the author's viewpoint or purpose. This difficulty in discerning the book's meaning is inherent in its basic premise, for the work records a stream of talk—actually one side of a dialogue—by a Frenchman who haunts a sleazy bar in the harbor district of Amsterdam and who does not trouble to hide the fact that most of what he says, including his name, is invented. Because he is worldly and cultivated, his talk is fascinating and seizes the attention of his implied interlocutor (who is also, of course, the reader) with riveting force. The name he gives himself is Jean-Baptiste Clamence, a name that evokes the biblical figure of the prophet John the Baptist as the voice crying in the wilderness (*vox clamantis in deserto*) and that coincides neatly with the occupation he claims to follow, also of his own invention: judge-penitent.

When Clamence remarks to his interlocutor, near the end of his five-day monologue, "I know what you are thinking: it is very difficult to distinguish the true from the false in what I am telling you. I confess that you are right," the reader feels that Camus has suddenly made a personal intervention into the novel in order to warn the reader that he or she has been deliberately manipulated by Clamence's playacting and has every right to feel bewildered. Camus thus signals to the reader that the book's troubling impact has been calculated and deliberate from the start. Only in the closing pages of the novel does he clarify the purpose of Clamence's invented narrative and the meaning of his invented calling, but the explanation comes too late—deliberately so, for the reader can never be free of doubt about whether Clamence's entire performance has been designed to raise questions concerning what is true and what is false, what is good and what is evil.

Clamence's "explanation" is, in fact, the most unsettling element in the book. He pointedly admits to his interlocutor that he has been penitently "confessing" his own sins in a carefully controlled pattern, only in order to induce his interlocutor to "confess" in turn, thus enabling Clamence to play the role of judge. Clamence begins his "confession" by describing his successful career in Paris as a much-admired lawyer known for his defense of "widows and orphans"—that is, the helpless and disadvantaged of society. He had every reason to see himself as a man of virtue, he says, until he began to "hear" a woman's mocking laughter whenever he looked at himself in the mirror with those feelings of self-satisfaction. The mocking laughter reminded him that his lawyerly altruism was only a mask for selfishness and forced him to recall an incident he had tried to forget: Crossing a bridge over the Seine one night, he had seen a young woman throw herself into the water and had made no effort to rescue her or to get help, instead walking hurriedly away without looking back. The mocking laughter was thus his conscience taunting him with the suppressed memory of his guilt: The admired man of virtue was in reality a fraud, a sinner like everyone else.

Clamence goes on to explain that thereafter he had found it increasingly difficult to continue his career in Paris and live with his guilt. At the same time, he could not give up his need to feel morally superior to others. His solution to this private inner conflict, he then declares, was his brilliant invention of a new career for himself as a judge-penitent. He closed his Paris office and moved to the harbor section of Amsterdam—which, he notes, is in the center of the concentric circles of Amsterdam's canals, like the ninth circle of Hell in Dante's *Inferno*, and is, moreover, "the site of one of the greatest crimes of modern history," meaning the Nazi destruction of the entire Jewish community of Amsterdam. In these new surroundings, he not only could assuage his guilt by the feeling that he was in the ninth circle of Hell, where he belonged, but also could have access to the endless succession of tourists who gravitated to that spot, whom he could "help," in such propitious surroundings, to recognize their own guilt as well. His "help" consisted of a recital of his own sins, so arranged as to emphasize their universality, thus subtly prompting his listener to confess the same sins in turn. In this way, Clamence uses his perfected performance as a penitent to put himself in the deeply satisfying position of judge, hearing his listener's confession while basking in the warm glow of his own moral superiority. Because everyone, without exception, is a guilty sinner, says Clamence, he has solved the dilemma of how to live happily with his nagging guilt. The essential secret, he says, is to accuse oneself first—and of all seven cardinal sins—thereby earning the right to accuse everyone else.

Clamence's "solution," which concludes *The Fall*, is a burlesque of moral reasoning, underscoring the bitterness of the satire that is at the heart of this novel. Like Camus's other novels, *The Fall* is an exploration of man's moral nature and his passionate search for happiness in a world that is indifferent to such spiritual values, but unlike any of his other works of fiction, *The Fall* is both unrelievedly pessimistic and irreducibly ambiguous. In Clamence's confession, is Camus's intention to castigate himself for having taken his own fame too seriously and thus expiate his personal sin of pride? Many critics read the book that way when it appeared in 1956. Or is he using Clamence, rather, to avenge himself on his enemies, whom he thought too quick to adopt a tone of moral superiority in judging his position on the Algerian Civil War? Many other critics saw *The Fall* that way. Generations later, it seems reasonable to suggest that both interpretations have validity. *The Fall* is a comic masterpiece, remarkably parallel in its tone, its themes, and its ambiguity to Camus's short story "Jonas," written about the same time—a story in which, everyone agrees, the author attempted to come to terms with his artistic sterility and with the conflict he felt between public obligation and the need for privacy.

"Jonas" ends with a celebrated verbal ambiguity: The painter-hero of the story, after long meditation, translates his thought to canvas by means of a single word, but it is impossible to discern whether that word is "solitary" or "solidary." It is tempting to conclude, using that short story as analogue, that the ambiguity of *The Fall* is also deliberate and that Camus meant his work both as private confession and public condemnation. Those two meanings, the one private and the other public, are surely intended to combine retrospectively in the reader's mind to form Camus's universal condemnation of man's moral bankruptcy. As the title is meant to suggest, *The Fall* is a modern parable about Original Sin and the Fall of Man.

There is reason to believe that the unrelenting pessimism of *The Fall* was not Camus's final word on humanity but was rather the expression of a temporary discouragement that he had almost succeeded in dispelling at the time of his death. In 1959, he was at work on a new novel, to be called "Le Premier Homme," the theme of which was to be a celebration of the formative experience of his Algerian youth. *The First Man* was not published until long after his death, in 1994; it addresses from a particularly personal perspective the subject that, at bottom, always animated Camus's fiction—the enigma of human beings' struggle against the indifference of creation and the unquenchable thirst for moral significance in life. Camus's unforgettable contribution to the ongoing dialogue inspired by that vast subject is embodied in the three great novels he managed to complete before his untimely death.

Murray Sachs

OTHER MAJOR WORKS

SHORT FICTION: *L'Exil et le royaume*, 1957 (*Exile and the Kingdom*, 1958).

PLAYS: *Révolte dans les Asturies*, pb. 1936 (with others); *Caligula*, pb. 1944 (wr. 1938-1939; English translation, 1948); *Le Malentendu*, pr., pb. 1944 (*The Misunderstanding*, 1948); *L'État de siège*, pr., pb. 1948 (*State of Siege*, 1958); *Les Justes*, pr. 1949 (*The Just Assassins*, 1958); *Caligula, and Three Other Plays*, 1958; *Les Possédés*, pr., pb. 1959 (adaptation of Fyodor Dostoevski's novel *Besy*; *The Possessed*, 1960).

NONFICTION: *L'Envers et l'endroit*, 1937 ("The Wrong Side and the Right Side," 1968); *Noces*, 1938 ("Nuptials," 1968); *Le Mythe de Sisyphe*, 1942 (*The Myth of Sisyphus*, 1955); *L'Homme révolté*, 1951 (*The Rebel*, 1956); *L'Été*, 1954 (*Summer*, 1968); *Carnets: Mai 1935-février 1942*, 1962 (*Notebooks: 1935-1942*, 1963); *Carnets: Janvier 1942-mars 1951*, 1964 (*Notebooks: 1942-1951*, 1965); *Lyrical and Critical Essays*, 1968 (includes "The Wrong Side and the Right Side," "Nuptials," and "Summer"); *Correspondance, 1939-1947*, 2000; *Camus à "Combat": Éditoriaux et articles d'Albert Camus, 1944-1947*, 2002 (*Camus at "Combat": Writing, 1944-1947*, 2006).

BIBLIOGRAPHY

Bronner, Stephen Eric. *Camus: Portrait of a Moralist*. Minneapolis: University of Minnesota Press, 1999. Provides a thorough, detailed account of the life and work of Camus, but assumes that the reader is familiar with key places and figures in Camus's life.

Carroll, David. *Albert Camus, the Algerian: Colonialism, Terrorism, Justice*. New York: Columbia University Press, 2007. Analyzes Camus's novels, short stories, and political essays within the context of the author's complicated relationship with his Algerian background. Concludes that Camus's work reflects his understanding of both the injustice of colonialism and the tragic nature of Algeria's struggle for independence. Includes bibliography and index.

Cruickshank, John. *Albert Camus and the Literature of Revolt*. 1959. Reprint. Westport, Conn.: Greenwood Press, 1978. Important work on Camus as writer and philosopher includes a general discussion of his principal ideas as they relate to the literature and historical events of the period. Offers interesting comments concerning American literary influences on Camus.

Hughes, Edward J., ed. *The Cambridge Companion to Camus*. New York: Cambridge University Press, 2007. Examines Camus's major works as well as his life, including his poverty-stricken childhood, his education, and his political beliefs. Includes reference citations in English and French.

Kellman, Steven G., ed. *"The Plague": Fiction and Resistance*. New York: Twayne, 1993. Discusses the novel in separate sections devoted to literary and historical context and to different readings of the work. Individual chapters examine major characters as well as the mysterious narrator.

King, Adele, ed. *Camus's "L'Étranger": Fifty Years On*. New York: St. Martin's Press,

1992. Addresses the contexts and influences of the novel, its reception and influence on other writers, textual studies, and comparative studies. Includes an informative introduction.

Lottman, Herbert R. *Albert Camus*. 1979. Corte Madera, Calif.: Gingko Press, 1997. Extremely well-documented biography is based on extensive interviews with people who knew Camus well.

McCarthy, Patrick. *Camus*. New York: Random House, 1982. A meticulous attempt to reconstruct Camus through his childhood and early influences. Also covers every major phase of the author's life and work. Includes notes and brief bibliography.

Rhein, Phillip H. *Albert Camus*. Rev. ed. Boston: Twayne, 1989. Useful introduction to Camus's life and work includes chapters on his childhood, his understanding of the absurd, his career in the theater, his view of humanity and rebellion. Includes notes and bibliography.

Rizzuto, Anthony. *Camus: Love and Sexuality*. Gainesville: University Press of Florida, 1998. Presents both biographical material and literary and psychological analysis in addressing the evolution of Camus's use of the themes of love and sex in his fiction. Includes bibliography and index.

Sprintzen, David. *Camus: A Critical Examination*. Philadelphia: Temple University Press, 1988. Delves into the biographical experience that informs Camus's work. Includes chapters on *The Stranger*, Camus's drama, his interpretation of social dislocation, society and rebellion, revolt and history, metaphysical rebellion, confrontations with modernity, and the search for a style of life. Includes notes and bibliography.

Todd, Olivier. *Albert Camus: A Life*. Translated by Benjamin Ivry. New York: Alfred A. Knopf, 1997. Making use of materials such as unpublished letters made available after the death of Camus's widow, this detailed biography reveals much about Camus's love affairs and his many important friendships.

JEAN COCTEAU

Born: Maisons-Laffitte, France; July 5, 1889
Died: Milly-la-Forêt, France; October 11, 1963
Also known as: Jean Maurice Eugène Clément Cocteau

PRINCIPAL LONG FICTION

Le Potomak, 1919
Le Grand Écart, 1923 (*The Grand Écart*, 1925)
Thomas l'imposteur, 1923 (*Thomas the Impostor*, 1925)
Le Livre blanc, 1928 (*The White Paper*, 1957)
Les Enfants terribles, 1929 (*Enfants Terribles*, 1930; better known as *Children of the Game*, 1955)
Le Fantôme de Marseille, 1933
La Fin du Potomak, 1939

OTHER LITERARY FORMS

Never limited by distinctions among genres, Jean Cocteau (kawk-TOH) was an important figure in many arts. After an early and not particularly interesting "dandyistic" phase in his poetry, including *La Lampe d'Aladin* (1909; Aladdin's lamp), *Le Prince frivole* (1910; the frivolous prince), and *La Danse de Sophocle* (1912; the dance of Sophocles), he was influenced by Futurism, Dadaism, and Surrealism, and he developed a classical rigor and purity mingled with linguistic and imaginative originality. *Le Cap de Bonne-Espérance* (1919; the Cape of Good Hope), for example, glorifies pilots and flying, emphasizing sensation. *L'Ode à Picasso* (1919; ode to Picasso) seeks the wellspring of creativity in the great artist. *Vocabulaire* (1922; vocabulary) exhibits further linguistic creativity, and *Discours du grand sommeil* (1922; discourse on the great sleep) explores the experience of World War I. Later works use the suggestions of mythology, classical simplicity, and the subconscious, particularly *Plain-Chant* (1923), *L'Ange Heurtebise* (1925), *Mythologie* (1934), *Allégories* (1941), *La Crucifixion* (1946), *Clair-obscur* (1954; chiaroscuro), *Gondole des morts* (1959), and *Cérémonial espagnol du phénix* (1961).

Cocteau was a witty playwright on similar themes in *Orphée* (pr. 1926; *Orpheus*, 1933), *La Voix humaine* (pr., pb. 1930; *The Human Voice*, 1951), *La Machine infernale* (pr., pb. 1934; *The Infernal Machine*, 1936), *Les Chevaliers de la table ronde* (pr., pb. 1937; *The Knights of the Round Table*, 1955), *Les Parents terribles* (pr., pb. 1938; *Intimate Relations*, 1952), *Les Monstres sacrés* (pr., pb. 1940; *The Holy Terrors*, 1953), *La Machine à écrire* (pr., pb. 1941; *The Typewriter*, 1948), the verse drama *Renaud et Armide* (pr., pb. 1943), *L'Aigle à deux têtes* (pr., pb. 1946; *The Eagle Has Two Heads*, 1946), and *Bacchus* (pr. 1951; English translation, 1955). He was director or writer, or both, of a

Jean Cocteau
(National Archives)

number of films that have become classics because of their striking visual imagery and their evocation of the archetypal and mythological. *Le Sang d'un poète* (1930; *The Blood of a Poet*, 1949), *La Belle et la bête* (1946; *Beauty and the Beast*, 1947), *Les Parents terribles* (1948; *Intimate Relations*, 1952), *Les Enfants terribles* (1950), *Orphée* (1950; *Orpheus*, 1950), and *Le Testament d'Orphée* (1959; *The Testament of Orpheus*, 1968) are considered his best. He also wrote ballet scenarios, including those for Erik Satie's *Parade* (pr. 1917), Darius Milhaud's *Le Boeuf sur le toit* (pr. 1920), and Les Six's *Les Mariés de la Tour Eiffel* (pr. 1921; *The Wedding on the Eiffel Tower*, 1937), and two musical dramas, *Antigone* (pr. 1922; English translation, 1961), with music by Arthur Honegger, and *Oedipus-Rex* (pr. 1927; English translation, 1961), with music by Igor Stravinsky.

Cocteau's nonfiction is witty and incisive and usually based on his life and role as a poet in the control of forces he does not understand. The books in this category include *Le Rappel à l'ordre* (1926; *A Call to Order*, 1926), *Lettre à Jacques Maritain* (1926; *Art and Faith*, 1948), *Opium: Journal d'une désintoxication* (1930; *Opium: Diary of a Cure*, 1932), *Essai de la critique indirecte* (1932; *The Lais Mystery: An Essay of Indirect Criticism*, 1936), *Portraits-souvenir, 1900-1914* (1935; *Paris Album*, 1956), *"La Belle et la bête": Journal d'un film* (1946; *"Beauty and the Beast": Journal of a Film*, 1950), *La Difficulté d'être* (1947; *The Difficulty of Being*, 1966), and *Poésie critique* (1960).

Achievements

Twentieth century art in many areas is indebted to Jean Cocteau. His accomplishments span the artistic and literary activities of his times, the diversity unified by his vision of all art as facets of the purest form: poetry. Whether working in film, fiction, theater, drawing, or verse, he considered himself to be revealing the poet in him. Critics now generally agree that his finest achievements are in the novel and the cinema. One of the most crystalline stylists among French writers of the twentieth century, Cocteau employed brilliant imagery and extraordinary visual qualities that make his novels powerfully evocative despite their terse style. Some regard him as a dilettante interested only in stylishness and facile demonstrations of his gifts; his classical style, however, allows him to transcend the limitations of ordinary novelists and their message-oriented prose to explore the resonances of mythology and archetype in a modern context. His versatility, irony, and playfulness encouraged his contemporaries to dismiss him, and he received few honors other than his 1955 election to the Académie Française. His novels are quirky, experimental, often chaotic, but filled with intriguing imagery and wit. *Children of the Game* is almost universally agreed to be his masterpiece.

Biography

Jean Cocteau's background was solidly Parisian bourgeois. Georges and Eugénie Lecomte Cocteau, his parents, were a cultivated couple who introduced Jean, his brother Paul, and his sister Marthe to the fine arts. Near their suburban home, Cocteau would recall, the children played on the grounds of a "magical" castle designed by François Mansart. When living in the city with his grandparents, Cocteau would wander through rooms that contained classical busts, vases, a painting by Eugène Delacroix, and drawings by Jean-Auguste-Dominique Ingres. The celebrated violinist Pablo de Sarasate often visited Cocteau's grandfather, who was a cellist, and they would play music together. What impressed the young Cocteau most, however, were his trips to the circus, the ice palace, and the theater, particularly the Comédie-Française. His memories of these trips, he would later come to realize, were even brighter than the real experiences. In his own productions years later, he would ask technicians to duplicate the lighting or brilliance of childhood theatrical events and be told it had been technically impossible to create such effects when he was a boy. Memory had heightened the splendor of the past, including the recollections of the castle and of his grandparents' house; his own life began to assume mythological dimensions.

At the Petit Lycée Condorcet, Cocteau was a poor student, especially after his father killed himself in 1899 because of financial pressures. He did, however, meet the haunting Pierre Dargelos, who would become the dark "god" of *Children of the Game*. At the Grand Condorcet, Cocteau was frequently truant, exploiting his illnesses to stay home. Like many creative people, he was irritated by institutions, and he much preferred having his German governess sew doll clothes for a model theater to sitting behind a school desk.

Réné Rocher, one of his best friends, often played with Cocteau's miniature theaters and, in adulthood, became a director himself.

Cocteau traveled with his mother to Venice, then began study for his *baccalauréat*. He was more interested, however, in his first love affair—with Madeleine Carlier, ten years his senior—and his deepening involvement in theater. He became a protégé of Édouard de Max, who acted opposite Sarah Bernhardt. All of these diversions contributed to Cocteau's failing the *bachot*.

De Max, however, thrust Cocteau into the public eye by organizing a reading of Cocteau's poetry by de Max, Rocher, and other prominent actors and actresses, at the Théâtre Fémina, on April 4, 1908. Several important literary critics and many of the elite of Paris attended. Cocteau's debut was a great success, and reviewers compared him to Pierre de Ronsard and Alfred de Musset. Subsequently, Cocteau met many literary notables, including Edmond Rostand, Marcel Proust, Charles-Pierre Péguy, Catulle Mendès, and Jules Lemaître. Comtesse Anna de Noailles particularly enchanted him, and he tried to write refined and sensual poetry like hers. He helped found the literary magazine *Schéhérazade*, dedicated to poetry and music, and moved into the Hôtel Biron, whose residents at the time included Auguste Rodin and his secretary, Rainer Maria Rilke.

Meeting the great impresario Sergei Diaghilev of the Ballets Russes caused Cocteau to abandon his previous enthusiasms for a while. He begged Diaghilev to let him write ballets. Diaghilev eventually said, "Étonne-moi!" ("Astonish me!"), perhaps to quiet him, but Cocteau took it as an order and a goal for the rest of his life's work. Though Diaghilev produced Cocteau's first ballet, *Le Dieu bleu* (pr. 1912), for the coronation of George V, it was not successful. Believing that the score rather than his scenario was at fault, Cocteau began to associate with composer Igor Stravinsky, even moving in with him for a while. During this period, Henri Ghéon of *La Nouvelle Revue Française* accused Cocteau of being an entirely derivative poet. Stung by the validity of the review (perhaps coauthored by André Gide), Cocteau began a search for himself as an artist. He underwent what he called a "molting" around 1914, rebelling against older writers who had influenced him, such as Rostand and the Comtesse de Noailles, and moving in the direction of poets such as Max Jacob and Guillaume Apollinaire. *Le Potomak*, with its radical mixture of prose, drawings, and verse, was completed while Cocteau was living with Gide and Stravinsky and is the first important, truly original expression of Cocteau's personality.

Cocteau's attempted enlistment at the outset of World War I was rejected because of his health. He nevertheless became an ambulance driver on the Belgian front (albeit illegally). He was discovered and ordered back to Paris immediately before the group to which he had attached himself was decimated in an attack. These experiences formed the basis for his novel and film *Thomas the Impostor*. As the war continued, Cocteau met artists Amedeo Modigliani and Pablo Picasso in Paris. The latter he introduced to Diaghilev, who put him to work on Satie's ballet *Parade*; the scenario was written by Cocteau, the costumes and set were by Picasso, and the ballet was choreographed by Léonide Massine.

The ballet's atonal music and radical set and costumes caused a near riot in the theater. Apollinaire, wearing his uniform and a dressing over his wounded head, barely managed to keep the spectators from assaulting the stage. Cocteau responded in the press, vigorously attacking the musical influence of Claude Debussy, Richard Wagner, and, surprisingly, Stravinsky, and aligning himself with the radical group called Les Six (Georges Auric, Louis Durey, Arthur Honegger, Darius Milhaud, Francis Poulenc, and Germaine Tailleferre).

Raymond Radiguet was fifteen, handsome, and a poetic genius, Cocteau believed, when he met and fell in love with him in 1919. Radiguet was a major influence in moving Cocteau toward a simpler, more classical style. Cocteau's energy revived, and he produced several new works, including *The Grand Écart* and the volume of poems *Plain-Chant*. When in December, 1923, Radiguet died of typhoid, Cocteau was devastated. Diaghilev took Cocteau to Monte Carlo to help him recover, but the discovery of opium there was Cocteau's only comfort. His friends and family were forced to persuade him to enter a sanatorium in 1925, when his addiction had become serious. Jacques Maritain, the Catholic philosopher, briefly restored Cocteau's faith in religion during the cure. The faith waned, but works such as *L'Ange Heurtebise*, *Orpheus*, and *Children of the Game* followed. Patching up his friendship with Stravinsky, Cocteau wrote the libretto for the oratorio *Oedipus-Rex*.

Though Cocteau contracted typhoid in 1931, his artistic output in the 1930's was astonishing. He wrote plays, poems, songs, ballets, art criticism, and a column for the newspaper *Ce Soir*. He published a journal chronicling a trip taken in imitation of Jules Verne's *Le Tour du monde en quatre-vingt jours* (1873; *Around the World in Eighty Days*, 1873). He also became the manager of bantamweight boxer Alphonse Theo Brown. His first attempt at *poésie cinématographique* (poetry of the film), however, was probably his most important activity. He wrote and directed the film *The Blood of a Poet*, which became a classic. His abilities in the visual arts and in visual imagery expressed themselves well in cinema, and he became responsible for a number of major films, including *Beauty and the Beast*, *Intimate Relations*, *The Testament of Orpheus*, and *Les Enfants terribles*.

During the German occupation of France, Cocteau was constantly vilified by the press. His play *The Typewriter* was banned. At one point, he was beaten by a group of French Nazis for not saluting their flag. He testified in court for thief, novelist, and Resistance fighter Jean Genet in 1942, despite much advice to the contrary. Cocteau gained respect for his courage and, after the war, found himself a "grand old man" of the artistic world.

His muse, however, would not let him retire. He traveled, made recordings, and wrote plays, journals, and films. His frescoes for the city hall at Menton, the Chapel of Saint Pierre at Villefranche-sur-Mer, the Chapel of Notre Dame in London, the Church of Saint Blaise-des-Simples in Milly-la-Fôret, and the Chapel at Fréjus, Notre-Dame-de-Jérusalem created controversy among art critics. He also designed fabrics, plates, and posters. In 1955, he was elected to the Royal Belgian Academy and to the Académie Française. In 1956, he was awarded an honorary doctorate of letters from Oxford University. He died on October 11, 1963, distressed at hearing of the death of his friend Edith Piaf earlier in the day.

Analysis

Le Potomak was a crucial work in Jean Cocteau's development, as he used it to break free of former influences and find an individual voice. Highly experimental, it is, however, not of compelling interest for any other reason, consisting as it does of an exploration of the subconscious through a hodgepodge of verse, prose, and drawings, all of which reveal Cocteau's talents but mostly demonstrate rebellion rather than a mature concept of the novelistic art. Its writing was interrupted by World War I, and the influence of the war is apparent in the revised edition. Under the influence of Radiguet, Cocteau wrote *The Grand Écart* and *Thomas the Impostor*. Mythologizing memories of his childhood, Cocteau based *The Grand Écart* on a childhood visit to Venice and his recollections of boarding school. One of his recurrent images appears indistinctly in this novel in the form of the Englishman Stopwell. Like Dargelos and the Angel Heurtebise, Stopwell is an angel in the form of a tempter who brings about annihilation or metamorphosis. *Thomas the Impostor* was based largely on Cocteau's own experiences during the war. Rejected for service, he posed as an ambulance driver on the Belgian front and was "adopted" by a group of Fusiliers Marins. When discovered by a superior officer, he was arrested and taken from the front. A day later, most of his comrades were killed. Rather than portraying the war as a horror, however, the novel turns it into a ghastly joke, a reflection of humanity's chaotic mind, a cruel trick played by a Euripidean god. Being an impostor is likened to being a poet, and reality and impostorship merge only when Thomas the Impostor is shot in the Waste Land. The "Prince of Frivolity," as Cocteau was known, uses flippant, humorous, outlandish imagery that accentuates the horror. The book is clearly one of his better novels, though not nearly equal to his next.

CHILDREN OF THE GAME

Children of the Game is considered to be Cocteau's most successful novel by far. In addition to being beautifully written, it is an extraordinary evocation of adolescent hopes, fears, dreams, and obsessions; it is said to have been regarded by French teenagers as capturing their alienation from adult society in the same way that J. D. Salinger articulated teen alienation in American culture. Perhaps because Cocteau, as an artist and a man, always held himself as a kind of alien visitor to the realms of the establishment from the world of subjectivity and irrationality, his sensitivity to adolescent alienation was enhanced. *Children of the Game* is not a realistic portrayal of adolescence, however. It is sensitive, but it is so overlaid with dream imagery and mythological overtones that whatever autobiographical elements and psychological truths it might contain are submerged.

Fragments from many mythological sources are identifiable upon even a cursory reading of the work. Cocteau was fascinated with mythology and at various times in his career wrote works dealing with Antigone, Orpheus, Bacchus, and the "Beauty and the Beast" motif. Cocteau wrote *Children of the Game* very rapidly—at the rate of seventeen pages a day for three weeks—while he was undergoing treatment for opium addiction, as if he were trying to let archetypal and subconscious elements flow freely onto the page. Too careful an artist to practice automatic writing without aesthetically manipulating the result, he nevertheless refused to make later changes in the text for fear of destroying the fabric of the book. Characters in *Children of the Game* quite often suggest beings from mythology, as Cocteau imbues people and events from his own life and imagination with a supernatural or divine aura.

Dargelos, for example, whose name is taken from a real boy whom Cocteau admired in his school days, takes on the characteristics of a god. Early in the book, Paul seeks Dargelos among the snowball wars in the Cité Monthiers. Paul's love for Dargelos is described as "sexless and purposeless," and his seeking him in order to fight beside him, defend him, and prove what he can do takes on religious overtones. Paul, however, is silenced by a snowball from one of his idol's acolytes, condemning him to Dargelos's wrath. Dargelos rises up in an immense gesture, his cheeks on fire and his hair in disorder, like a statue of Dionysus. Paul feels the blow of the snowball on his chest—a dark blow, the blow of a marble fist. As Paul loses consciousness, he imagines Dargelos upon a dais, in a supernatural light. Dargelos has struck Paul in the heart, with a snowball like Thor's hammer or Zeus's thunderbolt. Dargelos, throughout the rest of the book, is hardly mentioned; his presence, however, seems to loom over all subsequent events. As Wallace Fowlie has observed, he "grows into the figure of a dark angel who haunts the dreams and thoughts of the protagonist."

Eden is evoked when Paul, his sister Elisabeth, and Gérard find themselves alone without adult supervision. In "the Room," they are free of conventional worries about food and seem innocent of evil. Their childhood seems to be prolonged. Although the situation appears to be fraught with incestuous overtones—Paul and Elisabeth sleep in the same room and bathe together—there is instead a matter-of-fact sexlessness, a lack of shame. When a ball of poison (associated with Dargelos's snowball) causes the cold, outside world of snow and death to blow into their Eden, one may see an analogy to the expulsion from Eden, the coming of mortality into Eden.

One must not, however, treat *Children of the Game* as allegory. Cocteau is weaving a fugue of implications and mythological elements. One critic has found the novel to be about the impossibility of escaping bourgeois ideology; another has found it to be the playing out of fate in the form of Eros-Thanatos. There is certainly a hint of inevitability in the sequence of events. Tragedy is suggested from the beginning, and the classical structure and sparkling sentences help convey this impression. The characters are in the grip of forces beyond their control. When Michael, the rich American Jew, is killed, it seems as if the Room reaches out to protect itself. When Dargelos gives Paul the fist-sized ball of poison, one is reminded of the marble-hard snowball and the apple that destroyed Eden. A reddish gash in the ball is reminiscent of both a wound and female genitalia, suggesting an association between mortality and the loss of innocence. The end is destined, and nothing can hold it back. Childhood is doomed. As Cocteau himself wrote in *The Difficulty of Being:* "Childhood knows what it wants. It wants to emerge from childhood. The trouble starts when it does emerge. For youth knows what it does not want before it knows what it does want. But what it does not want is what we do want." Thus are the "holy terrors" doomed.

LA FIN DU POTOMAK

Le Fantôme de Marseille is a slight work containing associations and local color that Cocteau recalled from his running away to Marseilles at the age of fifteen. Later, in Le Picquey, in a hotel where he had stayed with Radiguet in 1923, Cocteau watched over the convalescence of a new love, actor Jean Marais, and returned to the inspiration of *Le Potomak* for his last novel. *La Fin du Potomak* is a curious mixture of fairy tales, aphorisms, riddles, and true stories recalling Cocteau's experiences after 1913. A revival of Cocteau's classicism has been seen in the work, but most often it is regarded as a mere shadow of *Le Potomak*, as if the author's creative interests had shifted away from *poésie de roman* (poetry of the novel). Brooding over the entire work is a disappointment with human nature and recurrent imagery of death, perhaps evoked by Marais's illness and the memory of Radiguet's sudden death. There is also an acceptance of the author's own death (which was many years in the future), indicated by some lines of poetry at the end: "Death, don't be clever/ . . . You see, I wait standing still/ I even offer you my hand/ . . . What does it matter? I leave behind a book/ That you will not take from me."

J. Madison Davis

OTHER MAJOR WORKS

PLAYS: *Antigone*, pr. 1922 (libretto; English translation, 1961); *Orphée*, pr. 1926 (*Orpheus*, 1933); *Oedipus-Rex*, pr. 1927 (libretto; English translation, 1961); *La Voix humaine*, pr., pb. 1930 (*The Human Voice*, 1951); *La Machine infernale*, pr., pb. 1934 (*The Infernal Machine*, 1936); *L'École des veuves*, pr., pb. 1936; *Les Chevaliers de la table ronde*, pr., pb. 1937 (*The Knights of the Round Table*, 1955); *Les Parents terribles*, pr., pb. 1938 (*Intimate Relations*, 1952); *Les Monstres sacrés*, pr., pb. 1940 (*The Holy Terrors*, 1953); *La Machine à écrire*, pr., pb. 1941 (*The Typewriter*, 1948); *Renaud et Armide*, pr., pb. 1943; *L'Aigle à deux têtes*, pr., pb. 1946 (*The Eagle Has Two Heads*, 1946); *Bacchus*, pr. 1951 (English translation, 1955); *Théâtre complet*, pb. 1957 (2 volumes); *Five Plays*, pb. 1961; *L'Impromptu du Palais-Royal*, pr., pb. 1962; *The Infernal Machine, and Other Plays*, 1964.

POETRY: *La Lampe d'Aladin*, 1909; *Le Prince frivole*, 1910; *La Danse de Sophocle*,

1912; *Le Cap de Bonne-Espérance*, 1919; *L'Ode à Picasso*, 1919; *Escales*, 1920; *Poésies, 1917-1920*, 1920; *Discours du grand sommeil*, 1922; *Vocabulaire*, 1922; *Plain-Chant*, 1923; *Poésie, 1916-1923*, 1924; *Cri écrit*, 1925; *L'Ange Heurtebise*, 1925; *Prière mutilée*, 1925; *Opéra*, 1927; *Morceaux choisis*, 1932; *Mythologie*, 1934; *Allégories*, 1941; *Léone*, 1945; *Poèmes*, 1945; *La Crucifixion*, 1946; *Anthologie poétique*, 1951; *Le Chiffre sept*, 1952; *Appogiatures*, 1953; *Clair-obscur*, 1954; *Poèmes, 1916-1955*, 1956; *Gondole des morts*, 1959; *Cérémonial espagnol du phénix*, 1961; *Le Requiem*, 1962.

SCREENPLAYS: *Le Sang d'un poète*, 1930 (*The Blood of a Poet*, 1949); *L'Éternel Retour*, 1943 (*The Eternal Return*, 1948); *Le Baron fantôme*, 1943; *L'Aigle à deux têtes*, 1946; *La Belle et la bête*, 1946 (*Beauty and the Beast*, 1947); *Ruy Blas*, 1947; *Les Parents terribles*, 1948 (*Intimate Relations*, 1952); *Les Enfants terribles*, 1950; *Orphée*, 1950 (*Orpheus*, 1950); *Le Testament d'Orphée*, 1959 (*The Testament of Orpheus*, 1968); *Thomas l'Imposteur*, 1965.

NONFICTION: *Le Coq et l'Arlequin*, 1918 (*Cock and Harlequin*, 1921); *Le Secret professionnel*, 1922; *Lettre à Jacques Maritain*, 1926 (*Art and Faith*, 1948); *Le Rappel à l'ordre*, 1926 (*A Call to Order*, 1926); *Opium: Journal d'une désintoxication*, 1930 (*Opium: Diary of a Cure*, 1932); *Essai de la critique indirecte*, 1932 (*The Lais Mystery: An Essay of Indirect Criticism*, 1936); *Portraits-souvenir, 1900-1914*, 1935 (*Paris Album*, 1956); *"La Belle et la bête": Journal d'un film*, 1946 (*"Beauty and the Beast": Journal of a Film*, 1950); *La Difficulté d'être*, 1947 (*The Difficulty of Being*, 1966); *Journal d'un inconnu*, 1952 (*The Hand of a Stranger*, 1956; also known as *Diary of an Unknown*, 1988); *The Journals of Jean Cocteau*, 1956; *Poésie critique*, 1960.

BALLET SCENARIOS: *Le Dieu bleu*, pr. 1912 (with Frédéric de Madrazo); *Parade*, pr. 1917 (music by Erik Satie, scenery by Pablo Picasso); *Le Boeuf sur le toit*, pr. 1920 (music by Darius Milhaud, scenery by Raoul Dufy); *Le Gendarme incompris*, pr. 1921 (with Raymond Radiguet; music by Francis Poulenc); *Les Mariés de la tour Eiffel*, pr. 1921 (music by Les Six; *The Wedding on the Eiffel Tower*, 1937); *Les Biches*, pr. 1924 (music by Poulenc); *Les Fâcheux*, pr. 1924 (music by Georges Auric); *Le Jeune Homme et la mort*, pr. 1946 (music by Johann Sebastian Bach); *Phèdre*, pr. 1950 (music by Auric).

TRANSLATION: *Roméo et Juliette*, 1926 (of William Shakespeare's play).

Bibliography

Brown, Frederick. *An Impersonation of Angels: A Biography of Jean Cocteau*. New York: Viking Press, 1968. Study of the life and work of Cocteau focuses on his artistic milieu and his collaborators and sources of inspiration, such as poet Guillaume Apollinaire, artist Pablo Picasso, novelist André Gide, and filmmaker Jean Marais. Includes illustrations and bibliography.

Crosland, Margaret. *Jean Cocteau: A Biography*. New York: Alfred A. Knopf, 1956. Charming biography written with the help and encouragement of Cocteau himself. The goal is to relate Cocteau's work to his life and to relate the different aspects of his work to one another. Offers lively comments by fellow artists as well as discussion and interpretation of individual works by Cocteau. Includes excerpts from letters of Cocteau and numerous illustrations.

Crowson, Lydia. *The Esthetic of Jean Cocteau*. Hanover: University of New Hampshire Press, 1978. Scholarly work devotes chapters to Cocteau's milieu, the nature of the real, and the roles of myth, consciousness, and power. Includes introduction and bibliography.

Fowlie, Wallace. *Jean Cocteau: The History of a Poet's Age*. Bloomington: Indiana University Press, 1966. General study defines Cocteau's originality by comparing him with other French writers and film directors of his lifetime. Proposes a very sensible evaluation of Cocteau's real accomplishments.

Knapp, Bettina L. *Jean Cocteau*. Updated ed. Boston: Twayne, 1989. Thorough study pursues both psychological and literary views of Cocteau's work, with chapters following a chronological approach. Includes chronology, notes, bibliography, and index.

Lowe, Romana N. *The Fictional Female: Sacrificial Rituals and Spectacles of Writing in Baudelaire, Zola, and Cocteau*. New York: Peter Lang, 1997. Highlights the sacrificial victim common in nineteenth and twentieth century French texts: woman. Traces structures and images of female sacrifice in the genres of poetry, novel, and theater with close readings of the works of Charles Baudelaire, Émile Zola, and Cocteau.

Mauriès, Patrick. *Jean Cocteau*. Translated by Jane Brenton. London: Thames and Hudson, 1998. Brief but excellent biography provides information that places Cocteau's works within the context of his life. Illustrated with many photographs.

Selous, Trista. *Cocteau*. Paris: Centre Pompidou, 2003. Retrospective catalog compiled by the Centre Pompidou and the Montreal Museum offers an illustrated review of Cocteau's creative output along with seventeen essays on his life and work.

Steegmuller, Francis. *Cocteau*. Boston: D. R. Godine, 1986. Major biography discusses Cocteau's childhood, the influence of his mother, and fellow poets. Defines Cocteau as a "quick-change artist" with a propensity for constant self-invention, discarding old views and activities and assuming new roles or guises with remarkable facility. Includes illustrations, twelve informative appendixes, bibliography, and index.

Williams, James S. *Jean Cocteau*. London: Reaktion Books, 2008. Biography chronicles the development of Cocteau's aesthetic and his work as a novelist, poet, dramatist, filmmaker, and designer. Concludes that Cocteau's oeuvre is characterized by a continual self-questioning.

CYRANO DE BERGERAC

Born: Paris, France; March 6, 1619
Died: Paris, France; July 28, 1655
Also known as: Hector Savinien de Cyrano

PRINCIPAL LONG FICTION

L'Autre Monde: Ou, Les États et empires de la lune et du soleil, 1656-1662 (*Comical History of the States and Empires of the Worlds of the Moon and Sun*, 1687; also known as *Other Worlds: The Comical History of the States and Empires of the Moon and the Sun*, 1965; includes *Histoire comique des états et empires de la lune*, 1656 [*Comical History of the States and Empires of the Moon*; also known as *The Government of the World in the Moon*, 1659], and *Histoire comique des états et empires du soleil*, 1662 [*Comical History of the States and Empires of the Sun*])

OTHER LITERARY FORMS

In the course of his brief and turbulent life, Cyrano de Bergerac (SEE-rah-noh deh BEHR-zheh-rahk) tried his hand at an array of genres and acquitted himself honorably in all of them. His tragedy *La Mort d'Agrippine* (pr. 1653) compares favorably with the lesser works of Pierre Corneille. Cyrano's one comedy, *Le Pédant joué* (pb. 1954; the pedant outwitted), though never staged in his lifetime, was almost certainly the unacknowledged source of two highly effective scenes in Molière's *Les Fourberies de Scapin* (pr., pb. 1671; *The Cheats of Scapin*, 1701). *Le Pédant joué* is essentially a burlesque of the pedantry and *préciosité* that were rife in Cyrano's day—though Cyrano himself could tap a "precious" vein when he chose.

The same gift for burlesque is evident in Cyrano's satiric poem, or *mazarinade* (attack on Cardinal Mazarin), of 1649, *Le Ministre d'état flambé* (the minister of state goes up in flames), and in the best of his letters. The latter were not genuine correspondence but showpieces designed for publication. They are of several kinds: love letters full of exaggerated compliments and reproaches, set off by far-fetched figures of speech in the worst *précieux* style; elaborate and fanciful descriptions of nature; satiric attacks on real and imagined enemies; and polemic pieces on a variety of political and philosophical issues. The letters "For the Sorcerers" and "Against the Sorcerers" are especially noteworthy for their satiric power and cogency of argument; they also anticipate the attacks on superstition and intolerance in *Other Worlds*, Cyrano's most important work.

ACHIEVEMENTS

It is a great irony of literary history that Cyrano de Bergerac, a minor but talented and aggressively ambitious seventeenth century writer, at last achieved world renown in the

Cyrano de Bergerac
(Library of Congress)

twentieth century—as a fictional character who scarcely resembles his original. To be fair to Edmond Rostand (the playwright whose *Cyrano de Bergerac*, staged in 1897, spread Cyrano's fame), the unexpurgated manuscripts that were to reveal the full extent of his hero's boldness and malice were as yet unpublished when he wrote; yet it took a deal of willful misreading—and, of course, imaginative reworking—to make a noble Platonic lover of the dissolute and misanthropic Cyrano. Whatever his failures as a man, the real Cyrano deserves to be remembered as a competent literary craftsman and an inspired satirist. There is no denying that his libertinism had its sordid side, but its essence was simply "freethinking," a rejection of the Catholic Church's exclusive claim to truth and an espousal of the cause of scientific investigation.

In his best works, the two volumes of *Other Worlds* and the letters for and against sorcerers, Cyrano anticipates the form and some of the major themes of Voltaire's *contes philosophiques* (philosophical tales—a distinct genre). Indeed, Voltaire's *Le Micromégas* (1752; *Micromegas*, 1753), as well as Jonathan Swift's *Gulliver's Travels* (1726), owes a debt of inspiration to Cyrano. Perhaps Cyrano's greatest single achievement was his astonishing vision of cultural pluralism and toleration in an age clouded by superstition and repression.

BIOGRAPHY

For serious readers of his works, the facts of Cyrano de Bergerac's life offer an important corrective to his legend. Though his family laid claim to noble status, the only basis for that claim was their ownership of two "fiefs," or manorial properties—Mauvières and Bergerac—in the valley of the Chevreuse near Paris. The Cyranos were in fact of bourgeois origin; their son was christened Hector Savinien de Cyrano, and he himself added the title "de Bergerac" as a young man (as he occasionally assumed the pretentious given names of Alexandre or Hercule). This was deceptive on two counts, for, aside from smacking of nobility, the title suggests a Gascon origin. Rostand thus portrays his hero as born and bred in Gascony, which the real Cyrano never visited.

Cyrano was born in Paris and christened there on March 6, 1619. Some of his childhood was spent on his father's properties in the Chevreuse valley, where he acquired a love of nature and a hatred of dogmatic authority. The hatred was inspired by a country priest to whom Cyrano was sent for schooling; it was to grow into a lifelong passion, reinforced by his experiences at the Collège de Beauvais in Paris, where he completed his education. (The headmaster of the collège, Jean Grangier—a man of considerable scholarly reputation—is mercilessly satirized in Cyrano's comedy, *Le Pédant joué*, while the country priest is pilloried in *Comical History of the States and Empires of the Sun*.) Once out of school, Cyrano gave free rein to his rebellious streak and joined the circles of *libertins*, or freethinkers—and free livers—who frequented certain Paris cabarets. Among his libertine friends were several pupils of the materialist philosopher Pierre Gassendi, including the avowed atheist Claude-Emmanuel Chapelle and possibly the young Molière. Whether he studied with Gassendi himself, Cyrano was heavily influenced by his ideas, which are discussed at length in *Other Worlds*.

At about this time, Cyrano's father suffered serious financial reverses and was forced to sell his fiefs; it has been suggested that Cyrano's gambling losses may have been a factor. Whatever the reasons, relations between father and son were strained, and they continued to be so until the father's death; according to records left by his lawyers, Abel de Cyrano suspected his two sons of robbing him as he lay on his deathbed. It is worth noting as well that Cyrano includes a bitter tirade against fathers in *Other Worlds* and depicts the sons of the moon people as exercising authority over their old fathers.

His financial straits, as well as the desire to make a name for himself, inspired Cyrano to seek a commission in the Guards, a company made up almost entirely of Gascons, whose reputation for bravado was apparently well deserved. One element of the Cyrano legend that seems to bear up under inspection is his reputation for bravery in the duels for which the Guards were notorious. After being wounded in two battles, however (at the sieges of Mouzon and Arras), he gave up the military life in disgust and turned to a literary career. Frédéric Lachèvre, who produced the first accurate biography of Cyrano in 1920, has suggested that the serious illness from which Cyrano suffered during this period also influenced his decision by forcing him to withdraw from other spheres of activity. The exact nature of the disease is unknown, but several biographers have accepted Lachèvre's suggestion that it may have been syphilis. Illness and poverty combined to reinforce the misanthropic strain in Cyrano's character; during this period, he broke with and reviled many of his former friends.

An opponent of Cardinal Mazarin at the outbreak of the Fronde in 1649, he changed sides—possibly for pay—and wrote a scathing letter, *Contre les Frondeurs* (1651; against the Frondeurs). Jacques Prévot, editor of Cyrano's complete works, suggested that one of the most violent of these ruptures may have had an erotic dimension: Charles d'Assoucy, a satiric poet, was known to be homosexual, and Cyrano seems to have shown little interest in women.

Unfortunately, Cyrano enjoyed no greater success as a writer during his lifetime than he did as a soldier. In an age of censorship, he was too bold for most publishers, and he succeeded in publishing his plays and some letters only after accepting the patronage of the duke of Arpajon, a man of limited intelligence who wished to make a name for himself as a patron of the arts. With his support, Cyrano staged his tragedy, *La Mort d'Agrippine*, but it was closed after a few performances by a group hired to boo his "atheistic" stance (the hirelings, ironically, missed the more daring speeches and booed at a line they simply misunderstood). Shortly thereafter, Cyrano was hit on the head by a log dropped by one of the duke's servants. It seems at least as likely that this was an accident as that someone hired the servant to ambush Cyrano (for fear of facing him in a fair fight, as Rostand would have it): By this time, Cyrano's dueling days were behind him. The incident precipitated a rupture with the duke, however, and forced Cyrano to take to his bed. Fourteen months later, on July 28, 1655, he died at the age of thirty-six.

Lachèvre suggests that the primary cause of death was tertiary syphilis, but a lack of definite evidence has left this surmise in doubt. Cyrano is said to have returned to the faith on his deathbed at the urging of his relative, Mother Marguerite of Jesus, and his oldest friend, Henry Le Bret. Le Bret became Cyrano's literary executor and published a heavily expurgated version of *Other Worlds* in 1657, two years after Cyrano's death.

Analysis: Other Worlds

Erica Harth, in *Cyrano de Bergerac and the Polemics of Modernity* (1970), claims Cyrano de Bergerac to have been "the first of the Moderns," forerunner of a position more clearly formulated later in the seventeenth century in the great Quarrel of the Ancients and

Moderns. Cyrano went beyond his contemporaries the *libertins*, Harth argues, by refusing to settle for a critique of received wisdom; the "destructive spirit" in which he attacks tradition and Church authority "is accompanied by a positive acceptance and propagation of the same scientific and philosophical ideas which, although not directly transmitted by Cyrano, were to have a profound impact on the minds of the eighteenth century *philosophes*."

Cyrano, however, was also undeniably a man of his own time, attracted to as well as repulsed by the excesses of *préciosité*, charmed as well as amused by the arcane theories of thinkers such as Tommaso Campanella, in which allegory and myth are still intertwined with rationalistic investigation. If we can trust the priest's report, Cyrano even returned to the faith in time to die "a good Christian death," and as one critic has shown, it is impossible to deduce a consistent atheistic view even from the unexpurgated manuscripts of *Other Worlds*. However one looks at Cyrano's masterpiece, contradictions emerge. Before examining these contradictions in detail, a brief description of the work is in order.

Although *Comical History of the States and Empires of the Sun* was first published separately from *Comical History of the States and Empires of the Moon*, it seems clear that this division does not reflect any intention of the author; the two works relate voyages of similar scope by a single narrator, and the second of these voyages is said to be motivated by persecution arising from a published account of the first. Combined, the voyages form a continuous narrative—as do, for example, the two parts of Miguel de Cervantes' *Don Quixote de la Mancha* (1605, 1615)—and may be referred to without distortion by the collective title *Other Worlds*. (The French title, literally translated, is "the other world," a phrase that in French as well as English usually refers to the abode of souls after death; Cyrano probably meant it to be taken ironically, for his aim is to suggest that there are "other worlds" in the here and now as well.) This was Cyrano's only work of prose fiction, but it proved to be the most effective vehicle for his fractious talents and libertine perspective. Because of its subject, it has often been classified as a work of utopian fiction, but the genre to which it really belongs is that of the *conte philosophique*, or philosophical tale, as practiced preeminently by Voltaire one hundred years later.

A PHILOSOPHICAL TALE

The essence of the *conte philosophique* is its unique combination of satiric, even farcical, elements with serious philosophical or ideological ones. Consistency or fullness of characterization and cogency of plot tend to be sacrificed to the primary goals of ridiculing an opposing (usually dogmatic) intellectual position and of suggesting more enlightened alternatives. Because of the variety of scientific and philosophical positions, many of them incompatible, that are detailed by different characters of *Other Worlds*, it has been maintained that Cyrano—admittedly a dilettante rather than a true scholar—was himself confused about the ideas he wished to advance. While the confusion may be real, Prévot, in *Cyrano de Bergerac, romancier* (1977), has argued for a subtler reading that qualifies the didactic intent of the work. Insofar as Cyrano has a "message," Prévot suggests, it is one of radical skepticism; Cyrano considers all doctrines, however scientific, inherently suspect, and having rid himself of one set is not at all eager to embrace another.

In addition to fitting Le Bret's description of his old friend's beliefs, this analysis would tally with Cyrano's own warnings, in the second chapter of his fragmentary treatise on physics (never completed but published in Prévot's edition of *Œuvres complètes*, 1977) against taking one's hypotheses for realities. There is, moreover, an anarchic streak in *Other Worlds*, corresponding to its satiric intent; in that respect, Cyrano is a worthy heir of Aristophanes, Lucian, and François Rabelais, from whom he may have borrowed specific motifs but whose satiric vein he made his own.

The narrator of *Other Worlds*, who speaks in the first person, is not named until the opening pages of the second volume; he is there called Drycona, an obvious anagram of Cyrano. On the strength of his anagrammatic name, many critics have assumed that the narrator speaks for the author. While at times it is hard to deny that he does, his own position fluctuates from scene to scene, enabling him to serve as a foil for a variety of interlocutors. Thus, in conversation with an avowed atheist he defends the faith, whereas in conversation with an Old Testament prophet he blasphemes. Nor is he always in opposition: He listens deferentially to speakers of the most disparate opinions. It seems best to admit, with Prévot, that Drycona is primarily a fictional creation—as are the other "real" characters who appear, such as Campanella and René Descartes.

THE VOYAGES

The narrator's first voyage is inspired by a moonlit walk with friends, who try to outdo one another in *précieux* descriptions of the full moon (an attic window on heaven, the sign outside Bacchus's tavern). His friends ridicule the narrator for suggesting that the moon may be "a world like this one, for which our world serves as a moon." On reaching home, however, the narrator finds that a book has mysteriously appeared on his desk and is lying open at the page where the author (Jerome Cardan, a sixteenth century mathematician and astrologer) describes a visit from two men who said they lived on the moon. The narrator, determined to verify his hunch, contrives a first mode of space travel: He covers himself with small flasks of dew, which the sun draws upward. He rises so quickly toward the sun, however, that he is obliged to break most of the flasks, and falls back to the earth—in Canada, at that time New France. There he is entertained by the viceroy, with whom he discusses his belief that the earth travels around the sun (still a heretical proposition in 1648); his own displacement from France to Canada is of course evidence that the earth rotates.

In a second attempt to reach the moon, he builds a flying machine, which at first crashes; while he is tending his bruises, the colonial troops outfit the machine with fireworks, transforming it into a multistage rocket. The narrator manages to jump in before it takes off and, when the last stage falls to earth, finds himself still being drawn to the moon by the beef marrow he had rubbed on his bruises. (It was a popular superstition that the waning moon "sucked up" animal marrow.) As luck would have it, he falls in the Earthly Paradise and strikes against an apple from the Tree of Life, whose juice revivifies and rejuvenates him. The prophet Elias, one of two inhabitants of the Earthly Paradise (the other is Enoch), tells him its history, but the narrator cannot resist the impulse to tell a blasphemous joke, and he is cast out of Paradise.

The rest of the moon is inhabited by a race of giants who resemble human beings but move about on all fours; indeed, they take the narrator for an animal because he walks on two feet, and they exhibit him as a kind of sideshow (an idea borrowed by Swift). He is befriended by a spirit whose native land is the sun but who has visited the earth in various ages and was once the Genius or monitory Voice of Socrates; the spirit speaks Greek with the narrator and arranges to have him brought to the royal court. There he is taken for a female of the same species as a Spaniard who has arrived before him (the Spaniard, Gonsales, was the hero of Francis Godwin's 1638 book *The Man in the Moone: Or, A Discourse of a Voyage Thither*).

In the hope of producing more "animals" of their species, the moon people have them share a bed, where they have long talks on various scientific problems. As the narrator learns the moon language (which is of two kinds, musical notes for the upper classes and physical gestures for the lower), a controversy arises over his status: Is he a man or an animal? The moon priests consider it "a shocking impiety" to call such a "monster" a man, so he is interrogated before the Estates General. He tries to defend the principles of Aristotle's philosophy but is unanimously declared an animal when he refuses—as he was taught in school—to debate the principles themselves. A second trial, occasioned by his claim that "the moon"—that is, our earth—"is a world," leads to acknowledgment of his human status, but he is forced to recant the "heresy" of the claim itself. For the remainder of his stay, he is the guest of a moon family in which—according to custom—the son has authority over the father. In a series of conversations, the young man explains his radical materialist views of the universe; he is defending his atheism when a devil appears to snatch him away. The narrator, who tries to help his host, is thus transported back to earth (presumably because Hell is at its center). Thus ends the first volume.

The second volume opens with a clear reference to the first. Urged by a friend who shares his philosophical and scientific interests, the narrator—hereafter known as Drycona—writes an account of his moon voyage. He becomes a local celebrity but is accused of witchcraft by a malevolent country priest, who exploits the people's ignorance and persuades them to arrest the "sorcerer." Drycona escapes from prison by building a new flying machine—this one using the principle of the vacuum—in which he takes off for the sun. Once again, the machine can get him only part of the way there; it is the force of his desire, drawing him to the sun as source of life, that enables him to complete the voyage (which takes twenty-two months). The sun is divided into many regions of differing "opacity" (suggested by the then-recent discovery of sunspots); there is a rough correspondence between the intensity of light and the "enlightenment" of the inhabitants.

One race—that of "spirits," such as the Genius of Socrates—can alter their outward forms as their imagination dictates.

The race of birds, who prevent abuses of power by choosing as king one of their weakest members (a dove), capture Drycona and put him on trial, as had the moon people; this time, however, the charge is simply "being a man"—belonging to a pernicious and destructive species. On the advice of a friendly bird, Drycona claims to be a monkey raised by humans, but he is convicted; he is on the point of being devoured by insects (included among the birds) when a parrot whom he had once freed on earth testifies on his behalf and obtains a pardon for him. After an encounter with a forest of talking trees, who try to convince him of their moral superiority, Drycona witnesses a battle between a Fire-Beast and an Ice-Animal (the latter is defending the trees). The battle is also observed by the philosopher Tommaso Campanella (author of *La città del sole*, 1602; *The City of the Sun*, 1880), who becomes Drycona's guide. Together, they visit the Lake of Sleep and the Streams of the Five Senses, which empty into the Rivers of Memory, Imagination, and Judgment. A couple from the Province of Lovers, on their way to the Province of Philosophers (where the soul of Socrates is to settle a dispute between them), give the two travelers a lift in a basket suspended from a giant bird. Campanella is returning to his province to greet the soul of Descartes, newly arrived (he died in 1650). The narrative of the second volume ends, unfortunately, at the moment that Drycona and Campanella meet Descartes; Cyrano's ill health during the last year of his life prevented him from finishing the manuscript.

DIMENSIONS OF THE NOVEL

A brief résumé can give only the faintest idea of the inventiveness and satiric verve of *Other Worlds*. Cyrano takes every opportunity to make minor but telling—and often cutting—observations on various aspects of the human condition. The chief defect of his masterpiece, lack of unity, is merely the excess of a virtue: the acknowledgment that there are more things in heaven and on earth than are dreamed of in any one human philosophy. Quick of wit and eye, Cyrano was ever ready to bolt off in new directions. This quality gives his narrative a certain inclusiveness and makes it consistently entertaining, despite long stretches of philosophical argument. It also, however, gives the work a chaotic quality, which seems to reflect both the temperament of the author and the intellectual ferment of his day. (This feature of *Other Worlds* has been aptly contrasted with the unity, in tone and perspective, of Swift's *Gulliver's Travels*.) Perhaps the only way to do justice to the many dimensions of *Other Worlds* is to isolate some of the most important ones and assess them individually. They are, in ascending order of importance, *préciosité*, utopianism, didacticism or popularization, and satire.

Cyrano's use of *préciosité* reveals a deep-seated ambivalence symptomatic of his relationship to his own age. The *préciosité*, or cultivation of extravagantly refined language, that flourished in seventeenth century France grew out of the court mentality fostered by centralization of the monarchy; the salons, where *préciosité* emerged, were miniature "courts" on the model of the royal one and could be stepping-stones to power for those who learned the "art of pleasing." The earliest of Cyrano's letters seem to have been undertaken as exercises in this courtly form of entertainment. That he longed for fame, and for public acceptance of his work, is clear, but it is equally clear that his wit was too sharp for his own good and that, instead of ingratiating, it often alienated his audience. This tendency was not altogether involuntary.

Cyrano was rebellious by nature and could not resist the shock value of a daring bon mot; he was also too intelligent not to see how easily *préciosité* could be turned to ridicule. Yet he had a truly lyric imagination, which lent itself to *précieux* elaboration, as in some descriptive passages of *Other Worlds*. The landscape of the Five Senses recalls Mademoiselle de Scudéry, the *précieuse par excellence*, and it is hard to deny the passage its charm, despite a hint of affectation. At his best, Cyrano manages to walk the fine line between *préciosité* and burlesque. He can indulge in witty definitions of the moon, ascribing them to Drycona's friends, and then allow his hero to deflate them by remarking that they serve only to "tickle the time, to make it go faster." Like Aristophanes, who made his characters trot out old jokes while affecting disdain for them, Cyrano usually manages to have it both ways.

In addition to its occasional *préciosité*, *Other Worlds* also contains a utopian vein, though it scarcely belongs to the utopian genre. This vein is chiefly visible in Cyrano's treatment of machines and practical inventions. The most prominent are, of course, the flying machines, which, though fanciful (and less than fully effective), are all posited on genuine physical principles—the vacuum, magnetism, evaporation. It was doubtless the sheer fluidity and daring of his imagination that enabled Cyrano to anticipate other inventions of whose physical bases he was wholly ignorant; most striking of these inventions is the "talking book," or phonograph. There are also some radical social and political innovations in Cyrano's vision of the "other worlds" his protagonist visits: Battles on the moon can be fought only between armies of perfectly equal numbers, while the most important "battles" are debates between the scholars and wits of the two sides; in the realm of birds, the king is seen as the servant, not the master, of his people. Some of these innovations are transparent wish fulfillments to one familiar with Cyrano's life; the most pointed is the role inversion of fathers and sons, but there are humorous ones as well, such as the use of poetry for money (with value based on quality, not quantity) and the recognition, among the moon people, that a large nose is the infallible sign of a noble and witty nature.

Despite such pleasant surprises, however, Drycona encounters no ideal society: The moon people have their bigoted priests and heresy trials; the sun people, their disputes and unequal "enlightenment." The realm of the birds, which comes closest to a model state, also has the Draconian stamp that makes many utopias (Plato's Republic, Swift's land of the Houyhnhnms) so unpalatable, and Cyrano acknowledges that—as did Swift, perhaps in emulation of Cyrano—human beings may not live there. Despite a certain escapist impulse, then, the book is never more than guardedly optimistic about the realization of ideals. It may be significant that the closest thing to an ideal state of affairs in *Other Worlds* is set in our world: This is Drycona's brief but happy stay with his friends Colignac and Cussan. In a passage reminiscent of Rabelais's Abbey of Thélème (*Gargantua*, 1534; chapter 53), he describes the material comfort and intellectual stimulation of their life together:

> The innocent pleasures of which the body is capable were only the lesser share. Of all those the mind can derive from study and conversation, we lacked none; and our libraries, united like our minds, summoned all the learned into our company.

The idyll is soon threatened, and then shattered, by the malice of a priest and the ignorance of the peasants, but it offers a glimpse of the conditions Cyrano considered most likely to foster human happiness.

The prominence of learning in this vision raises the questions of whether Cyrano had a didactic or pedagogical aim in writing *Other Worlds*. It has been claimed that he was essentially a popularizer, concerned to present the new scientific theories of his contemporaries in a form accessible to the commoner. As with the utopian view, there is clearly some warrant for this interpretation; again, however, it seems less than adequate to account for the work as a whole. Drycona's abortive first flight, which lands him in Canada, is surely designed as a concrete illustration of the Copernican theory; it is appropriately followed by a discussion of the theory, and of various objections to it, in the conversation between Drycona and the viceroy. The sheer amount of space devoted to similar conversations throughout the book is an indication of their importance to Cyrano. At times, as in Drycona's long exchange with the young atheist on the moon, the plot is allowed to atrophy entirely: The focus of interest is on the ideas discussed and on the arguments for or against them. Yet Prévot has done well to point out that in each such discussion personalities are involved; there is no omniscient narrator and no completely reliable speaker.

Moreover, the universe of the book is hardly constrained by any one of the theories it sets forth, and it sometimes operates according to superstitious or supernatural beliefs: A devil can carry a man off for impiety, and the waning moon can "suck" the beef marrow Drycona uses as a salve. It seems particularly striking that on *both* of Drycona's outward voyages, the "scientific" method gets him only halfway there at most; the beef marrow gets him to the moon, while the "strength of his desire" for the source of all life draws him to the sun. The fictional data thus undercut not only specific scientific accounts but also any thoroughgoing rationalistic perspective.

This is not to suggest that the author has no clear-cut attitudes to convey: He does indeed, but his medium is satire rather than exposition. Drycona's motive in leaving the earth may be to explore the heavens, but Cyrano's purpose is to find a radically different perspective from which to observe the human world. The heliocentric theory espoused by the Church is symptomatic of human vanity, which insists that the universe was made for humans and continues, literally and figuratively, to revolve around them. Cyrano's protagonist finds himself in a position from which he is forced to reexamine virtually all of his assumptions—scientific, philosophical, religious, and social. Indeed, he is twice put on trial, not as an individual but as a representative of the human species. Yet each of the extraterrestrial societies he visits displays some of the defects of human societies, so that the lesson is one of cultural relativism, and the necessity for tolerance is made obvious, as in Voltaire's *contes philosophiques*, by the mistreatment of the sympathetic protagonist. The satire of religious abuses is particularly prominent, as befitted an age in which the Church was the chief opponent of free speech and investigation. Yet, as Prévot has shown, Cyrano's quarrel is not with God so much as with his vicars, who abuse their moral authority to indulge their own base motives.

The satiric effectiveness of *Other Worlds* is fueled by a keen sense of the comic. Cyrano's attitude toward his fellow humans was a complex one, compounded of anger, amusement, occasional admiration, and occasional hatred. It is the amusement, however, that tends to predominate. In this respect, Cyrano resembles his compatriots Rabelais and Voltaire (the first of whom he read, and the second of whom read him) more than he resembles his great English emulator, Swift. Between philosophical debates, he finds time to tell how the moon people make sundials of their teeth by pointing their noses toward the sun, how a "hypervegetarian" abstains even from vegetables that have not died a natural death, how a man from the Province of Lovers is forbidden to use hyperbole on pain of death after nearly persuading a young woman to use her own heart as a boat—because it is so "light" (fickle) and can hold so many. As well as an eloquent plea for tolerance and freedom of thought, *Other Worlds* is a consistently entertaining book, whose author clearly deserves to be remembered as an original writer of fiction, not merely as a character in a play by Rostand.

Lillian Doherty

Other major works

PLAYS: *La Mort d'Agrippine*, pr. 1653; *Le Pédant joué*, pb. 1954.

NONFICTION: *Contre les Frondeurs*, 1651; *Lettres*, 1654 (*Satyrical Characters and Handsome Descriptions in Letters*, 1658).

MISCELLANEOUS: *Cyrano de Bergerac: Œuvres complètes*, 1977 (Jacques Prévot, editor).

Bibliography

Addyman, Ishbel. *Cyrano: Adventures in Space and Time with the Legendary French Hero.* New York: Simon & Schuster, 2008. Presents a precise, balanced, and well-documented study of Cyrano. Includes notes, select bibliography, and index.

Aldington, Richard. *An Introduction to "Voyages to the Moon and the Sun."* New York: Orion, 1962. Aldington, one of England's best critics and a translator of Cyrano's fiction, discusses the legend and life of Cyrano as well as his friends and works.

Alter, Jean. "Figures of Social and Semiotic Dissent." In *A New History of French Literature*, edited by Denis Hollier et al. Cambridge, Mass.: Harvard University Press, 1994. Alter's essay includes information about Cyrano and his contemporaries. It is one of many brief, chronologically arranged essays that in their totality provide a comprehensive survey of French literature.

Campbell, Mary Baine. "A World in the Moon: Celestial Fictions of Francis Godwin and Cyrano de Bergerac." In *Wonder and Science: Imagining Worlds in Early Modern Europe*. Ithaca, N.Y.: Cornell University Press, 1999. Campbell analyzes a number of early modern texts, including fiction by Cyrano and other French and English writers, to demonstrate how people responded with awe to the new geographic and scientific discoveries of the seventeenth century.

Harth, Erica. *Cyrano de Bergerac and the Polemics of Modernity*. New York: Columbia University Press, 1970. Contains a thoughtful analysis of Cyrano's criticism of core Christian beliefs and his development of a mechanistic view of the universe in which God is not necessary, according to Cyrano.

Muratore, Mary Jo. *Mimesis and Metatextuality in the French Neo-Classical Text, Reflexive Readings of La Fontaine, Molière, Racine, Guilleragues, Madame de La Fayette, Scarron, Cyrano de Bergerac, and Perrault*. Geneva: Droz, 1994. Analyzes Cyrano as a science-fiction writer. Muratore makes good use of late twentieth century criticism. In spite of some jargon, this book can be helpful even for beginning students.

Popkin, Richard H. *The History of Scepticism from Erasmus to Descartes*. New York: Humanities Press, 1964. Provides a good description of Cyrano's originality in relation to other European freethinkers of the sixteenth and seventeenth centuries. The one weakness of Popkin's book is that he links atheists, such as Cyrano, to liberal-minded Christians, such as Desiderius Erasmus and René Descartes.

Sankey, Margaret. "From Seventeenth-Century Clandestine Manuscript to Contemporary Edition: *L'Autre Monde* of Cyrano de Bergerac." In *The Editorial Gaze: Mediating Texts in Literature and the Arts*, edited by Paul Eggert and Margaret Sankey. New York: Garland, 1998. Examines Cyrano's novel from a postmodern perspective, analyzing how his work was altered by editing and how editing changed the relationship between the book and its readers.

Van Baelen, Jacqueline. "Reality and Illusion in *L'Autre Monde:* The Narrative Voyage of Cyrano de Bergerac." *Yale French Studies* 49 (1973): 178-184. An excellent literary study, concentrating on the structure of the novel.

ALEXANDRE DUMAS, PÈRE

Born: Villers-Cotterêts, France; July 24, 1802
Died: Puys, France; December 5, 1870
Also known as: Dumas Davy de la Pailleterie

PRINCIPAL LONG FICTION

Acté, 1838 (English translation, 1904)
Le Capitaine Paul, 1838 (*Captain Paul*, 1848)
La Salle d'armes, 1838 (includes *Pauline* [English translation, 1844], *Pascal Bruno* [English translation, 1837], and *Murat* [English translation, 1896])
La Comtesse de Salisbury, 1839
Le Capitaine Pamphile, 1840 (*Captain Pamphile*, 1850)
Othon l'archer, 1840 (*Otho the Archer*, 1860)
Aventures de Lyderic, 1842 (*Lyderic, Count of Flanders*, 1903)
Ascanio, 1843 (with Paul Meurice; English translation, 1849)
Le Chevalier d'Harmental, 1843 (with Auguste Maquet; *The Chevalier d'Harmental*, 1856)
Georges, 1843 (*George*, 1846)
Amaury, 1844 (English translation, 1854)
Une Fille du régent, 1844 (with Maquet; *The Regent's Daughter*, 1845)
Les Frères corses, 1844 (*The Corsican Brothers*, 1880)
Gabriel Lambert, 1844 (*The Galley Slave*, 1849; also known as *Gabriel Lambert*, 1904)
Sylvandire, 1844 (*The Disputed Inheritance*, 1847; also known as *Sylvandire*, 1897)
Les Trois Mousquetaires, 1844 (*The Three Musketeers*, 1846)
Le Comte de Monte-Cristo, 1844-1845 (*The Count of Monte-Cristo*, 1846)
La Reine Margot, 1845 (with Maquet; *Marguerite de Navarre*, 1845; better known as *Marguerite de Valois*, 1846)
Vingt Ans après, 1845 (with Maquet; *Twenty Years After*, 1846)
La Guerre des femmes, 1845-1846 (*Nanon*, 1847; also known as *The War of Women*, 1895)
Le Bâtard de Mauléon, 1846 (*The Bastard of Mauléon*, 1848)
Le Chevalier de Maison-Rouge, 1846 (with Maquet; *Marie Antoinette: Or, The Chevalier of the Red House*, 1846; also known as *The Chevalier de Maison-Rouge*, 1893)
La Dame de Monsoreau, 1846 (*Chicot the Jester*, 1857)
Les Deux Diane, 1846 (with Meurice; *The Two Dianas*, 1857)
Mémoires d'un médecin, 1846-1848 (with Maquet; also known as *Joseph Balsamo*; *Memoirs of a Physician*, 1846)

Les Quarante-cinq, 1848 (with Maquet; *The Forty-five Guardsmen,* 1847)
Le Vicomte de Bragelonne, 1848-1850 (with Maquet; *The Vicomte de Bragelonne,* 1857; also published as 3 volumes, *The Vicomte de Bragelonne,* 1893; *Louise de la Vallière,* 1893; and *The Man in the Iron Mask,* 1893)
La Véloce, 1848-1851
Le Collier de la reine, 1849-1850 (with Maquet; *The Queen's Necklace,* 1855)
La Tulipe noire, 1850 (with Maquet and Paul Lacroix; *The Black Tulip,* 1851)
Ange Pitou, 1851 (*Six Years Later,* 1851; also known as *Ange Pitou,* 1859)
Conscience l'innocent, 1852 (*Conscience,* 1905)
Olympe de Clèves, 1852 (English translation, 1894)
Isaac Laquedem, 1852-1853
La Comtesse de Charny, 1853-1855 (*The Countess de Charny,* 1858)
Catherine Blum, 1854 (*The Foresters,* 1854; also known as *Catherine Blum,* 1861)
Ingénue, 1854 (English translation, 1855)
Le Page du duc de Savoie, 1854 (*Emmanuel Philibert,* 1854; also known as *The Page of the Duke of Savoy,* 1861)
El Saltéador, 1854 (*The Brigand,* 1897)
Les Mohicans de Paris, 1854-1855
Salvator, 1855-1859 (with *Les Mohicans de Paris,* abridged as *The Mohicans of Paris,* 1875)
Charles le Téméraire, 1857 (*Charles the Bold,* 1860)
Les Compagnons de Jéhu, 1857 (*Roland de Montrevel,* 1860; also known as *The Companions of Jéhu,* 1895)
Les Meneurs de loups, 1857 (*The Wolf Leader,* 1904)
Ainsi-soit-il!, 1858 (also known as *Madame de Chamblay,* 1862; *Madame de Chamblay,* 1869)
Le Capitaine Richard, 1858 (*The Twin Captains,* 1861)
L'Horoscope, 1858 (*The Horoscope,* 1897)
Le Chasseur de sauvagine, 1859 (*The Wild Duck Shooter,* 1906)
Histoire d'un cabanon et d'un châlet, 1859 (*The Convict's Son,* 1905)
Les Louves de Machecoul, 1859 (*The Last Vendée,* 1894; also known as *The She Wolves of Machecoul,* 1895)
Le Médecin de Java, 1859 (also known as *L'Île de feu,* 1870; *Doctor Basilius,* 1860)
La Maison de Glace, 1860 (*The Russian Gipsy,* 1860)
Le Père la Ruine, 1860 (*Père la Ruine,* 1905)
La San-Felice, 1864-1865 (*The Lovely Lady Hamilton,* 1903)
Le Comte de Moret, 1866 (*The Count of Moret,* 1868)
La Terreur prussienne, 1867 (*The Prussian Terror,* 1915)

Les Blancs et les bleus, 1867-1868 (*The Whites and the Blues*, 1895)
Le Chevalier de Sainte-Hermine, 1869 (serial), 2005 (book; *The Last Cavalier: Being the Adventures of Count Sainte Hermine in the Age of Napoleon*, 2007)
The Romances of Alexandre Dumas, 1893-1897 (60 volumes)
The Novels of Alexandre Dumas, 1903-1911 (56 volumes)

OTHER LITERARY FORMS

Other novels are attributed to Alexandre Dumas, *père* (dyew-MAH pehr), that some scholarship, such as that by Douglas Munro, Gilbert Sigaux, and Charles Samaran, credits more to his collaborators. Of the many editions of Dumas's works, the standard edition, *Œuvres complètes* (1846-1877), in 301 volumes by Calmann-Lévy, is not always authoritative. The best editions of the novels are those in *Œuvres d'Alexandre Dumas* (1962-1967; 38 volumes), published by Éditions Rencontre, with excellent introductions to the novels by Sigaux. Munro lists at least fifteen English editions of Dumas prior to 1910, and countless others have appeared since. *The Romances of Alexandre Dumas*, published by Little, Brown and Company, has been updated several times. Virtually all of Dumas's novels are available in English and many other languages.

Dumas also wrote many plays, several in collaboration with other authors and a number based on his novels. A total of sixty-six are generally ascribed to him, among them *Henri III et sa cour* (pr., pb. 1829; *Catherine of Cleves*, 1831, also known as *Henry III and His Court*, 1904), *Christine: Ou, Stockholm, Fontainebleau, et Rome* (pr., pb. 1830), *Kean: Ou, Désordre et génie* (pr., pb. 1836, with Théaulon de Lambert and Frédéric de Courcy; *Edmund Kean: Or, The Genius and the Libertine*, 1847), *Mademoiselle de Belle-Isle* (pr., pb. 1839; English translation, 1855), *Un Mariage sous Louis XV* (pr., pb. 1841; *A Marriage of Convenience*, 1899), *Les Demoiselles de Saint-Cyr* (pr., pb. 1843; *The Ladies of Saint-Cyr*, 1870), and *L'Invitation à la valse* (pr., pb. 1857; adapted in English as *Childhood Dreams*, 1881). The plays are available in the *Œuvres complètes*, occupying twenty-five volumes in the Calmann-Lévy edition. The best contemporary edition is *Théâtre complet*, edited by Fernande Bassan.

Dumas's other writings include histories, chronicles, memoirs, travel notes, articles, and essays. Among the more interesting of these are "Comment je devins auteur dramatique" ("How I Became a Playwright"), "En Suisse" (in Switzerland), *Quinze Jours au Sinai* (1838; *Impressions of Travel in Egypt and Arabia Petraea*, 1839), *Excursions sur les bords du Rhin* (1841, with Gérard de Nerval; excursions on the banks of the Rhine), *Le Midi de la France* (1841; *Pictures of Travel in the South of France*, 1852), *Le Spéronare* (1842; travels in Italy), *Le Corricolo* (1843; travels in Italy and Sicily), *Mes Mémoires* (1852, 1853, 1854-1855; *My Memoirs*, 1907-1909), *Causeries* (1860), *Les Garibaldiens* (1861; *The Garibaldians in Sicily*, 1861), *Histoires de mes bêtes* (1868; *My Pets*, 1909), and *Souvenirs dramatiques* (1868; souvenirs of the theater).

Alexandre Dumas, père
(Library of Congress)

Achievements

The Larousse *Grand Dictionnaire du XIX siècle* of 1870 described Alexandre Dumas, *père*, as "a novelist and the most prolific and popular playwright in France." Today his novels are regarded as his most durable achievement; they are known to every French person and to millions of other people through countless translations. Indeed, for innumerable readers, French history takes the form of Dumas's novels, and seventeenth century France is simply the France of the Three Musketeers. Dumas was an indefatigable writer, and his production is impressive by its volume alone: more than one hundred novels, including children's stories and tales. Although Dumas worked with many collaborators—the most famous being Auguste Maquet, Paul Meurice, Hippolyte Augier, Gérard de Nerval, and Auguste Vacquerie—a Dumas novel is readily distinguishable by its structure and style, sparkle, wit, rapid action, and dramatic dialogue.

Dumas's narratives teem with action and suspense; like the works of Eugène Sue, Frédéric Soulié, Honoré de Balzac, and Fyodor Dostoevski, most of Dumas's novels were first published in serial form, appearing in *La Presse*, *Journal des débats*, *Le Siècle*, and *Le*

Constitutionnel, and later in his own journals, such as *Le Mousquetaire* and *Le Monte-Cristo*. He thus attracted a continuation. Sometimes he himself was uncertain what direction the plot of a given novel would take, and certain inconsistencies and discrepancies occasionally resulted from the serial format, but these are generally insignificant and surprisingly few in number. Often melodramatic, Dumas's novels nevertheless combine realism with the fantastic. Historical personages in his fiction maintain their roles in history yet sparkle with life: the haughty Anne of Austria, the inflexible Cardinal Richelieu, the independent Louis XIV. Like a careful puppeteer, Dumas never allows the intricate plot to escape him, nor does he resolve it until the end.

A gifted dramatist, Dumas was above all a master of dialogue. The critic Isabelle Jan has analyzed Dumas's dialogue as the very life's breath of his characters, noting that Dumas succeeded in making even the dumb speak—the mute Noirtier in *The Count of Monte-Cristo*. Dumas's characters communicate by gestures and body language as well as by speech; indeed, in Dumas's fictions even stovepipes and scaffold boards are eloquent. The action in a Dumas novel is carried forward through dialogue; a Dumas plot is not described, it is enacted.

Though Dumas did not possess Balzac's profound analytic intelligence, he shared Balzac's powers of observation. Lacking Victor Hugo's awareness of the abyss and his visionary gift, Dumas nevertheless had Hugo's sparkle and wit. Indeed, both Balzac and Hugo admired Dumas greatly, as did Nerval, one of his collaborators, with whom he shared a taste for the occult and the supernatural. Unlike Stendhal, whose unhappy Julien Sorel was created "for the happy few," yet, like him, a true Romantic in spirit, Dumas wrote for all, proving that the novel could be both popular and memorable.

Biography

On July 24, 1802, Alexandre Dumas was born in Villers-Cotterêts, a suburb of Paris with souvenirs of eighteenth century royalty that was to figure in many of his novels. From his father, Thomas-Alexandre Dumas Davy de la Pailleterie, a general in Napoleon I's service who dared to defy the emperor and hence lost possibilities of future honors, he received an adventurous spirit and a mulatto ancestry. His father died in 1806, and young Alexandre was brought up by his mother with little formal education and a love for the country and its woods. In 1818, Adolphe de Leuven and Amédée de la Ponce began to initiate him into German and Italian studies, and later into the works of William Shakespeare and a love for the theater.

In 1823, Dumas left Villers-Cotterêts and, with little more than a few coins and a letter of introduction (the minimum that d'Artagnan also carried), found a job as a copyist for the future Louis-Philippe through the intermediary of his father's former colleague General Foy. Dumas's passion for women developed alongside his love for the theater, and in 1824 he had a child, Alexandre Dumas, *fils*, by Catherine Labay. Dumas's first successful play, *Henri III and His Court*, was staged at the Comédie-Française in 1828. Thereafter his plays succeeded one another as rapidly as his liaisons, many with actresses, notably Mélanie Waldor; Mélanie Serre (Belle Krelsamer), the mother of Marie-Alexandrine Dumas; and Ida Ferrier, later his wife. He rapidly became acquainted with the most notable authors and artists, including Balzac, Hugo, Alfred de Vigny, and Eugène Delacroix. In 1831, Dumas officially recognized Alexandre as his son, separating son from mother and beginning a turbulent existence with his son that was to last his entire life.

After Dumas had received the Croix de la Légion d'Honneur and was reconciled with Hugo in 1836 (earlier, Dumas had thought that Hugo, whom he regarded as a close friend, had taken portions of *Christine* to use for his own work *Marie Tudor*, 1833), the two of them operated the famous Théâtre de la Renaissance. At this time, historical novels in the manner of Sir Walter Scott became popular in France, and Dumas tried his hand at them. With many collaborators, the most important being Auguste Maquet, Dumas produced a tremendous output of fiction, particularly between 1844 and 1855—so great that Eugène de Mirecourt, in his 1845 "Fabrique de romans: Maison Alexandre Dumas et Cie.," accused Dumas of running a "novel factory." As the result of a lawsuit, Mirecourt was convicted of slander, and Dumas continued to write prodigiously, acquiring an immense fortune and spending his money with equal prodigality. In 1847, he received six hundred guests at the housewarming of his Château de Monte-Cristo, a lavish estate that he was to occupy for little more than a year.

The Revolution of 1848 curtailed Dumas's career as it did Hugo's. The Théâtre Historique, which Dumas had founded principally as a showcase for his own works, closed, and Dumas, like Hugo, went to Belgium in 1851, though Dumas's reasons were less political than financial, for he was pursued by his creditors. After reaching an arrangement with them in 1853, he returned to Paris, where he undertook publication of successive journals, such as *Le Mousquetaire* (1853-1857) and *Le Monte-Cristo* (1857-1860). He traveled extensively, always writing travel impressions of each place he visited. In 1860, his liaison with Émilie Cordier led him to Italy and brought him another daughter, Micaëlla; he later visited Germany, Austria, and Russia. Among his many interests was cooking, and in 1869 he undertook a *Grand Dictionnaire de cuisine*, which was completed by Anatole France and published in 1873. In 1870, at the declaration of war, Dumas returned to Paris from the South. After a stroke, he returned to his son's home at Puys, where he died on December 5, 1870. In 1872, his remains were transferred to Villers-Cotterêts, and his fame continued to spread far and wide.

ANALYSIS

Alexandre Dumas, *père*, arrived at the novel indirectly, through the theater and an apprenticeship with history and chronicles. By the time he turned to the novel in the style of Sir Walter Scott, then intensely popular in France, he had already dealt with historical subjects in his plays and had explored the Hundred Years' War, the French Revolution, and the Napoleonic era in his chronicles. Indeed, one can follow French history from the Middle Ages, though rather incompletely, up to the nineteenth century through Dumas's novels. His most successful cycles are set in the sixteenth century (especially the reign of the Valois), the seventeenth (especially the periods of Richelieu and Cardinal Mazarin), and the French Revolution, and the novels set in these periods are his best-known works—with the exception of *The Count of Monte-Cristo*, which is not really a historical novel but is rather a social novel or a *roman de moeurs*. His best historical fiction was written in the years from 1843 to 1855. Dumas's novels after 1855 are chiefly concerned with the French Revolution, the Directory, and the nineteenth century, and are less well known than his earlier works.

Among Dumas's medieval novels are *Otho the Archer*, which evokes a German medieval legend; *Lyderic, Count of Flanders*, set in seventh century Flanders; and *The Bastard of Mauléon*, which covers the period from 1358 to 1369, the earlier part of the Hundred Years' War. Dumas treats the period from 1500 to 1570 in greater detail, in scattered novels from 1843 to 1858. *The Brigand* treats the period from 1497 to 1519 and focuses on the youth of Charles V. *The Two Dianas* and *Ascanio*, written with the collaboration of Meurice, treat the reign of François I and the presence of sculptor Benvenuto Cellini at the French court. The two Dianas are Diane de Castro and Diane de Poitiers. *The Page of the Duke of Savoy*, set in the years 1555 to 1559, with an epilogue that takes place in 1580, is a companion to *The Two Dianas*. The final novel of the series, *The Horoscope*, treats the beginning of the reign of François II.

The Valois cycle, which covers the period from August, 1572, to June, 1586, comprises three of the most successful and popular of Dumas's historical romances. *Marguerite de Navarre* treats the period from 1572 to 1575, beginning with the wedding of Marguerite de Valois and Henri de Navarre and focusing on their various romantic intrigues; the novel concludes with the famous Saint Bartholemew's Day Massacre. The second book in the cycle, *Chicot the Jester*, is the most popular and introduces one of Dumas's finest creations: Chicot, a rival of d'Artagnan and similar to him in many ways. The novel covers the period from 1578 to 1579 under Henri III and focuses on the death of Bussy d'Amboise. The last book in the cycle, *The Forty-five Guardsmen*, covers the years from 1582 to 1584; it tells of the Ligue, the duc de Guise, and the vengeance of the duc d'Anjou for Bussy's murder.

Unquestionably Dumas's best-written and most popular cycle, however, is that of d'Artagnan, which covers the period from 1625 to 1673. It includes *The Three Musketeers*, the immortal story of Athos, Porthos, and Aramis, who, together with d'Artagnan, interact in the stories of Richelieu, Louis XIII, Anne of Austria, and the Duke of Buckingham from 1625 to 1628. *Twenty Years After*, as the title indicates, takes place in 1648 and finds the same characters involved with Anne of Austria and Mazarin, the Fronde, and the Civil War in England. *The Vicomte de Bragelonne*, a lengthy account largely set in the period from 1660 to 1673, focuses less on the musketeers than on Louis XIV, Fouquet, and the Man in the Iron Mask. The intervening years (1628 to 1648) are covered in three less important novels, the best being *The War of Women*, which deals with the new Fronde of 1648 to 1650.

The century from 1670 to 1770 is the subject of four novels, of which the best known are the companion works *The Chevalier d'Harmental* and *The Regent's Daughter*, both of which deal with the Cellamare conspiracy of 1718. The Marie Antoinette cycle, often referred to collectively by the title of the first volume, *Memoirs of a Physician*, takes place between 1770 and 1791 and is also a very popular series. The first book in the cycle, written in collaboration with Maquet, covers the period between 1770 and 1774, including the death of Louis XV and the marriage of Marie Antoinette to Louis XVI. *The Queen's Necklace* focuses on the scandal of the Queen's diamond necklace and her love affair with Charny from 1784 to 1786. *Taking the Bastille* covers only four months in 1789, the period of the taking of the Bastille. Finally, *The Countess de Charny* begins in 1789, covers the King's flight to Varennes in 1791 and the destinies of Andrée and Charny, and concludes with the King's execution in 1793. Although the series lacks a strong central character, with the possible exception of Joseph Balsamo, it is important for its emphasis on women.

Five other novels cover the intervening period until 1800, of which *The Whites and the Blues*, showing the influence of the novelist Charles Nodier, is the best known. Six novels treat the Napoleonic period, the Restoration, and the reign of Louis-Philippe. Of these, *The Mohicans of Paris*, dealing with the revolution under the Restoration in the 1820's, and *Salvator*, its companion, together form Dumas's longest novel; although not his most popular, it is a highly representative work.

In Dumas's many social novels, there are frequent historical excursions; among his finest and most popular works in this genre is *The Count of Monte-Cristo*, which begins with Napoleon's exile at Elba, the Hundred Days, and the second Restoration. In the manner of Balzac, this great novel depicts the greed and selfishness of the Parisian aristocracy and the consuming passion of ambition. Dumas treated racial prejudice in *George*, set in Mauritius, and depicted his own native town in three novels known as the Villers-Cotterêts cycle: *Conscience*, *Catherine Blum*, and *The Wolf Leader*.

In virtually all of his novels, Dumas excels in plot and dialogue. His most successful works blend history or social observation with fantasy, and his plots nearly always involve mystery and intrigue. Usually they concern romantic involvements, yet there are relatively few scenes of romance.

Although Dumas's novels are rich with memorable characters, he does not focus on psychological development. A given character remains essentially the same from the beginning to the end of a work. Despite the disguises and the mysteries that often surround a character's name—even the three musketeers have strange aliases—there is never an aspect of personality that remains to be discovered. Dumas's characters are not inspired by moral idealism; they are usually motivated by ambition, revenge, or simply a love for adventure. Dumas does not instruct, but he also does not distort the great movements of history or of social interaction. He aims principally to entertain, to help his readers forget the world in which they live and to move with his characters into a fantastic world that is sometimes truer to life than reality.

The famous d'Artagnan trilogy, which is made up of *The Three Musketeers*, *Twenty Years After*, and *The Vicomte de Bragelonne*, has three differing basic texts: the first, the original published in *Le Siècle*; the second in pirated Belgian texts; the third published by Baudry; many other versions exist as well. The series covers the period from 1625 to 1673, focusing on the events during the period of Richelieu, Mazarin, and Louis XIV. The main characters, and even some secondary ones, have their sources in history, although their interaction with the major historical figures is often imaginary. Dumas's primary source is the *Mémoires de M. d'Artagnan* (1700), a fabricated account of d'Artagnan's life by Gatien de Courtilz de Sandras. The trilogy provides an excellent introduction to Dumas's use of historical sources, his storytelling technique, his dramatic power, and his creation of character.

THE THREE MUSKETEERS

The Three Musketeers begins in April, 1625, at Meung-sur-Loire, where the Quixote-like d'Artagnan, a young Gascon of eighteen years, is making his way to Paris with a letter of introduction to Monsieur de Tréville, the captain of the King's musketeers. It is here that he meets the Count of Rochefort, Richelieu's right-hand man, and "Milady," a beautiful and mysterious woman whose path will cross his throughout the novel and whose shadow will haunt him for the next twenty years. In Paris, d'Artagnan becomes fast friends with Athos, Porthos, and Aramis, the three musketeers who share his adventures throughout the novel. D'Artagnan falls in love with Constance Bonacieux, his landlord's wife, also a lady-in-waiting to the Queen, Anne of Austria. He thus becomes involved in recovering the Queen's diamond studs, a present from the King that she has unwisely given to her lover, the handsome Duke of Buckingham, Richelieu's rival in both political and amorous intrigue. D'Artagnan falls in love with the bewitching Milady and discovers her criminal past, for which knowledge she begins an inexorable pursuit of him.

Meanwhile, the siege of La Rochelle permits the four friends to display their bravery and to develop a plot against Milady, who in a very complex intrigue becomes an agent in Buckingham's assassination. Milady's revenge leads her to poison Constance, and for this final crime she is tried and condemned by the four musketeers and her brother-in-law, Lord de Winter. Since the siege of La Rochelle ends to Richelieu's advantage through the invaluable assistance of the musketeers, d'Artagnan becomes a friend of Richelieu and a lieutenant of the musketeers. Porthos marries his mistress, the widowed Madame Coquenard; Aramis becomes a priest; and Athos, or the Comte de la Fère, after a few more years of military service, retires to his estate in Roussillon.

TWENTY YEARS AFTER

Twenty Years After, as the title indicates, begins in 1648, twenty years after the conclusion of *The Three Musketeers*; Mazarin is at the helm of the government, and Paris is on the verge of the Fronde, a rebellion of the nobles against the regent. The lives of the four musketeers have been singularly without adventure during the preceding twenty years; d'Artagnan, still a lieutenant in the musketeers, lives with "the fair Madeleine" in Paris; Athos, Comte de la Fère, spends his time bringing up his son, Raoul de Bragelonne; Porthos, now Comte du Vallon and master of three estates, is dissatisfied with his lot and aspires to become a baron; Aramis, formerly a musketeer who aspired to be an abbé, is now the Abbé d'Herblay and longs to be a musketeer again.

The four men, now a bit distrustful of one another, are unable to join forces since Athos and Aramis are *frondeurs* and d'Artagnan and Porthos are cardinalists. They meet on opposite sides in their first encounter with the Duke of Beaufort, who escapes from d'Artagnan. Subsequently in England, during Cromwell's overthrow of Charles I, they find themselves opponents but join in an unsuccessful attempt to save the King. Their efforts in this and other intrigues are thwarted by Mordaunt, Milady's son, who seeks to avenge his mother and finally meets with a violent death at sea. Their united support of Charles I wins the four imprisonment from Mazarin, whom they in turn abduct and coerce into signing certain concessions to the *frondeurs*. At the end, d'Artagnan becomes captain of the musketeers and Porthos, a baron.

THE VICOMTE DE BRAGELONNE

The third novel in the series, *The Vicomte de Bragelonne*, which is twice as long as the two previous novels together, covers the period from 1660 to 1673, from Louis XIV's visit to Blois in 1659 and his marriage to Marie-Thérèse of Spain to the death of d'Artagnan. It has four centers of interest: the Restoration of Charles II of England; the love affair of Louis XIV and Louise de la Vallière; the trial of Fouquet; and the famous tale of the Man in the Iron Mask. The musketeers are no longer in the foreground; in fact, they do not even appear in several episodes, and the novel as a whole is more disconnected than its predecessors in the trilogy. The main character, Raoul de Bragelonne (Athos's son), is unconvincing, though Louis XIV in particular emerges as a well-developed figure. Indeed, the historical characters dominate the novel, giving it the quality of a "sweeping pageant," as Richard Stowe describes it.

The d'Artagnan novels, especially *The Three Musketeers*, are Dumas at his best. They include his most successful character portrayals, both the primary historical figures—Richelieu, Mazarin, Anne of Austria, and Louis XIV—and the musketeers, who also have a basis in history. D'Artagnan especially is an immortal creation, partaking at once of Don Quixote, the clown, and Ariel; he is a creature of the air and the night whose age hardly seems to matter and whose sprightly, carefree manner is balanced by his inflexible loyalty to his three musketeer friends and to his masters. The three books in the trilogy, more successfully than any others, combine history and fiction and are perhaps the most popular novels produced in the nineteenth century.

THE COUNT OF MONTE-CRISTO

Rivaling the d'Artagnan saga in popularity is *The Count of Monte-Cristo*. Incredible as the adventures of Monte-Cristo may seem, they are based on reality. In 1842, Dumas visited Elba with Prince Jérôme, son of Napoleon's youngest brother, and sailed around the island of Monte-Cristo. Dumas said that he would someday immortalize it. At about the same time, he was approached by Béthune and Plon to write a work titled "Impressions de voyage dans Paris" (travel impressions in Paris). Béthune and Plon did not want an archeological or scientific work, but rather a novel like Eugène Sue's *Les Mystères de Paris* (1842-1843; *The Mysteries of Paris*, 1843). Dumas found the germ of a plot in "Le diamant et la vengeance," a chapter in *Mémoires tirés des archives de la Police de Paris* (1837-1838) by Jacques Peuchet, referred to by Dumas in his *Causeries* as "État civil du 'Comte de Monte-Cristo.'" The main character of *The Count of Monte-Cristo* is based on an unjustly imprisoned shoemaker named François Picaud.

The Count of Monte-Cristo first appeared serially, in *Le Journal des débats*, with the spelling *Christo*, a spelling also used in the Belgian pirated editions. Unlike Dumas's historical novels, *The Count of Monte-Cristo* is set in contemporary France and, except for short passages relating to Napoleon and Louis XVIII, is almost totally a *roman de moeurs*.

The lengthy novel is divided into three unequal parts—based on the cities in which the action takes place: Marseilles, Rome, and Paris—the last being by far the longest. Part 1 opens in 1815, in Marseilles, where Dumas introduces the attractive first mate of the ship *Pharaon*, Edmond Dantès, soon to be promoted to captain. He is celebrating his impending marriage to his beautiful Catalan sweetheart, Mercédès, when he is suddenly arrested. Earlier, the dying captain of the *Pharaon* had given him a letter to deliver to a Bonapartist group in Paris, and because of this he has been accused of treason by two jealous companions: Danglars, the ship's accountant, and Fernand, Dantès's rival for the hand of Mercédès. Caderousse, a neighbor, learns of the plot against Dantès but remains silent. Villefort, the *procureur du roi*, is sympathetic to Dantès until he discovers that the letter is intended for his father, whose Bonapartist and Girondist political views he despises, seeing them as a threat to his own future. He therefore allows Dantès to be condemned to solitary confinement at the nearby Château d'If. Dantès, resentful and despairing, remains in prison for fourteen years, during which time he makes the acquaintance of the Abbé Faria (a character based on a real person), who instructs Dantès in history, mathematics, and languages and wills him the fabulous treasure that the Abbé has hidden on the island of Monte-Cristo. At the Abbé's death, Dantès changes places with his corpse in the funeral sack, is thrown into the sea, and swims to safety.

Once free, Dantès claims the treasure and learns the whereabouts of his betrayers: Danglars has become a successful banker, while Fernand, after acquiring wealth by betraying Pasha Ali in the Greek revolution, has gained the title of Count de Morcerf and has married Mercédès. Shortly afterward, Dantès, now the Count of Monte-Cristo, assumes the persona of Sinbad the Sailor and entertains the Baron Franz d'Épinay at Monte-Cristo. An atmosphere reminiscent of *The Arabian Nights' Entertainments* (fifteenth century) dazzles Franz, who hardly knows if what he sees is real or imaginary. Later, Franz, in the company of his friend Albert de Morcerf, the son of Mercédès and Fernand, again meets Monte-Cristo in Rome, where Monte-Cristo saves Morcerf from the kidnapper Luigi Vampa. Albert invites Monte-Cristo to visit him in Paris, thus introducing part 3.

Part 3 is, properly speaking, the story of Dantès's vengeance and takes place twenty-three years after he was first imprisoned. Disguised sometimes as Monte-Cristo, sometimes as the Abbé Busoni, sometimes as Lord Wilmore, Dantès dazzles all of Paris with his endless wealth, powerful connections, and enigmatic manner. Meanwhile, he slowly but surely sets the stage for his revenge. Directly attacking no one, he nevertheless brings his four enemies to total ruin by intricate and complex machinations. The greedy Caderousse, who gave silent assent to Dantès's imprisonment, is killed by an anonymous assassin while attempting to rob Monte-Cristo's rich hotel on the Champs-Élysées. Before his death, he learns Monte-Cristo's real identity. Danglars is the next victim; by means of false information, Monte-Cristo succeeds in ruining him financially and exposing his wife's greed and infidelity. Fernand is brought down in turn when Monte-Cristo, with the aid of his adopted daughter, Haydée (the natural daughter of Pasha Ali), brings to light several acts of cowardice of which Fernand was guilty during his army service. Fernand's son Albert challenges Monte-Cristo to a duel, but through the intercession of Mercédès, who recognizes her fiancé of many years before, Albert's life is spared.

The last victim is Villefort, whose daughter Valentine is in love with Maximilien Morrel, the son of a shipping master who had aided Dantès and his father long ago. Monte-Cristo encourages Madame de Villefort's greedy efforts to acquire the wealth of Valentine (who is her stepdaughter), and the Villefort family is all but destroyed by the poison Madame de Villefort administers as part of her plan; Valentine herself is an apparent victim. Saved by Monte-Cristo, she is at last reunited with her lover on the island of Monte-Cristo, which Edmond Dantès reveals to the lovers as the site of the treasure he bequeaths to them. He sails off in the distance, his revenge complete. The revenge has also brought about a second transformation in Dantès, for he is now a man who, "like Satan, thought himself for an instant equal to God, but now acknowledges, with Christian humility, that God alone possesses supreme power and infinite wisdom."

Irma M. Kashuba

OTHER MAJOR WORKS

PLAYS: *La Chasse et l'amour*, pr., pb. 1825 (with Adolphe de Leuven and P.-J. Rousseau); *La Noce et l'enterrement*, pr., pb. 1826; *Henri III et sa cour*, pr., pb. 1829 (*Catherine of Cleves*, 1831; also known as *Henry III and His Court*, 1904); *Christine: Ou, Stockholm,*

Fontainebleau, et Rome, pr., pb. 1830; *Antony*, pr., pb. 1831 (English translation, 1904); *Charles VII chez ses grands vassaux*, pr., pb. 1831; *Napoléon Bonaparte: Ou, Trente Ans dans l'histoire de France*, pr., pb. 1831; *Richard Darlington*, pr. 1831; *La Tour de Nesle*, pr., pb. 1832 (redrafted from a manuscript by Frédéric Gaillardet; English translation, 1906); *Le Fils de l'émigré: Ou, Le Peuple*, pr. 1832 (selections pb. 1902); *Le Mari de la veuve*, pr., pb. 1832; *Teresa*, pr., pb. 1832 (based on a draft by Auguste Anicet-Bourgeois); *Angèle*, pr. 1833; *Catherine Howard*, pr., pb. 1834 (English translation, 1859); *La Vénitienne*, pr., pb. 1834; *Cromwell et Charles I*, pr., pb. 1835 (with E.-C.-H. Cordellier-Delanoue); *Don Juan de Marana: Ou, La Chute d'un ange*, pr., pb. 1836; *Kean: Ou, Désordre et génie*, pr., pb. 1836 (with Théaulon de Lambert and Frédéric de Courcy; *Edmund Kean: Or, The Genius and the Libertine*, 1847); *Caligula*, pr. 1837; *Piquillo*, pr., pb. 1837 (libretto; with Gérard de Nerval); *Le Bourgeois de Gand: Ou, Le Secrétaire du duc d'Albe*, pr., pb. 1838 (with Hippolyte Romand); *Paul Jones*, pr., pb. 1838; *L'Alchimiste*, pr., pb. 1839 (with Nerval); *Bathilde*, pr., pb. 1839 (with Auguste Maquet); *Léo Burckart*, pr., pb. 1839 (with Nerval); *Mademoiselle de Belle-Isle*, pr., pb. 1839 (English translation, 1855); *Jarvis l'honnête homme: Ou, Le Marchand de Londres*, pr., pb. 1840 (originally credited to Charles Lafont); *Jeannic le Breton: Ou, Le Gérant responsable*, pr. 1841 (with Eugène Bourgeois); *Un Mariage sous Louis XV*, pr., pb. 1841 (*A Marriage of Convenience*, 1899); *Halifax*, pr. 1842 (with Adolphe D'Ennery?); *Lorenzino*, pr., pb. 1842; *Le Séducteur et le mari*, pr., pb. 1842 (with Lafont); *Les Demoiselles de Saint-Cyr*, pr., pb. 1843 (*The Ladies of Saint-Cyr*, 1870); *L'École des princes*, pr. 1843 (with Louis Lefèvre); *Louise Bernard*, pr., pb. 1843 (with Leuven and Léon Lhérie); *Le Mariage au tambour*, pr., pb. 1843 (with Leuven and Lhérie); *Un Conte des fées*, pr., pb. 1845 (with Leuven and Lhérie); *Le Garde forestier*, pr., pb. 1845 (with Leuven and Lhérie); *Les Mousquetaires*, pr., pb. 1845 (with Maquet; adaptation of Dumas's novel *Vingt Ans aprés*); *Sylvandire*, pr., pb. 1845 (with Leuven and Louis-Émile Vanderburch); *Échec et mat*, pr., pb. 1846 (with Octave Feuillet and Paul Bocage); *Une Fille du régent*, pr., pb. 1846; *Le Chevalier de Maison-Rouge*, pr., pb. 1847 (with Maquet; *The Chevalier de Maison-Rouge*, 1859); *Hamlet, prince de Danemark*, pr. 1847 (with Paul Meurice; adaptation of William Shakespeare's play); *Intrigue et amour*, pr., pb. 1847 (adaptation of Friedrich Schiller's play *Kabale und Liebe*); *La Reine Margot*, pr., pb. 1847 (with Maquet; adaptation of Dumas's novel); *Catilina*, pr., pb. 1848 (with Maquet); *Monte-Cristo*, parts 1 and 2, pr., pb. 1848 (with Maquet; *Monte-Cristo*, part 1, 1850); *Le Cachemire vert*, pr., pb. 1849 (with Eugène Nus); *Le Chevalier d'Harmental*, pr., pb. 1849 (with Maquet; based on Dumas's novel); *Le Comte Hermann*, pr., pb. 1849; *Le Connétable de Bourbon: Ou, L'Italie au seizième siècle*, pr., pb. 1849 (with Eugène Grangé and Xavier de Montépin); *La Guerre des femmes*, pr., pb. 1849 (with Maquet; based on Dumas's novel); *La Jeunesse des mousquetaires*, pr., pb. 1849 (with Maquet; based on Dumas's novel *Les Trois Mousquetaires*; *The Musketeers*, 1850); *Le Testament de César*, pr., pb. 1849 (with Jules Lacroix); *La Chasse au chastre*, pr., pb. 1850 (with Maquet?; based on Dumas's story); *Les Chevaliers du Lansquenet*, pr., pb. 1850 (with Grangé and Montépin); *Pauline*, pr., pb. 1850 (with Grangé and Montépin; based on Dumas's novel *Pauline*); *Urbain Grandier*, pr., pb. 1850 (with Maquet); *Le Vingt-quatre février*, pr., pb. 1850 (adapted from Zacharias Werner's play *Der 24 Februar*); *Le Comte de Morcerf*, pr., pb. 1851 (with Maquet; part 3 of *Monte-Cristo*); *Villefort*, pr., pb. 1851 (with Maquet; part 4 of *Monte-Cristo*); *Romulus*, pr., pb. 1854; *L'Orestie*, pr., pb. 1856; *L'Invitation à la valse*, pr., pb. 1857 (adapted in English as *Childhood Dreams*, 1881); *L'Envers d'une conspiration*, pr., pb. 1860; *Le Roman d'Elvire*, pr., pb. 1860 (with Leuven); *La Veillée allemande*, pr. 1863 (with Bernard Lopez); *Madame de Chamblay*, pr. 1868; *Les Blancs et les bleus*, pr., pb. 1869 (adaptation of part of Dumas's novel); *Théâtre complet*, 1873-1876 (25 volumes); *The Great Lover, and Other Plays*, 1979.

NONFICTION: *Gaule et France*, 1833 (*The Progress of Democracy*, 1841); *Impressions de voyage*, 1833, 1838, 1841, 1843 (*Travels in Switzerland*, 1958); *La Vendée et Madame*, 1833 (*The Duchess of Berri in La Vendée*, 1833); *Guelfes et Gibelins*, 1836; *Isabel de Bavière*, 1836 (*Isabel of Bavaria*, 1846); *Napoléon*, 1836 (English translation, 1874); *Quinze Jours au Sinai*, 1838 (*Impressions of Travel in Egypt and Arabia Petraea*, 1839); *Crimes célèbres*, 1838-1840 (*Celebrated Crimes*, 1896); *Excursions sur les bords du Rhin*, 1841 (with Gérard de Nerval); *Le Midi de la France*, 1841 (*Pictures of Travel in the South of France*, 1852); *Chroniques du roi Pépin*, 1842 (*Pepin*, 1906); *Jehanne la Pucelle, 1429-1431*, 1842 (*Joan the Heroic Maiden*, 1847); *Le Spéronare*, 1842; *Le Corricolo*, 1843; *Mes Mémoires*, 1852, 1853, 1854-1855 (*My Memoirs*, 1907-1909); *Souvenirs de 1830 à 1842*, 1854-1855; *Causeries*, 1860; *Les Garibaldiens*, 1861 (*The Garibaldians in Sicily*, 1861); *Histoires de mes bêtes*, 1868 (*My Pets*, 1909); *Souvenirs dramatiques*, 1868; *Grand Dictionnaire de cuisine*, 1873 (with Anatole France); *On Board the Emma*, 1929; *The Road to Monte-Cristo*, 1956.

TRANSLATION: *Mémoires de Garibaldi*, 1860 (of Giuseppe Garibaldi's *Memorie autobiografiche*).

CHILDREN'S LITERATURE: *La Bouillie de la Comtesse Berthe*, 1845 (*Good Lady Bertha's Honey Broth*, 1846); *Histoire d'un casse-noisette*, 1845 (*Story of a Nutcracker*, 1846); *Le Roi de Bohème*, 1853 (also known as *La Jeunesse de Pierrot*, 1854; *When Pierrot Was Young*, 1924); *Le Sifflet enchanté*, 1859 (*The Enchanted Whistle*, 1894).

MISCELLANEOUS: *Œuvres complètes*, 1846-1877 (301 volumes); *Œuvres d'Alexandre Dumas*, 1962-1967 (38 volumes).

BIBLIOGRAPHY

Beaujour, Elizabeth Klotsky. "Dumas's Decembrists: *Le Maitre d'Armes* and the *Memoirs* of Pauline Annenkova." *Russian Review* 59, no. 1 (2000): 38-51. Describes Dumas's meeting with the Russian subjects of a historical novel he had written eighteen years previously and considers the relationship between history and fiction in the author's works.

Bell, A. Craig. *Alexandre Dumas: A Biography and Study.* London: Cassel, 1950. Helpful and thorough guide pays significant attention to both the life and the work of Dumas. Introduction deals succinctly with the phenomenon of Dumas's popularity and the need for a careful treatment of his entire body of work.

Bell, David F. *Real Time: Accelerating Narrative from Balzac to Zola.* Urbana: University of Illinois Press, 2004. Cites examples from novels and short stories to explore how the accelerated movement of people and information in the nineteenth century was a crucial element in the work of Dumas and three other French authors.

Fabre, Michel. "International Beacons of African-American Memory: Alexandre Dumas père, Henry O. Tanner, and Josephine Baker as Examples of Recognition." In *History and Memory in African-American Culture*, edited by Genevieve Fabre and Robert O'Meally. New York: Oxford University Press, 1994. An examination of Dumas's African heritage is included in a collection of essays that focuses on how African Americans' historical identity has been represented in literature and other media.

Galan, F. W. "Bakhtiniada II, *The Corsican Brothers* in the Prague School: Or, The Reciprocity of Reception." *Poetics Today* 8, nos. 3/4 (1987): 565-577. Approaches Dumas's *The Corsican Brothers* using the critical apparatus of Russian literary critic Mikhail Bakhtin.

Lucas-Dubreton, J. *The Fourth Musketeer: The Life of Alexandre Dumas.* New York: Coward-McCann, 1938. Provides a lively introduction to Dumas's life and career for the general reader.

Maurois, André. *Alexandre Dumas: A Great Life in Brief.* Translated by Jack Palmer White. New York: Alfred A. Knopf, 1964. Offers a good introduction to the life of Dumas, providing the basic facts in readable but limited fashion, including information on the novels. Maurois is one of the recognized authorities on Dumas.

_____. *The Titans: A Three-Generation Biography of the Dumas.* Translated by Gerard Hopkins. 1957. Reprint. Westport, Conn.: Greenwood Press, 1971. A classic in Dumas studies by a seasoned biographer, recounting the life of Dumas, his father, and his son. Includes notes, bibliography, and illustrations.

Nesci, Catherine. "Talking Heads: Violence and Desire in Dumas *père*'s (Post-)Terrorist Society." *SubStance* 27, no. 2 (1998): 73-92. Presents a poststructuralist reading of two of Dumas's novels about the French Revolution, *The Thousand and One Ghosts* and *The Woman with a Velvet Necklace*.

Stowe, Richard S. *Alexandre Dumas père.* Boston: Twayne, 1976. One of the best short introductions to Dumas available in English, with a chapter of biography followed by chapters on Dumas's dramas, novels, and other fiction. Includes notes, chronology, and annotated bibliography.

ANATOLE FRANCE

Born: Paris, France; April 16, 1844
Died: La Béchellerie, near Tours, Saint-Cyr-sur-Loire, France; October 12, 1924
Also known as: Jacques-Anatole-François Thibault

PRINCIPAL LONG FICTION
Le Crime de Sylvestre Bonnard, 1881 (*The Crime of Sylvestre Bonnard*, 1890)
Les Désirs de Jean Servien, 1882 (*The Aspirations of Jean Servien*, 1912)
Thaïs, 1890 (English translation, 1891)
La Rôtisserie de la Reine Pédauque, 1893 (*At the Sign of the Reine Pédauque*, 1912)
Le Lys rouge, 1894 (*The Red Lily*, 1898)
L'Histoire contemporaine, 1897-1901 (collective title for the first 4 novels that follow; *Contemporary History*)
L'Orme du mail, 1897 (*The Elm Tree on the Mall*, 1910)
Le Mannequin d'osier, 1897 (*The Wicker Work Woman*, 1910)
L'Anneau d'améthyste, 1899 (*The Amethyst Ring*, 1919)
Monsieur Bergeret à Paris, 1901 (*Monsieur Bergeret in Paris*, 1922)
Histoire comique, 1903 (*A Mummer's Tale*, 1921)
L'Île des pingouins, 1908 (*Penguin Island*, 1914)
Les Dieux ont soif, 1912 (*The Gods Are Athirst*, 1913)
La Révolte des anges, 1914 (*The Revolt of the Angels*, 1914)

OTHER LITERARY FORMS

Of the twenty-five volumes that make up the standard French edition of the complete works of Anatole France (frahns), more than fifteen are given over to one form or another of prose fiction: ten novels (thirteen if one counts the tetralogy *Contemporary History* as four separate novels), ten collections of short stories, and four volumes of fictionalized autobiography. The remainder of the twenty-five-volume set exhibits a startling variety of literary forms: poetry, theater, biography, history, literary criticism, philosophy, journalism, and polemical writings.

France's first publication was a book-length critical study of the French Romantic poet Alfred de Vigny (1868), after which he published two volumes of his own poetry, one containing lyric poems, the other a play in verse, and several long narrative poems. In the 1880's and 1890's, he wrote a regular weekly column, mostly about books and the literary world, for a prominent Paris newspaper, *Le Temps*. The best of those columns were republished in five volumes under the title *La Vie littéraire* (1888-1892; *On Life and Letters*, 1911-1914). His major venture into the writing of history was *La Vie de Jeanne d'Arc* (1908; *The Life of Joan of Arc*, 1908), published after a quarter of a century of research.

119

Anatole France
(Library of Congress)

That same year, he published his one original prose work for the theater, *La Comédie de celui qui épousa une femme muette* (1903; *The Man Who Married a Dumb Wife*, 1915), a farce based on a well-known medieval fabliau.

France's major speeches and occasional writings, on such issues of the times as the Dreyfus affair, socialism, and pacifism, were collected and published in several volumes under the title *Vers les temps meilleurs* (1906, 1949). Philosophical meditations on human nature and civilization can be found in a volume titled *Le Jardin d'Épicure* (1894; *The Garden of Epicurus*, 1908), consisting of pieces on general subjects originally written for his weekly newspaper column and not included in the volumes of *On Life and Letters*. One may say, in sum, that France was the complete man of letters, who tried his hand at just about every form of writing practiced in the literary world of his time. It is nevertheless accurate to say that the writing of fiction so dominated his output, throughout his career, that it constituted his true vocation.

Achievements

The election of Anatole France to the French Academy in 1896 and his winning of the Nobel Prize in Literature in 1921 were the major public landmarks of the great success and recognition he achieved during his career as a writer, first in his own country and then in the international arena. At the height of his fame, in the early years of the twentieth century, he was widely regarded as France's greatest living author, celebrated for his wit, his wisdom, and his humanitarian vision. The paradoxes of that fame, however, were multiple and heavy with irony: The fame had been an unusually long time in coming (he was nearly fifty years old before he had his first significant success with the public), it was based largely on his association with public events rather than on his genuine but esoteric literary talent, and it lasted only briefly. Indeed, the greatest paradox of his fame was its bewilderingly rapid eclipse after his death. His reputation would not regain the luster of his glory years, around the turn of the twentieth century.

France himself lived long enough to be the saddened witness of a major erosion of his fame in a storm of bitter controversy, which made him an object of both worship and hatred but for purely nonliterary reasons. The truth is that the great fame he enjoyed, during a brief period of his life, was of the public sort, only indirectly occasioned by his writings, which, even at their most popular, appealed to a rather narrowly circumscribed audience. One must separate his fame from his achievements as a writer—which is not to say that his achievements were minor, but only that they were literary and aesthetic, hence accessible to relatively few at any time.

As a novelist and short-story writer, France made his mark in the fiction of ideas, and as a literary critic, he established, by personal example, the validity of subjective impressionism as a method. Those are the two major achievements of his career in letters, the accomplishments that have affected literary history. To those literary achievements, one should add a more personal achievement: the creation of a highly distinctive, instantly identifiable style of classic purity and elegance, with subtle rhythms and limpid clarity, which perfectly translated the skeptical and gently ironic view he held of the human condition.

Biography

Anatole France, born Jacques-Anatole-François Thibault in 1844, was the only child of a well-established Parisian bookdealer and was seemingly predestined to the world of books. His father, Noël-François Thibault, ran the sort of bookshop that was also a gathering place of the literati, who would come as not only customers but also friends. They would sit and talk with the owner, whom they called by the familiar diminutive France, an abbreviation of François. Once the son was old enough to help in the shop and participate in the daily conversations, he was naturally called le jeune France, a custom that suggested to young Anatole the pen name he would choose when he began to write.

Shy and unassertive by nature and unprepossessing physically, France matured into an unworldly and bookish young man, easily intimidated by the "real" world and much given to periods of solitude and quiet reverie. In his twenties, he did occasional research and editing chores for the publishers of dictionaries and encyclopedias, having definitely decided against following in his father's footsteps as a bookseller. Eventually, he became a reader of manuscripts for a publisher, wrote articles for ephemeral journals, and took a civil servant's position, working in the senate library, all the while using his leisure moments to learn the craft of writing. He was thirty-three years old, and a published but thoroughly obscure and unknown author, when he overcame his timidity long enough to marry, in 1877. The marriage produced one child, a daughter born in 1881, but was otherwise an unhappy relationship for both sides that ended in a bitter divorce in 1893, after a prolonged separation.

France's unhappy domestic life was the backdrop for his long personal struggle to find his own "voice" and establish himself as a writer. By the 1880's, he had abandoned poetry and was experimenting with different modes of prose fiction, trying both the novel and the short-story forms but attracting very little attention from the reading public. Only after he became the regular literary critic for *Le Temps* and had published a genuinely popular work, the novel *Thaïs*, did he feel securely established enough as a writer to give up his post at the senate library.

Thereafter, all through the 1890's, France's books sold well, and he rose rapidly in public esteem, aided in part by a newfound interest in and involvement with politics and public affairs. In particular, the Dreyfus affair outraged his sense of justice and galvanized him into public action for the first time in his life. He was then in his fifties, and he discovered, a bit to his own surprise, a radical social thinker beneath the placid and conservative exterior he had always presented to the world. During the first years of the new century, he became outspokenly anticlerical and socialistic in his views but was soon plunged into disillusionment when he saw that even victory, as in the Dreyfus affair, produced little real change in society, and that his own activism served only to make him controversial and the object of vicious attacks, which he found especially painful to endure. This mood of disillusionment drove him to withdraw into himself once more and to give up active involvement in public affairs. His work increasingly concerned the past and took on an unaccustomed satiric edge.

The outbreak of World War I tempted France briefly into the public arena once more, to proclaim his pacifist views, but when he was assailed as unpatriotic, he retreated, this time definitively, into the private world of letters. It is perhaps suggestive of the depth of his wounds from the public fray that his literary preoccupations during the final decade of his life were almost exclusively autobiographical. His career as a novelist had effectively ended with the publication of *The Revolt of the Angels* in 1914.

Analysis

The world of books into which Anatole France was born was surely the strongest influence in determining his vocation as a writer, but that influence went far deeper still, for it also determined the kind of writer he would be. Almost all the subjects he chose to write about, in his long career, were derived from or related to books in some way. He was a voracious reader all of his life, and the many books he wrote not only reflect that wide reading but also reveal that what he read was more immediate and more vital to him—more nourishing to his creative imagination, indeed more *real* to him—than the quotidian reality in which he lived. Even when most actively involved in public events, as he was in the years immediately before the end of the nineteenth century and the beginning of the twentieth, he tended to approach events as abstractions, dealing with them as intellectual issues, somehow detached from specific occurrences involving specific human beings. This conscious need to convert real events into matter for books can be seen most clearly in the tetralogy that he so pointedly titled *Contemporary History* and in which he contrived to write about current events as though they were already in the distant past or even the stuff of legend.

Concomitant with his irreducibly bookish view of the world was his almost instinctive taste for storytelling. Whether as reader or as writer, nothing charmed him more than the unfolding of a narrative. Even factual writing—history and biography, for example—he treated as an exercise in storytelling, going so far as to characterize good literary criticism as a kind of novel in which the critic "recounts the adventures of his soul among masterpieces," as he put it in the famous preface to *On Life and Letters*. The art of storytelling was the art he set out to master in his long and difficult apprenticeship, and the storytelling impulse can be identified as the very heart of his vocation as a writer.

To the mind of the man of letters and the instinct of the teller of tales must be added a third characteristic: the outlook of the determined skeptic. France trained himself, from an early age, to question everything and to discern the contradictions and ironies in all forms of human behavior, including his own. He cultivated a perspective of distance and detachment from both people and events, but he learned to temper the bleakness and isolation of such a perspective with feelings of sympathetic recognition of the folly common to all humankind. A subtle blend of pity and irony came to be the hallmark of his view of the affairs of this world, expressed in the tone of gentle mockery with which his celebrated style was impregnated in the works of his maturity. Indeed, all three central characteristics of France—the literary turn of mind, the narrative impulse, and the ironic perspective—can be found in everything he wrote, including the youthful works of poetry, fiction, and literary criticism through which he gradually learned the writer's trade. Those three traits can be seen fully developed for the first time in the novel that won for him his first public recognition, *The Crime of Sylvestre Bonnard*, in 1881.

THE CRIME OF SYLVESTRE BONNARD

Published to the accolades of the French Academy, *The Crime of Sylvestre Bonnard* provided France with his first taste of success. The improbable hero of the book is an elderly, unworldly scholar and bibliophile who explains, in his own words, in the form of diary entries, how he came to acquire a coveted medieval manuscript and how he rescued a young girl from poverty and oppression. What holds the reader's interest is not the trivial plot but the character of Sylvestre Bonnard, whose naïve narrative style, in his diary, constantly and unwittingly reveals his own bumbling incompetence in dealing with the practical side of life.

The reader quickly recognizes as comical the dramatic earnestness with which the simpleminded scholar narrates the only two "adventures" that have ever intruded into his serene existence. The ironic discrepancy between the excited tone of the narrator and the mundane character of the events he narrates is echoed suggestively in the title, which promises a thriller but delivers nothing more violent than a book lover's crime: Having promised to sell his personal library in order to create a dowry for the damsel in distress he has rescued, Bonnard confesses, at the end of the diary, that he had "criminally" withheld from the sale several items with which he could not bear to part.

Perhaps the greatest skill the author displays in this book is that of artfully concealing the inherent sentimentality of the material. The key device of concealment is mockery: Bonnard's interest in old books and manuscripts is magnified, in both incidents, into a grand and criminal passion by a transparently mock-heroic tone. This device distracts and amuses the reader, preventing inopportune reflections about the "fairy-tale" unreality of the happy ending of each incident. It is also true that the eccentric character of Bonnard is charming and that the novelty of a gentle fantasy, published at the height of the popularity of the naturalistic novel in France, must have struck many readers of the day as a welcome relief. It was for such reasons, no doubt, that the novel enjoyed mild critical acclaim and modest sales in 1881, even as its author, sternly self-critical, recognized its limitations of both form and content and set about immediately trying to do better.

What France retained from *The Crime of Sylvestre Bonnard* for future use was the tone of gentle and sympathetic irony about human foibles. In the decade that followed, he experimented with fictionalized autobiography, tales of childhood, and themes borrowed from history or legend, seeking above all a composition that he—and his readers—could recognize as a fully realized work of art. He reached that goal with the publication of *Thaïs* in 1890—his first critical and popular success.

Thaïs

The story of Thaïs, the courtesan of Alexandria, has a bookish source, as does most of France's fiction; he changed the legend of Thaïs, however, by giving the central role in the tale to the monk, Paphnuce, whose ambition for saintliness inspires in him the project of converting the notorious actor and prostitute to Christianity. The well-known plot, in which the saintly monk succumbs to sin even as the notorious sinner seeks salvation in piety, is thus, in France's version, seen almost exclusively from the point of view of the monk. The character of Thaïs is developed hardly at all, while the complex motivations of Paphnuce are analyzed and explored in detail. This imbalance in the point of view, however, does not affect the fundamental irony of the story. Thaïs, though superficially presented, is shown clearly to be a seeker of pagan pleasure and prosperity, who yet was influenced in early youth by piety, having been secretly baptized, and whose growing fear of death and damnation happens to make her receptive to the preaching of Paphnuce at that particular time of her life.

Paphnuce, on the other hand, has had a long struggle against his own sensuality in trying to live as a monk, and is unaware that his sudden project of converting Thaïs is really prompted by his unconscious but still unruly sensual yearnings. When the two meet, therefore, each is ignorant of the other's true disposition, and Paphnuce, moreover, is ignorant of his own desires. Their encounter is thus fated to be sterile, for by that time, Thaïs is already on her way to salvation, and Paphnuce is proceeding precipitously in the opposite direction. France exploits the irony of their opposing trajectories by making the occasion of their meeting the longest and most concentrated episode in the book. The effect is structural: The book is designed as a triptych, with the shorter first and last segments employed to introduce the protagonists and then to record the ultimate fate of each, while the middle segment, equal in length to the other two combined, examines and analyzes their encounter from every angle and demonstrates the impossibility of any fruitful contact between them, because by that time each is in an unanticipatedly different frame of mind.

The structure of the book is perhaps what critics and public admired most about *Thaïs*. It has a satisfying aesthetic quality that announced that France had mastered the sense of form necessary for the achievement of a work of art. The book's success must also, however, be attributed to the subtle complexity of the ideas the author was able to distill from what is, after all, little more than a mildly indecorous comic anecdote. *Thaïs* is a profound and suggestive exploration of the hidden links between religious feeling and sexual desire and, beyond that, of the intricate and unexpected interplay between pagan and Christian ideals and thought and between worldliness and asceticism as patterns of human behavior. In this novel, characterization and realistic description count for comparatively little, and in spite of the daring subject matter, there is not a hint of prurience. The best effects are achieved by a tasteful and harmonious blend of elegant style, well-proportioned structure, and subtle ideas, all presented with gentle irony through the eyes of an amused and skeptical observer. *Thaïs* remains a delight for the thoughtful and attentive reader, one of France's finest achievements.

At about the same time as *Thaïs* was being composed, France was also diligently exploring the short-story form. Employing similar material from history or legend, he was striving to find the ideal fusion of form and content that would yield a work of art in that genre also, and in some of the stories of the volume titled *L'Étui de nacre* (1892; *Tales from a Mother of Pearl Casket*, 1896), notably the famous "Procurator of Judea" and "The Juggler of Our Lady," he succeeded as fully as he had for the novel in *Thaïs*. Thereafter, having earned his artistic spurs in both the novel and the short story, France developed his career in both domains, alternating a novel and a volume of short stories with something approaching regularity over the next twenty years. What is notable in the work of those years is the visible effort he made to avoid the facile repetition of past successes, to explore and experiment with new techniques, and to strive to develop and grow as an artist. During the 1890's, for example, he followed the gemlike stories of *Tales from a Mother of Pearl Casket* with a comic fantasy of a novel called *At the Sign of the Reine Pédauque*, then used a trip to Florence, Italy, as inspiration for a volume of short stories, *Le Puits de Sainte-Claire* (1895; *The Well of Saint Clare*, 1909), and a surprisingly conventional love story, *The Red Lily*, appearing in 1894. Those publications confirmed his newly won stature as a major writer and earned for him election to the French Academy in 1896.

Contemporary History

France's next project, *Contemporary History*, began as a series of weekly newspaper articles commenting on current events by means of anecdotes and illustrative tales. Soon he began interconnecting the articles by using the same set of characters in each. The articles could have formed the basis for a volume of short stories, but instead, France conceived the notion of weaving selected articles from one year's output into a novel that would record the main events of that year in a kind of fictionalized history. It was a bold experiment, which eventually ran to four volumes and occasioned some brilliant writing and the creation of one truly memorable character, Monsieur Bergeret, a scholar and teacher of a wittily ironic turn of mind, who usually articulated the author's own skeptical view of public events.

Some consider *Contemporary History* to be France's finest work, but while it does make unflaggingly entertaining reading, as well as offer a valuable historical record, it may be too randomly structured and too variable in tone to be artistically satisfying for the sophisticated modern reader. It deserves respect, however, both as an interesting experiment in a new kind of fiction and as the inauguration of a new thematic vein in France's work: the overt exploitation of public events, especially politics, in the writing of fiction.

The novels and short stories published between 1900 and 1914 are almost all in this new political vein, sometimes seriously polemical, more often comic and satiric. The most widely read work of that period is the amusing and clever *Penguin Island*, which gives a brief and jaundiced view of French history as though it were a history of a society of penguins. The masterpiece of this period, however, and probably the finest of all France's novels, is his reconstruction of the atmosphere of the French Revolution, called *The Gods Are Athirst*, published in 1912.

The Gods Are Athirst

France's strong interest in the period of the French Revolution was undoubtedly inspired by his youthful browsing in his father's bookshop, which specialized in that subject. During the 1880's, France began work on a novel about the revolutionary period, but he abandoned it, rearranging some of the completed fragments into short stories that turned up, a few years later, in the collection *Tales from a Mother of Pearl Casket*. By 1910, when he began to work on a new novel of the Revolution, he had been through his own personal revolution—involvement in the Dreyfus affair and public espousal of socialism—only to suffer rapid disillusionment with the way human nature seems inevitably to distort and betray ideals. Something of that disillusionment must have shaped *The Gods Are Athirst*, for it concentrates on the process by which the Reign of Terror developed out of revolutionary zeal for liberty, equality, and fraternity and, by means of the inclusion of a large and varied cast of characters, seeks to depict how daily life was affected by this process. The novel is set in Paris and covers a time span of about two years, from 1792 to 1794.

At the very heart of the novel, France places a struggling young painter, a pupil of Jacques Louis David, whose name is Évariste Gamelin and who, in 1792, is active in the revolutionary committees of his quarter. Gamelin is depicted as a mediocre artist but one who is serious in his devotion both to art and to the humanitarian ideals of the new Republic. His seriousness is a function of his youthful innocence, which is unrelieved by any element of gaiety or humor but which endows him with a capacity for tender feelings of affection or sympathy. Those tender feelings are the noble source of his support for the Revolution, but he gets caught up in complex and emotionally charged events that he is incapable of understanding, and, as a member of a revolutionary tribunal, he unwittingly betrays his own humanitarian principles by voting for the execution of innocent people to satisfy the bloodthirsty mob of spectators. Gamelin thus embodies the book's fundamental and deeply pessimistic theme, which is that even decent individuals and noble ideals will fall victim to the winds of fanaticism. At the ironic end of the novel, Gamelin the terrorist is himself condemned and executed by the Reign of Terror.

Gamelin is surrounded by an array of different types who give magnificent density to the novel's re-creation of the past. Most memorable, perhaps, is Maurice Brotteaux, a neighbor of Gamelin and a former member of the nobility, now earning his living by making puppets to sell in toy shops. Brotteaux is a skeptic and a witty ironist—unmistakably the author's alter ego—who, though not unsympathetic to the Revolution, deplores its decline into fanaticism, consoling himself by reading his ever-present copy of Lucretius's *De rerum natura*. The author's intentional irony in this detail is that the Latin poet's work had the original purpose of explaining nature to his contemporaries without reference to the supernatural, in order thus to liberate his compatriots from their superstitious fear of the gods. As the novel's title suggests, Lucretius's noble project is a futile exercise when the gods thirst for blood. Gamelin's fiancé, the voluptuous Élodie, adds a fascinating psychological element to the novel, for as her lover Gamelin grows more and more savage in his condemnation of his fellow citizens, she is surprised to discover that, her horror of him notwithstanding, her sensual attraction to him intensifies: The more blood there is on his hands, the more uncontrollable her passion becomes.

The novel is masterful in its smooth handling of the welter of significant characters and details, the unobtrusive integration of known historical figures and events into an invented narrative, and the creation of both a sense of inevitable tragedy in the action and the feel of epic grandeur in the composition as a whole. It is an impressively vast canvas the author attempts to encompass here—the greatest and most complex of his career. Although there is, of necessity, much weaving back and forth from setting to setting and from one group of characters to another, the clarity and focus of the narrative line are never blurred, and the careful structure accentuates for the reader the inexorability of the mounting dramatic tension enveloping more and more of the novel's characters. In the manner of a classical tragedy, the novel closes with the return of uneasy calm after the catastrophe and the indication that the dead will be quickly forgotten and that life will go on as before. The final paragraph shows Élodie taking a new lover and employing the same endearments to him as she had used at the start of her affair with Gamelin.

The Gods Are Athirst does not quite attain the majestic historical sweep that a subject such as the French Revolution might be expected to command, perhaps because the figure at its center, Évariste Gamelin, is deliberately not cast in the heroic mold. Yet it is a fine and powerful novel, and its unforgettable images carry their intended message to issues beyond the events described, revealing something fundamentally important about human conduct in any revolution and, indeed, in any group situation subject to the volatile incitements of mob psychology. This brilliant novel, written when the author was nearly seventy years old, proved to be the artistic culmination of France's long career. The novel that followed it, *The Revolt of the Angels*, is a merry fantasy of anticlerical bent, amusing to read but making no artistic or intellectual claims to importance. It proved, simply, that this veteran teller of tales still had the skill and magic, at seventy, to hold the attention of the reading public.

THE RED LILY

As a writer of fiction, France has always eluded classification. He showed little interest in the precise observation of daily reality that was the hallmark of his naturalist contemporaries, nor did he strive to win fame with sensational plotting, flamboyant characters, or studies in spicily abnormal psychology. Though allied, at certain times, with the Parnassians and the Symbolists, he never submitted himself fully to their aesthetic discipline in his own art. He followed his own bent, and because he was so steeped in books and erudition, so unsociable and so fond of solitude, and so little driven by ambition, he tended to cut a strange and solitary figure in the literary world.

In both manner and matter, he was really quite unlike anyone else then writing. Probably nothing contributed more to his uniqueness as a writer than his absolute addiction to ideas. The originating inspiration for everything he wrote was neither an event nor a character nor a situation nor even a new literary trick to try out, but ever and always an idea, a concept, an abstraction that he wanted to bring to life by means of a story, a play, or a poem. Even his most conventional novel, *The Red Lily*, seems to be only a routine story of frustrated love and jealousy. What truly animates this novel is the daring concept of female independence, which entrenched social attitudes and the habits of male possessiveness in love relationships put out of the reach of even the most lucid and intelligent women, even in that haven of enlightened individualism, Florence.

Though not a great novel, *The Red Lily* penetratingly probes an idea that was very advanced for the time: the idea that a woman who conceives the ambition to be a person in her own right, rather than an accessory to someone else's life, faces tragically insuperable obstacles. One can identify a seminal idea of that kind at the very center of the concerns of every novel and every short story France wrote. Ideas are his trademark—not surprisingly, because his literary imagination was so completely grounded in books, rather than in life, and because his carefully maintained view of the world was a skepticism so systematic, and so bathed in irony, that it kept reality at a distance and made the life of the mind virtually the only life he knew. Such a writer is not for everyone, but in spite of the low ebb of his reputation since his death, his audience will never entirely vanish as long as there are those who relish the pleasures of the intellect.

Murray Sachs

OTHER MAJOR WORKS

SHORT FICTION: *Nos enfants*, 1886; *Balthasar*, 1889 (English translation, 1909); *L'Étui de nacre*, 1892 (*Tales from a Mother of Pearl Casket*, 1896); *Le Puits de Sainte-Claire*, 1895 (*The Well of Saint Clare*, 1909); *Clio*, 1900 (English translation, 1922); *Crainquebille, Putois, Riquet, et plusieurs autres récits profitables*, 1904 (*Crainquebille, Putois, Riquet, and Other Profitable Tales*, 1915); *Les Contes de Jacques Tournebroche*, 1908 (*The Merry Tales of Jacques Tournebroche*, 1910); *Les Sept Femmes de la Barbe-Bleue, et autres contes merveilleux*, 1909 (*The Seven Wives of Bluebeard*, 1920); *The Latin Genius*, 1924; *The Wisdom of the Ages, and Other Stories*, 1925; *Golden Tales*, 1926.

PLAYS: *La Comédie de celui qui épousa une femme muette*, pb. 1903 (*The Man Who Married a Dumb Wife*, 1915); *Crainquebille*, pb. 1903 (English translation, 1915).

NONFICTION: *Alfred de Vigny*, 1868; *La Vie littéraire*, 1888-1892 (5 volumes; *On Life and Letters*, 1911-1914); *Le Jardin d'Épicure*, 1894 (*The Garden of Epicurus*, 1908); *Vers les temps meilleurs*, 1906, 1949; *La Vie de Jeanne d'Arc*, 1908 (*The Life of Joan of Arc*, 1908); *Le Génie latin*, 1913 (*The Latin Genius*, 1924); *Sur la voie glorieuse*, 1915.

MISCELLANEOUS: *The Complete Works*, 1908-1928 (21 volumes); *Œuvres complètes*, 1925-1935 (25 volumes).

BIBLIOGRAPHY

Auchincloss, Louis. "Anatole France." In *Writers and Personality*. Columbia: University of South Carolina Press, 2005. Auchincloss, himself a novelist, has compiled his observations about writers in this collection. The chapter on France discusses how France's personality was reflected in his own fiction.

Axelrad, Jacob. *Anatole France: A Life Without Illusions.* New York: Harper & Brothers, 1944. In this dated but eminently readable biography, Axelrad focuses on France's impact as a social critic and partisan of justice. While the research is carefully undertaken and generally accurate, the point of view is overly sentimental, unabashedly admiring, and insufficiently critical and analytical.

Chevalier, Haakon M. *The Ironic Temper: Anatole France and His Time.* New York: Oxford University Press, 1932. Although dated, this book is insightful and engagingly written. Its purpose is to study a character, not to evaluate the artistic achievement of its subject. It sets an excellent analysis of France's ironic view of the world against a detailed portrait of the political climate in which he lived and wrote. Includes photographs and a bibliography.

Emery, Elizabeth. "Art as Passion in Anatole France's *Le Lys rouge.*" *Nineteenth Century French Studies* 35, no. 3/4 (2007): 641-652. An analysis of the novel *The Red Lily*, describing it as a "mordant satire of [France's] contemporaries' aesthetic pronouncements" and focusing on its detailed descriptions of fin-de-siècle aesthetic tastes and attitudes about art.

Hamilton, James F. "Terrorizing the 'Feminine' in Hugo, Dickens, and France." *Symposium* 48, no. 3 (Fall, 1994): 204-215. An analysis of France's novel *The Gods Are Athirst* and novels about the French Revolution by Victor Hugo and Charles Dickens. Hamilton argues that these authors repress the feminine side in their depiction of the Reign of Terror, relying on cold mechanical reasoning that creates a self-defeating force of violence.

Jefferson, Carter. *Anatole France: The Politics of Skepticism.* New Brunswick, N.J.: Rutgers University Press, 1965. This work emphasizes the historical and political, as opposed to the literary, ideas of France and is especially informative with respect to the complex and shifting political positions he assumed in the last two decades of his life. The book's five chapters cover the conservative, anarchist, crusader, socialist, and "bolshevik" stages of France's thought. Contains a bibliography.

Stableford, Brian M. "Anatole France." In *Supernatural Fiction Writers: Fantasy and Horror, 1: Apuleius to May Sinclair*, edited by Everett Franklin Bleiler. New York: Scribner's, 1985. Stableford provides a brief introduction to France's treatment of the Christian myth and to his fantastic fiction, discussing some of the individual works.

Virtanen, Reino. *Anatole France.* New York: Twayne, 1968. Intended as a general introduction to the author's work, this insightful volume is accurate and sound in its evaluation of France's life and career. It is also of use to general readers in its detailed analysis of France's most significant literary works.

JULIEN GREEN

Born: Paris, France; September 6, 1900
Died: Paris, France; August 13, 1998
Also known as: Julien Hartridge Green

PRINCIPAL LONG FICTION
Mont-Cinère, 1926 (*Avarice House*, 1927)
Adrienne Mesurat, 1927 (*The Closed Garden*, 1928)
Léviathan, 1929 (*The Dark Journey*, 1929)
L'Autre Sommeil, 1931 (*The Other Sleep*, 2001)
Épaves, 1932 (*The Strange River*, 1932)
Le Visionnaire, 1934 (*The Dreamer*, 1934)
Minuit, 1936 (*Midnight*, 1936)
Varouna, 1940 (*Then Shall the Dust Return*, 1941)
Si j'étais vous, 1947 (*If I Were You*, 1949)
Moïra, 1950 (*Moira*, 1951)
Le Malfaiteur, 1955 (*The Transgressor*, 1957)
Chaque homme dans sa nuit, 1960 (*Each in His Darkness*, 1961)
L'Autre, 1971 (*The Other One*, 1973)
Le Mauvais Lieu, 1977
Les Pays lointains, 1987 (*The Distant Lands*, 1990)
Les Étoiles du sud, 1989 (*The Stars of the South*, 1996)
Dixie, 1995

OTHER LITERARY FORMS

Julien Green first drew critical attention in the late 1920's as a writer of short fiction (*Le Voyageur sur la terre*, 1930; and *Les Clefs de la mort*, 1927) before attempting the longer narratives that became his forte. Green, however, is almost as well known for his autobiographical works as for his novels. His *Journal*, begun in 1928, has appeared in eighteen volumes published between 1938 and 2006 (partial translations in *Personal Record, 1928-1939*, 1939, and *Diary, 1928-1957*, 1964); a second series, begun in 1963, is more personal and frankly confessional in tone: *Partir avant le jour* (1963; *To Leave Before Dawn*, 1967), *Mille chemins ouverts* (1964; *The War at Sixteen*, 1993), *Terre lointaine* (1966; *Love in America*, 1994), and *Jeunesse* (1974; *Restless Youth, 1922-1929*, 1996). An additional volume, *Memories of Happy Days* (1942), was written and published in English during Green's self-imposed wartime exile in the United States.

Encouraged by Louis Jouvet to try his hand at writing plays, Green achieved moderate success as a playwright with *Sud* (pr., pb. 1953; *South*, 1955), *L'Ennemi* (pr., pb. 1954), and *L'Ombre* (pr., pb. 1956), but he soon concluded that his true skills were those of a novelist. In any case, Green's plays are seldom performed and are of interest mainly to readers already familiar with his novels.

Achievements

In 1971, shortly after publication of his novel *The Other One*) Green became, at the age of seventy, the first foreigner ever elected to membership in the French Academy; his election brought sudden and considerable attention to a long, distinguished, but insufficiently appreciated literary career. Green, born in France to American parents, had been writing and publishing novels in French since the age of twenty-five, attracting more critical attention in France than in the United States, despite the availability of his work in English translation. Even in France, however, his novels have not received extensive critical notice, owing in part to his work being difficult to classify.

Encouraged by the success of his earliest writings, Green lost little time in developing a characteristic mode of expression, alternately mystical and sensual, often both at once. Many critics, as if willfully blind to the erotic dimension of Green's work, sought to classify him as a "Catholic" writer in the tradition of Georges Bernanos and François Mauriac. Others, focusing on the oppressive atmosphere pervading many of his novels, sought to place Green closer to the gothic tradition. Neither classification is quite accurate, yet it was not until after Green's autobiography began to appear in 1963 that reassessment of his novels began in earnest.

Using a clear, ornament-free style that has been described as classical, Green quickly involves his readers in the solitary lives of tortured characters obsessed with the need to escape. Often, the compulsion toward escape leads to violence, madness, or death; when it does not, it produces an implied "leap of faith," which is not, however, totally satisfying to those who would see Green as a religious writer in the Catholic tradition. Even in those rare cases in which solutions are offered, it is still the problems that dominate the consciousness of author and reader alike. Endowed with keen powers of observation, Green excels in the portrayal of psychological anguish that any thoughtful reader can understand, even if he or she does not share it.

The publication of Green's autobiography beginning in the 1960's permitted at last a demystification of the novels—in Green's case, more help than hindrance. In the light of Green's frankness, many of the tortures undergone by his characters stood revealed as artistic transpositions of the author's own private anguish as he sought to reconcile his spiritual aspirations with a growing awareness of his homosexuality. Far from detracting from the power of Green's novels, such disclosures shed valuable light on his life in art, allowing critics and casual readers alike to appreciate the true nature of Green's novelistic achievement. Whatever their source, Green's novels remain powerful portraits of alienation and estrangement unmatched in contemporary French or American literature.

Biography

Julien Hartridge Green was born in Paris on September 6, 1900, the youngest of eight children. His father, Edward Moon Green of Virginia, had since 1895 served as European agent of the Southern Cotton Seed Oil Company. Green's mother, Mary Hartridge of Savannah, Georgia, dominated her son's early life with a curious blend of love and Puritan guilt; her death in 1914, instead of liberating the young Green from the tyranny of her moods and ideas, seems rather to have increased her hold upon his developing conscience. Green grew to adulthood torn between a strong, if repressed, sensuality and a mystical desire for sainthood, often equally strong. Converted to Catholicism within a year after his mother's death, he seriously considered entering a monastic order but deferred his plans for the duration of World War I. In 1917, he served as an ambulance driver, first for the American Field Service and later for the Red Cross; the following year, still (as he remained) a U.S. citizen, he obtained a commission in the French army by first enlisting in the Foreign Legion. Demobilized in 1919, he returned to Paris and soon renounced his monastic vocation, a loss that caused him considerable anguish.

Unable to decide on a career, he accepted with some reluctance the offer of a Hartridge uncle to finance his education at the University of Virginia. Enrolled as a "special student," Green read widely in literature, religion, and sociology; in 1921, after two years in residence, he was appointed an assistant professor of French. Still homesick for his native France, more at ease in French than in English, Green returned to Paris in 1922 to study art, gradually discovering instead his vocation as a writer and attracting the attention of such influential literary figures as Jacques de Lacretelle and Gaston Gallimard. By the age of twenty-five, already an established author with a growing reputation, Green had found his lifework.

During his thirties, Green read widely in mysticism and Eastern religions. Returning to the Catholic Church as early as 1939, Green was soon thereafter obliged to leave Paris by the onset of World War II. After the fall of France in 1940, he moved to the United States for the duration, teaching at various colleges and universities before and after brief service as a language instructor in the U.S. Army. Returning to Paris in September, 1945, he remained there, pursuing the life and career of a French man of letters until his death on August 13, 1998.

Analysis

Educated primarily in the French tradition) Green brought to his novels a distinctly French concern for the presentation and development of character. Whether his novels are set in France, the United States, or elsewhere, his characters are observed and portrayed with the psychological precision that has characterized French fiction from Madame de La Fayette down through Honoré de Balzac and Gustave Flaubert to Marcel Proust. With critical and seemingly pitiless exactitude, Green takes the reader inside his characters to show their thought and motivations, achieving considerable identification even when the characters tend toward violence or madness. On the surface, few of Green's characters would appear to invite identification on the part of the reader; they tend to be misfits of one sort or another, haunted by strange fears and insecurities. It is Green's singular talent, however, to present them and their thoughts in such a way that they seem almost instantly plausible and authentic, and to hold the reader's interest in what will happen to them. Life, as particularized in Green's characters, emerges as both threat and promise, most often as a trap set for the unwary.

Typically, Green's protagonists, often female with one surviving and insensitive parent, find themselves trapped in an existence that they can neither tolerate nor understand; not infrequently, they contribute to their own misfortune through a stubborn refusal to express themselves. Even so, the reader senses that to speak their minds would render them vulnerable to even greater assaults from a hostile environment. Locked within themselves, they suffer all the tortures of an earthly hell from which they yearn to escape. In his autobiography, Green observes that a feeling of imprisonment was a recurring childhood nightmare; in his novels, the theme is enlarged to archetypal proportions, assuming the authority of fable. Green's characters, for all their particularities, emerge as highly convincing exemplars of the human condition.

Escape, for all of its apparent promise, offers no relief to the suffering of Green's characters. Adrienne Mesurat, among the most convincing of Green's early heroines, gradually retreats into madness once she has achieved through an act of violence the freedom for which she has longed; Paul Guéret, the ill-favored viewpoint character of *The Dark Journey*, strikes and disfigures the young woman whose attentions he has sought, thereafter becoming a fugitive. Manuel, the title character of *The Dreamer*, retreats from the undesirable world into a fictional universe of his own making, only to die soon thereafter. Elisabeth, the protagonist of *Midnight*, seeks to escape with her lover, only to be killed with him in a fall. Clearly, the oppressive atmosphere that stifles Green's characters is internal as well as external; like Adrienne Mesurat, they remain imprisoned even when they are free to come and go as they please. Even in the later novels, such as *The Other One*, death is frequently the only means of escape available.

The power of Green's novels derives in no small measure from the author's skill in providing motivation for the behavior of his characters. In the case of Adrienne Mesurat, for example, Green quickly and convincingly shows normal desire stifled by silence until it becomes first an obsession, then true madness. Philippe Cléry, the main viewpoint character of *The Strange River*, passes the age of thirty before being obliged to examine his life; thereafter, he becomes most convincingly self-conscious, questioning his every move in an authentically ineffectual way. Sympathetic or not (and most are not), Green's characters are inescapably human and believable, commanding the reader's identification; although they seem to exist in a world of their own, they are unmistakably drawn from life, the products of Green's keen powers of observation.

It is possible, that, had Green not been reared in a time less tolerant than the twentieth century, his novels might never have come into being. Arguably, Green's expression has responded somewhat to the temper of the times, dealing more and more openly with homosexual attraction in such novels as *The Transgressor*; indeed, by the time Green wrote and published his autobiography in the 1960's, his revelations seemed less scandalous than timely and enlightening. The restraint that helped to shape his earlier works was in a sense no longer necessary. It seems likely, moreover, that the writing of the autobiographical volumes lessened the sense of creative urgency that marks the best of Green's earlier writing. In fact, Green's later novels (*Le Mauvais Lieu* in particular), while still holding the reader's attention, cover little new ground and move perilously close to self-parody.

THE CLOSED GARDEN

Green's second novel, *The Closed Garden*, written and published within a year after the success of *Avarice House*, ranks among his best and is perhaps the most memorable. Refreshingly normal at the start of the novel, eighteen-year-old Adrienne quickly erodes into madness and amnesia as a result of the stifling circumstances of her life. Recently out of school (the time is 1908), she lives in a provincial French town with her retired father and her thirty-five-year-old spinster sister, Germaine. A chronic invalid whose illness their autocratic father refuses even to recognize, Germaine rules over Adrienne with the authority of a mother but with none of the attendant love. As in Green's *Avarice House*, kinship is no guarantee of understanding or even friendship; indeed, the family emerges as perhaps the most inimical and threatening of human institutions. Using heavy irony, Green shows Adrienne's daily interaction with her hostile relatives; the reader, privy to Adrienne's innermost thoughts, looks on with horror as she is repeatedly unable to express them.

At the start of the novel, Adrienne is looking with healthy scorn at a group of family portraits to which she inwardly refers as "the cemetery," concluding with some satisfaction that her own features place her on the "strong" side of the family. Dressed as a servant, she is doing the family housework, exhibiting physical strength by moving heavy furniture with ease. It is precisely such apparent strength that will soon prove to be her undoing, as it turns inward upon herself, accomplishing in several weeks a deterioration that otherwise might take years. Deprived of normal human companionship, Adrienne becomes infatuated with a neighboring physician, Dr. Maurecourt, whom she has seen but once; such adolescent passion, harmless enough at face value, functions rather in Green's universe as an instrument of destruction. Adrienne, unable to confide to her father or sister the relatively innocent causes of her slightly irregular behavior, retreats further and further into her fantasy with each new demand for an explanation.

Steadfastly refusing to name the object of her secret passion, she soon finds herself literally locked up in the house, forbidden to leave but still dreaming of escape. Ironically, it is the nearly bedridden Germaine, rather than the healthy Adrienne, who in fact does manage to escape the father's tyranny, sneaking out of the house with Adrienne's help in order to seek refuge in a convent near Paris. Germaine's departure triggers a rare and violent dispute between Adrienne and her father, who reveals that he, like Germaine, has guessed the identity of Adrienne's lover. Overcome with shame and grief, Adrienne runs toward her father and pushes him downstairs; she is never quite sure whether she intended to kill him. In any case, he dies, and although Adrienne is never formally charged with his murder, she is eventually convicted of the crime by the tribunal of malicious gossip. Indeed, the entire village soon takes on the sinister aspect of Adrienne's now-absent family, hemming her within a circle of watchful and accusing eyes.

A brief attempt at leaving the village finds Adrienne drifting aimlessly from one provincial town to another, beset by nightmares as she sleeps fitfully in seedy hotels, imagining that she is being watched. Returning home to live among her tormentors, she falls physically ill; Dr. Maurecourt is summoned, and at the end of a lengthy and difficult conversation, she blurts out her unrequited love for him. Maurecourt, a frail widower of forty-five, is understandably nonplussed; with genuine compassion, he explains to Adrienne that he is mortally ill, having hardly more than a year left to live, while she, Adrienne, has her whole life ahead of her. For all practical purposes, however, Adrienne's life is as good as over; she again leaves the house, intending to escape but succeeding only in wandering aimlessly about the town until she is found suffering from amnesia.

Like other novels and plays of the period—John O'Hara's *Appointment in Samarra* (1934) and Jean Cocteau's *La Machine infernale* (1934; *The Infernal Machine*, 1936) come readily to mind—*The Closed Garden* is the carefully recorded history of what can happen to a human life and mind when everything possible goes wrong. Subjected to torture such as might be inflicted upon a steel rod in laboratory tests, Adrienne's mind eventually snaps. Until very near the end, however, Adrienne remains painfully lucid, aware of all that is happening to her yet powerless to stop it. Unlike such characters as O'Hara's Julian English and Cocteau's Oedipus, Adrienne seems singularly undeserving of her cruel fate; neither arrogant nor thoughtless, she seems to have been chosen almost at random by unseen forces bent upon destroying her for no good reason.

THE DARK JOURNEY

The Dark Journey, Green's third novel, breaks new ground in presenting several viewpoint characters and a number of interlocking subplots. Each of the main characters, reminiscent of Balzac's provincial "monomaniacs," is governed and identified by a ruling passion, much as Adrienne Mesurat is governed by her passion for the helpless Dr. Maurecourt. The main viewpoint character, whose life provides a link among the others, is Paul Guéret, an ill-favored and unhappily married man in his thirties who is obsessed by his passion for the young and attractive Angèle. A typical Green heroine, Angèle has been thrust by circumstances into a thankless and sordid existence from which she longs to escape, presumably in the loving company of a young man her own age. A launderer by day, she moonlights by sleeping with various gentlemen who frequent the restaurant owned and operated by the insatiably curious Madame Londe. In a sense, Angèle is less prostitute than spy, engaged by Madame Londe to supply her with useful information concerning the gentlemen's private lives. Guéret, to his consternation, is excluded from Angèle's regular clientele because he is simply not interesting enough, either as a person or because of his station in life, to warrant Madame Londe's interest. Angèle, meanwhile, is flattered by Guéret's awkward attentions, even if she cannot bring herself to return his love in kind.

Guéret, driven nearly to distraction by Angèle's flirtatiousness and inaccessibility, becomes increasingly obsessed with his need to possess the girl, and before long his obsession leads to violence. First, after a long and painful struggle to scale the wall of Angèle's building, he breaks into her room, only to find that she is not there. The next day, unable to tolerate her taunting behavior, he beats her and goes into hiding, leaving her for dead on a riverbank. Angèle survives, although disfigured for life. Guéret, meanwhile, is in fact guilty of murder, having bludgeoned to death an old man who stumbled upon his hiding place. After several months as a fugitive, he is given asylum by the bored and sadistic Eva Grosgeorge, mother of a boy he once tutored. Eventually, Madame Grosgeorge tires of Guéret and denounces him to the police against the protestations of Angèle, still convalescent, who does her best to rescue him. Unsuccessful, Angèle lapses into a dreamlike state and, like Adrienne Mesurat before her, wanders about town in what she thinks is an attempt to escape; delirious, she dies of exposure soon after being brought back to her room. Madame Grosgeorge, meanwhile, having shot herself melodramatically at the moment of Guéret's arrest, is expected to survive.

The Dark Journey differs from Green's earlier novels in both the depth and the scope of its character development. Although both Guéret and Angèle show clear lines of descent from Green's earlier protagonists, such characters as Madame Londe and the Grosgeorge couple bear witness to a broadening of Green's psychological and social observation; Eva Grosgeorge, in particular, is a most convincing grotesque, the bored and self-indulgent younger wife of a rather bovine industrialist. Guéret, the misfit, serves unwittingly as the link between these various social types, whose paths would otherwise be unlikely to cross. As elsewhere in Green's work, interpersonal love is shown to be an unattainable illusion. Guéret's passion for Angèle, among the more normal obsessions portrayed in the book, is doomed by its own intensity. Angèle, meanwhile, is too lost in her own romantic fantasies to see beyond Guéret's ugliness to her own genuine feelings toward him until it is too late for them both.

THE STRANGE RIVER

Less sensational in subject matter and in treatment than *The Closed Garden* or *The Dark Journey*, Green's fifth novel, *The Strange River*, remains one of his least known; nevertheless, it ranks among his best. Nearly devoid of external action or incident, *The Strange River* presents social and psychological analysis of rare accuracy and power, approaching Flaubert's ambition to write a book about "nothing." To a far greater degree than in *The Dark Journey*, Green reveals his seldom-used gifts as a social satirist, here portraying in painful detail the empty existence of the idle rich. *The Strange River* is, moreover, the only one of Green's novels to be set in Paris, where he himself resided.

As in *The Dark Journey*, Green derives considerable effect in *The Strange River* from the presentation of multiple viewpoints, primarily those of Philippe Cléry and his sister-in-law, Eliane, but not excluding that of Philippe's wife, Henriette. Philippe, rich through inheritance, suffers in his own ineffectual way the double torture of being superfluous and knowing it. As titular head of a mining company about which he knows nothing and cares even less, he need only appear (and remain silent) at monthly meetings in order to do all that society expects of him. The rest of the time, he is free to remain in his elegant apartment (he owns the building) or go for long walks dressed as the gentleman he is. At thirty-one, he is aware that his marriage has long since become as meaningless and hollow as his professional title; Henriette goes out on the town without him nearly every evening and has taken a lower-class lover to occupy the rest of her time. Their only child, ten-year-old Robert, spends most of the year out of sight and mind in boarding school; his rare presence during school vacations, when he has nowhere else to go, proves irritating to his parents and aunt, as they have no idea what to say to him. Philippe, meanwhile, unless he is out walking, usually finds himself in the company of Henriette's elder sister, Eliane, who secretly loves Philippe even as she comes to despise him for what he is.

Against such a background of silence and mistrust, Green sketches in the private thoughts and feelings of his characters, expressing the pain of existence in all of its contingency. The plot of *The Strange River*, such as it is, turns upon an incident that Philippe thinks he may have witnessed in the course of one of his long walks: A middle-aged, shabbily dressed couple appeared to be struggling on the banks of the Seine, and the woman may or may not have called out to Philippe for help. In any case, Philippe went on his way, not consulting the police until hours later. As the novel proceeds, the incident often returns to haunt Philippe with its implications.

Anticipating by some twenty-five years the central incident of Albert Camus's *La Chute* (1956; *The Fall*, 1957), Philippe's experience disrupts the balance of a previously unexamined life; Philippe, however, is already too weak to do much of anything with what he has learned about himself. For months after the incident, he scans the papers for reports of bodies fished from the Seine; at length he finds one, and it is quite likely that he was in fact witness to a murder. In the meantime, another of his nocturnal walks has provided him with further evidence of his own cowardice; accosted by a stranger, he hands over his billfold at the merest threat of violence. Attending a monthly board meeting, he impulsively takes the floor and resigns his post, to the astonishment of his sister-in-law and wife, who fear that he has lost his mind; his life, however, goes on pretty much as before, closely observed by the lovesick spinster Eliane. Like Adrienne Mesurat, Eliane is both powerless and lucid in her unrequited love, increasingly attached to Philippe even as she begins to deduce his guilty secret concerning the couple on the riverbank.

Unlike all but one of Green's other novels (*The Other Sleep*), *The Strange River* is open-ended, leaving the main characters with much of their lives yet before them. The action is not resolved in violence, as in *The Dark Journey*, or in madness, as in the case of Adrienne Mesurat. Philippe, of course, is too weak to do much of anything except worry about himself.

Not until *The Transgressor*, written a quarter of a century later, did Green again try his hand at the sort of social satire so successfully managed in *The Strange River*; despite his skill in such portrayal, it is clear that Greene's true interest lay elsewhere, deep within the conscience of the individual. *The Strange River* is thus in a sense a happy accident; Green, in order to probe the inmost thoughts of a Philippe Cléry, had first to invent Philippe and place him against a social background. The result is a most satisfying work, rather different from Green's other novels but thoroughly successful in accomplishing what it sets out to do.

For a period after *The Strange River*, Green's novels tended increasingly toward fantasy, taking place in a real or fancied dreamworld fashioned by individual characters. It is perhaps no accident that these novels, atypical of Green's work taken as a whole, were written during the time of Green's estrangement from Catholicism, when he was reading extensively in mysticism and Eastern religions. Reconciled with the Church in 1939, Green was soon thereafter to leave France and his career as a novelist for the duration of World War II. *Moira*, the first of Green's true postwar novels, returns to the familiar psychological ground of his earliest work, going even further in its portrayal of the conflict between the mystical and the sensual.

MOIRA

Returning to the time and setting of his American university experience, Green presents in *Moira* the thoughts and behavior of Joseph Day, a Fundamentalist rustic who is even more of an outsider to the university life than Green himself must have been. Joseph is at odds with the school from the first day of his enrollment, horrified by the license and corruption that he sees all around him. His landlady, Mrs. Dare, smokes cigarettes and wears makeup, and his classmates discuss freely their relations with the opposite sex. His missionary zeal fueled by a truly violent temperament to match his red hair, Joseph seeks to save the souls of those around him; thus inclined, he is quite unable to see either himself or his fellows as human beings. Derisively nicknamed "the avenging angel," he burns with a white heat, quite unaware of the eroticism at its source. Early on, he unwittingly rebuffs the sexual advances of a young, male art student, who later commits suicide as a result; meanwhile, Joseph feels mysteriously drawn to the elegant, aristocratic Praileau, who has made fun of Joseph's red hair. Challenging Praileau to a fight, Joseph is so overcome by an excess of clearly sexual frenzy that he nearly kills the young man, who tells him that he is a potential murderer.

Unable to reconcile his Protestant faith with his increasingly violent feelings and behavior, Joseph confides in a fellow ministerial candidate, David Laird, whose vocation is both stronger and less temperamental than Joseph's own. David, however sympathetic, is quite unprepared to deal with the problems of his tortured friend, who proceeds toward the date with destiny suggested in the book's title. Moira, it seems, is also the name of Mrs. Dare's adopted daughter, a licentious young woman who emerges as almost a caricature of the flapper. Even before he meets the girl, Joseph is scandalized by all that he has heard about her; even so, he is quite unprepared for her taunting, loose-mouthed treatment of him.

Another apparent gay man, Killigrew, tries and fails to get close to Joseph. Joseph does, however, vividly recall Killigrew's description of Moira as a she-monster whenever thoughts of the girl invade his daydreams. At length, Joseph, having changed lodgings, returns to his room to find Moira planted there as part of a prank perpetrated upon the "avenging angel" by his classmates. Moira, of course, is a most willing accessory, her vanity piqued by the one man, Joseph, who has proved resistant to her rather blatant charms. By the time the planned seduction occurs, it is Moira, not Joseph, who believes herself to have fallen in love. In the morning, however, Joseph strangles Moira in a fit of remorse over what they have done. After burying her body without incident, he twice considers the possibility of escape but finally turns himself in to the police, who have sought him for questioning.

Despite a plot almost too tightly rigged to seem quite plausible, *Moira* ranks with the best of Green's earlier novels, showing considerable development in the depth and scope of his literary art. As in *The Dark Journey* and *The Strange River,* Green shows himself to be a shrewd and discerning observer of society and its distinctions. Characteristically, however, he remains concerned primarily with the inner workings of the human mind and emotions, and the variety of characters portrayed in *Moira* affords him ample opportunity to display his talents. Freed from taboos (both internal and external) against the depiction of homosexuality in literature, Green in *Moira* seemed to be moving toward a new, mature frankness of expression. However, the novels that he wrote after *Moira,* though explicit, fail to match that work either in suggestive power or in tightness of construction. The first novel of Green's "mature" period thus remains quite probably that period's best.

David B. Parsell

OTHER MAJOR WORKS

SHORT FICTION: *Le Voyageur sur la terre,* 1930 (*Christine, and Other Stories,* 1930).

PLAYS: *Sud,* pr., pb. 1953 (*South,* 1955); *L'Ennemi,* pr., pb. 1954; *L'Ombre,* pr., pb. 1956.

NONFICTION: *Journal,* 1938-2006 (18 volumes; partial translations in *Personal Record, 1928-1939,* 1939, and *Diary, 1928-1957,* 1964); *Memories of Happy Days,* 1942; *Partir avant le jour,* 1963 (*To Leave Before Dawn,* 1967; also known as *The Green Paradise*); *Mille chemins ouverts,* 1964 (*The War at Sixteen,* 1993); *Terre lointaine,* 1966 (*Love* in America, 1994); *Jeunesse,* 1974 (*Restless Youth, 1922-1929,* 1996); *Memories of Evil Days,* 1976; *Dans la gueule du temps,* 1979; *Une Grande Amitié: Correspondance, 1926-1972,* 1980 (with Jacques Maritain; *The Story of Two Souls: The Correspondence of Jacques Maritain and Julien Green,* 1988); *Frère François,* 1983 (*God's Fool: The Life and Times of Francis of Assisi,* 1985); *Paris,* 1983 (English translation, 1991); *The Apprentice Writer,* 1993; *Jeunesse immortelle,* 1998.

BIBLIOGRAPHY

Armbrecht, Thomas J. D. *At the Periphery of the Center: Sexuality and Literary Genre in the Works of Marguerite Yourcenar and Julien Green.* Amsterdam: Rodopi, 2007. Ambrecht compares the representation of homosexuality in the work of Green and Yourcenar, comparing their depiction of gay characters in their novels and plays. Includes a bibliography.

Burne, Glenn S. *Julian Green.* New York: Twayne, 1972. Provides a comprehensive overview of the first forty-five years of Green's career, culminating in his induction into the French Academy in 1971. Includes a bibliography.

Dunaway, John M. *The Metamorphoses of the Self: The Mystic, the Sensualist, and the Artist in the Works of Julien Green.* Lexington: University Press of Kentucky, 1978. Dunaway's study traces the sources and evolution of Green's narrative art, exploring the biographical genesis of his major fiction. Includes a bibliography and an index.

O'Dwyer, Michael. *Julien Green: A Critical Study.* Portland, Oreg.: Four Courts Press, 1997. O'Dwyer provides a biographical introduction and a critical assessment of Green's novels, short stories, plays, autobiography, journals, and other miscellaneous writings. Highlights the importance of Green's American background for a full appreciation of his work. Includes a foreword by Green.

———. "Toward a Positive Eschatology: A Study of the Beginning and Ending of Julien Green's *Chaque homme dans sa nuit.*" *Renascence* 49, no. 2 (Winter, 1997): 111-119. An analysis of *Each in His Darkness* within the context of Green's ideas about the end of the world. Examines the negative elements of Green's spiritual vision, the identical structure of the first and final chapters, and the echoes, resonances, and parallels between these two chapters.

Peyre, Henri. *French Novelists of Today.* New York: Oxford University Press, 1967. Provides a good overview of Green's career, presenting him as standing outside both the French and the American traditions from which his work derives. Includes useful readings of Green's early and midcareer fiction.

Stokes, Samuel. *Julian Green and the Thorn of Puritanism.* 1955. Reprint. Westport, Conn.: Greenwood Press, 1972. A study of Green's novels, concentrating on the various intellectual influences that help explain the spiritual background of his work. Discusses Green's use of fiction to relate the lives of individuals to the society in which they live.

VICTOR HUGO

Born: Besançon, France; February 26, 1802
Died: Paris, France; May 22, 1885
Also known as: Victor-Marie Hugo

PRINCIPAL LONG FICTION
Han d'Islande, 1823 (*Hans of Iceland*, 1845)
Bug-Jargal, 1826 (*The Noble Rival*, 1845)
Le Dernier Jour d'un condamné, 1829 (*The Last Day of a Condemned*, 1840)
Notre-Dame de Paris, 1831 (*The Hunchback of Notre Dame*, 1833)
Claude Gueux, 1834
Les Misérables, 1862 (English translation, 1862)
Les Travailleurs de la mer, 1866 (*The Toilers of the Sea*, 1866)
L'Homme qui rit, 1869 (*The Man Who Laughs*, 1869)
Quatre-vingt-treize, 1874 (*Ninety-Three*, 1874)

OTHER LITERARY FORMS

Victor Hugo (YEW-goh) dominates nineteenth century literature in France both by the length of his writing career and by the diversity of his work. Indeed, it is difficult to think of a literary form Hugo did not employ. Lyric, satiric, and epic poetry; drama in verse and prose; political polemic and social criticism—all are found in his oeuvre. His early plays and poetry made him a leader of the Romantic movement. His political writing included the publication of a newspaper, *L'Événement*, in 1851, which contributed to his exile from the Second Empire. During his exile, he wrote vehement criticism of Napoleon III as well as visionary works of poetry. His poetic genius ranged from light verse to profound epics; his prose works include accounts of his travels and literary criticism as well as fiction.

ACHIEVEMENTS

The complete works of Victor Hugo constitute more nearly a legend than an achievement. In poetry, Hugo had become a national institution by the end of his life. He was a member of the Académie Française, an officer of the Légion d'Honneur, and a Peer of France under the monarchy of Louis-Philippe. When he died, he was accorded the singular honor of lying in state beneath Paris's Arc de Triomphe before his burial in the Panthéon.

During his lifetime, Hugo's novels accounted for much of his popularity with the public. Both sentimental and dramatic, they were excellent vehicles for spreading his humanitarian ideas among large numbers of people. His two most famous novels are *The Hunchback of Notre Dame* and *Les Misérables*. The former is an example of dramatic historical romance, inspired in France by the novels of Sir Walter Scott. It is said to have created in-

Victor Hugo
(Library of Congress)

terest in and ensured the architectural preservation of the Notre Dame cathedral in Paris. It is also a study in Romanticism, with its evocation of the dark force of fate and the intricate intertwining of the grotesque and the sublime.

Les Misérables testifies to Hugo's optimistic faith in humanitarian principles and social progress. The intricate and elaborate plot confronts both social injustice and indifference. It is typical of many nineteenth century attitudes in its emphasis on education, charity, and love as powerful forces in saving the unfortunate creatures of the lower classes from becoming hardened criminals. *Les Misérables* is a novel on an epic scale both in its historical tableaux and as the story of a human soul. Thus, even though Hugo's achievements in the novel are of a lesser scale than his poetry and drama, they are enduring and worthy monuments to the author and to his century.

Biography

Victor-Marie Hugo was born in Besançon, France, in 1802, the third son of Joseph-Léopold-Sigisbert Hugo and Sophie-Françoise Trébuchet. His father had been born in Nancy and his mother in Nantes. They met in the Vendée, where Léopold Hugo was serving in the Napoleonic army. His military career kept the family on the move, and it was during Major Hugo's tour of duty with the Army of the Rhine that Victor-Marie was born in Besançon.

Léopold and Sophie did not have a happy marriage, and after the birth of their third son, they were frequently separated. By 1808, Léopold had been promoted to general and was made a count in Napoleon I's empire. During one reunion of Hugo's parents, Victor and his brothers joined General Hugo in Spain, a land that fascinated Victor and left its mark on his poetic imagination.

In spite of their father's desire that they should study for entrance to the École Polytechnique, Victor and his next older brother, Eugène, spent their free time writing poetry, hoping to emulate their master, François-René de Chateaubriand. In 1817, Victor earned the first official recognition of his talent by winning an honorable mention in a poetry competition sponsored by the Académie Française. Because he was only fifteen, the secretary of the Académie asked to meet him, and the press displayed an interest in the young poet.

Eugène and Victor received permission from their father to study law in 1818 and left their boarding school to live with their mother in Paris. Sophie encouraged them in their ambition to become writers and never insisted that they attend lectures or study for examinations. Victor continued to receive recognition for his poems, and the brothers founded a review, *Le Conservateur littéraire*, in 1819. Unfortunately, the two brothers also shared a passion for the same young woman, Adèle Foucher. In love as well as in poetry, Eugène took second place to his younger brother. Adèle and Victor were betrothed after the death of Madame Hugo, who had opposed the marriage. The wedding took place in 1822. At the wedding feast, Eugène went insane; he spent nearly all the rest of his life in institutions.

Hugo's early publications were favorably received by the avant-garde of Romanticism, and by 1824, Hugo was a dominant personality in Charles Nodier's Cénacle, a group of Romantic poets united in their struggle against the rules of French classicism. The year 1824 also marked the birth of Léopoldine, the Hugos' second child and the first to survive infancy. She was always to have a special place in her father's heart. In 1827, the Hugos had another child, Charles.

The Hugos were acquainted with many of those writers and artists who are now considered major figures in the Romantic movement, among them Alexandre Dumas, *père*, Alfred de Vigny, and Eugène Delacroix. The sculptor David d'Angers recorded Hugo's youthful appearance on a medallion. (Decades later, sculptor Auguste Rodin would also preserve his impression of the aged poet.) The influential critic Charles-Augustin Sainte-Beuve also became a frequent visitor to the Hugos' apartment.

Momentum was building for the Romantic movement, and in December, 1827, Hugo published a play, *Cromwell* (English translation, 1896), the preface to which became the manifesto of the young Romantics. Two years later, his verse drama *Hernani* (pr., pb. 1830; English translation, 1830) would provide the battleground between Romanticism and classicism. In the meantime, General Hugo had died in 1828, and a son, François-Victor, had been born to Victor and Adèle.

The famous "battle of *Hernani*" at the work's premiere on January 10, 1830, was an outcry against outmoded conventions in every form of art. Artists sympathetic to Romanticism had been recruited from the Latin Quarter in support of Hugo's play, which breaks the rules of versification as well as the three unities of classical drama (time, place, and action). They engaged in a battle for modern artistic freedom against the "authorities" of the past. *Hernani* therefore had political significance as well: The restoration of the Bourbons was in its final months.

Stormy performances continued at the Théâtre-Français for several months, and, by the end, the tyranny of classicism had been demolished. In addition to artistic freedom for all, *Hernani* brought financial well-being to the Hugos. It also brought Sainte-Beuve increasingly into their family circle, where he kept Adèle company while Hugo was distracted by the *Hernani* affair.

In July of 1830, Victor and Adèle's last child, Adèle, came into the world to the sound of the shots of the July Revolution, which deposed Charles X, the last Bourbon "king of France." The new monarch was Louis-Philippe of the Orléans branch of the royal family, who called himself "king of the French." There was now a deep attachment between Madame Hugo and Sainte-Beuve. Although Adèle and Victor were never to separate, their marriage had become a platonic companionship.

In 1832, the Hugos moved to the Place Royale (now called the Place des Vosges), to the home that would later become the Victor Hugo museum in Paris. Scarcely a year passed without a publication by Hugo. By that time, he was able to command enormous sums for his work in comparison with other authors of his day. He was already becoming a legend, with disciples rather than friends. His ambition had always been fierce, and he was beginning to portray himself as a bard, a seer with powers to guide all France. Only in his family life was he suffering from less than complete success.

At the time, *Lucrèce Borgia* (pr., pb. 1833; *Lucretia Borgia*, 1842) was in rehearsal, and among the cast was a lovely young actor, Juliette Drouet. Soon after opening night, she and Hugo became lovers, and they remained so for many years. Juliette had not been a brilliant actor, but she abandoned what might have been a moderately successful career to live the rest of her life in seclusion and devotion to Hugo. In *Les Chants du crépuscule* (1835; *Songs of Twilight*, 1836), Hugo included thirteen poems to Juliette and three to Adèle, expressing the deep affection he still felt for his wife.

Critics were beginning to snipe at Hugo for what seemed to be shallow emotions and facile expressions. (Sainte-Beuve deplored Hugo's lack of taste, but Sainte-Beuve was hardly a disinterested critic.) The fashion for Hugo seemed to be somewhat on the wane, although adverse criticism did not inhibit the flow of his writing. The publication of *Les Rayons et les ombres* (1840) marked the end of one phase of Hugo's poetry. The splendor of the language and the music in his verse as well as the visual imagery were richer than ever, but Hugo was still criticized for lacking genuine emotion. He had by this time decided, however, to devote himself to his political ambitions.

He was determined to become a Peer of France, having been made an officer of the Légion d'Honneur several years before. In order to obtain a peerage, a man of letters had to be a member of the Académie Française. After presenting himself for the fifth time, he was elected to the Académie in 1841, and in the spring of 1845 he was named a Peer of France, a status that protected him from arrest the following summer, when police found him in flagrante delicto with the wife of Auguste Biard. Léonie Biard was sent to the Saint-Lazare prison, but Hugo's cordial relations with King Louis-Philippe helped calm the scandal, and Léonie retired to a convent for a short while before resuming her affair with Hugo.

An event of much deeper emotional impact had occurred in 1843, when Hugo's eldest daughter, Léopoldine, had married Charles Vacquerie. Hugo had found it difficult to be separated from his child, who went to live in Le Havre. That summer, in July, he paid a brief visit to the young couple before leaving on a journey with Juliette. In early September, while traveling, Hugo read in a newspaper that Léopoldine and Charles had been drowned in a boating accident several days before. Grief-stricken, Hugo was also beset by guilt at having left his family for a trip with his mistress. He published nothing more for nine years.

Eventually, the political events of 1848 eclipsed Hugo's complex relationship with his wife and two mistresses. During the Revolution of 1848, Louis-Philippe was forced to abdicate. The monarchy was rejected outright by the provisional government under the leadership of the Romantic poet Alphonse de Lamartine. The peerage was also abolished, and although Hugo sought political office, he was generally considered to be too dramatic and rhetorical to be of practical use in government. More than a few of his contemporary politicians viewed him as a self-interested opportunist. He seems to have longed for the glory of being a statesman without the necessary political sense.

On June 24, 1848, militant insurgents had occupied the Hugo apartment on the Place Royal. The family had fled, and Adèle had refused to live there again. One of the first visitors to their new apartment was Louis-Napoleon Bonaparte, nephew of Napoleon I. He was seeking Hugo's support of his candidacy for president of the new republic. Thereafter, Louis-Napoleon was endorsed in Hugo's newspaper, *L'Événement*, which he had founded that summer and which was edited and published by his sons.

Louis-Napoleon became president in December of 1848, but he did not long remain on good terms with Hugo. Hugo and *L'Événement* increasingly took leftist political positions as the new government was moving toward the Right. Freedom of the press was increasingly limited, and, in 1851, both of Hugo's sons were imprisoned for violating restrictions on the press and for showing disrespect to the government.

It was in this year that Juliette and Léonie attempted to force Hugo to choose between them. In the end, politics resolved the conflict. On December 2, 1851, Louis-Napoleon dissolved the National Assembly and declared himself prince-president for ten years. When Hugo learned of the coup d'état, he attempted to organize some resistance. There was shooting in the streets of Paris. Juliette is given credit for saving him from violence. She hid him successfully while a false passport was prepared, and on December 11, he took the train to Brussels in disguise and under a false name. Juliette followed him into exile.

From exile, the pen was Hugo's only political weapon, and he wrote *Napoléon le petit* (1852; *Napoleon the Little*, 1852) and *Histoire d'un crime* (1877; *The History of a Crime*, 1877-1878). Having been authorized to stay in Belgium for only three months, Hugo made plans to move to Jersey, one of the Channel Islands. His family joined him, and Juliette took rooms nearby. He began work on *Les Châtiments* (1853), poems inspired by anger and pride. France remained his preoccupation while he was in exile. Indeed, it has been said that exile renewed Hugo's career. Certainly, his fame suffered neither from his banishment nor from the tone of righteous indignation with which he could thus proclaim his contempt for the empire of Napoleon III.

There was a group of militant exiles on the island, and when, in 1855, they attacked Queen Victoria in their newspaper for visiting Napoleon III, Jersey officials informed them that they would have to leave. The Hugos moved to Guernsey, where they eventually purchased Hauteville House. At about the same time, in the spring of 1856, *Les Contemplations* was published, marking Hugo's reappearance as a lyric poet. Juliette moved to a nearby house that she called Hauteville-Féerie, where the lawn was inscribed with flowers forming a bright "V H." Although Hugo's prestige benefited immensely from his exile, his family suffered from their isolation, especially his daughter Adèle, who was in her early twenties. Eventually, she followed an army officer, Albert Pinson, to Canada, convinced that they would marry. After nine years of erratic, senseless wandering, she was brought home to end her life in a mental institution.

For her father, exile was a time to write. The first two volumes of *La Légende des siècles* (1859-1883; *The Legend of the Centuries*, 1894) was followed by *The Toilers of the Sea* and *The Man Who Laughs*, among other works. In 1859, Napoleon III offered amnesty of Republican exiles, but Hugo refused to accept it, preferring the grandeur of defiance and martyrdom on his rocky island.

After Adèle's flight, the island became intolerable for Madame Hugo. In 1865, she left for Brussels with the younger son, François-Victor, and spent most of her time there during the remainder of Hugo's exile. In his isolation, Hugo continued his work.

On the occasion of the Paris International Exposition in 1867, the imperial censors permitted a revival of *Hernani* at the Théâtre-Français. Adèle traveled to Paris to witness the great success of the play and the adulation of her husband. Another visitor to the Paris Exposition would be instrumental in ending Hugo's self-imposed banishment. Future German Chancellor Otto von Bismarck came to Paris ostensibly on a state visit from Prussia but secretly taking the measure of French armaments. Adèle died in Brussels the following year. Her sons accompanied her body to its grave in France; Hugo stopped at the French border and soon returned to Guernsey with Juliette.

One of Hugo's dreams had always been a United States of Europe, and in Lausanne in 1869, he presided over the congress of the International League for Peace and Freedom. Early in 1870, he was honored by the Second Empire with a revival of *Lucretia Borgia* and a recitation of his poetry before the emperor by Sarah Bernhardt. On July 14 of that year, the poet planted an acorn at Hauteville House. The future tree was dedicated to "the United States of Europe." By the following day, France and Prussia were at war.

The Franco-Prussian War brought an end to the Second Empire and to Hugo's nineteen years of exile. He returned in time to participate in the siege of Paris and to witness the cataclysmic events of the Commune. His own politics, however, although idealistically liberal and Republican, did not mesh with any political group in a practical way. He refused several minor offices that were offered to him by the new government and resigned after only a month as an elected deputy for Paris to the new National Assembly.

The following years were marked by family sorrows. Soon following Hugo's resignation from active politics, his elder son, Charles, died of an apoplectic stroke. Hugo was to remain devoted to his son's widow, Alice, and to his grandchildren, Jeanne and Georges. In 1872, Adèle was brought home from Barbados, insane. The following year, his younger son, François-Victor, died of tuberculosis. Only the faithful Juliette remained as a companion to Hugo in his old age.

He continued to write unceasingly in Paris, but in 1878 he suffered a stroke. This virtually brought his writing to an end, although works he had written earlier continued to be published. On his birthday in 1881, the Republic organized elaborate festivities in his honor, including a procession of admirers who passed beneath his window for hours. In May, the main part of the avenue d'Eylau was rechristened the avenue Victor-Hugo.

Juliette died in May of 1883. On his birthday in 1885, Hugo received tributes from all quarters as a venerated symbol of the French spirit. He became seriously ill in May, suffering from a lesion of the heart and congestion of the lungs. He died on May 22, 1885. Hugo's funeral was a national ceremony, the coffin lying in state beneath the Arc de Triomphe. He was the only Frenchman to be so honored before the Unknown Soldier after World War I. While Napoleon III lay buried in exile, the remains of Victor Hugo were ceremoniously interred in the Panthéon, France's shrine to her great men of letters.

Analysis

The earliest published full-length fiction by Victor Hugo was *Hans of Iceland*, begun when he was eighteen years old, although not published until three years later. In part a tribute to Adèle Foucher, who was to become his wife, it is a convoluted gothic romance in which it is not clear where the author is being serious and where he is deliberately creating a parody of the popular gothic genre. It is worthwhile to begin with this youthful work, however, because it contains many themes and images that were to remain important in Hugo's work throughout his life.

HANS OF ICELAND

The characters in *Hans of Iceland* are archetypes rather than psychologically realistic figures. In a sense, it is unfair to criticize Hugo for a lack of complexity in his characterizations, because he is a creator of myths and legends—his genius does not lie in the realm of the realistic novel. This is the reason his talent as a novelist is eclipsed by the other great novelists of his century, Stendhal, Honoré de Balzac, Gustave Flaubert, and Émile Zola. Hugo's last novels were written after Flaubert's *Madame Bovary* (1857; English translation, 1886) and after Zola's first naturalistic novels, yet Hugo's late books remain closer in tone to *Hans of Iceland* than to any contemporary novel.

It is thus more useful to consider *Hans of Iceland* as a romance, following the patterns of myths and legends, rather than as a novel with claims to psychological and historical realism. Although tenuously based on historical fact, set in seventeenth century Norway, the plot of *Hans of Iceland* closely resembles that of the traditional quest. The hero, Ordener Guldenlew (Golden Lion), disguises his noble birth and sets out to rescue his beloved, the pure maiden Ethel, from the evil forces that imprison her with her father, Jean Schumaker, Count Griffenfeld. Ordener's adventures take him through dark and fearsome settings where he must overcome the monster Hans of Iceland, a mysterious being who, although a man, possesses demoniac powers and beastly desires.

As in traditional romance, the characters in *Hans of Iceland* are all good or evil, like black and white pieces in a chess game. Ethel's father is the good former grand chancellor who has been imprisoned for some years after having been unjustly accused of treason. His counterpart is the wicked Count d'Ahlefeld, who, with the treacherous countess, is responsible for Schumaker's downfall. Their son Frédéric is Ordener's rival for Ethel's love. The most treacherous villain is the count's adviser, Musdoemon, who turns out to be Frédéric's real father. Opposed to everyone, good or evil, is the man-demon Hans of Iceland, who haunts the land by dark of night, leaving the marks of his clawlike nails on his victims.

Ordener's quest begins in the morgue, where he seeks a box that had been in the possession of a military officer killed by Hans. The box contains documents proving Schumaker's innocence. Believing it to be in Hans's possession, Ordener sets off through storms and danger to recover the box.

As the adventure progresses, Hugo begins to reveal his personal preoccupations and thus to depart from the traditional romance. Hans's ambiguous nature, grotesque as he is, has some unsettling sympathetic qualities. One begins to feel, as the story progresses and as the social villains become more devious and nefarious, that Hans, the social outcast, is morally superior in spite of his diabolically glowing eyes and his tendency to crunch human bones. Hugo appears to suggest the Romantic noble savage beneath a diabolic exterior. Because Ordener is a strangely passive hero, who fails to slay Hans or even to find the box, the reader's interest is transferred to Hans. In this monster with redeeming human qualities, it is not difficult to see the prefiguration of later grotesques such as Quasimodo in *The Hunchback of Notre Dame*.

The social commentary that is constant in Hugo's narratives has its beginning here in the figure of Musdoemon, the true evil figure of the work. This adviser to the aristocracy, whose name reveals that he has the soul of a rat, betrays everyone until he is at last himself betrayed and hanged. The executioner turns out to be his brother, delighted to have revenge for Musdoemon's treachery toward him years before.

At one point, Musdoemon tricks a group of miners (the good common people) into rebelling against the king in Schumaker's name. Ordener finds himself in the midst of the angry mob as they battle the king's troops. Hans attacks both sides, increasing the confusion and slaughter. Later, at the trial of the rebels on charges of treason, Ordener takes full responsibility, thus diverting blame from Schumaker. Given the choice of execution or marriage to the daughter of the wicked d'Ahlefeld, he chooses death. He and Ethel are married in his cell and are saved by the chance discovery of the documents. Hans gives himself up and dies by his own hand.

By comparing *Hans of Iceland* with another early novel, *The Noble Rival*, the reader can trace the preoccupations that led to *The Hunchback of Notre Dame* and *Les Misérables*. *The Noble Rival* is the story of a slave revolt in Santo Domingo, Dominican Republic. The hero of the title is a slave as well as the spiritually noble leader of his people. The Romantic hero is Léopold, a Frenchman visiting his uncle's plantation. Like Ordener, Léopold is pure but essentially passive. The heroic energy belongs to the outcast from society, Bug-Jargal. In both novels, Hugo's sympathy for the "people" is apparent. The miners and the slaves point directly to the commoners of Paris in *The Hunchback of Notre Dame*.

THE HUNCHBACK OF NOTRE DAME

At the center of *The Hunchback of Notre Dame* is the theme of fatality, a word that the author imagines to have been inscribed on the wall of one of the cathedral towers as the Greek *anankè*. The cathedral is the focus of the novel, as it was the heart of medieval Paris. It is a spiritual center with an ambiguous demoniac-grotesque spirit within. Claude Frollo, the priest, is consumed by lust for a Gypsy girl, Esmeralda. Quasimodo, the bell ringer, a hunchback frighteningly deformed, is elevated by his pure love for Esmeralda, whom he attempts to save from the pernicious Frollo. In an image central to the novel and to Hugo's entire work, Frollo watches a spider and a fly caught in its web. The web, however, stretches across a pane of glass so that even if the fly should manage to escape, it will only hurl itself against the invisible barrier in its flight toward the sun. The priest will be the spider to Esmeralda but also the fly, caught in the trap of his own consuming desire. All the characters risk entrapment in the web prepared for them by fate. Even if they somehow break free of the web, the glass will block escape until death releases them from earthly concerns.

Esmeralda believes she can "fly to the sun" in the person of the handsome military captain Phoebus, but he is interested in her only in an earthly way. Frollo's destructive passion leads him to set a trap for Esmeralda. For a fee, Phoebus agrees to hide Frollo where he can watch a rendezvous between Phoebus and Esmeralda. Unable to contain himself, the priest leaves his hiding place, stabs Phoebus, and leaves. Esmeralda is, of course, accused of the crime.

Quasimodo saves her from execution and gives her sanctuary in the cathedral, but she is betrayed again by Frollo, who orders her to choose between him and the gallows. Like the fly, Esmeralda tears herself away from the priest to collapse at the foot of the gibbet. Phoebus, who did not die of his wound, remains indifferent to her plight, but Quasimodo pushes Frollo to his death from the tower of Notre Dame as the priest gloats over Esmeralda's execution. Quasimodo, the grotesque, gains in moral stature throughout the novel, just as Frollo falls from grace. Two years later, a deformed skeleton is found in a burial vault beside that of the virtuous Esmeralda.

The Hunchback of Notre Dame and *Les Misérables* are justly Hugo's most famous novels because they combine the exposition of his social ideas with an aesthetically unified structure. By contrast, *The Last Day of a Condemned*, written in 1829, is basically a social treatise on the horrors of prison life. In the same way, *Claude Gueux*, a short work of 1834, protests against the death penalty. In both works, the writer speaks out against society's injustice to man, but it was with *Les Misérables* that the reformer's voice spoke most effectively.

LES MISÉRABLES

Les Misérables tells of the spiritual journey of Jean Valjean, a poor but honorable man, driven in desperation to steal a loaf of bread to feed his widowed sister and her children. Sent to prison, he becomes an embittered, morally deformed creature, until he is redeemed by his love for the orphan girl Cosette. The plot of the novel is quite complex, as Jean rises to respectability and descends again several times. This is true because, as a convict, he must live under an assumed name. His spiritual voyage will not end until he can stand once more as Jean Valjean. His name suggests the French verb *valoir*, "to be worth." Jean must become worthy of Jean; he cannot have value under a counterfeit name.

His first reappearance as a respectable bourgeois is as Monsieur Madeleine, Mayor of Montreuil-sur-Mer. He is soon called upon, however, to reveal his true identity in order to save another from life imprisonment for having been identified as Jean Valjean, parole breaker. He descends into society's underworld, eluding capture by his nemesis, the policeman Javert. In Hugo's works, the way down is always the way up to salvation. Just as Ordener descended into the mines, Jean must now pass through a valley (*Val*) in order to save Jean. Here, as in *The Hunchback of Notre Dame*, moral superiority is to be found among the lowly.

In order to save himself, Jean must be the savior of others. He begins by rescuing Cosette from her wicked foster parents. Later, he will save Javert from insurrectionists. His greatest test, however, will be that of saving Marius, the man Cosette loves and who will separate Jean from the girl who is his paradise. This episode is the famous flight through the sewers of Paris, a true descent into the underworld, whence Jean Valjean is reborn, his soul transfigured, clear, and serene. He still has one more trial to endure, that of regaining his own name, which, through a misunderstanding, brings a painful estrangement from Cosette and Marius. He begins to die but is reconciled with his children at the last moment and leaves this life with a soul radiantly transformed.

THE TOILERS OF THE SEA

Les Misérables was written partly in exile, and certain episodes begin to show a preference for images of water. *The Toilers of the Sea*, written on Guernsey in 1864 and 1865, is a novel dominated by the sea. The text originally included an introductory section titled "L'Archipel de la Manche" ("The Archipelago of the English Channel"), which Hugo's editor persuaded him to publish separately at a later date (1883). The two parts reveal that Hugo has separated sociology from fiction. It would seem that, at odds with the predominant novelistic style of his time, Hugo preferred not to communicate his social philosophy through the imagery and structure of his novels. Thus, the prologue contains Hugo's doctrine of social progress and his analysis of the geology, customs, and language of the Channel Islands. The larger section that became the published novel is once again the story of a solitary quest.

The hero, Gilliatt, is a fisherman who lives a simple, rather ordinary life with his elderly mother on the island of Guernsey. In their house, they keep a marriage chest containing a trousseau for Gilliatt's future bride. Gilliatt loves Déruchette, niece of Mess Lethierry, inventor of the steamboat *Durande*, with which he has made his fortune in commerce. When the villain, Clubin, steals Lethierry's money and wrecks his steamer, Gilliatt's adventures begin.

Like the king of myth or legend, Lethierry offers his niece's hand in marriage to whomever can salvage the *Durande*. Gilliatt sets out upon the sea. Ominously missing are the magical beasts or mysterious beings who normally appear to assist the hero as he sets off. Even Ordener, for example, had a guide, Benignus Spiagudry, at the beginning of his quest. It is entirely unaided that Gilliatt leaves shore.

He now faces nature and the unknown, completely cut off from human society. He survives a titanic struggle for the ship against the hurricane forces of nature, but he must still descend into an underwater grotto, where he is seized by a hideous octopus. Gilliatt is, in

Hugo's words, "the fly of that spider." The language of the passage makes it clear that in freeing himself from the octopus, Gilliatt frees himself from evil.

Exhausted, Gilliatt prays, then sleeps. When he wakes, the sea is calm. He returns to land a savior, bringing the engine of the ship as well as the stolen money. When he learns that Déruchette wishes to marry another, he gives her his own marriage chest and leaves to die in the rising tide. *The Toilers of the Sea* is considered by many to be the finest and purest expression of Hugo's mythic vision.

THE MAN WHO LAUGHS

Almost immediately after *The Toilers of the Sea*, Hugo turned his attention back to history. In 1866, he began work on the first novel of what he intended to be a trilogy focusing in turn on aristocracy, monarchy, and democracy. The first, *The Man Who Laughs*, is set in England after 1688; the second would have taken place in prerevolutionary France; and the third is *Ninety-three*, a vision of France after 1789. The role of fate is diminished in these last two novels because Hugo wished to emphasize man's conscience and free will in a social and political context.

In *The Man Who Laughs*, the disfigured hero, Gwynplaine, chooses to leave his humble earthly paradise when he learns that he had been born to the aristocracy. Predictably, the way up leads to Gwynplaine's downfall. Noble society is a hellish labyrinth (another type of web) from which Gwynplaine barely manages to escape. A wolf named Homo helps him find his lost love again, a blind girl named Déa. When she dies, Gwynplaine finds salvation by letting himself sink beneath the water of the Thames.

NINETY-THREE

Hugo's vivid portrayal of a demoniac aristocratic society justified the cause of the French Revolution in 1789, preparing the way for his vision of an egalitarian future as described in his last novel, *Ninety-three*. By choosing to write about 1793 instead of the fall of the Bastille, Hugo was attempting to deal with the Terror, which he considered to have deformed the original ideals of the Revolution.

Rather than the familiar love interest, Hugo places the characters Michelle Fléchard and her three children at the center of the novel. In Hugo's works, kindness to children can redeem almost any amount of wickedness. The monstrous Hans of Iceland, for example, is partially excused because he was avenging the death of his son. It is therefore not surprising to find in *Ninety-three* that each faction in the Revolution is tested and judged according to its treatment of Michelle and her children.

The extreme positions in the violent political clash are represented by the Marquis de Lantenac, the Royalist leader, and his counterpart, Cimourdain, a former priest and fanatic revolutionary. Both men are inflexible and coldly logical in their courageous devotion to their beliefs. The violent excesses of both sides are depicted as demoniac no matter how noble the cause. Human charity and benign moderation are represented in Gauvain, a general in the revolutionary army. He is Lantenac's nephew and the former pupil of Cimourdain. He is clearly also the spokesman for Hugo's point of view.

In the course of events, Lantenac redeems his inhumanity by rescuing Michelle's children from a burning tower. He is now Gauvain's prisoner and should be sent to the guillotine. Gauvain's humanity, however, responds to Lantenac's act of self-sacrifice, and Gauvain arranges for him to escape. It is now Cimourdain's turn, but he remains loyal to his principles, condemning to death his beloved disciple. Before his execution, Gauvain expounds his (Hugo's) idealistic social philosophy in a dialogue with Cimourdin's pragmatic view of a disciplined society based on strict justice.

In this final novel, Hugo's desire to express his visionary ideology overwhelms his talents as a novelist. At the age of seventy, he had become the prophet of a transfigured social order of the future. He would create no more of his compelling fictional worlds. It was time for Hugo the creator of legends to assume the legendary stature of his final decade.

Jan St. Martin

OTHER MAJOR WORKS

PLAYS: *Cromwell*, pb. 1827 (verse drama; English translation, 1896); *Amy Robsart*, pr. 1828 (English translation, 1895); *Hernani*, pr., pb. 1830 (verse drama; English translation, 1830); *Marion de Lorme*, pr., pb. 1831 (verse drama; English translation, 1895); *Le Roi s'amuse*, pr., pb. 1832 (verse drama; *The King's Fool*, 1842; also known as *The King Amuses Himself*, 1964); *Lucrèce Borgia*, pr., pb. 1833 (*Lucretia Borgia*, 1842); *Marie Tudor*, pr., pb. 1833 (English translation, 1895); *Angelo, tyran de Padoue*, pr., pb. 1835 (*Angelo, Tyrant of Padua*, 1880); *Ruy Blas*, pr., pb. 1838 (verse drama; English translation, 1890); *Les Burgraves*, pr., pb. 1843 (*The Burgraves*, 1896); *Inez de Castro*, pb. 1863 (wr. c. 1818; verse drama); *La Grand-mère*, pb. 1865; *Mille Francs de Recompense*, pb. 1866; *Les Deux Trouvailles de Gallus*, pb. 1881; *Torquemada*, pb. 1882 (wr. 1869; English translation, 1896); *Théâtre en liberté*, pb. 1886 (includes *Mangeront-ils?*); *The Dramatic Works*, 1887; *The Dramatic Works of Victor Hugo*, 1895-1896 (4 volumes); *Irtamène*, pb. 1934 (wr. 1816; verse drama).

POETRY: *Odes et poésies diverses*, 1822, 1823; *Nouvelles Odes*, 1824; *Odes et ballades*, 1826; *Les Orientales*, 1829 (*Les Orientales: Or, Eastern Lyrics*, 1879); *Les Feuilles d'automne*, 1831; *Les Chants du crépuscule*, 1835 (*Songs of Twilight*, 1836); *Les Voix intérieures*, 1837; *Les Rayons et les ombres*, 1840; *Les Châtiments*, 1853; *Les Contemplations*, 1856; *La Légende des siècles*, 1859-1883 (5 volumes; *The Legend of the Centuries*, 1894); *Les Chansons des rues et des bois*, 1865; *L'Année terrible*, 1872; *L'Art d'être grand-père*, 1877; *Le Pape*, 1878; *La Pitié suprême*, 1879; *L'Âne*, 1880; *Les Quatre vents de l'esprit*, 1881; *The Literary Life and Poetical Works of Victor Hugo*, 1883; *La Fin de Satan*, 1886; *Toute la lyre*, 1888; *Dieu*, 1891; *Les Années funestes*, 1896; *Poems from Victor Hugo*, 1901; *Dernière Gerbe*, 1902; *Poems*, 1902; *The Poems of Victor Hugo*, 1906; *Océan*, 1942.

NONFICTION: *La Préface de Cromwell*, 1827 (English translation, 1896); *Littérature et philosophie mêlées*, 1834; *Le Rhin*, 1842 (*The Rhine*, 1843); *Napoléon le petit*, 1852 (*Napoleon the Little*, 1852); *William Shakespeare*, 1864 (English translation, 1864); *Actes et paroles*, 1875-1876; *Histoire d'un crime*, 1877 (*The History of a Crime*, 1877-1878); *Religions et religion*, 1880; *Le Théâtre en liberté*, 1886; *Choses vues*, 1887 (*Things Seen*, 1887); *En voyage: Alpes et Pyrénées*, 1890 (*The Alps and Pyrenees*, 1898); *France et Belgique*, 1892; *Correspondance*, 1896-1898.

MISCELLANEOUS: *Œuvres complètes*, 1880-1892 (57 volumes); *Victor Hugo's Works*, 1892 (30 volumes); *Works*, 1907 (10 volumes).

BIBLIOGRAPHY

Bloom, Harold, ed. *Victor Hugo*. New York: Chelsea House, 1988. Collection of twelve essays discusses all aspects of Hugo's career. Two essays are devoted to analysis of *Les Misérables*. Includes introduction, chronology, and bibliography.

Brombert, Victor. *Victor Hugo and the Visionary Novel*. Cambridge, Mass.: Harvard University Press, 1984. Study by one of the most distinguished scholars of modern French literature includes an especially informative chapter on *Les Misérables*. Provides detailed notes and bibliography.

Frey, John Andrew. *A Victor Hugo Encyclopedia*. Westport, Conn.: Greenwood Press, 1999. Comprehensive guide to the works of Hugo includes introductory and biographical material. Addresses Hugo as a leading poet, novelist, artist, and religious and revolutionary thinker of France. The balance of the volume contains alphabetically arranged entries discussing his works, characters, and themes as well as relevant historical persons and places. Includes a general bibliography.

Grossman, Kathryn M. *"Les Misérables": Conversion, Revolution, Redemption*. New York: Twayne, 1996. Examination of the novel, aimed at students and general readers, recounts the historical events leading up to the novel's publication, discusses the importance of the book, describes how Hugo's political and philosophical ideas are expressed in the work, and analyzes the character of protagonist Jean Valjean. Includes bibliographical references and index.

Maurois, André. *Olympio: The Life of Victor Hugo*. Translated by Gerard Hopkins. New York: Harper & Row, 1956. This work, originally published in French in 1954, is probably as close an approach as possible to an ideal one-volume biography dealing with both the life and the work of a monumental figure such as Hugo. Of the sparse illustrations, several are superb; the bibliography, principally of sources in French, provides a sense of Hugo's celebrity and influence, which persisted well into the twentieth century.

_____. *Victor Hugo and His World*. London: Thames and Hudson, 1966. The 1956 English translation of Maurois's text noted above was edited to conform to the format of a series of illustrated books. The result is interesting and intelligible, but rather schematic. In compensation for the vast cuts in text, a chronology and dozens of well-annotated illustrations have been added.

Porter, Laurence M. *Victor Hugo*. New York: Twayne, 1999. Study of Hugo and his works provides a biography, separate chapters analyzing *The Hunchback of Notre Dame* and *Les Misérables*, and discussions of Hugo's plays and poetry. Includes bibliography and index.

Raser, Timothy. *The Simplest of Signs: Victor Hugo and the Language of Images in France, 1850-1950*. Newark: University of Delaware Press, 2004. Analyzes the relationship of Hugo's works to French architecture and other visual arts, examining how Hugo used language to describe time, place, and visual details, his aesthetics and politics, and the language and methods of French art criticism.

Richardson, Joanna. *Victor Hugo*. New York: St. Martin's Press, 1976. Well-written, scholarly biography of Hugo is divided into three sections: "The Man," "The Prophet," and "The Legend." Includes detailed notes, extensive bibliography, and index.

Robb, Graham. *Victor Hugo*. New York: W. W. Norton, 1998. Thorough biography reveals many previously unknown aspects of Hugo's long life and literary career. Robb's introduction discusses earlier biographies. Includes detailed notes and bibliography.

Vargas Llosa, Mario. *The Temptation of the Impossible: Victor Hugo and "Les Misérables."* Princeton, N.J.: Princeton University Press, 2007. Provides a fascinating look at Hugo's writing of *Les Misérables*, including an examination of the work's structure and narration. Includes comparisons to modern novels and critics' reactions to the novel in Hugo's day.

MARCEL PROUST

Born: Auteuil, France; July 10, 1871
Died: Paris, France; November 18, 1922
Also known as: Valentin Louis Georges Eugène Marcel Proust

PRINCIPAL LONG FICTION

Du côté de chez Swann, 1913 (*Swann's Way*, 1922)
À l'ombre des jeunes filles en fleurs, 1919 (*Within a Budding Grove*, 1924)
Le Côté de Guermantes, 1920-1921 (*The Guermantes Way*, 1925)
Sodome et Gomorrhe, 1922 (*Cities of the Plain*, 1927)
Albertine disparue, 1925 (*The Sweet Cheat Gone*, 1930)
La Prisonnière, 1925 (*The Captive*, 1929)
Le Temps retrouvé, 1927 (*Time Regained*, 1931)
À la recherche du temps perdu, 1913-1927 (collective title for all of the above; *Remembrance of Things Past*, 1922-1931, 1981)
Jean Santeuil, 1952 (English translation, 1955)

OTHER LITERARY FORMS

In addition to his magnum opus, *Remembrance of Things Past*, Marcel Proust (prewst) wrote a number of less well-known works. His first book, *Les Plaisirs et les jours* (1896; *Pleasures and Regrets*, 1948), a collection of stories and some verse, was published in 1896. Its primary value lies in its preliminary statement of themes that are developed more fully in *Remembrance of Things Past*, as Edmund Wilson has pointed out.

Proust's fascination with John Ruskin led to prefaces for and translations of Ruskin's *The Bible of Amiens* (1880-1885) in 1904 and of his *Sesame and Lilies* (1865) in 1906. Before turning his full attention to the novel, Proust also wrote a series of parodies of his favorite French writers, which were published in *Le Figaro*. Of considerable interest to Proust scholars is *Contre Sainte-Beuve* (*By Way of Sainte-Beuve*, 1958), written in 1908 but not published until 1954. In it, Proust uses a variety of essays, autobiographical pieces, and fiction to attack criticism that claims to be scientific and objective. Proust argues instead that only memory and the unconscious can break through the barriers of habit that impede art. Of somewhat less interest is *Pastiches et mélanges*, a volume of miscellaneous pieces published in 1919. Proust's brother, Robert, collected magazine and newspaper articles written by Proust as late as 1921 and published them in *Chroniques* (1927).

ACHIEVEMENTS

Marcel Proust's monumental achievement in writing *Remembrance of Things Past* consists not simply in the work's multivolume length or the complexity of the extended and intermingled lives of its characters, although these elements alone are impressive. It is

Marcel Proust
(Library of Congress)

above all the intense psychological realism with which the novel's characters—particularly the author's alter ego, Marcel—are rendered that has influenced other writers and has drawn critical acclaim. That "realism" is internal: Proust was fascinated by the interplay between external events and the mind, especially by the way human perception synthesizes and interprets events in time—by "the symbolic omnitemporality of an event fixed in a remembering consciousness," as Erich Auerbach put it. These concerns are reflected in much of twentieth century literature—notably in the works of James Joyce, Thomas Mann, and Virginia Woolf—and Proust may be said to have introduced their full exposition in his magnum opus.

Although, at the beginning of his writing career, Proust received little recognition outside his literary milieu, he was awarded the Prix Goncourt in 1919 for *Within a Budding Grove*. This recognition helped establish him as a serious and significant author, and since his death, his reputation and influence have continued to grow.

Biography

Marcel Proust was born in Auteuil, a suburb of Paris, on July 10, 1871. He was the son of the happily married Dr. Adrien Proust and Jeanne Weil. Adrien Proust had left the devoutly Catholic home of his candlemaker father in Illiers to go to Paris, where he ultimately found acclaim as a professor and hygienist. Adrien's family returned to Illiers, the "Combray" of *Remembrance of Things Past*, for frequent holidays. The home there of Adrien's sister, Elisabeth, became the model for the famous house and garden of Marcel's Aunt Léonie. Marcel's mother was the daughter of a wealthy Jewish family from Lorraine. Although Marcel was baptized a Catholic, he remained close to his mother's family throughout his life. His novels reveal little interest in religion other than aesthetic pleasure in church architecture, and Proust practiced no religion during his adult life.

From his birth, Proust was plagued by ill health; indeed, his parents feared he would die shortly after his birth. In spite of careful attention given to his well-being, he suffered a severe attack of asthma at the age of nine. Such frailty doubtless contributed to his acute sensitivity. While both his father and younger brother, Robert (later also a doctor), were committed to science, duty, and routine, Marcel and his mother were of a more emotional, artistic, and intellectual sensibility.

Poor health did not restrict Proust's movement entirely. He attended the Lycée Condorcet, and during his years there (1882-1889), he played in the gardens of the Champs-Elysées, where he fell in love with Marie de Banardaky. Although he had numerous friendships at school, even at that early age he found pleasure in the solitary task of writing. That did not, however, prevent him from attending the salons of his classmates' mothers. At the age of seventeen, Proust had already entered the world of Parisian society that he would depict so brilliantly in *Remembrance of Things Past*.

After receiving his *baccalauréat* in 1889, Proust volunteered for his one year of military duty. It was one of the happiest, most "normal" years of his life. He became friends with Gaston Arman de Caillavet, one of the models for Robert de Saint-Loup. On his return to Paris, he studied at the Sorbonne and at the École des Sciences Politiques, where he was deeply influenced by the lectures of the French philosopher Henri Bergson. In spite of his father's wish that he enter diplomatic service, Proust found himself more attracted to the worlds of society and literature. He became a favorite in the salons of both the haute bourgeoisie and the nobility. At the salon of Madame Arman de Caillavet, he met Anatole France, a meeting that provided the model in part for Bergotte. Although women such as the Comtesse Greffulhe and Princess Mathilde provided invaluable opportunities for Proust to observe the mannerisms and style of the pinnacle of Parisian society, it was perhaps the salon of Madame Straus, widow of Georges Bizet and mother of Marcel's Condorcet friend, Jacques, that was most influential in Proust's development. Madame Straus was noted for her beauty and wit, and along with the Comtesse de Chevigné, she contributed significantly to the characterization of the chief denizen of Proust's fictional Parisian suburb Faubourg Saint-Germain, Madame de Guermantes.

In his mid-twenties, Proust gradually withdrew from the brilliant world he had both participated in and observed so carefully. From an early age he had felt that artistic endeavor and social life were largely incompatible; he may also have grown disillusioned with the vanities of high society.

During these early years of maturity, Proust developed intense platonic relationships with both men and women. His sexual interest was primarily in men. Among his earliest affairs was one with Reynaldo Hahn, a composer. It was Comte Robert de Montesquieu, however, who served as chief model for Proust's greatest gay character, the Baron de Charlus. Perhaps Proust's most compelling involvement was with Alfred Agostinelli, who served as his chauffeur and secretary. Agostinelli, who enrolled in aviation school under the name Marcel Swann, drowned as the result of an airplane crash off the French coast in 1914. It has been suggested frequently that Proust's tortured experience with Agostinelli was the inspiration for the characterization of Albertine.

Proust's father died in 1903, and his mother's death in 1905 left Proust utterly grief-stricken. Within a year after his mother's death, he began an early version of *Remembrance of Things Past*. In the remaining years of that decade, he wrote widely, penning parodies, some fiction, and essays in criticism. In January, 1909, Proust returned on a snowy evening to the warmth of his kitchen for a cup of tea and dry toast; while idly savoring the humble repast, he involuntarily recalled precious childhood memories. The significance of spontaneous memory as a condition for art struck Proust, providing the missing link in his theory of literature. This revelation was to shape his writing of *Remembrance of Things Past* as he labored in his cork-lined Paris apartment.

Proust was physically unfit to serve during World War I, although the suffering of France affected him deeply. During the war, his life was more solitary than ever before, although he dined so frequently at a famous Paris hotel that he became known as Marcel of the Ritz. Thus, the image of the dandy, the snob, the fop followed Proust throughout most of his life. Nevertheless, he had a huge coterie of loyal friends and servants and a reputation for courage (he once fought a duel with a libelous critic) and generosity. Before his death from asthma in 1922, he not only had been awarded the Prix Goncourt but also had received the recognition of his contemporaries as a genius.

Analysis

Like Gustave Flaubert, Marcel Proust believed that of all literary forms, the novel most fully reveals the temperament of its writer. As George Painter's exhaustive biography of Proust demonstrates, there are innumerable, indeed seemingly endless, parallels between the lives of Marcel Proust and Marcel, the narrator of *Remembrance of Things Past*.

Remembrance of Things Past

While the novel reveals much of Proust's character and values, it is not an autobiography but a work of fiction in which the raw materials of personal experience and remembrance are transformed by the imagination into art of the highest order. Rather than yield to the temptation of a biographical reading of the novel, it is perhaps more profitable to concentrate on the development of the themes and to note the techniques that Proust employs to create his vision of humankind in their emotional, moral, and aesthetic worlds.

Like Dante and Honoré de Balzac before him, Proust creates a vast and teeming world, depicting the immense social changes that took place in French life between the end of the Franco-Prussian War in 1871 and the post-World War I era. While *Remembrance of Things Past* focuses on the wealthy bourgeois and nobility of Paris, it by no means excludes other classes. The detailed and sympathetic characterizations of Jupien the tailor, Françoise, and Aimé, the headwaiter at the Grand Hotel, testify to the social range of the novel. Given the work's considerable time span and its scope of social inquiry, it is not surprising that Proust is able to develop a variety of themes: the Dreyfus affair, homosexuality, the difficulties of love, the growth of the artist, the vanity of society, and so on. By doing this, Proust invests the worlds of Paris, Combray, and Balbec with solidity and seriousness. Each thematic concern is ultimately registered on the growing consciousness of the protagonist, Marcel; all themes are subordinated to the dominant thematic concern of the novel: Marcel's attempt to overcome the disappointments of love, the false social expectations and the faulty imaginings and appearances that separate him from reality. With the aid of memory, prompted involuntarily by physical stimuli, Marcel ultimately defeats time, and through art, he finds the joy that has eluded him in love and social life. It is difficult, therefore, to understand Wilson's characterization of the novel as "the gloomiest book ever written"; while Proust's world is obviously complex and borders on the tragic, the existence in it of a sensuous and moral art belies the charge of pessimism.

The need to give structure and unity to a work as thematically ambitious as *Remembrance of Things Past* was a major challenge for Proust. While Wilson may have been off the mark thematically, his observation that the novel's structure is symphonic, a series of shifting images with "multiplied associations," is accurate. In so describing Proust, Wilson, like other critics, emphasized Proust's debt to Symbolism specifically and Romanticism generally. Proust's appreciation of introspection, his attentiveness to and enthusiasm for the natural world, his awareness of the power of the subjective and unconscious, and his use of image as symbol—all are variations on themes and techniques developed by nineteenth century French Romantics. Proust's affinity with the Symbolists was reinforced by his appreciation of the metaphysics of Henri Bergson, who was one of Proust's professors and a cousin by marriage. Although Proust denied any debt to Bergson, he, like Bergson, appreciated the role of intuition as a source of knowledge. Bergson also believed, as Wallace Fowlie has pointed out in his book *A Reading of Proust* (1964), that the capacity of an object to stimulate the memory lies in the individual himself, not in the object. By embracing the Symbolists and Bergson, Proust aligned himself clearly with those who resisted a purely scientific interpretation of reality.

Proust employs a variety of specific means to give shape to his world. Most important, perhaps, is the organization of *Remembrance of Things Past* into three major quests undertaken by the protagonist, Marcel. The first is the quest for love, a search that prompts much subjective analysis by the protagonist. In contrast, the second quest, Marcel's emergence into society, draws upon Proust's brilliant and often comic observations of both manners and morals. The quest for love begins with young Marcel's desperate desire for a goodnight kiss from his mother, a desire frustrated by Swann's call on his parents. Marcel's subsequent infatuations with Gilberte, the Duchess de Guermantes, and Albertine are paralleled by other, equally vain quests for love by Swann for Odette, Robert de Saint-Loup for Rachel, and Baron de Charlus for Morel. The quest for love is symbolized in part by Swann's Way, one of the two paths that leads young Marcel and his family from their home in Combray to the outside world. The other road, the Guermantes Way, symbolizes the quest for society that leads Marcel from the secure world of family, servants, and neighbors in Combray to the drawing room of Odette Swann and, later, to a higher echelon of society symbolized by the salon of the slightly déclassé "bluestocking" Madame de Villeparisis. From there, Marcel finds his way into the much sought-after world of the Duke and Duchess de Guermantes and ultimately to the most socially exalted milieu of all, the soirees given by Prince and Princess de Guermantes.

In the same way that Swann's Way and Guermantes Way are finally united when Swann's daughter marries a Guermantes, these two quests, one private, one public, come together in mutual disillusionment. What saves the novel from utter despair is the persistence of those things that are not defeated by time and human vanity: Marcel's memories of his grandmother's selflessness and love, his involuntary recollection of sensations that produced great happiness, his realization of the eternity that lies within art. Thus, failure in the first two quests allows for success in the third: Marcel's pursuit of a career as an artist. The quest for art, initially overshadowed by love and society, is hinted at, however, by the presence in the novel of three artists who, in spite of their foibles and miseries, have created enduring works of art: the novelist Bergotte, the painter Elstir, and the composer Vinteuil. Indeed, although the emphasis shifts from book to book, all three quests figure in each of the seven novels that together make up *Remembrance of Things Past*.

SWANN'S WAY

Swann's Way, the chronicle of Marcel's childhood, begins and ends with memories of the protagonist, the mature Marcel. The first memory, recounted in a section called "Overture," is preceded by a description of the disorientation and pleasure that come from awakening in a darkened room at night. This sensation is one that Marcel has learned to relish, because it leads him to recall other rooms, particularly those of Combray, his childhood home. Marcel recalls the particular evening when Swann called on his family. Wealthy, Jewish, suave, and sophisticated, Swann visits Marcel's family frequently when he is home from Paris. Swann's visit upsets Marcel because it interrupts the ritual of his mother's nightly kiss. In his room, young Marcel grows so desperate that he sends Françoise, the cook, to deliver a note to his mother. His mother does not come until Swann leaves, but Marcel's stern father suggests unexpectedly that she sleep in Marcel's room to comfort him. The triumph of Marcel, touching yet disturbing in its power to manipulate, proves to be paradoxical. Even though he possesses his mother's attention, Marcel senses that such happiness, such a moment of unexpected success, is fleeting. "I knew that such a night could not be repeated." One function of this incident is clear: Marcel's quest for love has a most ambiguous beginning.

Immediately following the famous scene of the mother's kiss, Proust draws a crucial distinction between two types of memory. The first is voluntary, or recollection associated with intellect, "an exercise of the will." Voluntary memory is largely sterile and in vivid contrast to the sensations created by the second type, involuntary memory. Proust makes this distinction clear by recounting the episode of *la petite madeleine*, or little cake. The adult Marcel comes home on a winter day to tea and cakes. The crumbs in the spoon of tea give him exquisite pleasure, much to his surprise and delight. Initially puzzled by the sensation, Marcel suddenly recovers the memory: His Aunt Léonie had once given him tea and madeleines. An entire vision of forgotten elements of Combray surges over him. The incident is charming in itself, but it also anticipates a larger movement in the novel, Marcel's quest for the source of artistic inspiration.

Having resurrected memories of his youthful home in the madeleine incident, Proust logically moves to the next section, titled "Combray." Here emerges Marcel's childhood as it is shaped by family, an occasional school friend such as the pugnacious Bloch, and his reading of novels, particularly the works of Bergotte, an acquaintance of Swann. While Proust has been accused of being careless, casual, and prolix, the Combray section indicates quite the opposite. The characters and the quest motifs and themes are introduced without diverting the reader's attention away from the immediate concern, the characterization of Marcel's early years. Like Charles Dickens, Proust creates characters that seem to have their own independent lives. The bedridden Aunt Léonie, for example, delights the reader with her quixotic pursuit of local gossip, yet her attachment to her sickroom clearly anticipates Marcel's own frequent retirements to his bed.

The Combray section also introduces the two "ways" that will influence Marcel's life, Swann's and Guermantes'. These two walks, the first represented by the lover Swann and the second by the socially prominent Duchess de Guermantes, will be the symbolic means by which Marcel will come to know the world outside Combray. While walking Swann's Way, Marcel first sees Swann's daughter, Gilberte, who will be the object of Marcel's first quest outside the confines of family. In an irony that is distinctly Proustian, Gilberte, standing under the pink hawthorns, makes an obscene gesture that to Marcel has the appearance of anger and rejection. The adult Marcel discovers that the reality was quite the opposite: Gilberte's youthful intentions were entirely sexual. This misreading of appearances emerges as one of the novel's central themes.

The Combray incidents are followed by what may seem an unlikely sequel, a novel within a novel titled "Swann in Love." Although audacious technically, its position within the larger work is logical and effective. Swann's affair with Odette contributes to the whole in terms of both style and theme. Proust reveals first of all his flexibility in use of point of view. The entire episode is told by an omniscient narrator; Proust recognizes that there is no way that either the youthful or the adult Marcel could be privy to the history of Swann's romance. Focusing on the sophisticated Swann also allows Proust to characterize the social world of Paris that Marcel will someday pursue. Of particular interest is Proust's use of the Verdurins and their "little nucleus" of friends. Not only do they enlarge one's knowledge of the teeming social life of Paris, but also they form a comic, ironic backdrop for Swann's tender love. Comically vulgar, the Verdurins are on the bottom rung of the social ladder—bohemians, as Marcel's grandfather calls them. Madame Verdurin will ultimately become much more than a backdrop, however; she will marry the Prince de Guermantes and prove herself to be the most vivid example of the immensity of the social change that occurs in the full novel's fifty-year time span. Another theme, similar in its social character, is also introduced in "Swann in Love." It occurs in a passing comment made by Oriane, the Princess des Laumes, about Swann's being a Jew. While apparently irrelevant in the early part of *Remembrance of Things Past*, the question of anti-Semitism, raised by the Dreyfus affair, later divided France profoundly.

This section's title indicates the primary focus of "Swann in Love." Swann's obsession with Odette, replete with ironies and contradictions, foreshadows Marcel's own loves; Swann is indeed the archetype of the Proustian lover. Whether heterosexual or "inverted" (Proust's term for homosexual), the lover chooses as his object someone who at best only obliquely shares his values. Swann—a member of the Jockey Club, a friend of the Prince of Wales, a man whose eye is so sensitive that he sees reflections of Giotto's *Charity* in a kitchen maid, the very spiritual and artistic father of Marcel—is also a man who seeks after prostitutes. He is continually vulnerable to "the sight of healthy, abundant, rosy human flesh." Similarly, the elegant, manly Robert de Saint-Loup is obsessed with the plain, whorish Rachel, and the Baron de Charlus freely spends his social, moral, and emotional capital on the unscrupulous grandson of a valet, Morel. While Odette de Crécy is no ordinary courtesan, she nevertheless has little of Swann's sophistication and sensibility. Once Swann has possessed Odette physically, their love is composed of lies, infidelities, perhaps lesbian sexuality on Odette's part, and jealousy and obsession on Swann's. Most significant, "this malady, which was Swann's love," will afflict Marcel as perniciously in his quest of Albertine.

A particularly brilliant scene, Swann attending a soiree at Madame de Sainte-Euverte's, illustrates both the function of Swann in the larger work and the tightly woven texture of Proust's art. Wishing to leave a drawing room—a room off-limits to Odette—Swann is irritated that he has been entrapped by the beginning of a musical piece. He soon recognizes a series of notes that proves to be a phrase from a sonata by the fictional composer Vinteuil, the same piece Swann had earlier called the national anthem of his love for Odette. Swann's experience as he listens to the piece foreshadows Marcel's most profound discoveries: involuntary memory as the source of revelation and disappointment in love. As he listens, Swann "could see it all: the snowy, curled petals of the chrysanthemum ... the address 'Maison Dorée' embossed on the note paper ... the frowning contraction of her eyebrows." From the moment he hears the sonata, Swann knows he can never revive his love for Odette.

Not only does Swann's epiphany, rooted in involuntary memory, foreshadow Marcel's in the final volume of the novel, but also it indicates how Proust develops a number of themes simultaneously. The party at Madame de Sainte-Euverte's is also fine social satire, one of Proust's major concerns. The important theme of music, represented by Vinteuil, is present. The works of Vinteuil will eventually play as large a role in Marcel's life as in Swann's. Most important, Swann is, as Vladimir Nabokov, in his *Lectures on Literature* (1980), calls him, "a kind of fancy mirror of the narrator himself," one who "sets the pattern." Significant, too, is the pervading sense of paradox and irony that attends Swann's realization of love gone stale. The scene unobtrusively knits together elements of plot and theme that preceded it, renders them with clarity in a fully realized present, and anticipates further enrichments of plot and theme to come. The scene does not conclude Swann's concern for Odette; their love goes through death throes described in images of disease and decay. As "Swann in Love" ends, it appears that Swann and Odette have separated permanently; as it turns out, however, only Swann's love has been lost.

Swann's Way concludes with a section titled "Place-Names: The Name." The reader has reentered the world of Marcel's childhood, now set in Paris. Thematically, even in matters of plot, this last section is still clearly connected to "Swann in Love." Marcel wishes to travel; the names of Venice, Florence, and Balbec are magical to him. Because of his health, however, Marcel is forced to remain in Paris. While playing in the Champs-Elysées, he meets Gilberte, Odette, and Swann's daughter, the same girl he had seen in Combray. Initially, Gilberte is kind to Marcel; she gives him an agate marble and an essay by Bergotte on Jean Racine. Gilberte's enthusiasm is in contrast to Marcel's, however, much as her mother's feelings had been for Swann. Marcel is aware that he loves alone, but he still maintains his keen interest for her parents. He tries to imitate Swann's mannerisms, and when Gilberte chooses not to be available, he watches the resplendent Odette walk along the Allée des Acacias. In this same locale twenty years later, the adult Marcel makes the closing observations of *Swann's Way*. On a somber November day, Marcel finds that "vulgarity and fatuity" have replaced the standards of elegance that Odette had set years before. More important, Marcel is led to reflect on memory and its relationship to reality: "The reality that I had known no longer existed." The sadness of Marcel as he feels the onslaught of fugitive time is not yet assuaged by the knowledge that time can, in fact, be regained with all of its color and truth. All he knows is that physical space, in this instance the Bois de Boulogne, does not contain the reality of the past. Marcel can remember Odette, but he experiences none of the ecstasy associated with involuntary memory. Thus, the melancholy tone of these closing pages indicates clearly that Marcel's goals of love, society, and an artistic vocation have not yet been achieved.

WITHIN A BUDDING GROVE

Even though Marcel's exact age is not stated, *Swann's Way* concerns itself generally with the years of Marcel's childhood, while *Within a Budding Grove* develops his adolescence. A sign of Marcel's increasing independence is his frequent visits to the drawing room of Madame Swann, whom Marcel's parents will not receive, despite their warm feelings for her husband. Thus, the first long chapter of *Within a Budding Grove* is titled "Madame Swann at Home." The second, somewhat shorter section, "Place-Names: The Place," and the third and concluding chapter, "Seascape, with Frieze of Girls," depict Marcel's first venture away from his parents. Even though his grandmother accompanies him for reasons of health to the seaside hotel at Balbec, Marcel experiences considerable freedom. He mingles with the lower classes, young women, the members of the aristocratic Guermantes family, and the Impressionist painter Elstir (who, like the composer Vinteuil, is a composite of several real artists), all of whom contribute to his largely unconscious search for the real. Indeed, appearances still make their claim on Marcel, but new realities begin to make themselves felt.

In spite of *Within a Budding Grove*'s concentration on Marcel's life apart from parental influence, its first great scene occurs within the confines of the family; furthermore, it is one of the few scenes in which Marcel's father emerges with much clarity. The occasion is a small dinner for the Marquis de Norpois, a distinguished member of the Foreign Office (Marcel's father is Permanent Secretary there). While Norpois reappears frequently in later novels, his primary function at the dinner is to introduce subtly the themes that will find elaboration in subsequent scenes. Marcel's career as a writer, the major concern of *Remembrance of Things Past*, is first discussed openly at the dinner. Norpois champions the vocation of writer, an important gesture, because Marcel's father has opposed it. In the hands of Dickens, Norpois would be the archetype of the good uncle who intervenes on behalf of a young boy beset by an incompetent or hostile father figure.

While Proust's method of characterization does seek out the type in the individual, as Swann sees the Botticellian possibilities in Odette, the type is always fully rounded, almost to the point of contradicting the type. Françoise is the good, faithful servant, but her limitations are never ignored. Similarly, Swann is the connoisseur, yet, as Norpois points out, since his marriage to Odette he has at times played the parvenu. In the case of Norpois, while he promotes Marcel's writing career, he nearly cuts it short by agreeing with Marcel's falsely modest assertion that his first writing exercise was "childish scribbling." Norpois goes on to attack Marcel's beloved Bergotte, judging him precious and an "evil influence." In a manner typical of him, Proust makes twofold use of Norpois's literary remarks. They obviously frustrate and antagonize the sensitive Marcel; they also contain many of the objections that Proust's own novels met critically. Norpois particularly dislikes "all those Chinese puzzles of form," saying that "all these deliquescent mandarin subtleties seem to me to be quite futile." Ironically, when Marcel soon thereafter meets Bergotte at Odette's, he is immensely disappointed and recalls Norpois's assessment.

Marcel's lofty vision of the novelist, inferred from his work, is mocked by Bergotte's disappointing physical qualities and his snobbery and ambition.

In addition to its effect on Marcel's writing career, Norpois's conversation reminds the reader of other topics and themes. Norpois's personal political credentials are established by his recollections of service to France under reactionary and radical governments; later he appears as the most reasonable of the anti-Dreyfusards. While Swann's Jewishness is not mentioned by Norpois, he does provide the missing exposition on Swann's marriage, and the reader is once again reminded of the love theme, which is reinforced by Norpois's insistence that Marcel be allowed to see the famous actress Berma perform as Phèdre in Jean Racine's great play. Norpois also plays a minor but important role in Marcel's growing social awareness; his influence extends from Odette's drawing room to the court of kings, yet he will not honor Marcel's simple, enthusiastic request that he mention his, Marcel's, name to Odette.

Before his journey to Balbec, Marcel does find admittance to Odette's salon. Marcel himself describes his time spent at Swann's house as a stage in his movement upward in society. Ironically, it was Marcel's quest for love, not society, that originally attracted him to Swann's. His first visit comes after Gilberte invites him to tea following his attack of asthma. He continues to call, but Odette takes more pleasure in his presence than does Gilberte. Finally, while coyly refusing to see Gilberte, Marcel remains faithful to Odette, among her chrysanthemums and coterie of bourgeois acquaintances. Marcel discontinues his visits when he learns another fact of love: Absence breeds forgetfulness. He still visits the Bois de Boulogne, knowing the exact time when Odette walks there, the very personification of Woman as she strolls with her mauve parasol, followed by Swann and his friends from the Jockey Club. This particular vision of Odette leads the adult Marcel to conclude that one's memories of "poetical sensations" are much greater than one's memory of suffering.

Two years pass before Marcel takes the 1:22 train to Balbec with his grandmother. The summer and fall Marcel passes there greatly increase his knowledge of society and, to a lesser extent, his knowledge of love. Although he longs to die when he first sees the unfamiliar room in the Grand Hotel, habit and the presence of Françoise and his grandmother soon make this new world bearable, even pleasurably exciting.

The much-desired world of society appears at first to be closed off to Marcel. He must resign himself to the presence of chattering, vulgar provincials and disdainful members of the local aristocracy. Circumstances, however, prove kind, and an accidental meeting between his grandmother and the Marquise de Villeparisis, her old schoolmate, slowly opens up a new world to Marcel. The Marquise is a member of the distinguished Guermantes family, and she proves to be an indispensable step in Marcel's movement to the very top of the social hierarchy. To demonstrate her fondness for Marcel, she takes him on carriage rides about the countryside. Proust identifies her closely with the arts; her family owns paintings by Titian, and her father entertained Stendhal. She herself will write a highly regarded memoir. She is also, unbeknown to Marcel, the Marquis de Norpois's lover. Madame de Villeparisis illustrates one of the central principles of Proust's world: A character's identity cannot be known at once; time will unfold its secrets, and the reader comes to see, as Nabokov has put it, that Proust's characters wear a series of masks.

Madame de Villeparisis also introduces Marcel to her nephews, two characters who figure prominently in the evolution of a variety of themes, including love and the analysis of society. Marcel's first impression of the handsome, elegant Robert, Marquis de Saint-Loup, is negative. His apparent insolence, however, masks a generosity that conquers both Marcel and his unpretentious, socially indifferent grandmother. The other, older nephew, Palamède, Baron de Charlus, wears an even more impenetrable mask. To characterize the Baron for Marcel, Robert relates an incident that illustrates both the Baron's virility and his hostility to inversion; Robert clearly is unaware that the Baron, who has stared fixedly at Marcel, is, in fact decidedly homosexual. Robert also points out with some family pride that the Baron, who moves with ease in the Faubourg Saint-Germain, the pinnacle of Parisian society, has a list at the Jockey Club of two hundred members to whom he would not permit himself to be introduced.

The Baron will play one of the central roles in Marcel's drama. His two major functions, furthering Marcel's social awareness and explicating the homosexual theme, are joined by a third: His formal social demeanor provides a vivid contrast to the crude behavior of Bloch, Marcel's Jewish friend. Part of Marcel's social education is his exposure to the Bloch family as well as to the Guermanteses. Lest Proust's portrayal of the vulgarity of the Blochs be seen as anti-Semitic, however, one must recall that Proust's mother and her family, whom he loved and honored, were Jewish, as were many of his closest friends. As in his treatment of other minorities—ethnic, social, and sexual—Proust proves to be compassionate without indulging in apologies or sentimentality. No character would have been more offended by the Bloch family's lack of decorum than the Jewish Swann. Also, Robert's Jewish mistress, Rachel, while seen as manipulative, "had opened his mind to the invisible, had brought a serious element into his life, delicacy into his heart."

While Marcel finds pleasure in his new acquaintances at Balbec, his attention is most avidly focused on a band of young girls whom he sees about the town and countryside. He meets them through an unexpected source, the famous painter Elstir. Marcel's easy access to Elstir brings to mind one of the most frequent criticisms of the novel: The young, inexperienced Marcel makes a quick conquest of almost everyone he meets, from duchesses and novelists to lift boys. The reader's only direct clue to Marcel's charm is found in *The Guermantes Way*, when Marcel wittily entertains Robert's friends at the army town of Doncières. Marcel is usually passive both in tête-à-têtes and in society. Elstir nevertheless takes Marcel seriously enough to deliver a stirring monologue on aesthetic matters and the nature of wisdom. Marcel, however, seems more concerned with the failure to appear of a young girl who occasionally visits Elstir's studio. Marcel does eventually meet this young girl, Albertine. His immediate response to her is distinctly Proustian: The real Albertine is less than the imagined one. Following an innocent courtship that thrives on games played in the sand dunes with a band of girls, Marcel chooses Albertine to be his love interest. When Marcel makes advances toward her, however, she repulses them, and Marcel's initiation into the larger world of Balbec ends, as does *Swann's Way*, on a melancholy, cool note. The novel has, however, furthered Marcel's quest for love and prepared for his entry into the salons of Parisian society.

THE GUERMANTES WAY

The Guermantes Way begins with a mundane fact, but one crucial to the success of Marcel's dual quest for love and society. Marcel's family has moved to the Hôtel Guermantes, the Paris residence of the Duke and Duchess de Guermantes and Madame de Villeparisis; there, too, is Jupien's tailor shop. While it is conceivable that Marcel might have made his way into the most distinguished drawing rooms of Paris without this change, it clearly makes Proust's plotting easier, even though plot is, perhaps, comparatively a lesser concern in such an expansive, comprehensive work as *Remembrance of Things Past*. Proust's keen psychological analyses, his brilliant use of metaphors to give depth and clarity to his themes, his elegance of style, and his sense of comedy are his chief virtues. Perhaps of all the novels of Proust's epic, *The Guermantes Way* best illustrates the truth of such a proposition.

The key organizing principle of *The Guermantes Way* is a series of social engagements: matinees, dinners at restaurants, and evening parties. Their only interruption, by what might appear to be an incongruity, is the death of Marcel's grandmother. There is, however, a unity of action provided by Marcel's growing consciousness, fostered by his exposure to the world of the Guermanteses. Once exposed, Marcel, relieved of his obsession with Oriane, the Duchess de Guermantes, states that "what troubled me now was the discovery that almost every house sheltered some unhappy person.... Quite half of the human race was in tears." He discovers the disparity between the romance that envelops a royal name and the reality of the royal person. Proust makes Marcel's disillusionment clearer by the use of metaphor. Marcel observes that

> each of my fellow guests at dinner, smothering the mysterious name under which I had only at a distance known and dreamed of them with a body and with a mind similar or inferior to those of all the people I knew, had given me the impression of flat vulgarity which the view on entering the Danish port of Elsinore would give to any passionate admirer of *Hamlet*.

Having met and conquered two of the members of the Guermantes family in Balbec, Madame de Villeparisis and Robert de Saint-Loup, Marcel, at the beginning of *The Guermantes Way*, sets his sights on Oriane, the beautiful Duchess de Guermantes. Marcel's own dreamlike state is reinforced by the magic of the great Berma's performance in Jean Racine's *Phèdre* (1677.) To Marcel's utter surprise, the Duchess acknowledges him with a wave of her hand. In comedy reminiscent of Dickens, Marcel thereafter stalks the Duchess, loitering in the streets in the hope of seeing her. When word reaches Marcel that his infatuation irritates the Duchess, he employs a new tactic: He goes to the military camp at Doncières to visit Robert de Saint-Loup, hoping to gain access to the Duchess through Robert's influence.

Even though Robert is unable to help Marcel, the rekindling of their friendship allows Proust the novelist to develop themes previously introduced. Robert's obsession with his mistress Rachel reminds the reader of Swann's relationship with Odette and anticipates both the Baron de Charlus's mad pursuit of Morel and, most important, Marcel's tortured relationship with Albertine. Even an apparently insignificant incident in which Robert strikes a gay man is preparation for Robert's own sexual inversion later.

Robert's pursuit of his mistress brings him and Marcel back to Paris. Marcel is encouraged by his father to attend a matinee at the home of Madame de Villeparisis. While this occasion is of greater social significance than the gatherings Marcel had previously attended at Odette Swann's, it has limited status. Madame de Villeparisis, from the point of view of the Faubourg Saint-Germain, has been careless of her famous family name. She has married beneath her station, has had liaisons, and has associated herself closely with the academic and artistic worlds. Although the Duchess de Guermantes and the Baron de Charlus attend the matinee, they do so out of family loyalty. The matinee, essentially comic in tone, focuses in part on the foibles of guests such as Legrandin, a shameless flatterer, and Marcel's boyhood friend Bloch, who upsets a vase of apple blossoms. Few of Proust's scenes are as comic as that of Madame de Villeparisis pretending to be asleep when the humiliated Bloch comes to bid her farewell. The comic, however, is interwoven with themes of tragic potential, such as Norpois's discussion with Bloch about the Dreyfus affair and the pervasive evidence of vicious snobbery. Most important, Marcel and the reader gain a clearer picture of the complexity of the Guermanteses: Oriane, the Baron, and Madame de Marsantes, the mother of Robert. The Baron's comically indirect, elegant propositioning of Marcel as he leaves the matinee develops the homosexual theme and reveals Marcel's naïveté.

A hiatus of sorts follows Marcel's initiation into the world of the Guermanteses. First, Marcel's grandmother dies. Having been convinced by an eminent physician, Dr. de Boulbon, that her ill health is psychosomatic, Marcel's grandmother follows his advice and accompanies Marcel to the Champs-Élysées. She rather suddenly interrupts their stroll to go into a public toilet. During the interim, Marcel talks to "la marquise," who attends the toilet, to which she refers as her "salon." Her conversation, coming so soon after the de Villeparisis matinee, is brutally satiric, as is Marcel's experience with a doctor, Professor E——, to whom he turns when it is apparent that the grandmother has suffered a stroke. Although he does examine her, Professor E—— is clearly more concerned with the mending of a buttonhole, a repair that is necessary before he calls on the Minister of Commerce. The protracted suffering of the grandmother and the devotion of Marcel's mother to her are set in stark contrast to the vanity, insinuations, and archness of the drawing room. Marcel will continue his social ascent, but the vision of his grandmother's love will provide a vivid contrast to the falseness of the *beau monde.*

Deeply touched by his grandmother's death, Marcel's attention nevertheless turns again to women. Although he successfully pursues a Madame de Stermaria, he is consoled by the reappearance of Albertine, finding that she no longer repulses his physical advances. Albertine's return coincides with a number of discoveries by Marcel. In spite of the kind of attention that Robert de Saint-Loup gives him, Marcel concludes that friendship is basically incompatible with the vocation of writing. Most important, he discovers that he has grown indifferent to the Duchess de Guermantes, as he had to Gilberte. This realization occurs ironically when Marcel receives an invitation from the Duchess to dine with her. Marcel's observations during the dinner, more than one hundred pages in length, are an excellent example of what Nabokov calls "Marcel the eavesdropper." Marcel's personality and concerns intrude little, if at all, in the description of the Guermanteses at home. At the center is Oriane, the Duchess herself. One learns that as a young woman she was, by the Guermanteses' standards, poor. What distinguished her was her beauty, her style, and her spirit: "She had had the audacity to say to the Russian Grand Duke: 'Well, Sir, I hear you would like to have Tolstoy murdered?'" In spite of her liberal views, she was most careful to marry well. With the aid of her aunt, Madame de Villeparisis, she married the Prince des Laumes, the future Duke de Guermantes. Their marriage has scarcely been a happy one. The Duke is tight with money but profligate in his affection for other women. The Duke admires his wife, however, particularly her sharp "Guermantes wit," which in reality often consists of terrible puns, poor imitations, cruel characterizations of her friends and family, and fatuous literary judgments. Marcel nevertheless finds something of value in the Faubourg Saint-Germain world that she represents. Like the peasants, the great noblemen still have a concern for the land, for history, for custom. In this way, they are superior to the bourgeoisie, who are interested only in money.

Although Marcel's social education is not yet complete, his evening with the Duchess does much to strip away the appearances and the magic of the world of names. Before the evening is out, however, Marcel will receive one more lesson. Invited by the Baron de Charlus to call on him after dinner, Marcel encounters a hostile Baron, who accuses Marcel of ingratitude and talebearing. Marcel retaliates by trampling the Baron's new silk hat and begins his exit. The formerly imperious Baron seems sobered by Marcel's anger. A civilized conversation follows, one that reveals the Baron's quixotic intelligence and sensitivity, as well as his appreciation for his family. The scene, both comic and touching, reveals him in his fullness and has led Wilson to compare Proust's characterization of the Baron to William Shakespeare's characterization of Falstaff.

In the final scene of *The Guermantes Way,* Proust provides—as he had in the episode of the grandmother's death—a brilliant gloss on the artificiality and vacuity of the Guermanteses' world. Marcel has received an invitation from the Princess de Guermantes, and being unsure of its authenticity, he goes to visit the Duke and Duchess upon their return to Paris. While he is there, Swann arrives with a photograph for a book he is writing on the knights of the Order of Malta. Oriane claims a great interest in Swann's project, but the Duke hurries her off to a dinner at a relative's. As they leave, Swann announces that he is dying. Although Swann is one of her oldest friends, the Duchess yields to her husband's demands that they leave for the dinner. The Duke tells Swann that he will outlive them all. The detail that fully reveals the cruelty of the Guermanteses, however, is the Duke's concern for Oriane's forgotten red shoes. The Duke and his world chose to ignore whatever unpleasant reality discomforts them in favor of a dramatic appearance.

CITIES OF THE PLAIN

Cities of the Plain, a novel of brilliantly contrasted scenes, records the beginning of Marcel's descent into his own personal hell, fuller description of which occurs in *The Captive* and *The Sweet Cheat Gone*. In *Cities of the Plain*, Marcel moves from the pinnacle of Parisian society, symbolized by the soiree given by the Prince and Princess de Guermantes, downward to the ridiculously comic Wednesdays at the Verdurins' home at La Raspelière. More significantly, Marcel himself reluctantly changes from detached observer to subjective sufferer because of the emergence of the phenomenon that dominates the novel: homosexuality.

One of the lingering criticisms of *Remembrance of Things Past* is that it gives excessive attention to the homosexual theme, thus presenting a distorted picture of society as it was in Paris at the beginning of the twentieth century. Some consider Proust's fascination with the subject merely self-indulgent; others, seeking to justify the theme, have called it a symbol of Original Sin or a symbol of the corruption and coming destruction of the aristocracy. Both the critics and Proust's defenders miss the point. Within the self-contained world of the larger novel, homosexuality functions primarily as an aesthetic device. Without its presence, there would be no Baron de Charlus, Proust's most brilliantly drawn character. Homosexuality also contributes to other major concerns of the novel, such as the characterization of much of the aristocracy, the love theme, and the education of the narrator. Without homosexuality, the central plot would not advance; had Albertine not mentioned her friendship with the lesbian who was the companion of Vinteuil's daughter, Marcel would not have urged her to come to Paris. One may further assume that the heterosexual Marcel's inability to find human love is directly connected to his ultimate quest for salvation in art. To see the function of homosexuality in terms of plot, theme, and characterization does not, however, negate its intrinsic interest. Like the characterization of the aristocracy and the descriptions of life in a provincial French town or sea resort, homosexuality resonates with the tragicomic complexity of human experience.

Cities of the Plain begins as an apparent extension of Marcel's pursuit of the world of the Guermanteses. In a flashback, Marcel awaits the return of the Duke and Duchess de Guermantes to ask about the authenticity of an invitation he has received from the Princess de Guermantes. Marcel sees instead the Baron de Charlus meeting Jupien, the tailor. Although Marcel could scarcely be ignorant of the Baron's sexual proclivities, he is still surprised by the cooperation of Jupien in such matters. Marcel is, nevertheless, fascinated by the coquetry that takes place, and he uses an extended botanical metaphor, comparing Jupien to an orchid and the Baron to a bee. The effect of the metaphor is to suggest that, while the encounter is unusual, it is in the larger scheme of things natural, "a miracle."

Jupien is just another member of the "human herbary" that intrigues Marcel, a "moral botanist." Samuel Beckett has noted the importance of Proust's use of "vegetal" images, stating,

> This preoccupation accompanies very naturally his complete indifference to moral values and human justices. Flowers and plants have no conscious will. They are shameless exposing their genitals. And so in a sense are Proust's men and women.

Although Beckett perhaps overstates the case, there is indeed no moral censure on young Marcel's part; neither is there a defense of homosexuality. Marcel concludes that gays are essentially men-women and that in spite of the Baron's pretension of virility, he, in fact, has the sensibility of a woman. Marcel concludes that homosexuals are like "an Oriental colony, cultured, musical, malicious, which has certain charming qualities and intolerable defects." Proust's objective characterization of homosexuals is perfectly consistent with those of other minorities: Jews, aristocrats, artists, and so on. Thus, Marcel later says that, like his extremely moral grandmother, he also "enjoyed the diversity of other people without expecting anything of them or resenting anything that they did."

There is another Marcel in *Cities of the Plain* who does not take such a sanguine view of humankind or homosexuality. The Marcel who captures the comedy, homosexual and otherwise, of the soiree at the Guermanteses' (where the Baron shamelessly pursues two vapid brothers in the presence of their unwittingly cooperative mother) is quite different from the Marcel who returns to Balbec and discovers that he is not immune to the sting of "vice."

Marcel's return to Balbec with his mother marks a general movement toward a more somber, reflective, subjective protagonist. Upon reaching his old room at the Grand Hotel, Marcel takes off his boots, and involuntarily his memory returns to his grandmother. For the first time, he feels the effect of her death and learns from Françoise of the courage and sacrifice his grandmother concealed from him during their earlier stay at Balbec. His suffering diminishes, however, with Albertine's return to town. His comfort proves to be short-lived. While visiting a casino with Cottard, the doctor, Marcel sees Albertine dancing with Andrée. Cottard casually remarks that the two women are aroused. Unlike his detached response to the Baron de Charlus and Jupien, Marcel is deeply distressed by the possibility of a lesbian liaison between Albertine and Andrée. From this point on, *Cities of the Plain* develops the torturous relationship of Marcel and Albertine, a relationship that reveals the sometimes sadistic, paranoiac, and self-indulgent aspects of Marcel's character.

In *Cities of the Plain*, Proust does not yet entirely extricate Marcel and Albertine from the larger social fabric. Their physical but loveless affair grows within the context of life at the Grand Hotel and, more important, the Wednesdays at the Verdurins' home. The "nucleus" that gathers around "The Mistress" has changed little since they first appeared in *Swann's Way*. If possible, they are even more ridiculously savage in their comedy. The evenings at La Raspelière are the supreme achievement of Proust's comedy. Whether it is the Faithful mistaking Meyerbeer for Claude Debussy, or Madame Cottard falling asleep, or the Baron de Charlus revealing his sexual proclivities by choosing strawberry juice rather than orangeade, the comedy is sublime. Madame Verdurin herself has become even more imperious and amoral. To her, the death of Deschampes the pianist is essentially a nuisance that threatens to spoil her first entertainment in her new country residence. Besides, she has a new protégé, the violinist Charles Morel. Morel, the grandson of Marcel's Uncle Adolphe's valet, emerges as one of Proust's greatest achievements in characterization. A fit companion for the Verdurins, Morel is utterly amoral, available either to men or women, entirely free of any loyalty, and he almost proves to be the Baron's nemesis. The Baron is so in love with Morel that he suffers the vulgarities and ignorance of the Verdurins and their circle in order to promote the young man's career and simply be in his presence. Like Odette and Albertine, Morel is one of those faithless creatures that ironically have the power to enslave a sensibility finer than their own. Morel's affair with the Baron is one panel in Proust's triptych of the vanity of human love.

In time, Marcel's jealousy and paranoia concerning Albertine lead him to resemble the Baron in his pursuit of Morel. At Balbec, however, Marcel's feelings are at best ambivalent. He is indeed possessive of Albertine and even jealous of her attention to his old friend Robert de Saint-Loup. So corrosive is the effect of this attachment on his moral behavior that he refuses to leave her alone with Saint-Loup in order to speak even briefly to Bloch's father. Marcel still dreams of traveling, however, and he finally resolves that he will abandon her. Only when Marcel inadvertently discovers that Albertine is an old friend of the lover of Vinteuil's daughter does the specter of lesbian sexuality rise up to shatter his resolution. It is scarcely the same detached Marcel, the moral botanist who watched Jupien lure the Baron, who announces to his mother that he will return to Paris and marry Albertine. While *The Guermantes Way* reveals Marcel's disillusionment in his quest for society, *Cities of the Plain* does the same for his quest for love. Salvation, if it exists it all, has thus far eluded Marcel.

THE CAPTIVE

Coupled with *The Sweet Cheat Gone, The Captive* has as its central concern Marcel's destructive relationship with the elusive Albertine. Although the love theme appears earlier, in the histories of Swann and Odette, Robert and Rachel, and the Baron de Charlus and Morel, it is in the painstaking treatment of Marcel's paranoid obsession with Albertine that Proust most fully explores the paradoxes of love. Wilson describes their relationship as "trying" at best: "It is quite without tenderness, glamour, or romance." There is in it neither "idealism [nor] enjoyment." This extended episode is crucial to the central concern of the novel, however: Marcel's discovery of his true vocation as an artist. Once love has proved itself impossible for Marcel, the only salvation is the world of art—as the final volume of *Remembrance of Things Past* will show.

Although *The Captive* includes one of Proust's most brilliant social scenes, the Verdurins' quarrel with the Baron de Charlus, it begins and ends with Marcel's life with Albertine. The novel opens with Marcel in his bedroom in Paris. As a number of critics have pointed out, the bedroom functions as one of the primary motifs in the work. Marcel's recurring bouts of ill health make his stays in bed, be it at Combray, Balbec, or Paris, credible; however, the emphasis in each instance is elsewhere. Consciously or not, Marcel's retirements represent a power struggle of sorts. His delicate health as a child guarantees the attention of his mother, and the famous scene at Combray where Marcel awaits and ultimately receives his mother's kiss represents an ambivalent victory for Marcel over his father. At his Balbec hotel room, the adolescent Marcel, although he is unaware of it, has a rival for his grandmother's attention: death itself. Again, Marcel temporarily wins the struggle. As an adult, Marcel once again retires to his bedroom and uses this withdrawal to imprison the third important woman in his life, Albertine. Her presence is in part a repetition of earlier experience. Marcel himself twice sees Albertine's kisses late at night as a reenactment of his mother's visit to his side after Swann had left that fateful night in *Swann's Way*. As was true with his mother and grandmother, Marcel has a rival for Albertine, her probable inclinations toward lesbian sexuality.

It has been suggested that Albertine's presence in the home of Marcel's parents violates credibility. Bourgeois values would not have allowed it. Proust does, however, cover his tracks. First, Marcel's father is away on diplomatic business, and his indulgent mother is conveniently in Combray, attending a sick relative. Only the disapproving Françoise is present. Moreover, Marcel conceals Albertine's residency from friends. Most important, Marcel has never particularly adhered to social strictures, as is indicated by his moral indifference to the male citizens of Sodom and Gomorrah.

While Marcel the social observer is admirably tolerant, Marcel the lover has little to recommend him other than his lucid candor; why Albertine accepts Marcel's paranoia and jealousy as long as she does is not clear. Marcel's motives and behavior, on the other hand, are scrutinized uncompromisingly. Marcel tells Albertine that the doctor has ordered him to stay in bed. In truth, Marcel is so jealous of Albertine that he cannot bear to see her responses to other people in public. Thus, the tyrant Marcel permits Albertine to go out only with Andrée or alone with the chauffeur, but he also asks both, in effect, to spy on her.

Marcel's desire for control over Albertine leads him to like her best when she is sleeping or just awakening. Marcel compares the waking Albertine to Eve come from the side of Adam—"astonished and submissive." So consuming is Marcel's jealousy that he finds he is less interested in Albertine's frequent intelligent comments than he is in some unguarded remark that will fuel his paranoia.

While his jealousy proves intensely painful to Marcel, he does find some pleasure in life with Albertine. He both admires and takes some credit for her intelligence. She does provide him physical titillation and satisfaction. His greatest pleasure seems to reside in his capacity simply to control her, to hold her captive. Whether he is choosing her clothing after consultation with the Duchess de Guermantes or begging her to return home from the Trocadéro, Marcel seeks to reduce Albertine to merely an instrument of his will. Marcel is fully conscious not only that his attachment to Albertine prevents him from traveling and working but also that he himself has become a captive to Albertine's lies and his own mania. Although unable to act on his knowledge, Marcel sees clearly that "I had clipped her wings, she had ceased to be a Victory, was a burdensome slave of whom I would fain have been rid."

The Captive does not develop Marcel's relationship with Albertine exclusively. Another love story, the Baron de Charlus's obsession with Morel, is also carried to a disastrous climax at the musical soiree held at the Verdurins'. The humiliation of the imperious Baron at the hands of the Verdurins is but one of the important events that this brilliant scene develops. Its objectively cruel satire, directed toward the aristocrats and the members of the Verdurins' circle, provides a necessary contrast in tone and texture to the Albertine-Marcel story. The playing of Vinteuil's lost septet during the soiree also allows Marcel to consider questions crucial to his development as an artist.

In *The Captive*, the theme of the artist is like an underground stream that slowly makes its way to the surface. Marcel points out early in the novel that when he is not with the Duchess, he examines an album of Elstir's work, or one of Bergotte's books, or Vinteuil's sonata. Later, Marcel learns of Bergotte's death as he is viewing a Vermeer at an exhibition. Proust, anticipating *Time Regained*, suggests that the dead Bergotte's books, arranged three by three, are the symbol of his resurrection, his salvation. Marcel, while awaiting Albertine's return from the Trocadéro, plays Vinteuil's sonata. Fowlie points out that this scene is of primary importance in the transition of Marcel from lover to artist. After the sonata, Marcel plays a score of Richard Wagner's *Tristan und Isolde* (1859), and this arouses a number of questions in him. He admires the giants of the nineteenth century—Wagner, Honoré de Balzac, Victor Hugo—and their capacity to produce "Vulcan-like" massive works leaves Marcel unhappy and unsure whether a commitment to art is preferable to life as he leads it. At the Verdurins', Marcel hears Vinteuil's septet, and he realizes that Vinteuil's later work has been enriched by his love and suffering for his daughter. In this septet, Vinteuil, like Bergotte, has found a means of defeating time.

In contrast to the violet mist in which Vinteuil's immortal work is shrouded is the unheroic world of the Verdurins. The Baron's aristocratic guests ignore Madame Verdurin, and to get revenge, she poisons Morel's mind against the Baron. Even in this atmosphere of snobbery and viciousness, Proust avoids caricature. At evening's end, the Verdurins decide to provide anonymously for the financially broken Saniette, whom they have abused in the past. More dramatic, however, is the Queen of Naples, who returns to the Verdurins' for a misplaced fan and rather magnificently comes to the aid of the devastated Baron de Charlus. Thus, the major concerns that propel the previous novels—homosexuality, the development of the artist, the vanity of love, the emptiness of the aristocracy, the Janus-like nature of reality—are in this scene recapitulated seamlessly.

Marcel returns home to Albertine. They quarrel, and Marcel asks Albertine to leave. A reconciliation follows, but Marcel learns more disquieting facts about Albertine's past. Albertine herself grows restless, as symbolized by her violent opening of her window. When Marcel plans to end the relationship, Albertine ensures his continued bondage to jealousy by leaving him first. It would appear that Marcel's quest for love has reached its nadir. The descent, however, is not yet complete.

THE SWEET CHEAT GONE

The Sweet Cheat Gone, more than any of the novels that precede it, concerns itself with Marcel's loss of innocence. Proust emphasizes this theme by ending the novel with Marcel's return to the Combray of his childhood. There he finds the youthful object of his imagination and love, Gilberte, living in a fallen world. For Marcel, not only has Gilberte lost her appeal, but also her husband and his friend, Robert de Saint-Loup, seems stripped of nobility. Most poignant, the once beautiful Vivonne is now little more than "a meagre, ugly rivulet."

The novel begins with Marcel's desperate strategies to bring Albertine back to him. He recognizes the irony of seeking the return of one who afforded him mediocre pleasures while preventing him from realizing loftier goals. Alas, she had become a habit. No longer having Albertine about to lie to him, Marcel lies to himself. He persuades himself that her departure is an attempt to negotiate better terms. He therefore dispatches a letter telling Albertine that her departure is final, while Robert de Saint-Loup is sent to bribe Albertine's aunt. A second letter reveals an even baser Marcel; in it, he suggests that a Rolls-Royce and a yacht might be in the offing. The final communication, a telegram, asks Albertine to name her terms; all he wants is to hold her three times a week. So summarized, Marcel's actions are comic. The news of Albertine's death in a riding accident alters the tone, as does her last letter, in which she asks Marcel to take her back on any terms. Proust, however, makes no attempt to sentimentalize her death. There is a peculiar flatness in its description that undercuts any pronounced emotional response. The reader has known so little of Albertine that he is moved only by the irony of events.

The ironic tone is sustained in the treatment of Marcel's grief. The former captor is now enslaved by memory, and Marcel discovers that each season brings with it a new set of painful recollections. Temporarily affectionate memories of Albertine replace his former suspicions. Marcel feels guilt, as though he had murdered her. He deifies her, calls her "my sister, my child, my tender mistress." The exaggerated, unexpected sincerity of Marcel's grief once again approaches comedy. He begins to believe that Albertine is not dead and considers the possibility of immortality. At the same time, Marcel has commissioned

Aimé, a former headwaiter at Balbec, to investigate Albertine's life at the resort; Aimé writes that Albertine had been an active lesbian. Aimé, on a second mission, discovers a laundress from whom Albertine had received profound pleasure, and Aimé believes the laundress's report because she has excited him sexually as well. Such revelations Marcel both believes and doubts. He continues his quest for the true Albertine, and while Andrée admits to having lesbian feelings, she denies any involvement with Albertine. Marcel is thus frustrated in his attempt to locate the one, the absolute Albertine. Instead, he discovers that memory crumbles, and the time will soon come when Albertine's room will be occupied by someone else.

Although Marcel's relationship with Albertine will surface again, the novel abandons it in favor of another and crueler kind of oblivion, which has taken place without Marcel's knowledge. Marcel is introduced in the drawing room of the Duchess de Guermantes to Mademoiselle de Forcheville, who is Gilberte Swann. While she had earlier recognized Marcel, Marcel had thought, indeed hoped, that she was a young woman of easy virtue whom Robert de Saint-Loup had once known. The return of Gilberte allows Proust to recall the aftermath of Swann's death. To everyone's surprise, Odette exhibited a long and sincere grief. She then married Forcheville, who in time adopted Gilberte. Gilberte has inherited an immense fortune from an uncle and has thus been received in aristocratic houses. Even the Duchess de Guermantes receives her, an event devoutly desired by Swann but denied to him during his life. Although Gilberte has inherited her father's tact and charm, she contributes to Swann's oblivion by addressing Forcheville as father, and soon no one mentions Swann's name in her presence. Her hypocrisy and snobbery are seen in her signature, "G. S. Forcheville." The Guermanteses, whom Marcel now describes as "people whose lives have no purpose," aid in the destruction of Swann's memory. When Gilberte notices some Elstir sketches in the Guermanteses' drawing room, the Duchess remarks that "some friends" recommended Elstir rather than embarrass Gilberte with the name of Swann.

While the scene serves the necessary function of reintroducing Gilberte to the plot, it also reveals the growth of Marcel, who no longer is enamored of names and rank. The concerted attempt to erase Swann's memory is particularly offensive to Marcel, because it was Swann who so unobtrusively provided a type of paternal authority for Marcel. In his affair with Albertine, Marcel constantly sees Swann's life with Odette as the prototype of love. Swann has also introduced Marcel to Bergotte and to an appreciation of Vinteuil. Had it not been for Swann's remarks about the Persian quality of the church at Balbec, Marcel believes, he might never have met Albertine or Elstir. Appropriately, the connoisseur of art, Swann, will himself be immortalized in the art of his aesthetic son, Marcel.

Albertine has not yet been forgotten either. Marcel speaks again with Andrée, from whom he receives "a terrible revelation." Andrée has lied previously about her lack of contact with Albertine; moreover, she tells Marcel that Albertine and Morel together enticed virginal girls into occasional orgiastic revels. Suggesting that while Albertine lived with

Marcel she had reformed and looked to him to save her, Andrée further implies that Albertine's death was a suicide related to a lesbian scandal. The effect of Andrée's tales, however, is less than might be expected. Marcel no longer feels the need to believe in Albertine's innocence; so detached has he become that he now realizes that Albertine's lesbian orientation was perhaps a precondition for her frank and open manner, one that permitted their special camaraderie. Marcel realizes he will never know the truth about Albertine, and sorrow is finally replaced by exhaustion. Marcel knows that oblivion has made a conquest of him when, in Venice, he receives a telegram from Gilberte that at first appears to be from Albertine. Even the possibility that Albertine is alive does not interest him.

Once the Albertine theme has reached its inevitable conclusion, Proust uses the closing pages of the novel to foreshadow the major concerns of the final volume, *Time Regained*. Foremost among them is the theme of time. While visiting Venice with his mother and an old friend, Madame Sazerat, Marcel sees Madame de Villeparisis seated with her old lover, Monsieur de Norpois. Time has grievously altered the Marquise; Madame Sazerat, whose father was ruined by a youthful affair with the noblewoman, can scarcely believe that the woman once "beautiful as an angel, wicked as a demon" is now "hunch backed, red-faced . . . hideous." A second theme, the social change brought by time, is contained in the news of two marriages: Gilberte to Robert de Saint-Loup and Jupien's niece to the nephew of Legrandin. In the union of Gilberte and Robert, Swann's Way and Guermantes Way unexpectedly come together. More startling is the story of Jupien's niece. Adopted by the Baron de Charlus and given a name, she dies shortly after her marriage to an impoverished member of the provincial aristocracy. This young girl, enamored of and abused by Morel, through her death sends the royal houses of Europe into mourning. It is the same sense of irony and dramatic change that will permeate *Time Regained*.

The Sweet Cheat Gone concludes with a series of revelations that further strip away from Marcel any remaining romantic illusions. Gilberte's marriage to Robert is not a happy one; Robert appears to have inherited both his uncle's proclivities and his infatuation with Morel. Gilberte tries to make herself look like Rachel in a vain attempt to stop his infidelity, but she reaps only lies and melodramatic confessions of guilt. Marcel learns also that Gilberte's childhood gesture under the arch of hawthorns had been intentionally vulgar, a revelation that serves to reinforce one of Proust's central tenets. There is not a single Gilberte, but many Gilbertes: the little girl amid the hawthorns, the loving daughter of Swann, the snob, the suffering wife. What exists is not an absolute Gilberte but a series of Gilbertes relative to time and place. Even places fail to present an absolute image, as Marcel's disappointment in his walks in Combray reveals. Innocence has been stripped away. The only quest left is the one for art.

The final installment of an ambitious and lengthy chronicle has a considerable number of tasks to perform. The reader nurtured on the nineteenth century novel expects to see the numerous loose threads of the plot knotted and the conflicts resolved. Themes must evolve, ripen, and produce; the characters that reflect such truths must complete their move from ignorance to greater knowledge. Most of all, there must be a sense of the conclusion's inevitability. Proust brilliantly fulfills such expectations in the final volume of *Remembrance of Things Past*. The matinee at the new mansion of the Prince and Princess de Guermantes allows Marcel to arrive at a knowledge that has eluded him previously in his various quests for society and love. Marcel, no longer young, himself victim of the onslaughts of time, discovers that, indeed, he is capable of the literary vocation that he had previously considered beyond his grasp. *Time Regained* is nothing less than a gallery of transformations. The guests at the matinee have aged so that Marcel first thinks he has come to a masquerade. French society itself has undergone a massive upheaval. Most significant, however, is the transformation in Marcel after he fortuitously steps on the uneven paving stones outside the Guermantes mansion.

TIME REGAINED

Time Regained begins in Combray, where Marcel lives among the shattered images of his youth. His own first love, Gilberte, now suffers from the same-sex infidelities of Marcel's dearest friend, Robert de Saint-Loup. In addition to these disappointments, a book given to Marcel by Gilberte, an unpublished *Journal* of the Goncourt brothers, convinces Marcel that he has no vocation in literature. A passage from the *Journal* describes an evening at the Verdurins'. The description of Cottard and other members of the clan makes Marcel feel that he lacks the capacity to see and hear accurately. Also, if the Goncourts' work is genuine art, then art lies, for Marcel knows that the circle surrounding the Verdurins has little of the glamour that the Goncourts' account suggests. Although realistic in its detail, the passage has failed, because it has not penetrated the surface. Marcel recalls that Bergotte succeeded where the *Journal* fails, because he had the ability to become a mirror that reflected life accurately. His reading of the *Journal* leaves Marcel in a state of artistic depression, one that will not be relieved until he steps on the uneven stones.

The Goncourt *Journal* has a second function: Its description of society prepares the way for Marcel's return to the Paris of World War I. Although the war rages less than an hour away, Paris seems largely unaffected; the feud between Madame Verdurin and the Baron de Charlus continues. Although Madame Verdurin, with the aid of Morel's journalistic pieces, appears to have turned society against the supposedly pro-German Baron, he has lost none of his intellectual or sexual fervor. What the Baron dislikes about wartime France is its love of the hypocritical chauvinistic cant written by men such as Norpois and Brichot. The Baron, however, does find the soldiers attractive; indeed, when Marcel encounters him, he is following two Zouaves. By chance, Marcel also learns of the Baron's preference for the sexually bizarre. Jupien has come to operate a male brothel for the sake of the Baron's pleasures, among which is a whipping administered to him while he is chained to an iron bed. Robert de Saint-Loup also frequents Jupien's establishment, but the war has restored his old nobility: Robert dies when he returns to the front in order to cover the retreat of his men. Gilberte, in the meantime, is in Tansonville, and Marcel learns from her that the Méséglise Way of his childhood has been the scene of an eight-month battle in which 600,000 Germans have died.

The final scene in the novel comes several years after the war has ended. Marcel has returned to Paris from a sanatorium. He continues to regret his lack of talent for literature; even his desire to produce a great work is apparently dying. Having thus no reason to avoid society, banal as it is, he accepts the invitation of the Prince and Princess de Guermantes to a matinee. The afternoon produces two major surprises. First, Marcel discovers that the past can be profoundly recaptured, although involuntarily; then, he witnesses the shocking effect time has wrought on the people he has known. His afternoon reaffirms his judgment that society has little to offer and that his one hope is to cheat death long enough to complete the work he now knows he must write.

Marcel's discoveries begin as he walks the last, short distance to the Guermanteses' new mansion. He encounters an aged Baron de Charlus supported by Jupien. The Baron brings to Marcel's mind the image of great tragic figures such as Lear and Oedipus. In this accidental meeting, the larger spectacle of aging apparent at the matinee is anticipated. Filled with gloom, Marcel approaches the mansion, but, in avoiding a passing car, he trips against the uneven paving stones. Immediately, a happiness like that evoked by the madeleine his Aunt Léonie had fed him, the trees at Balbec, and the music of Vinteuil dispels his melancholy. He then remembers the experience that lies at the source of this pleasure: The uneven stones have produced the same sensation he experienced when he stood on similar stones in the baptistery of Saint Mark's. Once inside the Guermanteses' mansion, Marcel continues to savor such memories: The sound of a spoon, the stiffness of a napkin invoke involuntary recollections. As Marcel relives the past, he is conscious of moving outside time.

Once cognizant of his ability to recapture past time, Marcel explores its relevance to creativity. In a profusion of brilliant, often aphoristic observations, Marcel indicates that the role of the artist is that of a translator of the impressions and sensations that lie within him into spiritual equivalencies. As Proust's own prose reveals, this transformation is accomplished primarily through the use of metaphor. Metaphor aids the artist in his search for the truths that lie obscured by conventional knowledge: "Through art alone are we able to emerge from ourselves, to know what another person sees of a universe which is not the same as our own." Unlike ordinary men, the artist understands that the images of daily life, the people one meets, are symbols waiting to be interpreted and read. As Wilson points out, Proust sees the role of the artist as prophetic and moral. Ideally, as Marcel states, "every reader is, while he is reading, the reader of his own self."

As Marcel savors his discoveries about the nature of art, he also perceives that Swann has indeed been his primary mentor and inspiration. Through Swann's influence, he has gone to Balbec and subsequently made the acquaintance of both the Guermanteses and Albertine. Marcel observes that even the Guermantes Way has emanated from Swann's Way, an idea reinforced when he meets Mademoiselle de Saint-Loup at the matinee. In this granddaughter of Swann, the two ways have literally become one. This recollection of Swann also provides a smooth transition back to Marcel's immediate concern, the matinee. With irony characteristic of the novel as a whole, Marcel discovers, with something akin to horror, the destructive effect of time precisely at the moment that he conceives of a work that depends on memories existing outside time. Gathered at the Guermanteses' home are most of the personages—the "interwoven threads," as Marcel calls them—that have populated the novel: Bloch, Legrandin, Gilberte, Odette, the Baron, the Duke and Duchess de Guermantes, Morel, even Rachel, Robert de Saint-Loup's old mistress. Marcel discovers curious reversals and startling revelations: The Duchess de Guermantes now patronizes Rachel, whom she once had snubbed; the Duke, described as a "magnificent ruin," loves Odette; most shocking of all, the new Princess de Guermantes is Madame Verdurin. Marcel is struck by the vast change that has taken place in a society that he once considered stable, monumental, and without flux.

The vivid display of decay and cruelty that Marcel sees at the matinee, coupled with the news of the tragic death of the great actress, Berma, produces the appropriate effect on Marcel and the reader. The physical world, awash in the tide of time, is rendered absurd by the inevitability of suffering and death. For Marcel, the visceral knowledge of such a fact is the necessary spur to action. Rather than sink into despair, he sees that life can be restored to its "pristine shape" only within the confines of a book; he repeatedly insists that his purpose in writing such a work is that others may examine their own lives.

The end of *Remembrance of Things Past* is also its beginning. Marcel removes himself from society, and, under the shadow of its own approaching death, he begins the work that will immortalize Swann, the Guermanteses, Albertine, and himself. While the quests for love and society fail or lead to disappointment, the greater quest for immortality in art succeeds.

John K. Saunders

Other Major Works

SHORT FICTION: *Les Plaisirs et les jours*, 1896 (*Pleasures and Regrets*, 1948); *The Complete Short Stories of Marcel Proust*, 2001.

NONFICTION: *Pastiches et mélanges*, 1919; *Chroniques*, 1927; *Contre Sainte-Beuve*, 1954 (wr. 1908; *By Way of Sainte-Beuve*, 1958); *Marcel Proust: Selected Letters, 1983-1992* (3 volumes; Philip Kolb, editor); *Letters of Marcel Proust*, 2006 (Mina Curtiss, editor).

TRANSLATIONS: *Le Bible d'Amiens*, 1904 (of John Ruskin's *The Bible of Amiens*); *Sésame et les lys*, 1906 (of Ruskin's *Sesame and Lilies*).

Bibliography

Aciman, André, ed. *The Proust Project*. New York: Farrar, Straus and Giroux, 2004. Twenty-eight authors discuss their favorite passages in Proust's *Remembrance of*

Things Past. Among the contributors are Judith Thurman, Edmund White, and J. D. McClatchy.

Bales, Richard, ed. *The Cambridge Companion to Proust.* New York: Cambridge University Press, 2001. Collection of essays about *Remembrance of Things Past* includes discussions of the novel's birth and development, the novel's structure, its narrator, and love, sex, and friendship in the novel. Also addressed are the changes seen in French society from the belle époque to World War I.

Bloom, Harold, ed. *Marcel Proust.* New York: Chelsea House, 1987. Collection features essays by Proust's most distinguished critics, including Germaine Brée, Samuel Beckett, and Walter Benjamin. Topics covered include Proust's reading and his handling of time, narrative, and metaphor. Begins with an informative editor's introduction and includes a chronology and a bibliography.

_____. *Marcel Proust's "Remembrance of Things Past."* New York: Chelsea House, 1987. Overlaps somewhat with Bloom's other edited volume of essays (above) but contains important essays by Georges Bataille ("Proust and Evil") and Georges Poulet ("Proustian Space"). Includes an introduction, chronology, and bibliography.

Brady, Patrick. *Marcel Proust.* Boston: Twayne, 1977. Good introductory study presents discussion of Proust's voice and tone as well as selves, relationships, things, symbols, patterns, memories, and art in his works. Includes chronology, notes, and annotated bibliography.

Brown, Stephen Gilbert. *The Gardens of Desire: Marcel Proust and the Fugitive Sublime.* Albany: State University of New York Press, 2004. Provides a psychological critique of *Remembrance of Things Past*, applying theories of Sigmund Freud, Jacques Derrida, and Otto Rank to analyze the origins of the novels' creative impulse.

Cano, Christine M. *Proust's Deadline.* Urbana: University of Illinois Press, 2006. Interesting history describes the publishing and reception of *Remembrance of Things Past.* Includes discussion of how the later discovery of unpublished drafts touched off a debate about the novel's authenticity.

Carter, William C. *Marcel Proust: A Life.* New Haven, Conn.: Yale University Press, 2000. Meticulous account of Proust's life and literary career traces his development as a writer. Demonstrates how his earlier writings, including the abandoned novel *Jean Santeuil*, led him to create *Remembrances of Things Past.*

Hodson, Leighton, ed. *Marcel Proust: The Critical Heritage.* New York: Routledge, 1989. Carefully tracks the reception of the author's work, from contemporary reviews to later critical essays. Includes a bibliography.

Murphy, Michael. *Proust and America.* Liverpool, England: Liverpool University Press, 2007. Interprets Proust's work within the context of American art, literature, and culture. Describes how the French writer was influenced by American authors Ralph Waldo Emerson and Edgar Allan Poe as well as by American neurologist George Beard's writings on neurasthenia and "American nervousness."

Painter, George. *Proust: The Early Years*. Boston: Little, Brown, 1959.

_____. *Proust: The Later Years*. Boston: Little, Brown, 1965. Two-volume work is renowned not only as a great biography of Proust but also as an exemplary work of biography in and of itself. Painter is noted for his extraordinary grasp of the autobiographical materials from which *Remembrance of Things Past* evolved.

White, Edmund. *Marcel Proust*. New York: Viking, 1999. Excellent concise biography of Proust. White, a gay literary critic and novelist, perceptively and honestly discusses Proust's homosexuality. Includes bibliographical references.

FRANÇOIS RABELAIS

Born: La Devinière, near Chinon, France; c. 1494
Died: Paris, France; April, 1553

PRINCIPAL LONG FICTION
Pantagruel, 1532 (English translation, 1653)
Gargantua, 1534 (English translation, 1653)
Tiers Livre, 1546 (*Third Book*, 1693)
Le Quart Livre, incomplete 1548, complete 1552 (*Fourth Book*, 1694)
Le Cinquième Livre, 1564 (*Fifth Book*, 1694)
Gargantua et Pantagruel, 1567 (includes all previous titles; *Gargantua and Pantagruel*, 1653-1694, 1929)

OTHER LITERARY FORMS

In preparation for his doctoral degree, François Rabelais (RAHB-uh-lay) composed commentaries on the *Aphorisms* of Hippocrates and the *Ars medicinalis* of Galen in editions of these works that Rabelais published in 1532. After his first trip to Rome, he edited a *Topographia antiquae Romae*, based on a work by Bartolome Marliani, which was published by Sébastien Gryphe in 1534. *La Sciomachie et festins* (simulated combats and feasts), published in Lyons by Gryphe in 1549, also refers to Rabelais's journeys. It is also known that Rabelais composed poetry. Many of his letters, especially letters that he wrote while in Rome, are available in various editions.

ACHIEVEMENTS

With François Rabelais, French literature entered into a new phase. After the great medieval epics and romances of the twelfth and thirteenth centuries, there had been a steady decline until the sixteenth century. In France, the new learning brought about by the rediscovery of ancient Greek manuscripts, the invention of printing, and the great voyages of discovery found its first expression in Rabelais. *Gargantua and Pantagruel* breathes the spirit of enthusiasm, liberation, and discovery that inspired the rebirth of culture and learning.

Nevertheless, there is in Rabelais much of the medieval. In fact, he chose as his inspiration a book popular at the time, *Grandes et inestimables cronicques du grant et énorme géant Gargantua* (1532; great and inestimable chronicles of the great and enormous giant Gargantua), based on the story of a giant associated with King Arthur, Merlin, Morgan, and Mélusine. Rabelais proposed a sequel in which he continued the popular comic of the *cronicques*. He enriched his legend with notes on history, geography, local custom, and theater; his is a Renaissance interpretation of a medieval carnival.

As the critic Jean Plattard noted, Rabelais maintained the medieval spirit of the farces

François Rabelais
(Library of Congress)

and fabliaux in his violent imagery, his vulgarity, and his preoccupation with sexual matters. At the same time, Rabelais introduced the spirit of the Renaissance with his rejection of Scholasticism, his confidence in antiquity, his faith in science, and his belief in human progress.

Rabelais did not write a novel in the modern sense of the word, nor did he intend to compose one. As Jacques Boulenger observed, Rabelais wanted to embroider a vast canvas both with fantasies and with scenes from real life; in his encyclopedic ambition, he was typical of the Renaissance. Rabelais's achievement lies above all in his style, in a remarkable exploitation of all the possibilities of language. His giants are polyglots, and so is their creator. He uses French and Latin with ease; he creates words in torrents. He is equally adept in dialect, patois, argot, and scientific terminology. Boulenger described Rabelais's styles as "verbal intoxication in the dionysiac sense," yet when the occasion demands, as in the description of Badebec's death, Rabelais is a master of economy. The first French prose writer with genuine artistic talent and one of the greatest examples of the *esprit gaulois* found in the *Roman de Renart* (c. 1175-1205), the fabliaux, Molière, and Voltaire, Rabelais was truly a turning point in French literature.

Biography

Much of François Rabelais's biography is lost in obscurity, but modern scholars have established the principal events of his life. The year of Rabelais's birth, believed to be 1494, is still uncertain, but it is known that his father, Antoine, was a lawyer at the royal court of Chinon and was associated with the most enlightened men of his day. Rabelais spent his childhood at Chinon, especially at the family's country home, La Devinière, often mentioned in his works, and at Angers, his mother's birthplace. He was probably educated at the Benedictine abbey of Seuillé, evoked in Friar John's monastery in *Gargantua and Pantagruel*.

By 1521, Rabelais was a Franciscan monk at Fontenay-le-Comte in Bas Poitou; it was there that he met Pierre Amy, one of the outstanding Hellenists of the time, and entered into correspondence with the eminent French Hellenist Guillaume Budé. Rabelais translated some of Herodotus from Greek into Latin, and also contributed to André Tiraqueau's treatise on the laws of marriage, "De legibus connubialibus," echoes of which appear in book 3.

In 1523, the Greek books of the monastery were confiscated under orders from the Sorbonne, and shortly afterward Rabelais transferred to the Benedictines of Saint-Pierre-de-Maillezain, where he came into contact with the scholarly bishop Geoffroy d'Estissac. In 1527, Rabelais left the monastery and toured the same universities his Pantagruel visits in book 2. In 1532, he received his bachelor's degree in medicine from the University of Montpellier and assumed a post in Lyons, at that time the capital of the Renaissance. He also continued his classical commentaries and the same year published *Pantagruel*, censured by the Sorbonne for obscenity. Jean du Bellay, bishop of Paris, became Rabelais's protector in 1534, taking him to Rome as his personal physician. It was upon Rabelais's return that he published *Gargantua*, likewise censured because of its unfortunate coincidence with the Affair of the Placards.

Rabelais attempted briefly the life of a secular priest; by 1537, he was a doctor of medicine in Lyons. In 1541, he published a new edition of *Gargantua and Pantagruel*, with the attacks against the Sorbonne expurgated. The publication of book 3 in 1546 still provoked censure, as did that of the complete book 4 in 1552. His later days included more travel in Italy, especially with du Bellay. It is fairly certain that Rabelais died in Paris, at the beginning of April, 1553.

Analysis

François Rabelais is universally regarded as one of the major figures in the Western literary tradition, in the company of Dante, Geoffrey Chaucer, William Shakespeare, and Miguel de Cervantes, yet he is more often praised than read. Indeed, in the judgment of scholar Mikhail Bakhtin, "Of all the great writers of world literature, Rabelais is the least popular, the least understood and appreciated."

The difficulty of Rabelais, the quality that discourages many modern readers from making headway in his work, is not the strategic obscurity of a James Joyce or an Ezra Pound; rather, it resembles the difficulty that one experiences in "getting" a joke, the humor of which is not immediately apparent. To read Rabelais is essentially to laugh, but humor is notoriously elusive, dependent on a wide range of local cultural assumptions and linguistic practices and thus quick to be lost in time and in translation. Here, there is a comparison with Shakespeare: One vein of Shakespearean humor, closely related to the humor of Rabelais, is accessible to the modern reader only via scholarly explication of wordplay, allusions, implicit cultural assumptions, and so on, but Shakespeare remains highly readable even when many of his bawdy puns, for example, are entirely missed.

The difficulty in grasping the spirit of Rabelais's jokes, their underlying intent, is confirmed by ongoing critical debate. Even such a fundamental issue as Rabelais's attitude toward Christianity and the Church has been the subject of bitter controversy. Throughout *Gargantua and Pantagruel* there are frequent satiric jabs at the rites and institutions of the Church. While Rabelais ridicules monasticism and the Papacy, however, and while his parodies of Christian ritual could be deemed sacrilegious if not blasphemous, he stops short of the open atheism of the Enlightenment.

Critics such as Abel Lefranc have argued that Rabelais was in fact a thoroughgoing rationalist who, unable to express his convictions openly, presented them in a humorous guise. According to such critics, Rabelais thus anticipated the skepticism of the Enlightenment. On the other hand, critics such as Lucien Febvre, who devoted a massive volume to a refutation of Lefranc, have argued that Rabelais's satire was directed against institutional abuses of the Church, not against the heart of Christian belief.

Although such questions may never be definitively resolved, one helpful approach to Rabelais's humor is that taken by Bakhtin, who places Rabelais in what he calls the carnival tradition, a tradition of folk humor with roots in the ancient past, encompassing such festivities as the Roman Saturnalia and still vital in the Middle Ages: "Celebrations of a carnival type represented a considerable part of the life of medieval men, even in the time given over to them. Large medieval cities devoted an average of three months a year to these festivities."

Bakhtin suggests that it is Rabelais's indebtedness to this folk tradition, an expression of popular culture still largely unexplored by literary scholars, that accounts for the relative failure of modern readers to appreciate his work. In the carnival atmosphere, all of the sacred values of medieval society were parodied in a ritualistic manner—often with the full participation of the clergy. Rabelais's humor is thus characterized by the systematic inversion typical of carnival: parody, blasphemy, gross physical images, and so on.

By placing *Gargantua and Pantagruel* in this context, Bakhtin shifts the emphasis from an interpretation of Rabelais's values—that is, the personal beliefs informing his work—to the folk tradition of which his work was the supreme expression even as it marked the decisive break between the Renaissance and the Middle Ages.

GARGANTUA AND PANTAGRUEL

Rabelais's Renaissance spirit is nowhere more apparent than in his style, an overflowing fountain of verbal exuberance, a rich compound of slang, odd words, jargon of the various professions, interminable lists, and other heterogeneous elements. *Gargantua and Pantagruel* is full of puns that are difficult to translate: *service du vin/service divin* (the wine service/the divine service); Grandgousier's name, from *Que grand tu as (gosier)* (What a big gullet you have); or Epistemon, who has *la coupe tétée* (his chop headed off).

This exuberance is also evident in Rabelais's characterizations. Although he created types rather than flesh-and-blood people, his characters are unforgettable. Grandgousier, the progenitor of the illustrious family of giants, is the most shadowy. He appears as the noble lord, just and forgiving after the Picrocholine Wars and a good father to Gargantua. His son is curious, witty, garrulous, and loving. After the beginning of book 2, Grandgousier appears rarely, but always with concern for his son. Pantagruel, Gargantua's son, is the real hero of the story. After a well-delineated education, he becomes a kind lord, and his earlier wit changes to wisdom. Perhaps the best-portrayed characters are Friar John and Panurge. Friar John is the garrulous monk who always has something of the cloister about him; kind, generous, and witty, he enlivens all the adventures from the Picrocholine Wars to the voyage for the Divine Bottle. Panurge, the perpetual trickster and inventor of farces, changes his character in book 3 to that of a man caught in a dilemma: to marry or not to marry? To choose action or inaction? There are few female characters in *Gargantua and Pantagruel*; they are limited to Gargamelle, Grandgousier's wife, and Badebec, Gargantua's wife, who dies as she is giving birth to Pantagruel. Basically, the story is a very masculine one; as in the medieval farces, women are little more than bearers of children and objects of sexual desire.

GARGANTUA

Although published two years after *Pantagruel*, in 1534, *Gargantua* is known as book 1 because of its chronology. Gargantua is the father of Pantagruel, and the book tells of his miraculous birth, adolescence, education, and maturity. The prologue describes a *silenus*, a little box for rare drugs, which Rabelais compares to Socrates, and indeed to his own work: ugly from the outside but precious on the inside.

After Rabelais has made a Genesis-like presentation of Gargantua's genealogy, birth, and naming, the reader learns his first words: *à boire* (drink), symbolic of the thirst of the Renaissance man for the new learning. Much of book 1 is concerned with education; the critic Thomas M. Greene considers its essential theme to be the process of development in the young giant as he progresses from the "random equality of childhood experience ... to poise and sophistication without losing his capacity for naïve joy." First educated in a haphazard manner by the Sophists, he is purged by Ponocrates and learns more by ear than by eye to integrate all activities—physical, mental, and spiritual—and grow from chaos to discipline and from ignorance to truth and justice.

A lengthy episode treats the wars between Picrochole, King of Lerné, and Grandgousier, Gargantua's father, a noble and peace-loving lord. Lefranc sees historical and biographical material in this unjust war, as it takes place around La Roche-Clamard, near Seuillé, in Rabelais's native Chinon. As the war progresses, Friar John of the Funnels, the vibrant and impetuous monk, becomes Grandgousier's staunch ally. In the words and actions of Friar John, one finds some of Rabelais's finest satire of the monastic life he knew so well.

In recompense for his help in the war won by Grandgousier, Friar John receives the Abbey of Thélème, Rabelais's ideal for an elite community. This semiutopian monastery, modeled on the château of Bonnivet, admits both men and women of outstanding physical and moral traits, inviting them to spend their time in pursuit of culture and eventually to leave and marry. It is governed by only one rule: "Fay ce que voudras" (do what you wish). An enigmatic inscription in poetry concludes the book and invites the reader to continue the search for truth in the Renaissance spirit.

Pantagruel

Book 2, *Pantagruel*, is the least coherent of the first four volumes. It reveals the author's unmistakable style and wit and gives promise of more adventures in the future. As in *Gargantua*, Rabelais traces the genealogy of Pantagruel in a burlesque parody of the Bible and Pliny the Elder's *Natural History* (77 C.E.), as he emphasizes his hero's gigantic appetite and prodigious strength. Because Pantagruel will later liberate himself and others from the bonds of ignorance, he frees himself as a child from the constraint of his cradle.

Education plays an important role here also, especially in chapter 8, in which Gargantua tells his son Pantagruel to become "an abyss of knowledge." Pantagruel also tours the famous universities of his day: Toulouse, a center of dance and fencing; Montepellier, noted for its wine; Avignon, for its women; Bourges, for its poor laws; and Angers, which he avoids because it is infested with the plague. He visits libraries, which Rabelais uses to satirize many spiritual texts and the immoral lives of those who read them.

In book 2, Pantagruel meets Panurge, who is to become his friend for life. Panurge is one of a long line of picaros; he introduces himself in many languages, a performance typical of his pranks, which, as Greene observes, "mingle in various measures humor, cunning, perversity, creative inspiration and malice." Rabelais describes Panurge as proper-looking, a bit of a lecher, always short of money (which he always finds by cunningly perpetrated larceny), and a perpetual trickster. His clever and often crude tricks form much of the wit of books 2 and 4.

In the courtly tradition, Panurge and Pantagruel go off to battle in Utopia, where Gargantua has been transferred by the fairy Morgue. Rabelais seems to return to the spirit of the *cronicques* as he ends his disjointed but highly original portrayal of the giants.

In contrast to the looseness of book 2, book 3 is the most unified of the entire series. In the prologue, Rabelais compares himself to Diogenes, who, though physically unfit for war, rolled his tub so as not to appear lazy. In the first six chapters, Panurge appears as the traditional spendthrift; having inherited an estate, he rapidly squanders his inheritance on feasting. In the remainder of the book, he engages in lengthy discussions on whether to marry. Many critics trace Rabelais's treatment of marriage and cuckoldry in book 3 to the medieval farces; others, such as Greene, see the search for truth and the importance of action as forming the real subject of the book.

Panurge consults various sources to resolve his dilemma: the *sortes vergilianae* (a book of Vergil opened at random), a fortune-teller, the poet Raminagrobis, the magician Herr Trippa. All give him the same response: If he marries, he will be cuckolded, beaten, and robbed. The theologian Hippothadée encourages him to choose someone like Solomon's "valiant woman"; the doctor Rondibilis tells him of woman's foibles; the philosopher Trouillogan has no definite answer. After a final consultation with the fool Triboulet, no more satisfactory than all the others, Pantagruel convinces Panurge to consult the Oracle of the Divine Bottle in Cathay. Thus, the stage is set for the adventures that occupy books 4 and 5.

In book 4, inspired by the accounts of navigation so prominent at the time, especially those of Jacques Cartier, Rabelais composed the travelogue or odyssey of his heroes—a fantastic account of imaginary places and allegorical people, filled with the marvelous and touching on science fiction, such as the frozen words that melt and begin to speak. There are many realistic allusions to Rabelais's own day, such as the Decretals, the base of canonical jurisprudence; the officers of law and justice, portrayed in the Chicanous; and the wars between Protestants and Catholics, symbolized by the battle with the Andouilles.

Rabelais also satirizes perennial vices such as gluttony and its opposite, a sterile asceticism based on pride rather than on genuine piety. Panurge reassumes the character of the trickster and in a famous episode drowns the sheep of the avaricious merchant Dindenault. The travelers have not reached the Divine Bottle by the end of book 4, but Rabelais's imagination and invention are here at their height.

Originally published posthumously as *L'Isle sonante* in 1562, book 5 differs so radically from the preceding ones that critics today still question its authenticity; it is bitter, rambling, and far less creative than its predecessors. In it, the story of the navigation continues through many more fantastic islands.

The Isle Sonante (ringing island), with its perpetually clanging bells, is inhabited by birds that resemble men and women and whose names refer to the clergy and members of religious orders. The Chats-fourrés (furry cats) are the officers of the Parlement of Paris, who refused Michel de l'Hospital's proposal for an edict of toleration for the Protestants. The Apedeftes, or ignoramuses, are the tax collectors and clerks in the counting houses.

After many other such adventures, the travelers finally reach the Divine Bottle and admire the magnificent temple in which it is located. The priestess Bacbuc invites Panurge to hear the long-awaited pronouncement, which consists of one word: "Drink." The priestess

JEAN-JACQUES ROUSSEAU

Born: Geneva (now in Switzerland); June 28, 1712
Died: Ermenonville, France; July 2, 1778

PRINCIPAL LONG FICTION
Julie: Ou, La Nouvelle Héloïse, 1761 (*Eloise: Or, A Series of Original Letters*, 1761; also known as *Julie: Or, The New Eloise*, 1968; better known as *The New Héloïse*)

OTHER LITERARY FORMS

Like many of the great figures of the Enlightenment, Jean-Jacques Rousseau (rew-SOH) wrote on a wide variety of topics and explored both literary and nonliterary forms. His first serious effort at writing—the one with which he hoped to launch his career upon his arrival in Paris in 1742—was a proposal for a new system of musical notation that he presented to the Académie des Sciences. Although his proposal did not win an overly enthusiastic reception, Rousseau was recognized as knowledgeable in music. Cardinal Richelieu asked him to adapt the verses and the music of a ballet by Voltaire and Jean-Philippe Rameau titled *Les Fêtes de Ramire* (1745). Rousseau's interlude *Le Devin du village* (pr. 1752; *The Cunning-Man*, 1766) met with much success at its first performance before King Louis XV at Fontainebleau. When the editors of *L'Encyclopédie* (1751-1780) were later soliciting authors for the various sections of this voluminous work, Rousseau was engaged to write the articles on music along with the article "Économie politique" ("Political Economy"). He also dabbled in theater, writing, among other plays, *Narcisse: Ou, L'Amant de lui-même* (1752). It was, however, particularly with his two anthropological essays, or discourses—*Discours sur les sciences et les arts* (1750; *The Discourse Which Carried the Praemium at the Academy of Dijon*, 1751; better known as *A Discourse on the Arts and Sciences*, 1913) and *Discours sur l'origine et les fondements de l'inégalité parmi les hommes* (1755; *A Discourse upon the Origin and Foundation of Inequality Among Mankind*, 1761)—that Rousseau established himself as an original writer of profound insight. The discourses set the stage for much of Rousseau's subsequent work: his epistolary novel, *The New Héloïse;* a retort to Jean d'Alembert's *L'Encyclopédie* article on Geneva, *Lettre à d'Alembert sur les spectacles* (1758; *A Letter to M. d'Alembert Concerning the Effects of Theatrical Entertainments*, 1759); a treatise on education, *Émile: Ou, De l'éducation* (1762; *Emilius and Sophia: Or, A New System of Education*, 1762-1763); a work of political theory, *Du contrat social: Ou, Principes du droit politique* (1762; *A Treatise on the Social Contract: Or, The Principles of Political Law*, 1764; commonly known as *The Social Contract*); and a short interpretive piece on language, *Essai sur l'origine des langues* (1781; *On the Origin of Languages*, 1967). In his later years, Rousseau turned to autobiographical writing and composed *Les Confessions de J.-J. Rousseau* (part 1, 1782; part 2, 1789; *The Confessions of J.-J.*

GARGANTUA AND PANTAGRUEL

Rabelais's Renaissance spirit is nowhere more apparent than in his style, an overflowing fountain of verbal exuberance, a rich compound of slang, odd words, jargon of the various professions, interminable lists, and other heterogeneous elements. *Gargantua and Pantagruel* is full of puns that are difficult to translate: *service du vin/service divin* (the wine service/the divine service); Grandgousier's name, from *Que grand tu as (gosier)* (What a big gullet you have); or Epistemon, who has *la coupe têtée* (his chop headed off).

This exuberance is also evident in Rabelais's characterizations. Although he created types rather than flesh-and-blood people, his characters are unforgettable. Grandgousier, the progenitor of the illustrious family of giants, is the most shadowy. He appears as the noble lord, just and forgiving after the Picrocholine Wars and a good father to Gargantua. His son is curious, witty, garrulous, and loving. After the beginning of book 2, Grandgousier appears rarely, but always with concern for his son. Pantagruel, Gargantua's son, is the real hero of the story. After a well-delineated education, he becomes a kind lord, and his earlier wit changes to wisdom. Perhaps the best-portrayed characters are Friar John and Panurge. Friar John is the garrulous monk who always has something of the cloister about him; kind, generous, and witty, he enlivens all the adventures from the Picrocholine Wars to the voyage for the Divine Bottle. Panurge, the perpetual trickster and inventor of farces, changes his character in book 3 to that of a man caught in a dilemma: to marry or not to marry? To choose action or inaction? There are few female characters in *Gargantua and Pantagruel*; they are limited to Gargamelle, Grandgousier's wife, and Badebec, Gargantua's wife, who dies as she is giving birth to Pantagruel. Basically, the story is a very masculine one; as in the medieval farces, women are little more than bearers of children and objects of sexual desire.

GARGANTUA

Although published two years after *Pantagruel*, in 1534, *Gargantua* is known as book 1 because of its chronology. Gargantua is the father of Pantagruel, and the book tells of his miraculous birth, adolescence, education, and maturity. The prologue describes a *silenus*, a little box for rare drugs, which Rabelais compares to Socrates, and indeed to his own work: ugly from the outside but precious on the inside.

After Rabelais has made a Genesis-like presentation of Gargantua's genealogy, birth, and naming, the reader learns his first words: *à boire* (drink), symbolic of the thirst of the Renaissance man for the new learning. Much of book 1 is concerned with education; the critic Thomas M. Greene considers its essential theme to be the process of development in the young giant as he progresses from the "random equality of childhood experience ... to poise and sophistication without losing his capacity for naïve joy." First educated in a haphazard manner by the Sophists, he is purged by Ponocrates and learns more by ear than by eye to integrate all activities—physical, mental, and spiritual—and grow from chaos to discipline and from ignorance to truth and justice.

A lengthy episode treats the wars between Picrochole, King of Lerné, and Grandgousier, Gargantua's father, a noble and peace-loving lord. Lefranc sees historical and biographical material in this unjust war, as it takes place around La Roche-Clamard, near Seuillé, in Rabelais's native Chinon. As the war progresses, Friar John of the Funnels, the vibrant and impetuous monk, becomes Grandgousier's staunch ally. In the words and actions of Friar John, one finds some of Rabelais's finest satire of the monastic life he knew so well.

In recompense for his help in the war won by Grandgousier, Friar John receives the Abbey of Thélème, Rabelais's ideal for an elite community. This semiutopian monastery, modeled on the château of Bonnivet, admits both men and women of outstanding physical and moral traits, inviting them to spend their time in pursuit of culture and eventually to leave and marry. It is governed by only one rule: "Fay ce que voudras" (do what you wish). An enigmatic inscription in poetry concludes the book and invites the reader to continue the search for truth in the Renaissance spirit.

Pantagruel

Book 2, *Pantagruel*, is the least coherent of the first four volumes. It reveals the author's unmistakable style and wit and gives promise of more adventures in the future. As in *Gargantua*, Rabelais traces the genealogy of Pantagruel in a burlesque parody of the Bible and Pliny the Elder's *Natural History* (77 C.E.), as he emphasizes his hero's gigantic appetite and prodigious strength. Because Pantagruel will later liberate himself and others from the bonds of ignorance, he frees himself as a child from the constraint of his cradle.

Education plays an important role here also, especially in chapter 8, in which Gargantua tells his son Pantagruel to become "an abyss of knowledge." Pantagruel also tours the famous universities of his day: Toulouse, a center of dance and fencing; Montepellier, noted for its wine; Avignon, for its women; Bourges, for its poor laws; and Angers, which he avoids because it is infested with the plague. He visits libraries, which Rabelais uses to satirize many spiritual texts and the immoral lives of those who read them.

In book 2, Pantagruel meets Panurge, who is to become his friend for life. Panurge is one of a long line of picaros; he introduces himself in many languages, a performance typical of his pranks, which, as Greene observes, "mingle in various measures humor, cunning, perversity, creative inspiration and malice." Rabelais describes Panurge as proper-looking, a bit of a lecher, always short of money (which he always finds by cunningly perpetrated larceny), and a perpetual trickster. His clever and often crude tricks form much of the wit of books 2 and 4.

In the courtly tradition, Panurge and Pantagruel go off to battle in Utopia, where Gargantua has been transferred by the fairy Morgue. Rabelais seems to return to the spirit of the *cronicques* as he ends his disjointed but highly original portrayal of the giants.

In contrast to the looseness of book 2, book 3 is the most unified of the entire series. In the prologue, Rabelais compares himself to Diogenes, who, though physically unfit for war, rolled his tub so as not to appear lazy. In the first six chapters, Panurge appears as the traditional spendthrift; having inherited an estate, he rapidly squanders his inheritance on feasting. In the remainder of the book, he engages in lengthy discussions on whether to marry. Many critics trace Rabelais's treatment of marriage and cuckoldry in book 3 to the medieval farces; others, such as Greene, see the search for truth and the importance of action as forming the real subject of the book.

Panurge consults various sources to resolve his dilemma: the *sortes vergilianae* (a book of Vergil opened at random), a fortune-teller, the poet Raminagrobis, the magician Herr Trippa. All give him the same response: If he marries, he will be cuckolded, beaten, and robbed. The theologian Hippothadée encourages him to choose someone like Solomon's "valiant woman"; the doctor Rondibilis tells him of woman's foibles; the philosopher Trouillogan has no definite answer. After a final consultation with the fool Triboulet, no more satisfactory than all the others, Pantagruel convinces Panurge to consult the Oracle of the Divine Bottle in Cathay. Thus, the stage is set for the adventures that occupy books 4 and 5.

In book 4, inspired by the accounts of navigation so prominent at the time, especially those of Jacques Cartier, Rabelais composed the travelogue or odyssey of his heroes—a fantastic account of imaginary places and allegorical people, filled with the marvelous and touching on science fiction, such as the frozen words that melt and begin to speak. There are many realistic allusions to Rabelais's own day, such as the Decretals, the base of canonical jurisprudence; the officers of law and justice, portrayed in the Chicanous; and the wars between Protestants and Catholics, symbolized by the battle with the Andouilles.

Rabelais also satirizes perennial vices such as gluttony and its opposite, a sterile asceticism based on pride rather than on genuine piety. Panurge reassumes the character of the trickster and in a famous episode drowns the sheep of the avaricious merchant Dindenault. The travelers have not reached the Divine Bottle by the end of book 4, but Rabelais's imagination and invention are here at their height.

Originally published posthumously as *L'Isle sonante* in 1562, book 5 differs so radically from the preceding ones that critics today still question its authenticity; it is bitter, rambling, and far less creative than its predecessors. In it, the story of the navigation continues through many more fantastic islands.

The Isle Sonante (ringing island), with its perpetually clanging bells, is inhabited by birds that resemble men and women and whose names refer to the clergy and members of religious orders. The Chats-fourrés (furry cats) are the officers of the Parlement of Paris, who refused Michel de l'Hospital's proposal for an edict of toleration for the Protestants. The Apedeftes, or ignoramuses, are the tax collectors and clerks in the counting houses.

After many other such adventures, the travelers finally reach the Divine Bottle and admire the magnificent temple in which it is located. The priestess Bacbuc invites Panurge to hear the long-awaited pronouncement, which consists of one word: "Drink." The priestess has another word of wisdom: *in vino veritas* (in wine is truth). The engimatic conclusion has as many interpretations as there are critics, for essentially it tells readers to interpret their own destinies for themselves.

Irma M. Kashuba

OTHER MAJOR WORKS
NONFICTION: *La Sciomachie et festins*, 1549.
EDITED TEXTS: *Aphorisms*, 1532; *Ars medicinalis*, 1532; *Topographia antiquae Romae*, 1534.
MISCELLANEOUS: *Pantagruéline Prognostication*, 1532 (occasional verses and letters).

BIBLIOGRAPHY
Berry, Alice Fiola. *The Charm of Catastrophe: A Study of Rabelais's "Quart Livre."* Chapel Hill: University of North Carolina, Department of Romance Languages, 2000. Analyzes *Le Quart Livre*, the last novel by Rabelais published in the author's lifetime, demonstrating how the work expresses the elderly writer's despair over failing to achieve his youthful dreams.
Bowen, Barbara C. *Enter Rabelais, Laughing*. Nashville: Vanderbilt University Press, 1998. Focuses on the humor in Rabelais's work, describing why it was funny to his sixteenth century contemporaries and placing him within the tradition of Renaissance comic writings. Includes notes and bibliography.
Carron, Jean-Claude, ed. *François Rabelais: Critical Assessments*. Baltimore: Johns Hopkins University Press, 1995. Selection and revision of papers concerning Rabelais that were delivered at a 1991 symposium at the University of California, Los Angeles. Among the topics addressed are realism, feminism, and cultural connections in Rabelais's works.
Chesney, Elizabeth A., and Marcel Tetel. *Rabelais Revisited*. New York: Twayne, 1993. Provides a good introduction to the novels, with an annotated bibliography of important studies on Rabelais. Examines the relationships between men and women in Rabelais's works.
Coleman, Dorothy Gabe. *Rabelais: A Critical Study in Prose Fiction*. New York: Cambridge University Press, 1971. Presents a meticulous analysis of Rabelais as a prose stylist and of the genres in which he wrote. Includes bibliography.
Frame, Donald M. *François Rabelais: A Study*. New York: Harcourt Brace Jovanovich, 1977. Detailed study of Rabelais's life and work includes several chapters on his major fiction and on topics such as obscenity, comedy, satire, fantasy, storytelling, giantism, humanism, evangelism, characters, and fortunes in Rabelais's writings. Supplemented with detailed notes and an annotated bibliography.
Gauna, Max. *The Rabelaisian Mythologies*. Madison, N.J.: Fairleigh Dickinson Univer-

sity Press, 1996. Rabelais described his novels as "mythologies," and this study analyzes the mythological elements in *Pantagruel*, *Gargantua*, *Tiers Livre*, and *Le Quart Livre*. Includes bibliography.

Greene, Thomas M. *Rabelais: A Study in Comic Courage.* Englewood Cliffs, N.J.: Prentice-Hall, 1970. Excellent analysis of Rabelais's works is often cited as the best introductory study of the writer. Includes bibliography.

O'Brien, John, and Malcolm Quainton, eds. *Distant Voices Still Heard: Contemporary Readings of French Renaissance Literature.* Liverpool, England: Liverpool University Press, 2000. Collection of paired essays on five major authors applies modern critical theories to French Renaissance literature. The two essays on Rabelais provide a structuralist reading of *Pantagruel* and examine the methodology of *Tiers Livre*.

Zegura, Elizabeth Chesney, ed. *The Rabelais Encyclopedia.* Westport, Conn.: Greenwood Press, 2004. Alphabetically arranged collection of articles covers a wide range of topics, including Rabelais's characters, references to Renaissance and historical figures in Rabelais's works, themes and allusions in his works, and key influences on his writing. Also features a chronology of major events in his life and literary career.

JEAN-JACQUES ROUSSEAU

Born: Geneva (now in Switzerland); June 28, 1712
Died: Ermenonville, France; July 2, 1778

PRINCIPAL LONG FICTION
Julie: Ou, La Nouvelle Héloïse, 1761 (*Eloise: Or, A Series of Original Letters*, 1761; also known as *Julie: Or, The New Eloise*, 1968; better known as *The New Héloïse*)

OTHER LITERARY FORMS

Like many of the great figures of the Enlightenment, Jean-Jacques Rousseau (rew-SOH) wrote on a wide variety of topics and explored both literary and nonliterary forms. His first serious effort at writing—the one with which he hoped to launch his career upon his arrival in Paris in 1742—was a proposal for a new system of musical notation that he presented to the Académie des Sciences. Although his proposal did not win an overly enthusiastic reception, Rousseau was recognized as knowledgeable in music. Cardinal Richelieu asked him to adapt the verses and the music of a ballet by Voltaire and Jean-Philippe Rameau titled *Les Fêtes de Ramire* (1745). Rousseau's interlude *Le Devin du village* (pr. 1752; *The Cunning-Man*, 1766) met with much success at its first performance before King Louis XV at Fontainebleau. When the editors of *L'Encyclopédie* (1751-1780) were later soliciting authors for the various sections of this voluminous work, Rousseau was engaged to write the articles on music along with the article "Économie politique" ("Political Economy"). He also dabbled in theater, writing, among other plays, *Narcisse: Ou, L'Amant de lui-même* (1752). It was, however, particularly with his two anthropological essays, or discourses—*Discours sur les sciences et les arts* (1750; *The Discourse Which Carried the Praemium at the Academy of Dijon*, 1751; better known as *A Discourse on the Arts and Sciences*, 1913) and *Discours sur l'origine et les fondements de l'inégalité parmi les hommes* (1755; *A Discourse upon the Origin and Foundation of Inequality Among Mankind*, 1761)—that Rousseau established himself as an original writer of profound insight. The discourses set the stage for much of Rousseau's subsequent work: his epistolary novel, *The New Héloïse;* a retort to Jean d'Alembert's *L'Encyclopédie* article on Geneva, *Lettre à d'Alembert sur les spectacles* (1758; *A Letter to M. d'Alembert Concerning the Effects of Theatrical Entertainments*, 1759); a treatise on education, *Émile: Ou, De l'éducation* (1762; *Emilius and Sophia: Or, A New System of Education*, 1762-1763); a work of political theory, *Du contrat social: Ou, Principes du droit politique* (1762; *A Treatise on the Social Contract: Or, The Principles of Political Law*, 1764; commonly known as *The Social Contract*); and a short interpretive piece on language, *Essai sur l'origine des langues* (1781; *On the Origin of Languages*, 1967). In his later years, Rousseau turned to autobiographical writing and composed *Les Confessions de J.-J. Rousseau* (part 1, 1782; part 2, 1789; *The Confessions of J.-J.*

Jean-Jacques Rousseau
(Library of Congress)

Rousseau, 1783-1790), *Les Dialogues: Ou, Rousseau juge de Jean-Jacques* (first dialogue, 1780; complete edition, 1782), and, finally, *Les Rêveries du promeneur solitaire* (1782; *The Reveries of the Solitary Walker*, 1783).

ACHIEVEMENTS

With the publication of his first discourse, for which he won a prize at the Académie de Dijon, Jean-Jacques Rousseau vaulted to fame in the European world of letters. Montesquieu, Voltaire, and Rousseau rank as the seminal thinkers of the French Enlightenment. No one could ignore Rousseau's claim that civilization had corrupted humankind. The assertion gave new life to the quarrel between the ancients and the moderns.

As the debate over the contributions of the sciences and the arts raged on, Rousseau found himself increasingly isolated. His friends among the philosophes, who had championed the advancement of reason against intolerance and fanaticism, found themselves reluctant to accept the full implications of Rousseau's thesis once it was more amply elaborated in his second discourse. Ultimately, Rousseau was proposing a theory that would ensure human freedom from the undue constraints of society. As he wrote in *The Social Contract,* "Man is born free, and everywhere he is in chains."

In giving primacy to the individual's legitimate wants and needs, Rousseau came to promote sensibility rather than reason as the characteristic feature of humankind. According to Rousseau, nowhere are human beings more capable of remaining in touch with themselves and their world than in nature, which provides a reflecting mirror for the human *état d'âme* (state of soul). By calling renewed attention to human sensibility and humankind's close ties with nature, Rousseau and his disciple Jacques-Henri Bernardin de Saint-Pierre were to influence profoundly the work of Romantic writers such as François-René de Chateaubriand and Alphonse de Lamartine.

Repercussions from Rousseau's oeuvre did not cease, however, in the early nineteenth century. The "Citizen of Geneva," as he was fond of calling himself, considerably reworked the tradition of confessional writing begun by Saint Augustine and continued by Michel Eyquem de Montaigne. His very self constituted the subject of *The Confessions of J.-J. Rousseau,* and he rightly concluded, in the opening lines of that work, that it was unique: "I am forming a project that has never had a precedent." As he composed his autobiographical pieces, Rousseau integrated his life's story by using sensation and feeling in a novel way to reinforce his memory. The modern reader finds in Rousseau's work not only many passages prefiguring Marcel Proust but also a generous introduction to the literature of the self.

Biography

Jean-Jacques Rousseau was born in Geneva, Switzerland, on June 28, 1712, to a Protestant family. His mother died nine days later. His father and his Aunt Suzanne reared him until Rousseau's father had to flee Geneva because of a quarrel with a military officer. The ten-year-old boy was placed in the Lambercier pension at Bossey, and it was there that Rousseau acquired a taste for country life that never left him. Once back in Geneva, Rousseau attempted an apprenticeship, first as a notary, then as an engraver, but considered the work boring and oppressive. Returning from a walk late one day in 1728, he found the gates to the city locked and decided to leave Geneva and seek his fortune elsewhere.

Rousseau's departure from the city of his birth marked the beginning of a life of constant roaming from one place to the next, a life of exile with relatively few moments of tranquillity. One of these periods occurred, however, shortly after his flight from Geneva, when he met Madame de Warens in Annecy, France. This gentle and devout woman left a lasting impression on the young Rousseau. He would return to visit her several times during the next four years, before establishing residency at her home in Chambéry. Rousseau's brief but idyllic stay there—during which time he taught himself a variety of subjects—ended in disillusionment, however, when he discovered upon returning from one of his excursions that someone else had caught the eye of his "Maman." Not long thereafter, in 1742, he moved to Paris and met Thérèse Levasseur, a simpleminded girl with whom he would live almost continuously for the rest of his life. Their union produced five children, all of whom were placed in orphanages.

After the publication of Rousseau's second discourse, the couple moved to the area of Montmorency, where Rousseau was patronized at various times by Madame d'Épinay and the duc de Luxembourg. At the Ermitage, the lodge provided by Madame d'Épinay, Rousseau became an ardent admirer of his benefactor's sister-in-law, the Comtesse d'Houdetot. The passion he felt for this lovely woman no doubt influenced *The New Héloïse*, which he was writing at the time. The six years of solitude that Rousseau experienced in this area were extremely productive ones for him.

His serenity ended abruptly, however, in 1762. In that year, *The Social Contract* and *Emilius and Sophia* appeared in print. The condemnation heaped upon these works by political and religious institutions alike forced Rousseau henceforth to lead a life on the run. He was at first pursued by the police in France; his books were burned in Geneva. Moreover, at Môtiers, in the Prussian principality of Neuchâtel, his house was stoned. For a short time, Rousseau, offered asylum by the philosopher David Hume, lived in England, where he began preparing *The Confessions of J.-J. Rousseau*. His increasing sense of universal persecution, however, caused him to break off his friendship with Hume—as he had already done with many of his other friends—and leave England.

Rousseau returned to Paris in 1770 and remained there for eight years, until the Marquis de Girardin invited him to live on his property in Ermenonville. A few months after he had moved to his new residence, Rousseau died; he was buried on the premises in the restful setting of the Island of Poplar Trees. In 1794, during the French Revolution, Rousseau's remains were by special decree transferred to the Panthéon in Paris.

Analysis

Man, according to Jean-Jacques Rousseau, is innately good. If he has become corrupt, it is society that has corrupted him. In the lace, frills, wigs, and pervasive artifice of the eighteenth century, Rousseau saw only a distortion of reality and an attempt to cover up the true nature of man. To peel away the accumulated layers of contact between man and society, Rousseau postulated for conceptual purposes a man of nature. Presumably, nature in this sense represented all that was furthest removed from the civilized world. In it, primitive men lived in relative isolation and enjoyed freedom in their simple, everyday activities.

When notions of property became widespread, however, the pure state of nature ceased to exist. Men moved into close contact with, and became dependent on, one another. Social classes established themselves, and inequities arose among them. A previous *amour de soi* (self-love)—based on self-preservation and giving rise to love and, concomitantly, pity of one's fellow human beings—yielded to *amour propre* (selfish love), a concern primarily with aggrandizement of oneself or one's possessions. Men's actions no longer came about spontaneously and from heartfelt emotions; they resulted, rather, from carefully contrived plots.

Notwithstanding his harsh attack on society, Rousseau did find in it some sources of hope. As long as man in society could feel pity, which Rousseau considered as perhaps the last vestige of primitive man, there remained the possibility of his self-betterment. Rousseau believed that man is a "perfectible" creature and predicated his educational and political theories on this belief. Sifting the various aspects of society, Rousseau came upon reason and government as key areas by which to reestablish morality. Reason, although not as reliable a guide as man's feeling or conscience, can ultimately lead him to enlightenment. As a young boy, Emilius, in the semifictional work named after him, receives an education in reason, but only after assimilating the full worth of his sensations and feelings. Moreover, the reason to which his tutor introduces him takes on a "sensitive" character. Its content has essential meaning only insofar as it has the deeper cognitive backing of feeling. Government, in its turn, should also give full force to the individual's feeling and will. In his view of the state as seen in *The Social Contract*, Rousseau balanced the individual will with the general will by closely associating the one with the other. According to his scheme of things, each individual "uniting with all obeys, however, only himself and remains as free as before."

Rousseau's dogged pursuit of a virtuous individual freedom paralleled his search for truth and authenticity in his own life and in his works. He took as his motto a saying from Juvenal's *Saturae* (100-127 C.E.; *Satires*,1693): *vitam impendere vero* (to devote one's life to truth). When Rousseau criticized d'Alembert's article on Genevan theater, it was less out of any personal distaste for dramatic performances than out of his belief that the integrity of the spectators was being compromised. In the theater, they watched only feigned emotions and staged appearances without coming to any enhanced awareness of themselves or their fellow human beings. Rousseau countered this alienating experience with the public festival, or *fête*, in which participating members demonstrated what critic Jean Starobinski has called "transparency" in their behavior.

The privileged place that Rousseau granted simplicity, openness, and spontaneity in interpersonal relations led him not only to create in his fictional writing characters that illustrated these traits but also to attempt to exemplify them himself. In his autobiographical works, Rousseau established one of the closest rhetorical relationships yet seen in the history of literature between narrator and reader. While perusing the pages of *The Confessions of J.-J. Rousseau*, the dialogues, and *The Reveries of the Solitary Walker*, one comes to a new sense of realism in literature—almost able if not to touch then certainly to feel *intùs et in cute* (on the inside and under the skin) the writer of these works.

THE NEW HÉLOÏSE

In his only major novel, *The New Héloïse*, which bore the subtitle *Lettres de deux amants, habitants d'une petite ville au pied des Alpes, recueillies et publiées par J.-J.*

Rousseau (*Letters of Two Lovers, Inhabitants of a Small Town at the Foot of the Alps, Collected and Published by J.-J. Rousseau*), Rousseau brought together many of his utopian ideas concerning humankind and society. The novel has a dreamlike quality; indeed, the subtitle reflects Rousseau's own predilection for an idyllic life in the country. Because he was composing *A Letter to M. d'Alembert*, *The Social Contract*, and *Emilius and Sophia* at the same time, echoes from these works found their way into *The New Héloïse*. They are particularly evident in the grape-harvest scene, the way of life, and the system of education chosen for Julie d'Étange's children at Clarens, the town in which she settles after turning away from the lover of her own choosing, Saint-Preux, and accepting her father's marital choice for her, Monsieur de Wolmar.

The grape harvest offers a positive example of the *fête* that Rousseau described to d'Alembert. It takes place outdoors in a public forum in which all members of the community can see one another. None of the theatrical devices or conventions that allow actors to hide behind masks and curtains and foster a mere representation of human feelings are operative there. The air of simple gaiety, combined with the industriousness of the event itself, conspires to effect an aesthetic and political ideal dear to Rousseau—an admixture of the pleasant (*l'agréable*) with the useful (*l'utile*).

The very house at Clarens has been modified to reflect the lifestyle of its inhabitants. Simple and practical furniture has replaced the former, richly decorated pieces. Another vegetable garden is cultivated where flower beds stood earlier. As for the community's society, however paternalistic it may be, its workers often act among themselves both independently and with one voice. When an individual's request agrees completely with the general will, it is automatically granted. The person's thanks, however, go not to another individual but to the group.

After Saint-Preux receives Wolmar's permission to join Julie and him at Clarens, he is charged with the instruction of their children. Although Saint-Preux no doubt possesses the requisite sensitivity to teach, Julie and Wolmar find it necessary to clarify with him their position on educating a child properly. Their system of education reflects Rousseau's own approach to this activity, which he felt was all too often preoccupied with making reason instead of nature the guiding force. Julie and Wolmar wish their children to be educated naturally, so that each step in the learning process follows the preceding one at an appropriate time and place. Should any outside factor disturb or rush this process, one ends up, as Julie notes, with "young doctors and old children." It is the tutor's foremost responsibility to develop rather than correct what nature has already given a child.

Despite some of its similarities to his other writings, *The New Héloïse* distinguishes itself in Rousseau's literary canon primarily by its subject matter. It is the one work in which the author, inspired by the correspondence between Abélard and Héloïse in the Middle Ages, integrates his thought around the central notion of love. In so doing, he not only accurately depicts the dialectics of desire but also offers an alternative to *amour-passion* in virtue. The book thus has a moralizing tone that Rousseau considered necessary for the society of his day. The vital struggle between a passionate love and a virtuous love—both of which inherently yield certain freedoms—underlies the entire novel.

Though very much in love, Julie and Saint-Preux must ultimately part company. Their separation, in conjunction with their intense feelings, lends aesthetic and dramatic plausibility to the novel's epistolary form. When Julie marries Wolmar, she undergoes a religious conversion that leads her to a new life of piety. In her letters to Saint-Preux, she attempts to tell him of the joys of virtue, which for him represents a renunciation of his desire for Julie. After several years and numerous trips, Saint-Preux, in the style of a bildungsroman character, is finally won over to virtue. What henceforth characterizes their relationship and, indeed, what has always characterized that between the novel's other major figures, Claire d'Orbe and Édouard Bomston, is a lasting friendship. Immune to the vagaries of passionate love, friendship becomes a source of peace and happiness. If Julie's death at the novel's end proves the intransmutability of passion, it does not altogether efface the intimate friendship among the remaining characters. In her absence, it is, by necessity, all that they have left as they hope to join Julie themselves.

John C. O'Neal

Other major works

PLAYS: *Les Muses galantes*, pr. 1745 (opera); *Le Devin du village*, pr. 1752 (*The Cunning-Man*, 1766); *Narcisse: Ou, L'Amant de lui-même*, pb. 1752.

NONFICTION: *Dissertation sur la musique moderne*, 1743; *Discours sur les sciences et les arts*, 1750 (*The Discourse Which Carried the Praemium at the Academy of Dijon*, 1751; better known as *A Discourse on the Arts and Sciences*, 1913); *Discours sur l'origine et les fondements de l'inégalité parmi les hommes* (1755; *A Discourse upon the Origin and Foundation of Inequality Among Mankind*, 1761); *Lettre à d'Alembert sur les spectacles*, 1758 (*A Letter to M. d'Alembert Concerning the Effects of Theatrical Entertainments*, 1759); *Émile: Ou, De l'éducation*, 1762 (*Emilius and Sophia: Or, A New System of Education*, 1762-1763); *Du contrat social: Ou, Principes du droit politique*, 1762 (*A Treatise on the Social Contract: Or, The Principles of Politic Law*, 1764; commonly known as *The Social Contract*); *Le Sentiment des citoyens*, 1764; *Quatre lettres à M. le président de Malesherbes contenant le vrai tableau de mon caractère et les vrais motifs de toute ma conduite*, 1779; *Les Dialogues: Ou, Rousseau juge de Jean-Jacques*, 1780, 1782; *Essai sur l'origine des langues*, 1781 (criticism; *On the Origin of Languages*, 1967); *Les Confessions de J.-J. Rousseau*, 1782, 1789 (*The Confessions of J.-J. Rousseau*, 1783-1790); *Les Rêveries du promeneur solitaire*, 1782 (*The Reveries of the Solitary Walker*, 1783); *Political Writings*, 1915, 1954; *Religious Writings*, 1970.

MISCELLANEOUS: *The Works*, 1763-1773 (10 volumes); *The Miscellaneous Works*, 1767 (5 volumes); *Œuvres complètes*, 1780-1789 (33 volumes); *Œuvres complètes de Jean-Jacques Rousseau*, 1959-1969 (4 volumes).

BIBLIOGRAPHY

Coleman, Patrick. *Reparative Realism: Mourning and Modernity in the French Novel, 1730-1830.* Geneva, Switzerland: Librairie Droz, 1998. Examines *The New Héloïse* and novels by Abbé Prévost, Benjamin Constant, Madame de Stäel, and Honoré de Balzac to describe how issues of grief and bereavement were handled in eighteenth and nineteenth century French fiction.

Cranston, Maurice William. *Jean-Jacques: The Early Life and Work of Jean-Jacques Rousseau, 1712-1754.* New York: W. W. Norton, 1982.

———. *The Noble Savage: Jean-Jacques Rousseau, 1754-1762.* Chicago: University of Chicago Press, 1991.

———. *The Solitary Self: Jean-Jacques Rousseau in Exile and Adversity.* Chicago: University of Chicago Press, 1997. Monumental three-volume biography has been hailed by some critics as the definitive account of Rousseau's life and work. Covers all of Rousseau's writings, including *The New Héloïse*.

Damrosch, Leo. *Jean-Jacques Rousseau: Restless Genius.* Boston: Houghton Mifflin, 2005. Biography represents a useful addition to Rousseau scholarship, providing an incisive, accessible account of Rousseau's life and contributions to philosophy and literature. Includes illustrations, time line, bibliography, and index.

Dent, Nicholas. *Rousseau.* New York: Routledge, 2005. Provides an overview of the entire range of Rousseau's philosophy, paying particular attention to the theories of democracy and freedom outlined in *The Social Contract*. Also explains Rousseau's concept of the "general will."

Havens, George R. *Jean-Jacques Rousseau.* Boston: Twayne, 1978. Concise introductory account of Rousseau's life and career is coupled with analyses of his major works. Includes bibliography and index.

Howells, Robin. *Regressive Fictions: Graffigny, Rousseau, Bernardin.* London: Legenda, 2007. Analyzes *The New Héloïse* and works by two other writers to describe how the French novel changed in the mid-eighteenth century. Prior to that time, Howells maintains, novels reflected a worldly society, characterized by wit, social sophistication, and sexual experience; novels in the last half of the century were set in idealized, imaginary worlds characterized by originality, closeness to nature, and innocence.

Hulliung, Mark. *The Autocritique of Enlightenment: Rousseau and the Philosophes.* Cambridge, Mass.: Harvard University Press, 1994. Explains how Rousseau both reflected and departed from the main currents in Enlightenment philosophy, particularly the ideas of Voltaire and Denis Diderot. Includes bibliography and index.

Morgenstern, Mira. *Rousseau and the Politics of Ambiguity: Self, Culture, and Society.* University Park: Pennsylvania State University Press, 1996. Analyzes Rousseau's political theory and its historical context, demonstrating how Rousseau's thought introduced notes of ambiguity that remain in current political life. Includes bibliography and index.

Riley, Patrick, ed. *The Cambridge Companion to Rousseau.* New York: Cambridge University Press, 2001. Collection of essays includes an overview of Rousseau's life and work, discussions of his philosophy, and a consideration of the images of authority in *The New Héloïse* and other works.

Wokler, Robert. *Rousseau: A Very Short Introduction.* 2d ed. New York: Oxford University Press, 2001. Provides a concise and lucid introduction to Rousseau's life and works, with information about his fiction and his educational and religious writings as well as discussion of his theories about politics, history, and music.

GEORGE SAND
Amandine-Aurore-Lucile Dupin

Born: Paris, France; July 1, 1804
Died: Nohant, France; June 8, 1876
Also known as: Amandine-Aurore-Lucile Dupin; Baronne Dudevant

PRINCIPAL LONG FICTION
Indiana, 1832 (English translation, 1833)
Valentine, 1832 (English translation, 1902)
Lélia, 1833, 1839 (English translation, 1978)
Mauprat, 1837 (English translation, 1870)
Spiridion, 1839 (English translation, 1842)
Le Compagnon du tour de France, 1840 (*The Companion of the Tour of France*, 1976; also known as *The Journeyman Joiner*, 1847)
Consuelo, 1842-1843 (English translation, 1846)
La Comtesse de Rudolstadt, 1843-1844 (*The Countess of Rudolstadt*, 1847)
Jeanne, 1844
Le Meunier d'Angibault, 1845 (*The Miller of Angibault*, 1847)
La Mare au diable, 1846 (*The Devil's Pool*, 1929; also known as *The Enchanted Lake*, 1850)
Lucrezia Floriani, 1846 (English translation, 1985)
Le Péché de M. Antoine, 1847 (*The Sin of Monsieur Antoine*, 1900)
La Petite Fadette, 1848-1849 (*Fanchon the Cricket*, 1864; also known as *Little Fadette*, 1850)
François le champi, 1850 (*Francis the Waif*, 1889)
Les Maîtres sonneurs, 1853 (*The Bagpipers*, 1890)
Elle et lui, 1859 (*She and He*, 1902)
Le Marquis de Villemer, 1861 (*The Marquis of Villemer*, 1871)
La Ville noire, 1861
Mademoiselle la Quintinie, 1863
Mademoiselle Merquem, 1868 (English translation, 1868)
Marianne, 1876 (novella; English translation, 1883)
Historic and Romantic Novels, 1900-1902 (20 volumes)

OTHER LITERARY FORMS

George Sand, who was famous during her lifetime primarily as a novelist, earned a living for many years as a journalist. Some of her essays on art, literature, politics, and social questions are collected in two posthumous volumes, *Questions d'art et de littérature* (1878) and *Questions politiques et sociales* (1879). Her twenty-volume autobiography,

George Sand
(Library of Congress)

Histoire de ma vie (1854-1855; *History of My Life*, 1901), is considered by some to be her masterpiece. Georges Lubin produced an excellent annotated edition of this work and other autobiographical writings for Gallimard in 1970. Other important nonfictional works include *Lettres d'un voyageur* (1837; *Letters of a Traveller*, 1847), *Lettres à Marcie* (1837), and *Un Hiver à Majorque* (1841; *Winter in Majorca*, 1956). Sand's plays were published in five volumes in 1877. She wrote more than nineteen thousand letters and was called by André Maurois "the best French epistolary writer." From 1964 onward, Lubin devoted himself to a new multivolume edition of Sand's letters, many of which were previously unpublished or had been published only in truncated form. The twenty-sixth and final volume of that series was published in 1995.

Achievements

To her contemporaries, George Sand was a great novelist and a fallen woman. The controversy surrounding her life has continued into the twenty-first century. Until the late 1980's, scholars neglected her enormous production of literary works to concentrate on biographical quarrels. She was recognized as a major novelist by Honoré de Balzac, Ivan

Turgenev, Victor Hugo, and Henry James. She was widely read in the United States and Great Britain, where she influenced writers such as the Brontë sisters (Anne, Charlotte, and Emily) and George Eliot. In Russia, where political treatises were banned, her novels passed on progressive ideas and inspired political thinkers such as Mikhail Bakunin as well as novelists such as Fyodor Dostoevski. Gustave Flaubert called Sand "My Dear Master," and Marcel Proust's most poignant childhood memories involved his mother reading Sand's rustic novels to him.

This picture of Sand's pastoral or rustic novels persists in France today, where the average reader considers her a writer of sentimental stories for children. Because of this image, she has been attacked by political liberals who accuse her of supporting the status quo with her tales of happy peasants. Scholars, on the other hand, regard her rustic novels as the perfection of a literary genre. To the nineteenth century public, Sand's novels calling for the emancipation of women (and men) from arranged marriages, equality between the sexes, and education for women seemed outrageously feminist. Her novel *Lélia* shocked readers with its explicit analysis of female sexuality. Modern-day feminists, however, point to the limits of Sand's feminism, especially to her opposition to the participation of women in political affairs, for she felt that women should be educated before they were given the right to vote.

Because of the volume of Sand's work and the speed at which she was forced to write to support her family, her artistic circle, and her charitable contributions, the quality of her fiction is uneven, yet literary critics admire her fluid style and her techniques of psychological analysis. All agree in considering *Mauprat*, *Consuelo*, and the rustic novels as powerful masterpieces.

BIOGRAPHY

George Sand was born Amandine-Aurore-Lucile Dupin in Paris on July 1, 1804, to parents who had been married scarcely a month. Her father, Maurice Dupin, was a descendant through bastard lines of the king of Poland, Augustus the Strong, and her mother, Sophie Delaborde, was a camp follower and the daughter of a Paris bird seller. Thus, from the beginning, Sand was exposed to the class struggle. When she was four years old, her father was killed in a fall from a horse; three years later, her mother gave up custody of her to her aristocratic maternal grandmother, who brought her up as a lady at her country estate of Nohant in the Berry region. Sand nevertheless reached out to her mother in Paris and the working class she represented.

In 1817, Sand returned to Paris, where she entered the Couvent des Anglaises for her education. In 1820, she returned to the country while her grandmother attempted to arrange a suitable marriage for her; Sand preferred to read books and ride horses. After the death of her grandmother in 1821, Sand returned to Paris to live with her mother. This arrangement proved unsatisfactory because of her mother's violent temper, and the girl sought refuge at the country estate of her father's friends, the Roëttiers. Through the

Roëttiers, she met Casimir François Dudevant, the illegitimate but recognized son of a baron; she married Dudevant in 1822.

At first, the couple seemed happy enough, but after the birth of their son Maurice in 1823, their incompatibility became evident. A second child, Solange, was born in 1828. After a fight with her husband, Sand arranged to spend half of each year in Paris, where Dudevant would send her an allowance from the revenues of her land. In 1831, she left for Paris to live with Jules Sandeau, a law student who aspired to become a writer. To supplement her meager pension, Sand obtained a job writing for *Le Figaro*, a newspaper run by Hyacinthe de Latouche. In collaboration with Sandeau, Sand wrote several short stories and at least one novel, which was signed "J. Sand." When Sand wrote *Indiana* alone at Nohant and returned to Paris to publish it, de Latouche suggested that she keep the name "Sand" and choose another Christian name. She chose "Georges" (soon anglicized to George) because it seemed to her to be typical of the Berry region. *Indiana*, the first novel signed "George Sand," was published in 1832. More than seventy others were to follow.

In 1833, Sand fell in love with the poet Alfred de Musset and left with him for Venice, the city that all the Romantic writers dreamed of visiting. There they both fell ill. Following several violent incidents resulting from Musset's overindulgence in wine and women, they agreed to separate. When Musset's illness recurred, Sand nursed him faithfully but fell in love with his Italian doctor, Pietro Pagello. Barely restored to health, Musset returned to Paris while Sand and Pagello stayed in Italy. Sand addressed much of her correspondence in *Letters of a Traveller* to Musset in Paris. In 1834, she returned to Paris with Pagello but neglected him, feeling herself drawn again to Musset. Musset wrote some of his most famous poems about this relationship and analyzed it in his *La Confession d'un enfant du siècle* (1836; *The Confession of a Child of the Century*, 1892). After Musset's death in 1857, Sand reevaluated their adventure in *She and He*.

After many painful scenes, Sand finally broke with Musset in 1835. Later that year, she met and fell in love with the Republican lawyer Michel de Bourges. When she returned to Nohant, she had a definitive fight with her husband and sued for a legal separation, since divorce did not exist in France at that time. De Bourges acted as her lawyer.

In 1838, Sand began a relationship with Frédéric Chopin, whom she met through a mutual friend, Franz Liszt. For nine years, Sand was Chopin's mother, mistress, and nurse, protecting him and enabling him to write some of his best music. The most famous event in their years together was the ill-fated trip they took with Sand's children to Majorca in the winter of 1838-1839, which she describes in *Winter in Majorca*. Most literary critics agree that Sand was satirizing her relationship with Chopin in her novel *Lucrezia Floriani*. Sand and Chopin separated in 1847, disagreeing over the marriage of her daughter Solange to the sculptor Jean-Baptiste Auguste Clésinger.

In 1848, Sand returned to Paris as soon as she received word that the monarchy had been overthrown. She wrote most of the official bulletins for the new Republican government, which included many of her old friends. When the Republicans were arrested in

May, Sand took refuge at Nohant. Although she continued to intercede with the Emperor Napoleon III for her friends, Sand has been accused of turning her back on the Revolution to write bourgeois pastoral novels.

After 1848, Sand spent more time at Nohant than in Paris, but she returned to Paris often, frequently for the openings of her plays. From 1850 to 1865, Alexandre Manceau, an engraver and a friend of her son Maurice (who was an artist, a pupil of Eugène Delacroix), was Sand's private secretary and lover. In 1864, Manceau bought a small house near Paris, where they lived in order to leave Nohant to Maurice and his new wife, Lina, the daughter of the engraver Luigi Calamatta, an old friend of Sand. After Manceau's death from tuberculosis in 1865, Sand traveled, lived in Paris, visited Flaubert at Croisset, and went to the Ardennes region to document a novel, but she considered Nohant her home again. There, she received Flaubert and Turgenev as well as other friends. She died at Nohant of a painful intestinal blockage on June 8, 1876.

Analysis

Faced with the enormous number of George Sand's novels, literary critics quickly moved to divide them into categories. The traditional categories include feminist novels, socialistic novels, and rustic novels. While this oversimplification is inaccurate, it does help the reader to identify the major themes that recur in most of her novels.

Valentine

Valentine is a good example of the critics' dilemma. The novel recounts a love story of a married noblewoman and an educated peasant that ends tragically with the death of the lovers. The plot is a Romantic one, both in the sense of "a love story" and in the literary-historical sense of the term, for it contains several of the essential themes of French Romanticism: the passing of time, the passing of love with time, and a search for the meaning of the universe beyond the limits of human life. In *Valentine*, Sand's Bénédict is a melancholy, meditative person who resembles François-René de Chateaubriand's René. He is killed accidentally by a jealous husband, but Valentine, the heroine, dies from sorrow soon after his death. At first reading, the novel seems to be primarily Romantic, yet Valentine's fruitless attempts to find personal happiness and satisfaction, despite her financially arranged marriage and her indifferent and absent husband, suggest classification among the feminist novels. The beautiful descriptions of the Berry countryside and details of the daily life of the peasants are characteristic of her rustic novels. The love affair between two people of different social classes suggests classification as a socialistic novel. The conclusion is obvious: Most of Sand's novels contain Romantic elements, Romanesque elements, feminist elements, rustic elements, and socialist elements.

The novels that contain the highest percentage of feminist elements are the early ones. Clearly, Sand's unhappy personal experiences were reflected in novels such as *Indiana*, in which the heroine leaves her despotic husband, is betrayed by her lover, and ultimately finds happiness with her cousin, who serves as a father figure for her and becomes her lover on a lush tropical island in a primitive paradise that owes something to Jean-Jacques Rousseau and Jacques-Henri Bernardin de Saint-Pierre. Sand's feminist novel par excellence is *Lélia*, which reinterprets the metaphysical dilemma of the Romantic hero in feminine terms.

Sand's socialistic novels are generally less successful artistically than her work in other genres, perhaps because her theoretical digressions are not well integrated into the plots. One exception, *The Companion of the Tour of France*, was reedited by the University Press of Grenoble in the late 1980's and then began to receive long-overdue critical attention. In addition to its story of the love between the lady of a manor and a carpenter-artist, the novel contains a study of secret trade guilds and a portrait of the daily life of workers—a class that was neglected by Balzac in *La Comédie humaine* (1829-1848; *The Comedy of Human Life*, 1885-1893, 1896; also known as *The Human Comedy*, 1895-1896, 1911). *The Miller of Angibault* is also a successful socialistic novel, but it contains many elements of the rustic novels as well. *The Sin of Monsieur Antoine* and *La Ville noire* expose the problems of factory workers, making Sand the only French novelist before Émile Zola to analyze seriously the effects of the Industrial Revolution.

Jeanne

Sand's experiments with the rustic novel began with *Jeanne*, whose peasant heroine is compared to Joan of Arc and Napoleon. In the rustic novels, Sand saw herself as an intermediary between Paris and Nohant, between bourgeois and peasant. She hoped to bring about a reconciliation between the two by portraying the best qualities of the country folk to make them acceptable to urban readers. She did not, however, neglect the very real problems of rural life. Her peasants are often hungry and overworked, but they have a noble character that enables them to conquer all obstacles and a resourcefulness that comes from living in harmony with nature.

Sand never claimed to be a realist, even though she documented her novels carefully. There are realistic elements in her psychological analyses, in her landscapes, and in her portrayal of the everyday life of workers and peasants. Nevertheless, what counted for Sand, as she states in the introduction to *The Devil's Pool*, was "ideal truth" rather than "a slice of life." She wanted to inspire readers to live up to their potential, in contrast to the productions of the realist and naturalist schools, which, she felt, depressed people by showing the ugly side of life. In her autobiography, she quotes Balzac as saying to her, "You search for man as he should be, while I take him as he is. Believe me, we are both right."

Lélia

Lélia is a flawed masterpiece. Its lyric tone and mystical examination of God, love, the universe, and the nature of truth make it both a profound philosophical work and a difficult novel for most readers. The characters tend toward allegory: Lélia represents doubt, according to a document published in *Sketches and Hints* (1926); Trenmor, expiation and stoicism; Sténio, poetry and credulity; Magnus, superstition and repressed desire; and Pulchérie, the senses (as opposed to the mind or soul). They also represent different aspects of Sand's own personality. She wrote in *Journal intime* (1926; *The Intimate Journal*, 1929), which was published with *Sketches and Hints*, "Magnus is my childhood; Sténio, my youth; Lélia is my maturity; Trenmor will perhaps be my old age. All these types have been in me."

When Sand published *Lélia* in 1832, it had a *succès de scandale*. A novel by a woman treating explicitly the problem of female frigidity, briefly touching on lesbian sexuality, and creating a superior heroine to rival melancholy Romantic heroes (Chateaubriand's René, Étienne de Senancour's Obermann, Johann Wolfgang von Goethe's Werther, and Benjamin Constant's Adolphe) was more than even Paris was prepared to accept. Sand's passionate cry of suffering was so revealing, however, that Musset and many of her contemporaries called her "Lélia."

Sand, who ordinarily did not rewrite novels, rewrote *Lélia*, cutting out the sexually explicit passages and transforming its profoundly skeptical and pessimistic tone into a more positive and progressive one. The second version, published in 1839, was chosen by the author to be included in an edition of her complete works. After that, the 1832 edition disappeared from view until André Maurois titled his 1952 biography *Lélia: Ou, La Vie de George Sand* (*Lélia: The Life of George Sand*, 1953). Maurois asserted that the first *Lélia* was, with *Indiana* and *Consuelo*, one of Sand's finest novels and artistically superior to the 1839 version. In 1960, Pierre Reboul published the text of the 1832 *Lélia*, and scholars now generally agree with Maurois. Östen Södergård published a comparison of the two editions in 1962 and showed how and why Sand changed her novel.

In the first *Lélia*, the heroine is presented to the reader as seen from afar by the young poet Sténio, who worships and fears her. The question the first part of the novel asks is whether Lélia will be able to love Sténio. Trenmor, a rehabilitated gambler resigned to a calm philosophical life, says no. Lélia is older and wiser than Sténio and so frustrated by unsatisfying love affairs that she is no longer capable of physical love. She proposes a more spiritual love, but the poet insists that ideal love unites the senses with the spirit. After many vain power struggles, Lélia leaves Sténio with her courtesan-sister Pulchérie, with whom he makes love, believing her to be Lélia. In this way, Lélia hopes to teach him that sensual love is unreliable. Instead, Sténio, disillusioned by the experience, decides that pleasure alone is real and throws himself into debauchery. Finally, he drowns himself in a lake; while Lélia weeps over his body, she is strangled by Magnus, a priest who has become an atheist and has been driven insane by his desire for Lélia. At the end, Lélia and Sténio, the lovers who could not agree on earth, are united as stars in Heaven; and the philosopher Trenmor continues his pilgrimage alone.

The love story at the center of *Lélia* is less important than Lélia's desperate search for

God, herself, and truth—what Maria Espinosa, the translator of the original version of *Lélia* into English, calls the "spiritual odyssey" of Lélia and, of course, of Sand herself. Lélia searches for a man who is perfect, like God; not finding one, she makes a god of the man she loves. When she realizes her mistake, it is too late for her ever to obtain the fresh, pure love of which she dreams. She has lived too much without enjoyment, and her fantasies surpass any possible realization. This makes her doubt God and hate herself while she is filled with a burning and insatiable physical desire. Seeking relief in a year's voluntary claustration, Lélia waits in vain to achieve the stoic resignation of Trenmor, who is emotionally dead. Since, for her, physical love represents a submission of the woman to the man, she finds it distasteful and tries to solve her dilemma by taking the dominant male role in love scenes. For this reason, she treats Sténio like her son and loves him most when he is passive—sleeping or dead. Unable to find a solution to her problems, Lélia is finally content to be killed by Magnus.

In the 1839 version, Lélia becomes a nun who teaches girls how to resist men and reforms the Church. Trenmor becomes a reformed murderer and acquires a secret identity as Valmarina, a benefactor of the poor and needy as well as the head of a mystico-political secret society somewhat like the Italina Carbonaros. Even though Lélia dies in disgrace at the end of the second version, the reader feels that she will be vindicated. Both Trenmor and Lélia thus find meaningful things to do with their lives as Sand passes from Romantic pessimism to preach active reform of society.

Mauprat

The reader who finds the lyric and philosophical passages of *Lélia* long and painful will be enchanted by *Mauprat*. The latter, a more traditional novel, combines the beautiful exterior scenes of Sand's rustic novels with a historical adventure story of the type written by Sir Walter Scott or Alexandre Dumas, *père*. Political and philosophical reflections are carefully woven into the fabric of the work so as not to impede the swift movement of the plot toward its suspense-filled conclusion, for *Mauprat* also contains a detective story. These disparate elements are skillfully united to form a bildungsroman. The central focus of the novel is the education of Bernard de Mauprat, that is, the transformation of a wild barbarian interested only in sensual gratification into a sensitive, loving, and cultured man. This transformation is the work of Bernard's cousin Edmée, who uses his love for her to force him to change.

From the outside, Edmée seems to resemble Lélia. She is cold and proud; she dominates Bernard and treats him like her son. Edmée is not frigid, however; she merely appears that way because she suppresses her own desire for Bernard and patiently waits for him to become her equal, emotionally and morally, before she agrees to marry him. Meanwhile, like Sand herself, Edmée carries a knife with which to commit suicide if necessary to protect her virtue.

Bernard, who was taken at age seven by his grandfather Tristan de Mauprat to a disintegrating castle, grew up in an atmosphere of violence and crime as his marauding uncles filled the countryside with terror, re-creating in the eighteenth century their family's feudal domination of the peasants. Bernard's slow progress from this life of darkness to the light of civilization begins when Edmée de Mauprat, the sole heir of the respectable younger branch of the family, loses her way in the forest and is captured by the evil uncles. She convinces Bernard, who only wants to make love to her, to rescue her and flee from the castle with her. In order to do this, she promises Bernard that she will belong to no other man before him.

This solemn promise shapes the future of both the young people. Bernard, who is seeking only instant physical gratification, slowly and painfully discovers that Edmée will withhold this from him for many years, while he, like the medieval knight, is forced to overcome obstacles to merit her love. Chivalrous motifs are reinforced by a young man named Arthur, who serves as Bernard's friend and guide in the American Revolution, explaining to him what he must do to earn the favors of the fair maiden. The medieval knight had to conquer dragons (exterior enemies) while Bernard must conquer his own savage nature. For Edmée, on the other hand, this promise to make love is tantamount to a promise of marriage.

Sand states in her preface to *Mauprat* that the trauma of the legal separation from her husband made her begin to reflect upon the dream of an ideal marriage and an eternal love; thus, Bernard de Mauprat, who narrates his story at the age of eighty, tells his listeners that he loved only one woman in his entire life, before his marriage, during his marriage, and after her death. This is certainly a strong response to Sand's contemporaries, who criticized her for attacking the institution of marriage.

As the love story gives unity to the plot, the theme of the perfectibility of humankind forms the center of the philosophical framework of the novel. Here, Sand is undoubtedly following one of her first mentors, Rousseau. In a sense, Edmée is like Julie in Rousseau's *Julie: Ou, La Nouvelle Héloïse* (1761; *Eloise: Or, A Series of Original Letters*, 1761; also known as *Julie: Or, The New Eloise*, 1968; better known as *The New Héloïse*), who moves from a passionate lover, Saint-Preux, to a reasonable husband, Wolmar, creating a utopia out of her farm. The major difference is that Sand unites Saint-Preux and Wolmar to form one character, Bernard. Edmée does create a utopia with the aid of Patience, an old hermit who gives up his solitary lifestyle to help Edmée build a life of dignity and honor for the peasants. Bernard and Edmée are happy to give up their wealth with the arrival of the French Revolution, which they see as a step toward a more equitable society.

In *Mauprat*, Sand uses the medieval trappings, the plot of an adventure story, and the psychological developments of a love story to interest her reader in the essential message—that the human race can improve with education. This progressive theme signals Sand's own movement toward a more optimistic view of the world.

Consuelo

Consuelo and its sequel, *The Countess of Rudolstadt*, form, like *Mauprat*, a bildungsroman. This time, however, the person who learns and grows by overcoming obstacles is a woman. *Consuelo*, considered by many to be Sand's masterpiece, has been called France's answer to Goethe's saga of Wilhelm Meister. The novel is set in the eighteenth century, in Venice, Bohemia, Vienna, and Berlin—for Consuelo is a talented singer, born in Spain of a Gypsy mother, who travels in Europe perfecting her voice and developing her career. The character is roughly based on Pauline Garcia Viardot, a close friend of Sand; as a prototype of the Romantic artist, Consuelo also shares many traits with Sand herself. Consuelo has the misfortune of being ugly until she is transformed by her music. As Béatrice Didier has pointed out, her ugliness may not be a disadvantage after all, because it saves her from easy success and venal protectors, enabling her to keep her independence and grow in her art.

The bildungsroman operates on three levels, as Consuelo follows an artistic itinerary that leads to her becoming a composer, a political itinerary that makes her aware of the evils of despotism and dedicated to helping the poor and suffering, and a spiritual itinerary that culminates in her initiation into the secret society of the Invisibles, who work to correct social injustice. Consuelo's artistic voyage begins when the famous maestro Porpora agrees to give the poor girl free music lessons in Venice. After Porpora teaches her the fundamentals of her art, Consuelo becomes an opera star. At this point, Porpora feels he must warn her to beware of men—both would-be protectors such as Count Justiani and would-be lovers such as Anzoletto, her childhood friend. Porpora persuades Consuelo to devote her life to art and sends her off to the Castle of the Giants in Bohemia to give music lessons to the young Baroness Amélie.

In this castle, which has all the subterranean passageways and mysteries of the gothic novel, Consuelo meets Albert de Rudolstadt, Amélie's cousin, who is subject to temporary mental disorders during which he imagines that he is the reincarnation of the Prince Podiebrand or the Hussite hero Jean Ziska. He plays violin music that has a magical influence on Consuelo. Albert and his deranged peasant friend Zdenko teach her the history of Bohemia and its suffering under political and religious oppression. They introduce her to folk music and begin her initiation into the occult. After saving Albert's life by carrying him through secret underground passages, tunnels, and wells, Consuelo becomes ill and is nursed back to health by Albert, who falls in love with her. She refuses to marry him and leaves the castle for Vienna to pursue her study of music.

On the trip to Vienna, Consuelo dresses up like a man to protect herself. This loss of female identity gives her a freedom that helps her develop as an artist. She accidentally meets young Joseph Haydn, who accompanies her on the long trip on foot. As a result of this journey, she learns about war, despotism, and the oppression of the peasants. In Vienna, she finds Porpora again and learns about tyranny from Maria Theresa.

As she is leaving Vienna for Berlin, Consuelo receives a message that Albert is dying.

She rushes to the Rudolstadt castle and agrees to marry him *in extremis*. After his death, she renounces his wealth and title and continues on to Berlin, where she is imprisoned by Frederick the Great for conspiracy. In prison, she discovers the joys of musical composition and memorizes her creations, moving even closer to traditional folk music. She is freed from prison by the Invisibles, who take her to a palace where she studies their mysteries and decides to become a member of their secret society. She falls in love with her mysterious rescuer Liverani, only to discover that Albert is still alive and an Invisible. Forced to choose between love and duty, Consuelo follows her higher instincts and chooses Albert, who reveals that he is Liverani. After her initiation into the Invisibles, which takes place in another castle, with the symbolic name of Castle of the Grail, the marriage of Consuelo and Albert is renewed.

In the epilogue, the reader learns that the Invisibles have been forced underground and that Consuelo has lost her voice and Albert his reason. She has become a composer writing music for Albert's poems. They wander with their children through the countryside, bringing hope to the poor and needy. Consuelo is thus as poor at the end of the novel as she was at the beginning, but she has become the "Good Goddess of Poverty." She has fulfilled her artistic destiny by becoming a creator—a complete Romantic artist. She has fulfilled her political and spiritual destiny by helping the needy. Finally, she has fulfilled her destiny as a woman by uniting physical and spiritual love in her relationship with Albert. She is the whole woman Lélia wanted to be. She lives up to her name "Consuelo" by bringing "consolation" to those around her.

The religious and political philosophy of Albert and the Invisibles, which Consuelo adopts at the end of the novel, was inspired by Pierre Leroux, a Socialist thinker whom Sand admired. In *Consuelo*, the Invisibles base their doctrine on a belief in absolute equality between sexes and classes. They also proclaim the right of the people to participate as fully as the priests in religious sacraments. Their motto, The Cup to the People, refers to the communion chalice. This desire to reform the Catholic Church was a constant preoccupation of Sand, best expressed in *Spiridion*, which develops a religious philosophy of history. Parallel to her desire to reform the Church is her desire to reform society, which finds in *Consuelo* its most complete expression.

This novel, which is epic in scope, has been called a novel of initiation as well as a bildungsroman. Because of its length, it is a challenge to most modern readers. Its beautiful landscapes, fascinating characters, and exciting plot, however, reward readers for their perseverance.

THE DEVIL'S POOL

If *Consuelo* can be likened to an epic poem, *The Devil's Pool* is more like a folk song. Considered the perfect example of Sand's rustic novels, it is short, simple, and tightly structured. The novel has only two major characters, Germain, a thirty-year-old widower with three children, and Marie, a poverty-stricken sixteen-year-old girl. The title of the novel leads one to think that the occult might play as large a role in this novel as in *Consuelo*. Actually, the Devil's Pool, which forms the center of the narrative structure, is magic only because it makes people lose their way in the forest at night. Marie and Germain, accompanied by Germain's oldest child, Pierre, lose their way near this pool and there discover the truth about themselves—that they love each other. The major theme of the novel is thus quasi-biblical: "Those who think they are lost are found," or "One finds one's way by losing it."

The conflict in the plot arises from the fact that Germain must remarry to ensure the economic viability of the family unit, although at first he has no desire to do so. Marie is considered an unfit wife for him because of her youth and poverty. In the forest, however, she shows her true character—she is provident, attuned to nature, and clever at caring for children. After Germain recognizes her special gifts, he still has to persuade the elders of his family that she is an appropriate bride for him. Until the end of the story, he is uncertain whether Marie returns his love.

The ideological basis of this novel springs from Rousseau's theories about the purity of country life and the corruption of the cities. Germain and Marie, the innocent country people, find their opposites in the vain, materialistic Cathérine Guérin, a widow whom Germain was supposed to marry, and the Farmer of Ormeaux, the licentious master who attempts to seduce Marie. It is important to note that they are both members of the middle class as well as inhabitants of a village. Sand's vision of the country, however, is more than simply an ideological construct. She grew up in the country, and her portraits of the peasants of Berry have done much to preserve the language and folklore that were beginning to disappear.

There is an innate conflict in the rustic novels between Sand's desire to conserve and preserve a disappearing way of life and her avowed purpose of reforming society by promoting understanding between the bourgeois and the peasant. Her rustic novels have been read for more than a century as tributes to the status quo and have been used by the French educational system to keep people in their place. This is clearly not what Sand intended when she wrote in the introduction to *The Devil's Pool*, "It is necessary for Lazarus to leave his dungheap so that the poor will no longer rejoice in the death of the rich. It is necessary that all be happy so that the happiness of the few may not be criminal and cursed by God." In this introduction, Sand explains that the novel was inspired by an engraving by Hans Holbein the Younger showing death as the only recompense for a life of hard labor in the fields. Sand believed that nineteenth century laborers should have life rather than death as a reward and that inequities should be rectified on earth rather than in Heaven. In this way, *The Devil's Pool* joins the technical perfection of a new genre of novel with an expansion of Sand's constant concern for the suffering of humanity.

Lucy M. Schwartz

OTHER MAJOR WORKS

SHORT FICTION: *Contes d'une grand'mère*, 1873, 1876 (*Tales of a Grandmother*, 1930).

PLAY: *Théâtre complet de George Sand*, 1877 (5 volumes).

NONFICTION: *Lettres à Marcie*, 1837; *Lettres d'un voyageur*, 1837 (*Letters of a Traveller*, 1847); *Un Hiver à Majorque*, 1841 (*Winter in Majorca*, 1956); *Histoire de ma vie*, 1854-1855 (20 volumes; *History of My Life*, 1901); *Questions d'art et de littérature*, 1878; *Questions politiques et sociales*, 1879; *Letters*, 1896 (9 volumes); *Journal intime*, 1926 (*The Intimate Journal*, 1929); *Sketches and Hints*, 1926; *Correspondance*, 1964-1995 (26 volumes); *Œuvres autobiographiques*, 1970-1971 (2 volumes).

MISCELLANEOUS: *Works*, 1887 (38 volumes).

BIBLIOGRAPHY

Atwood, William G. *The Lioness and the Little One: The Liaison of George Sand and Frédéric Chopin*. New York: Columbia University Press, 1980. Offers a careful and scholarly account of a part of Sand's life and career that has often been distorted and sensationalized.

Barry, Joseph. *Infamous Woman: The Life of George Sand*. Garden City, N.Y.: Doubleday, 1977. Presents an illuminating overview of Sand's life and writing. Chronicles her development as an artist, her tumultuous love affairs, her relationships with her children and her mother, her role in French politics, and her stand against traditional female roles.

Cate, Curtis. *George Sand*. Boston: Little, Brown, 1975. Sound, comprehensive biography includes a preface that provides an insightful discussion of Maurois's classic biography (cited below) and the fluctuations of Sand's literary reputation.

Crecelius, Kathryn J. *Family Romances: George Sand's Early Novels*. Bloomington: Indiana University Press, 1987. Informative study discusses topics such as Sand's handling of heroic romance and bourgeois realism and her role as a woman artist. Separate chapters cover her novels *Lélia*, *Mauprat*, and *Valentine*.

Eisler, Benita. *Naked in the Marketplace: The Lives of George Sand*. New York: Basic Books, 2006. Biography draws on Sand's substantial body of correspondence to explore the complicated personality of the radical nineteenth century feminist. Focuses especially on Sand's impressively active and lengthy love life and its impact on her literary output.

Goodwin-Jones, Robert. *Romantic Vision: The Novels of George Sand*. Birmingham, Ala.: Summa, 1995. Presents a thematic analysis of about forty of Sand's novels, including *Valentine*, *Indiana*, *Mauprat*, and *The Companion of the Tour of France*. Includes an introductory discussion of Sand as a novelist.

Harkness, Nigel. *Men of Their Words: The Poetics of Masculinity in George Sand's Fiction*. London: Legenda, 2007. Examines questions of masculinity in Sand's fiction within the context of the nineteenth century French novel, describing how Sand's novels repeatedly depict the connections among masculinity, power, and language.

Jack, Belinda Elizabeth. *George Sand: A Woman's Life Writ Large*. New York: Vintage Books, 1999. Biography pays especial attention to Sand's childhood and its influence on her later life and career. Includes illustrations and index.

Massardier-Kenney, Françoise. *Gender in the Fiction of George Sand*. Atlanta: Rodopi, 2000. Argues that Sand's novels express a complex and extremely modern conception of gender in which she questions prevalent patriarchal modes of discourse and redefines masculinity and femininity.

Maurois, André. *Lélia: The Life of George Sand*. New York: Harper and Brothers, 1953. Classic biography by one of the genre's most renowned practitioners. Less scholarly than Cate's biography (cited above), but written with verve and a sure grasp of both the subject and her period.

Powell, David A. *George Sand*. Boston: Twayne, 1990. Provides an excellent introduction to Sand's life and works. Approaches Sand as a major Romantic and feminist writer and places her work within the context of French social history.

JEAN-PAUL SARTRE

Born: Paris, France; June 21, 1905
Died: Paris, France; April 15, 1980
Also known as: Jean-Paul Charles Aymard Sartre

PRINCIPAL LONG FICTION
 La Nausée, 1938 (Nausea, 1949)
 L'Âge de raison, 1945 (The Age of Reason, 1947)
 Le Sursis, 1945 (The Reprieve, 1947)
 La Mort dans l'âme, 1949 (Troubled Sleep, 1950; also known as Iron in the
    Soul; previous three novels collectively known as Les Chemins de la liberté,
    in English as The Roads to Freedom)

OTHER LITERARY FORMS

Around the time that he published *Nausea*, Jean-Paul Sartre (SAHR-truh) drew considerable attention as a promising writer of short fiction with the stories collected in *Le Mur* (1939; *The Wall, and Other Stories*, 1948). Trained as a philosopher, Sartre went on to define and develop his concept of existentialism in *L'Être et le néant* (1943; *Being and Nothingness*, 1956), turning also to the theater with such famous plays as *Les Mouches* (pr., pb. 1943; *The Flies*, 1946), *Huis clos* (pr. 1944; *In Camera*, 1946; better known as *No Exit*, 1947), and *Les Mains sales* (pr., pb. 1948; *Dirty Hands*, 1949), in which the basic tenets of his thought are brilliantly executed and easily grasped. He is known also for essays and reviews collected in several volumes of the journal *Situations* as well as for psychological criticism of such authors as Charles Baudelaire, Gustave Flaubert, and Jean Genet. In 1964, he published a partial autobiography, *Les Mots* (*The Words*, 1964).

ACHIEVEMENTS

For students and readers of long fiction, Jean-Paul Sartre is perhaps most notable as the author of *Nausea*, an unsettling and groundbreaking work that exercised considerable influence over developments in the novel during the postwar era. His later efforts in the genre—the unfinished tetralogy *Roads to Freedom*—are viewed less charitably by most of his commentators, who would contend that Sartre had by that time turned his finest efforts toward the drama. Some scholars, however, have argued that Sartre's later novels have simply been obscured by the sensational publicity afforded his plays and other writings. In any event, Sartre himself appears to have lost interest in the writing of fiction, preferring such alternative forms as his essays on Baudelaire and Flaubert. Nevertheless, Sartre's influence on fiction, both long and short, has been considerable. In 1964, Sartre was awarded the Nobel Prize in Literature, which he declined to accept.

Jean-Paul Sartre
(Library of Congress)

Biography

Born in Paris in 1905, Jean-Paul Sartre grew up in a book-filled, if fatherless, household. Sartre was a brilliant student, and his secondary schooling at the time-honored Lycée Henri IV was followed by competitive admission to the École Normale Supérieure. Although he failed his first attempt at the likewise competitive *agrégation*, or teaching credential, before successfully retaking it in 1929, Sartre had opted early for a life of the mind and had written at least one novel (later destroyed for want of a publisher) while still in his teens. He had also made the acquaintance of Simone de Beauvoir, a fellow philosophy student who would remain his companion for life, even as both rejected as "inauthentic" the "bourgeois" institution of marriage. During the 1930's, Sartre taught philosophy in *lycées* at Le Havre and elsewhere, traveling during vacations with the help of a small inheritance, before settling into the life of the professional writer and thinker as author of *The Wall, and Other Stories* and *Nausea*.

Briefly incarcerated by the Germans as a prisoner of war in 1940 and 1941, Sartre was nevertheless able to pursue his literary and philosophical work during the Occupation with a minimum of interference. As founding editor of the liberal periodical *Les Temps modernes* (ironically named for the 1936 Charles Chaplin film *Modern Times*, which both he and Beauvoir admired), Sartre became perhaps the most frequently quoted spokesman of the intellectual French Left, even as he "kept his options open" and refrained from the ultimate commitment of membership in the Communist Party. As the leading proponent of existentialism, Sartre also attracted the attention of the print and broadcast media, achieving during the postwar years celebrity status as existentialism was widely discussed and misinterpreted, seen by many commentators as the immediate ancestor of such phenomena as the Beat generation. His plays, meanwhile, shone brightly as the strongest and most durable of his creative efforts, performed worldwide before increasingly appreciative audiences.

During his later years, Sartre traveled widely and, when in Paris, spent most of his time and energy on his psychobiographical study of Flaubert, *L'Idiot de la famille: Gustave Flaubert, 1821-1857* (1971-1972; partial translation *The Family Idiot: Gustave Flaubert, 1821-1857*, 1981, 1987), a massive work conceived in much the same spirit as his earlier studies of Baudelaire and Jean Genet. Sartre died in Paris on April 15, 1980.

Analysis

Hailed in the immediate prewar years as a rising master of prose fiction, Jean-Paul Sartre soon deserted the form and would leave unfinished the fourth and final volume of *The Roads to Freedom*, originally announced as a tetralogy. As it turned out, his creative talents were perhaps indeed better suited to the theater; encouraged by the eminent director Charles Dullin, Sartre, between 1943 and 1959, turned out eight original plays, fully half of which survived him and are still included in the world's repertory. Unlike his onetime friend and colleague Albert Camus (1913-1960), who repeatedly tried and failed to apply his gifts to the stage, Sartre possessed a particularly dramatic imagination that proved especially well suited to the exposition even of the most difficult philosophical concepts originally expounded in his essays. To be sure, a number of his concepts found their earliest, albeit undeveloped, expression in *Nausea* and in the stories to be collected in *The Wall, and Other Stories*; nevertheless, Sartre found fiction a comparatively inefficient vehicle for the communication of his ideas.

Nausea

Completed as early as 1936 under the working title of "Melancholia" (inspired by Albrecht Dürer's engraving *Melancholia I*, 1514), *Nausea* proved to be as unconventional in content as it was apparently conventional in form. Cast in the more or less familiar format of a diary discovered after the death (or disappearance) of its author, a convention in turn derived from the time-honored epistolary form, Sartre's first novel bodied forth a disoriented, disorienting vision of the world as perceived through the eyes of its rapidly changing protagonist and narrator: Antoine Roquentin, a thirty-year-old historian and former teacher, finds himself suddenly overcome by the sensation of his own existence, a sensation that soon evokes in him the nausea of the book's eventual, publisher-selected title. Overwhelmed by the evident contingency of his own being, Roquentin soon senses the same contingency in others, and in inanimate objects as well: In one memorable scene, Roquentin watches and describes his own hand as if it were a monstrous creature quite divorced from his existence, a beached crab with hair; in another scene, a glass of beer appears to be spying on him. His eventual and perhaps inevitable conclusion is that he is superfluous (*de trop*), a quality shared by most of the things and people around him.

Had Sartre limited *Nausea* to Roquentin's record of the changes taking place in his own mind, the book might well have been dismissed as an inventive simulacrum of a psychological case history. What assures the viability and power of *Nausea* is the nature and aptness of Roquentin's powers of observation, powers that alternately feed on and are fed by the operations of his mind. Even without the record of Roquentin's depression, *Nausea* might well have earned a respectable place in French literary history as a rare work of biting yet perceptive social satire in which few conditions of life are spared. To his credit, Sartre in *Nausea* repeatedly manages portraits that closely approach caricature yet stop short of straining the reader's credulity.

Trained as a historian, Roquentin is perhaps well chosen as an observer, yet not even he is presented wholly without satire. Dissatisfied with teaching, able to survive (if barely) on a small but regular unearned income, Roquentin probably is superfluous, at least by certain people's standards; in 1932, when he begins his journal, he has been working for some three years on the study of one Marquis de Rollebon, a minor survivor of the French Revolution whose descendants have willed the Marquis's papers to the city of Bouville (Mudville, equated by most of Sartre's commentators with the port city of Le Havre). Roquentin's daily work at the public library of Bouville has exposed him to a small but highly memorable cast of characters, including the Corsican librarian and especially the Self-taught Man (*l'autodidacte*), a drab civil servant and World War I veteran who spends all of his free time in the library, attempting to educate himself by reading all of the books in alphabetical order, as filed under the author's name: "He has passed brutally from the study of coeleopterae to the quantum theory," observes Roquentin, "from a work on Tamerlaine to a Catholic pamphlet against Darwinism, he has never been disconcerted for an instant." Later in the novel, the Self-taught Man will emerge as a deeply committed if somewhat fuzzy-minded Socialist not unlike those satirized around the same time by George Orwell in Britain; Roquentin, decreasingly proud (or even certain) of his own humanity, will turn a deaf ear to his acquaintance's declarations of predigested humanism. In a brief scene near the end of the book, the Self-taught Man stands cruelly revealed and judged as a barely repressed pederast, permanently expelled by the Corsican from the library that has come to represent his entire life. The greater part of Sartre's satire and Roquentin's scorn is reserved for the bourgeois "city fathers," however, whose portraits hang proudly on the walls of the civic museum—"*les salauds*," Roquentin calls them, using a term perhaps best rendered into English as "the bastards." For Sartre, as for Roquentin, the *salauds* are perhaps the most superfluous of all, born into a system that was set in place by their ancestors and that they themselves accept without question even as they perpetuate it; such individuals were to serve as models for Sartre's diatribes against inauthentic or "received" behavior. Roquentin, perversely fascinated by one portrait of particularly fearsome aspect, makes no secret of his pleasure upon learning that the man portrayed stood barely five feet tall.

Inevitably, Roquentin abandons his work on the life and career of Monsieur de Rollebon, having long since begun to suspect its futility. A brief visit to Paris and his former girlfriend, Anny, yields little more of consequence; Anny, a second-rate actor apparently addicted to striking poses, freely announces that she has become another man's "kept woman" and that, moreover, she is about to leave the country. Roquentin notes with some satisfaction that Anny has grown quite fat and wonders, between the lines of his journal, why he ever lent his collusion to her endless poses and "game-playing." With love thus discredited, Roquentin then moves on to the oddly Proustian conclusion that art alone offers a possible clue to life's meaning, if any, and a potential cure for his "nausea." Perhaps, he thinks, he might have found more meaning in life if he had written a novel. In any case, it is now too late, and the journal trails off into nothingness.

Throughout the diary, to be sure, Roquentin's only solace against his disquieting revelations has come through art, *authentic* art as opposed to the commissioned excrescences on display in the Bouville museum. A particular favorite is a jazz tune that he first heard on the lips of American soldiers during 1917, now preserved on a record on the jukebox in the Railwaymen's Café. As he continues his journal, the record grows in importance until, toward the end, Roquentin conjures up a vision of a Jewish musician and a black woman vocalist, who in less than five minutes of recorded playing time have achieved their immortality. The song, initially associated in Roquentin's mind with Anny, has long since acquired an authentic life of its own; by then, however, Roquentin has tacitly rejected the option of creative salvation for himself. Instead, he simply disappears, leaving the diary behind.

From the 1940's onward, it was customary to read *Nausea* in the reflected light of Sartre's subsequent efforts, finding Roquentin's memoirs complete illustration of such Sartrean categories as "essence," "existence," "anguish," and "bad faith." As James Arnold and other scholars have shown, however, the novel originally conceived as "Melancholia" represents a somewhat earlier stage in the evolution of Sartre's thinking, and such examples as there are (such as the implicit "bad faith" of the *salauds*) must be seen as prototypical rather than exemplary; those in search of specific illustrations might be better advised to consider such plays as *The Flies*, *No Exit*, or *Dirty Hands*. To be sure, Sartre's particular concept of "existence" receives its first exposition in *Nausea*, as Roquentin discovers and explores the "unjustified" fact of his being in all of its contingency; the "nausea" that overwhelms him as a result might likewise be interpreted as an early manifestation of the state later described as *angoisse* (anguish). Still *Nausea* demands to be read and appreciated as an independent work of art rather than as an existentialist manifesto. As Arnold has pointed out, moreover, the novel is also rich in autobiographical elements, however skillfully reworked and transposed; the character of Anny, for example, was drawn quite closely from life, in the person of an artist-actor with whom a very young Sartre once believed himself to be in love and whose perennial posing provided him with an invaluable object lesson in the "art" of inauthentic behavior. Like "The Wall" and its companion stories, *Nausea* must thus be seen, regardless of its thought-provoking "content," above all as a work of literary art.

It was not until well after *Nausea*, during the wartime and postwar years, that Sartre would truly emerge as an original and provocative thinker. His ideas, afforded scholarly and rather ponderous exposition in *Being and Nothingness*, soon gained widespread exposure through his plays, particularly *The Flies* and *No Exit*, as well as in essays and columns initially published in *Les Temps modernes*. Soon a coherent existentialist attitude began to emerge, roughly delineated as follows: Of all beings, Sartre maintains, only the "human animal" is capable of *creating* itself through continual, fully conscious acts of *choice*; at birth, people share *essence* with rocks, plants, and other animals, but they must then proceed toward a uniquely human *existence* of their own choosing. Those who refuse to choose, or to accept responsibility for choices already made, are guilty of "bad faith" (*mauvaise foi*) in renouncing their potential "existence" (*pour-soi*) for a subhuman fixed "essence" (*en-soi*) that is tantamount to death. Indeed, as the godless prefigured hell of *No Exit* makes abundantly clear, those who reject the "anguish" of perpetual free choice for the illusory comfort of self-applied "labels" are in fact already dead to the world. Only after real, physical death should it be possible to draw the bottom line, to add up the total of a human life; until that time, any effort to complete the phrase "I am . . ." with a predicate, adjective, or noun identifies the speaker as a person "in love with death," one who has forsaken the unique human privilege and potential of existence. Sartre applies this theory with particular clarity in his *Réflexions sur la question juive* (1946; *Anti-Semite and Jew*, 1948), in which bigotry is portrayed not as an "opinion" or "reaction" but rather as a "passion," a predisposition that antedates its object. Bigots, Sartre maintains, are at bottom terrified of their own freedom, of their own capacity for change; they have therefore opted, in conscious or unconscious bad faith, for the fixed essence of a position that they perceive as self-protective: Refusing to consider the possibility that the world is simply ill-made, they choose to blame all of its ills on a particular minority—Jews, blacks, or Arabs, for example. "If the Jew did not exist," concludes Sartre with the persuasion of simple logic, "the anti-Semite would have to invent him."

As Hazel E. Barnes has pointed out, much of Sartre's argument against anti-Semitism, and against bigotry in general, is outlined in his prewar novella *L'Enfance d'un chef* (*Childhood of a Boss*), the longest of the tales collected in *The Wall, and Other Stories*. Frequently too broad in its satire of bourgeois mentality and morality to be thoroughly credible, *Childhood of a Boss* nevertheless announces, even more clearly than *Nausea*, the provocative blend of philosophy, psychology, and politics that would become characteristic of Sartre's mature output: The life of Lucien Fleurier is a life lived almost totally in bad faith, including a constant search for comforting, self-applied labels and dilettantish flirtation with the artistic "fads" of the time, most notably Surrealism. Insecure from his earliest childhood onward, Lucien constantly seeks to hide behind something larger and stronger than himself, ultimately finding refuge in Fascist anti-Semitism. Haunted also by suspicions of his homosexuality, he relates to women only insofar as he can "objectify" them, to be objectified by them in his turn. In the end, Lucien is so strengthened by his reactionary politics as to have crystallized into the archetypal, unbending capitalist "boss" of the title, not unlike the *salauds* of Bouville.

THE ROADS TO FREEDOM

In the projected tetralogy *The Roads to Freedom*, begun around the same time as *Being and Nothingness* and the early plays, Sartre endeavors to illustrate his developing philosophy through the lives of several continuing characters, most of whom are fortunately drawn less close to caricature than the hapless Lucien Fleurier. Although narration throughout is in the objective, "affectless" third person, the apparent central character in the three published novels is one Mathieu Delarue, a disaffected intellectual in his thirties who resembles Sartre even more than does Antoine Roquentin. The first volume, ironically titled *The Age of Reason*, deals mainly with Mathieu's efforts to secure an abortion for his unloved and unlovely live-in mistress, Marcelle; only at the end, having met with odd opposition from unexpected quarters, will Mathieu ruefully conclude that he has at last reached "the age of reason." Among the more intriguing characters of *The Age of Reason* and its sequels is Mathieu's friend Daniel, a gay man who nevertheless cherishes his clandestine friendship with Marcelle and refuses Mathieu a loan for the abortion, claiming that he does not have the money when in fact he does. A protracted earlier scene has shown Daniel contemplating suicide, planning first to drown his three beloved cats in order to be free of his last responsibilities; unable to kill the cats, he will likewise lack the nerve to carry out his projected self-annihilation. At the end of *The Age of Reason*, he will astound the reader and his fellow characters alike by choosing to marry Marcelle, ostensibly to assure her unborn child a home and father but also, and perhaps more likely, to lock himself into a situation in which he will be condemned to feel false, deserving of contempt as well.

For Barnes, Daniel is perhaps the archetypal character in existentialist fiction, defined not by heredity or environment, as in the traditional novel, but rather, simply by choice. As Barnes points out, nothing is revealed of Daniel's parentage, childhood, or early sexual encounters; Daniel is shown only *in situa*, defining himself (however negatively) through continuous and conscious acts of choice. It is Daniel's *choice* to be reviled and hateful, for whatever unknown reasons. Like Lucien Fleurier—although with far greater lucidity, reflecting the subsequent evolution of Sartre's thought—Daniel is so terrified of his potential freedom that he repeatedly uses that freedom to turn himself into a detestable object, a walking testimonial to the negative effects of bad faith. Mathieu, in turn, "has discovered his freedom but does not know what to do with it." Less interesting as a character than is

Daniel, although perhaps equally complex, Mathieu functions throughout the existing trilogy less as protagonist than as catalyst, a common acquaintance shared by the variety of characters portrayed. Toward the end of the third novel of the series, *Troubled Sleep*, which portrays the end of the "phony war" and the start of the Vichy regime, Mathieu falls in battle and is apparently left for dead, his "central" position being assumed by the committed Communist Brunet; from Sartre's descriptions of the projected fourth volume, however, as well as from excerpts from it published in *Les Temps modernes* during 1949, it was clear that Mathieu would survive his wounds and that Daniel, perhaps too predictably, would collaborate with Occupation forces.

As in *Nausea*, Sartre in *The Roads to Freedom* proves to be a keen observer of human nature as well as a social satirist of no mean talent; among his more skillful portraits are those of Mathieu's brother Jacques, a successful lawyer (who in turn will refuse to lend Mathieu the abortion money) and Jacques's wife, Odette, an intelligent but bored (and boring) bourgeoise. By the early 1940's, however, social satire had lost ground in relative importance to the development of Sartre's philosophical and political attitudes; diverting though the social portraiture may be, it is clear throughout *The Roads to Freedom* that what really matters are the choices facing, and made by, each of the characters, whether consciously or unconsciously. As early as 1939, Sartre had addressed himself as a critic to the delineation of character in fiction, calling for a clear-cut distinction between exposition and "advocacy" on the part of a supposedly omniscient narrator, berating François Mauriac, in particular, for assuming a "godlike" attitude in denying his characters their "freedom." "God is no novelist," Sartre opined in a now-famous statement, "and neither is François Mauriac."

In *The Roads to Freedom*, Sartre appears to have been quite determined to allow his characters their freedom, even at the cost of plausibility; taking care to preserve their integrity by denying his personages the customary justifications of heredity and/or environment, Sartre frequently strains readers' credulity by asking them to accept the validity of voluntary, seemingly unmotivated actions, a practice perhaps derived from André Gide's earlier concept of the *acte gratuit*, or unmotivated gesture, exemplified in the murder of Fleurissoire in *Les Caves du Vatican* (1914; *The Vatican Swindle*, 1925; better known as *Lafcadio's Adventures*, 1927). Perhaps not surprisingly, Sartre's ideas received considerably more credible and effective presentation in his plays, in which actors could accomplish the necessary mediation between text and audience; one is reminded, in particular, of Electra's sudden but thoroughly plausible recourse to bad faith in *The Flies*.

In all of Sartre's published fiction, perhaps the best illustration of his developing theories is to be found in his story "The Wall," narrated throughout by an unprivileged first-person narrator from inside a situation that threatens him with imminent extinction; that Pablo survives to tell the tale at all is surely among the greater, and more skillfully managed, ironies in all modern fiction. In the longer form, however, Sartre proved somewhat less skillful at bridging the gap between theory and practice; indeed, few of his commentators expressed any real surprise when his tetralogy was left unfinished.

With or without the support of Sartre's unfolding existentialism, *The Roads to Freedom* appears not to have stood the test of time. However carefully observed, the disaffected, often marginal characters of the trilogy seem unlikely to capture or maintain the reader's interest, perhaps least of all in what might have become of them in the projected fourth volume. Of the existing volumes, *The Reprieve* has perhaps deservedly received the greatest critical attention, owing mainly to Sartre's skillful experiments with time and simultaneity, a technique admittedly borrowed from the cinema by way of John Dos Passos. On balance, however, Sartre was doubtless well advised to turn his talents elsewhere.

David B. Parsell

OTHER MAJOR WORKS

SHORT FICTION: *Le Mur*, 1939 (*The Wall, and Other Stories*, 1948).

PLAYS: *Les Mouches*, pr., pb. 1943 (*The Flies*, 1946); *Huis clos*, pr. 1944 (*In Camera*, 1946; better known as *No Exit*, 1947); *Morts sans sépulture*, pr., pb. 1946 (*The Victors*, 1948); *La Putain respectueuse*, pr., pb. 1946 (*The Respectful Prostitute*, 1947); *Les Jeux sont faits*, pr., pb. 1947 (*The Chips Are Down*, 1948); *Les Mains sales*, pr., pb. 1948 (*Dirty Hands*, 1949); *Le Diable et le Bon Dieu*, pr. 1951 (*The Devil and the Good Lord*, 1953); *Kean: Ou, Désordre et génie*, pb. 1952 (adaptation of Alexandre Dumas, père's play; *Kean: Or, Disorder and Genius*, 1954); *Nekrassov*, pr. 1955 (English translation, 1956); *Les Séquestrés d'Altona*, pr. 1959 (*The Condemned of Altona*, 1960); *Les Troyennes*, pr., pb. 1965 (adaptation of Euripides' play; *The Trojan Women*, 1967).

NONFICTION: *L'Imagination*, 1936 (*Imagination: A Psychological Critique*, 1962); *Esquisse d'une théorie des émotions*, 1939 (*The Emotions: Outline of a Theory*, 1948); *L'Imaginaire: Psychologie phénoménologique de l'imagination*, 1940 (*The Psychology of Imagination*, 1948); *L'Être et le néant*, 1943 (*Being and Nothingness*, 1956); *L'Existentialisme est un humanisme*, 1946 (*Existentialism*, 1947; also known as *Existentialism and Humanism*, 1948); *Réflexions sur la question juive*, 1946 (*Anti-Semite and Jew*, 1948); *Baudelaire*, 1947 (English translation, 1950); *Qu'est-ce que la littérature?*, 1947 (*What Is Literature?*, 1949); *Situations I-X*, 1947-1975 (10 volumes; partial translation, 1965-1977); *Saint-Genet: Comédien et martyr*, 1952 (*Saint Genet: Actor and Martyr*, 1963); *Critique de la raison dialectique, précédé de question de méthode*, 1960 (*Search for a Method*, 1963); *Critique de la raison dialectique, I: Théorie des ensembles pratiques*, 1960 (*Critique of Dialectical Reason, I: Theory of Practical Ensembles*, 1976); *Les Mots*, 1964 (*The Words*, 1964); *L'Idiot de la famille: Gustave Flaubert, 1821-1857*, 1971-1972 (3 volumes; partial translation *The Family Idiot: Gustave Flaubert, 1821-1857*, 1981, 1987); *Un Théâtre de situations*, 1973 (*Sartre on Theater*, 1976); *Les Carnets de la drôle de guerre*, 1983 (*The War Diaries of Jean-Paul Sartre: November, 1939-March, 1940*, 1984); *Lettres au Castor et à quelques autres*, 1983 (2 volumes; volume 1, *Witness to My Life: The Letters of Jean-Paul Sartre to Simone de Beauvoir, 1926-1939*,

1992; volume 2, *Quiet Moments in War: The Letters of Jean-Paul Sartre to Simone de Beauvoir, 1940-1963*, 1993); *Le Scénario Freud*, 1984 (*The Freud Scenario*, 1985).

BIBLIOGRAPHY

Aronson, Ronald, and Adrian van den Hoven. *Sartre Alive*. Detroit, Mich.: Wayne State University Press, 1991. Provides a judicious and well-informed introduction to Sartre's work followed by sections on Sartre's continuing political relevance, on his political and philosophical thought, on his fiction and biography, on his relationships with Simone de Beauvoir and other writers, and on concluding assessments of his career.

Bloom, Harold, ed. *Jean-Paul Sartre*. Philadelphia: Chelsea House, 2001. Collection of critical essays on Sartre is supplemented by an editor's introduction, a brief biography, and a chronology of events in Sartre's life. Includes bibliography and index.

Fournay, Jean-François, and Charles D. Minahen, eds. *Situating Sartre in Twentieth-Century Thought and Culture*. New York: St. Martin's Press, 1997. Sartre scholars offer varied interpretations on the significance of Sartre's philosophical and literary works.

Hayman, Ronald. *Sartre: A Life*. New York: Simon & Schuster, 1987. Well-written biography shows the historical contexts within Sartre wrote various works, suggesting how and why Sartre explored different literary genres in search of the most accessible vehicle for his ideas.

Hill, Charles G. *Jean-Paul Sartre: Freedom and Commitment*. New York: Peter Lang, 1992. Discusses Sartre's qu est for freedom and authentic actions as well as his recognition of the ambiguities of commitment. Chapter 2 discusses the novel *Nausea*. Includes chronology, notes, and bibliography.

Howells, Christina, ed. *Sartre*. New York: Longman, 1995. Collection of essays presents critical analyses of Sartre's dramatic works and literary fiction, including all his novels. Includes bibliography and index.

McBride, William L., ed. *Existentialist Literature and Aesthetics*. Vol. 7 in *Sartre and Existentialism*. New York: Garland, 1997. This volume, part of a multivolume series on Sartre and his philosophy, examines his literary works and how existentialism is expressed in them. Includes bibliography.

Rowley, Hazel. *Tête-à-Tête: Simone de Beauvoir and Jean-Paul Sartre*. New York: HarperCollins, 2005. Chronicles the relationship between the two French writers, discussing their writings, their politics, their philosophical legacy, and their commitment to each other. Includes bibliography and index.

Silvester, Rosalind. *Seeking Sartre's Style: Stylistic Inroads into "Les Chemins de la liberté."* Lewiston, N.Y.: Edwin Mellen Press, 2003. Offers a detailed philosophical and linguistic analysis of *The Roads to Freedom*, analyzing Sartre's use of language in the novel trilogy. Includes bibliography and index.

Van den Hoven, Adrian, and Andrew Leak, eds. *Sartre Today: A Centenary Celebration.*

New York: Berghahn Books, 2005. Collection of essays includes discussion of Sartre's existential philosophy and his thoughts on psychology and politics.

Wardman, Harold W. *Jean-Paul Sartre: The Evolution of His Thought and Art.* Lewiston, N.Y.: Edwin Mellen Press, 1992. Critical examination of Sartre's literary works traces the author's philosophical development through his writings, charting his changing ideas about religion, art, human relationships, and politics. Includes bibliography and index.

JULES VERNE

Born: Nantes, France; February 8, 1828
Died: Amiens, France; March 24, 1905
Also known as: Jules Gabriel Verne

PRINCIPAL LONG FICTION
  Cinq Semaines en ballon, 1863 (*Five Weeks in a Balloon*, 1876)
  Voyage au centre de la terre, 1864 (*A Journey to the Centre of the Earth*, 1872)
  Voyages et aventures du capitaine Hatteras, 1864-1866 (2 volumes; includes *Les Anglais au pôle nord*, 1864 [*English at the North Pole*, 1874], and *Le Désert de glace*, 1866 [*Field of Ice*, 1876]; also known as *Adventures of Captain Hatteras*, 1875)
  De la terre à la lune, 1865 (*From the Earth to the Moon*, 1873)
  Les Enfants du capitaine Grant, 1867-1868 (3 volumes; *Voyage Round the World*, 1876-1877; also known as *Captain Grant's Children*; includes *The Mysterious Document*, *Among the Cannibals*, and *On the Track*)
  Vingt mille lieues sous les mers, 1869-1870 (*Twenty Thousand Leagues Under the Sea*, 1873)
  Autour de la lune, 1870 (*From the Earth to the Moon . . . and a Trip Around It*, 1873)
  Une Ville flottante, 1871 (*A Floating City*, 1876)
  Aventures de trois russes et de trois anglais, 1872 (*Meridiana: The Adventures of Three Englishmen and Three Russians in South Africa*, 1873)
  Le Tour du monde en quatre-vingts jours, 1873 (*Around the World in Eighty Days*, 1873)
  L'Île mystérieuse, 1874-1875 (3 volumes; includes *Les Naufrages de l'air*, *L'Abandonné*, and *Le Secret de l'île*; *The Mysterious Island*, 1875)
  Le Chancellor, 1875 (*Survivors of the Chancellor*, 1875)
  Michel Strogoff, 1876 (*Michael Strogoff*, 1876-1877)
  Hector Servadac, 1877 (English translation, 1878)
  Les Cinq Cents Millions de la Bégum, 1878 (*The Begum's Fortune*, 1880)
  La Maison à vapeur, 1880 (*The Steam House*, 1881; includes *The Demon of Cawnpore* and *Tigers and Traitors*)
  La Jangada, 1881 (2 volumes; *The Giant Raft*, 1881; includes *Down the Amazon* and *The Cryptogram*)
  Mathias Sandorf, 1885 (English translation, 1886)
  Robur le conquerant, 1886 (*The Clipper of the Clouds*, 1887)
  Sans dessus dessous, 1889 (*The Purchase of the North Pole*, 1891)
  Le Château des Carpathes, 1892 (*The Castle of the Carpathians*, 1893)

L'Île à hélice, 1895 (*Floating Island*, 1896; also known as *Propeller Island*, 1965)
Face au drapeau, 1896 (*For the Flag*, 1897)
Le Sphinx des glaces, 1897 (*An Antarctic Mystery*, 1898; also known as *The Mystery of Arthur Gordon Pym*)
Le Superbe Orénoque, 1898 (*The Mighty Orinoco*, 2002)
Le Village aérien, 1901 (*The Village in the Treetops*, 1964)
Maître du monde, 1904 (*Master of the World*, 1914)
L'Invasion de la mer, 1905 (*Invasion of the Sea*, 2001)
La Chasse au météore, 1908 (*The Chase of the Golden Meteor*, 1909; also known as *The Meteor Hunt*, 2006)
Les Naufrages du Jonathan, 1909 (*The Survivors of the Jonathan*, 1962)
Le Secret de Wilhelm Storitz, 1910 (*The Secret of Wilhelm Storitz*, 1965)
L'Étonnante Aventure de la mission Barsac, 1920 (2 volumes; *Into the Niger Bend*, 1919; *The City in the Sahara*, 1965)
Paris au XXe siècle, 1994 (*Paris in the Twentieth Century*, 1996)

Other literary forms

Jules Verne's initial ambition was to be a playwright, and several of his plays and operettas were produced in Paris during the 1850's. The first was *Les Pailles rompues*, produced by Alexandre Dumas, *père*, in 1850, which also appeared in print. Others were the librettos *Colin Maillard* (pb. 1853) and *Les Compagnons de la Marjolaine* (pr. 1855). A number of Verne's short stories appeared in periodicals during the same period; some were collected along with the novelette "Une Fantasie du docteur Ox" in 1874. A collection of later stories was assembled for publication by Verne's son, Michel Verne, appearing under the title *Hier et demain* (1910; *Yesterday and Tomorrow*, 1965). Verne also wrote various nonfictional works on the history of exploration and took over from Théophile Lavellée a multivolume project called *Géographie illustrée de la France et de ses colonies*, which was issued in the period 1867-1868. Many of his novels were adapted to dramatic form and were usually represented as collaborations when produced or subsequently published as plays. Of his early articles, the most important is an essay on Edgar Allan Poe that he published in 1864 in the journal *Musée des familles*.

Achievements

Jules Verne is remembered today chiefly as one of the two most notable writers of science fiction in a time before that term existed. I. O. Evans has described Verne as the "founder" of science fiction, and Peter Costello has called him the "inventor" of science fiction. The claim is justified, but it should be remembered that Verne did not see himself in this way—he was quite sincere in seeing no real literary relationship between his own work and that of H. G. Wells, with whom he was frequently compared during the last de-

Jules Verne
(Library of Congress)

cade of his life. What Verne actually set out to do, consciously and methodically, was to use geography as an ideative resource in the same way that Alexandre Dumas, *père*, had used history. Only a fraction of his work can be described as science fiction, yet all of it fits into a single pattern that is suggested by his use of the term *les voyages extraordinaire* as a kind of series title for his oeuvre. The medium that Verne invented and developed might more appropriately be called "the novel of imaginary tourism"; the science-fiction element in his work arose out of his occasional ambitions to send his tourists to places never before visited by humans (the North Pole, the moon, and cave systems beneath the earth's surface). In some instances, he had to devise new modes of travel—Barbicane's space-gun and Robur's flying machine—but, for the most part, he was content to employ conventional means of transport or slightly more luxurious versions of already existing machines (balloons and submarines).

There is a sense in which Verne's reputation has been distorted by the emphasis on his achievements as a precursor of modern science fiction. He has been described by Franz

Born as "the man who invented the future" and by Peter Haining as "the master of prophecy," but these descriptions are plainly absurd. Apart from two whimsical essays and his last, most somber, short story, "L'Eternel Adam" (written c. 1900 and included in *Yesterday and Tomorrow*; "The Eternal Adam"), Verne wrote nothing set in the future. Many of his novels deal with achievements not yet accomplished in the real world, but they were all achievements that Verne believed to be perfectly possible in the context of his own times. Even in his own day, Verne was hailed as the inventor, in his imagination, of technological devices later realized, but Verne always disclaimed any such achievement. In relation to the most commonly quoted example—the submarine described in *Twenty Thousand Leagues Under the Sea*—Verne pointed out, when questioned, that there had been submarines around for at least sixty years (he had probably seen *Le Plongeur*, built in 1864, on display at the Paris Exhibition of 1867) and that all the innovations he had attributed to the *Nautilus* actually remained unrealized.

Verne's real achievement was simply to notice the impact that the revolution in transportation was having on the world. When he saw the *Great Eastern* under construction in London in 1859, he had the wit to realize what a difference steamships would make to the business of travel and to the accessibility of distant parts of the world. He realized that a revolution in exploration was under way quite as important as the great navigations of the fifteenth and sixteenth centuries, and that new technologies would shrink the world very dramatically. If his novel *Around the World in Eighty Days* seemed sensational, it was only because of the ignorance of the audience; Thomas Cook had already advertised the first tour around the world for anyone who cared to go, and a Bostonian named George Francis Train had already gone around the world in eighty traveling days, though his total journey time was extended by a few sojourns in foreign jails.

Verne's enthusiasm for the Industrial Revolution was undoubtedly based on a one-sided view of its consequences; the same might be said, however, of the many writers who saw and bemoaned the social consequences of the revolution—the growth of the industrial poor—without realizing the historical significance of technological advancement. Verne had little to say about the future of technology, but he was aware of the fact that the process of innovation would continue and would be important in its impact on human affairs. This makes him a wiser man than most of the political economists of the day—including Karl Marx—who grossly underestimated, or even mistook, the significance of technological change.

Verne has never been taken very seriously as a novelist. Partly this is because he was considered popular, and thus vulgar—all the more so because Pierre-Jules Hetzel, his publisher, dealt mainly in juvenile fiction. In Britain, Verne's books were published in butchered translations as "boys' books," and it is only in recent years that unmutilated translations of a few of his more famous works have become available. In France, interest in Verne has revived. Michel Butor wrote an excellent essay titled "The Golden Age in Jules Verne" (1960), and even Roland Barthes paid wry homage to Verne in one of the brief essays in *Mythologies* (1957; English translation, 1972). The contribution made by Verne to nineteenth century consciousness is now openly acknowledged, if not universally admired. The literary skills displayed in Verne's novels are limited, and the very processes of change that he was celebrating have robbed his stories of their excitement and conviction, leaving to them only historical interest and a certain naïve charm. For these reasons, modern readers have great difficulty in reading Verne for pleasure; his appeal is anchored in a lost past from which today's reader is far removed. Nevertheless, his achievements, seen in their appropriate historical context, should not be underestimated.

Biography

Jules Gabriel Verne was born in 1828, the son of Pierre Verne, a lawyer, and Sophie, née Allotte de la Fuye. He was born in Nantes, on the Île Feydeau, an island in the Loire River that has since been connected to the bank. His family appears to have been a bastion of middle-class respectability, desperately concerned with keeping up appearances. This fact appears to have had a profound effect on Verne's life, a subtle but important influence on his work, and to be the cause of some misrepresentation in the biographies written by members of his family—even the one published in 1973 by Jean Jules-Verne (his grandson).

Verne's life story seems to have been one of constant and unsuccessful rebellion against the standards and lifestyle that his family tried to impose on him. He never escaped the clutches of middle-class respectability and seems to have spent the last forty years of his life maintaining a facade for the sake of the expectations of his family. Under such circumstances, it is perhaps not surprising that he took full advantage of the opportunity to become a voyager in the imagination—a champion escapist.

Verne studied law in his father's office for a while before going to Paris, ostensibly to continue his studies there. Actually, he wanted to be a playwright, and he threw himself into the bohemian life of the student quarter of the Left Bank, where he met Victor Hugo and Alexandre Dumas, *père*. Dumas encouraged his literary endeavors and produced Verne's first one-act comedy at the Théâtre Historique. Verne's attempts to establish himself in the literary world were, however, less than wholly successful. While he wrote plays, short stories, and operettas in the early 1850's, he was for three years secretary of the Théâtre Lyrique, but by the end of 1855, he had had enough. In 1856, he planned to marry a young widow, Honorine Morel, and in order to be able to support her, he asked his father to buy him a share in a stockbroking business.

This business provided Verne with an income, but he still had other ambitions and began collecting articles that he hoped might help him to carve out a niche for himself as a novelist exploiting geography in the same way Dumas had exploited history. He traveled extensively, visiting Britain in 1859 and Scandinavia in 1861, and produced more light plays with music. His son Michel was born in August, 1861.

Around this time, Verne appears to have become partly estranged from his wife. They had no more children and occupied separate beds, but they continued to maintain the appearance of a happy marriage. Verne retreated more and more frequently to his club—the Cercle de la Presse Scientifique—where he met and became friendly with Félix Tournachon, a photographer and aeronaut who used the pseudonym "Nadar." Out of the interest in aeronautics inspired by this association came a documentary novel about ballooning, which Verne took to the publisher Hetzel (who himself wrote, under the pseudonym P. J. Stahl) in 1862. Hetzel suggested sweeping revisions, which Verne carried out in only two weeks. Verne put to Hetzel, soon after the publication of *Five Weeks in a Balloon*, his idea for an extended series of *les voyages extraordinaires*, and Hetzel encouraged him to go ahead. By September, 1863, when the Verne family moved to Auteuil, Verne was well established as a novelist. He was, however, apparently under great personal strain. He suffered a good deal from stress-related facial paralysis, which eventually had to be relieved by electric shock treatment.

Verne seems to have been grateful to Hetzel, and his first biographer, Marguerite Allotte de la Fuye (his niece), alleges that Hetzel treated him with the utmost generosity. In fact, Hetzel's financial records reveal that Hetzel made about five times as much from Verne's books as Verne did and, although Verne eventually became quite well-off, his family certainly struggled for a while in the 1860's and may have suffered mild financial embarrassments later in his career, when his sales fell off dramatically.

In 1870, Ferdinand de Lesseps solicited the Légion d'Honneur for Verne; it was awarded in 1870 immediately before the fall of the Third Republic. He was honored by the Académie Française in August, 1872, but was never elected to it. During the Franco-Prussian War, Verne set up a coast-guard unit at Crotoy, where he had been living for some years, and afterward had to return to the Bourse for a while because of the effect of the war on the book trade. This did not last long, however, and in 1872, he settled permanently in Amiens, devoting himself from then on to full-time writing.

Verne's son Michel proved a great disappointment to him. As a boy, Michel was a delinquent, and he was estranged from his parents for a long time, living a turbulent personal life. When he finally settled down, however, he and his father were reconciled. Michel's third son, Jean Jules-Verne, eventually became one of Verne's biographers.

Verne's main relaxation during his years at Amiens was his involvement with a series of small boats, all of which he called *St. Michel*, the third and last of which he bought in 1877. He spent a great deal of time on these boats, and the third one was actually large enough to allow him to undertake some voyages of his own. He visited Britain and Scandinavia in 1877, went cruising in the Baltic in 1880, and toured parts of the Mediterranean in 1884. On the last trip, in particular, he was exposed to a great deal of publicity and was hailed as a celebrity wherever he went. He tried to avoid this, but his wife reveled in it and frustrated his attempts to remain unnoticed. He sold the third *St. Michel* in 1886, possibly because of financial problems—throughout the 1880's, sales of his new books plummeted. Whereas, at the peak of his career, *Around the World in Eighty Days* had sold more than a hundred thousand copies in the trade edition, by 1880, his new works frequently sold less than twenty thousand copies, and the books he wrote in the last decade of his life sold less than ten thousand copies.

In March, 1886, Verne was shot in the foot by a would-be assassin—his nephew Gaston. Gaston was confined to an asylum; the incident was so shocking to the family that, according to Peter Costello's 1978 Verne biography, no one in the family would discuss the matter almost one hundred years later. Verne remained lame for the rest of his life, but that did not prevent him from going into local politics the following year. This represented a modest emergence from his shell, in that he stood as a radical, undoubtedly offending his staunchly conservative family. It is interesting that Verne's political radicalism is occasionally evident in his wry asides but is never given free expression in his works. The same is true of his religious beliefs. Though his family was staunchly Catholic (and the family biographers maintain that Verne was also), Verne appears to have become an agnostic, if not an atheist, as early as the 1850's. Religiosity was part of the facade that he maintained throughout his life, and his novels do very little to suggest his true opinions, except in certain sly remarks. This self-conscious hypocrisy is, at times, willfully subverted by the author, as in *The Village in the Treetops*, in which a token denial of belief in Darwinism is then made to look absurd by a story about apes with quasi-human intelligence—living "missing links." The difficulty of penetrating this facade was increased when Verne, in 1898, burned a number of his personal papers, including manuscripts and account books.

Even after Verne's death, the business of keeping up appearances continued. Michel became his father's literary executor and seems to have taken a hand in revising one or two of his manuscripts for posthumous publication. The authorship of the novel translated into English in two volumes as *Into the Niger Bend* and *The City in the Sahara*, in particular, is rather dubious. A ghostwriter named Georges Montignac may well have been involved, as well as Michel. Certain other works published under Jules Verne's name are most likely the work of Michel, although this may apply only to shorter pieces.

What is remarkable about Verne's life, insofar as it affected his literary career, was the extent to which everything that really mattered to him remained private. He was a man whose "real" life was lived inside his head, quite disconnected from the daily routine of going through the motions of respectable middle-class life. Even in his books, his innermost thoughts remain covert, peeping out only occasionally, and then in disguise. The best of his fantasies concern ordinary people snatched by circumstance into isolation and imprisonment, which they accept with relief and guilty joy. He was the archetypal armchair traveler, a man who found solace in his dreams and worked to add a special verisimilitude to those dreams, researching indefatigably to fill in their background. He pretended to be satisfied with his lot in life, but his stories are the work of a deeply disappointed and frustrated man.

Analysis

Most of Jules Verne's novels, including the ones for which he is best known, are imaginary travelogues whose initial appeal to readers is that they will provide access to the remote regions of the world and allow readers to participate in adventures that could take place only there. In the first ten years of his career, Verne's imaginary travels took him to all the most inaccessible corners of the globe: Captain Hatteras went to the North Pole; the children of Captain Grant circumnavigated the Southern Hemisphere; and the protagonists of *Five Weeks in a Balloon* and *Meridiana* crossed darkest Africa at a time when "darkest" still meant obscure and unknown. Other characters undertook still bolder voyages: Axel and Professor Lidenbrock never did reach the center of the earth, but they did get under its skin, and though Barbicane and his companions failed to land on the moon (mercifully, as they had no means of return), they did get a trip around it.

We know today that all these stories are unrealistic, but Verne's audience could not know that, and they were compelled to be impressed by the elaborate methods Verne used to create an atmosphere of verisimilitude. His attention to detail, particularly the detail of scientific instrumentation and measurement, gives his travelers a vital sense of purpose. They are researchers, collecting information with the same intellectual curiosity and dedication that guided Verne's collecting of research materials. It may well be that the scientifically minded heroes have less serious companions who are along for the ride (and who usually provide comic relief), but there is no doubt as to where the real value of the works is located.

A JOURNEY TO THE CENTRE OF THE EARTH

The best of the early works is *A Journey to the Centre of the Earth*, because it is at once the most painstaking, the most imaginative, and the most elegantly plotted. The notion of an enclosed world inhabited by primeval monsters is one that has been copied many times since, and though it is the kind of wild invention of which Verne rather disapproved (he never did anything similar again), it seems perfectly appropriate to this particular literary exercise. Significantly, however, *A Journey to the Centre of the Earth* was not the most popular of the early works, and it does not enjoy the highest reputation—that distinction goes to *Twenty Thousand Leagues Under the Sea*.

TWENTY THOUSAND LEAGUES UNDER THE SEA

There are many reasons for the popularity of *Twenty Thousand Leagues Under the Sea*. The undersea world that it displays is bound to seem meager, and sometimes laughable, to modern readers who have seen and become familiar with films made by Jacques Cousteau. The contemporary reader knows what a strange and wonderful world it is, and how many bizarre inhabitants it has. In 1870, however, there was no underwater photography, the first skin-diving equipment had not yet been designed, and the undersea world was as alien as the planet Mars. The mysterious menace of the sea was legendary and had been spectacularly recalled to the public attention in 1861, when the French naval vessel

Alecton encountered a so-called giant octopus (actually a giant squid), which the crew nearly succeeded in harpooning and hauling aboard.

In fact, *Twenty Thousand Leagues Under the Sea* is the least reliable of all Verne's novels as far as its informational content is concerned. Almost every invention in it, no matter how modest, missed the mark. Although the illustrations imply that the diving suits in the novel are rather like the pressurized suits that later became widespread, in reality the ones Verne describes would be lethal. Despite the credit given to Verne for "inventing" the modern submarine, the *Nautilus* is rather an absurd vessel, in terms of its scientific plausibility. All of this, of course, would not have affected the contemporary reader, who could quite easily swallow the whole story, hook, line, and sinker.

Quite apart from these considerations, however, the book offers powerful attractions. Captain Nemo and the *Nautilus* may not be particularly realistic, but they are most certainly charismatic. They are only disguised as rational creations; in fact, they are myth figures whose significance reveals a good deal about the spirit of Verne's work.

Barthes, in *Mythologies*, claims that what Verne's characters are always seeking is seclusion and that the many vessels employed in Verne's stories are to be seen not so much as the means of reaching faraway destinations but as microcosmic private worlds where "claustrophilic" heroes can live in comfort, safe from the chaotic and confusing world that flows by outside the windows. In this respect, the *Nautilus* is by far the best of the Verne ships. It has every possible comfort—Nemo not only has the best of everything, but his best also reaches a standard unknown to the aesthetes of Paris. It is also sealed tight; Aronnax is so completely enclosed that he is a helpless prisoner—even the power of self-determination has been taken away from him, so that he can relax utterly and completely into a security greater than anything he has undergone since the womb.

This desire for seclusion and the retreat into a private microcosm is by no means all there is to Verne—it is often the case that his characters cannot seclude themselves and are forced to fight a dogged battle for survival—but it is something that shows up strongly in his romantic and most personal stories. The fantasy of being held prisoner by a benevolent captor, maintained in luxury, and removed from the hurly-burly of the actual world is a common one, and in *Twenty Thousand Leagues Under the Sea*, it finds almost perfect expression. The wonders and dangers of the undersea world are most important here as a kind of emphatic counterpoint, standing in for the uncertainties of life. Nemo's obsessive crusade against the world's shipping is basically a strategy of rejection and retreat that, though it can be admired, envied, and temporarily shared, must ultimately be refused as a viable mode of conduct. The real world, after all, does have to be faced; one cannot help but deal with it even if one's dealings constitute a facade and one's heart is elsewhere.

THE MYSTERIOUS ISLAND

It is significant that Captain Nemo makes his reappearance in Verne's own favorite among his novels—the long and languid *The Mysterious Island*. This was the first and best of Verne's several robinsonades, in which the island on which the protagonists are cast away becomes an ideal microcosm where (with a little help from an unknown friend) they carefully reconstruct a world of middle-class comfort. Significantly, it is an all-male world strongly reminiscent of a gentlemen's club. The discovery, late in the novel, that the *Nautilus* is hidden deep in the bowels of the island is a magnificently naïve emphasis of the fact that, in terms of Verne's private mythology, the island and the submarine are really the same in terms of their function.

The Mysterious Island belongs to the second decade of Verne's career, a decade in some ways very different from the first. It commenced with the most popular of his nonfantastic works, *Around the World in Eighty Days*, which constitutes a travelogue rather different from his earlier ones in that the emphasis is on speed rather than leisurely seclusion. Significantly, it is from the closed world of a Victorian club that Phileas Fogg emerges, and to which he intends to return in the minimum possible time, once he has demonstrated that the world can be encircled (and therefore, in a sense, brought under control) on an unexpectedly tight schedule.

The travelogues that Verne wrote after *Around the World in Eighty Days* are markedly different in character from those that he wrote before. The emphasis on scientific research is largely abandoned, though the characters are always subject to occasional lapses into careful observation of odd phenomena and debates about their significance. There are no more expeditions of the kind undertaken by Professor Lidenbrock—Verne takes care to provide his characters with more urgent and more personal motives for travel and thus begins to rely more and more on shipwreck and catastrophe as motive forces.

It may be significant that the highly self-indulgent *The Mysterious Island* was followed by the grim horror story *Survivors of the Chancellor*, the story of a ship beset by a chain of catastrophes leaving the survivors to face further appalling ordeals. The contrast reflects the tension in Verne's work to which Barthes does not do full justice—the author was quite well aware of the cozy romanticism that occasionally dominated his stories, and he shared with Barthes the suspicion that there was something unhealthy about it and that it might even be something to be despised. It is almost as if, after 1874, Verne made a conscious effort to distance his work from his own daydreams, to free himself from dependence on their emotional charge in order to become a genuine literary craftsman. He went on after *Survivors of the Chancellor* to write the adventure story *Michael Strogoff*, the plot of which is built around a journey but which can under no circumstances be accounted a novel of imaginary tourism. When, in *Hector Servadac*, he made a conscious return to imaginative territory similar to that covered in *From the Earth to the Moon . . . and a Trip Around It*, he was noticeably halfhearted about it and allowed the novel to decay into confusion. Not until 1881, when he published *The Giant Raft*, did he really recapture something of the spirit of his early travel-adventure novels.

THE BEGUM'S FORTUNE

One of the most interesting experiments of this second decade was *The Begum's Fortune*, an exercise in social speculation in which an enormous inheritance split between two legatees is used to build two very different cities—the utopian Frankville and the militaristic Stahlstadt. In imagining this sharp contrast between the ideals of a French social scientist and a German militarist, Verne was reflecting on the intellectual legacy of the Franco-Prussian War, but his vision of Stahlstadt proved to be rather more prophetic than he would have wished. Verne was, in reality, interested in politics and in town planning— there was a streak of authentic utopianism in him—but that was one of the few occasions when he allowed his interest to affect his literary work, and it does so only in a rather stylized manner; both Frankville and Stahlstadt are deliberately oversimplified almost to the point of caricature, as if to emphasize the fact that Verne had no wish to deal in serious speculations about the possible future developments in French or German society. He seems to have believed that there would be a kind of impropriety in so doing, and this belief may be connected with his curiously hostile reaction to the idea that he belonged in the same literary category as Wells.

For the whole of his career as a novelist, Verne maintained a steady productivity. His books were released at the rate of one or two a year, and he left behind enough of a stockpile for the publishers to maintain this schedule for five years after his death. The decline in his popularity in the 1880's, however, reflected a genuine decline in the appeal of his work. He might with justification have wondered at that, believing himself to be demonstrating much greater versatility in his work, but it is ironically true that he echoed his earlier vitality only when he was virtually plagiarizing himself. Many of his later works are interesting, for one reason or another, but few of them are really memorable. *The Clipper of the Clouds* and its sequel, *Master of the World*, are effective pastiches of *Twenty Thousand Leagues Under the Sea*, reduced dramatically in effect by virtue of the fact that the skies patrolled by the flying machine are no substitute for the submarine world of the *Nautilus*. A rather more interesting "microcosmic fantasy" is provided in *Propeller Island*, but Verne deliberately does not treat the notion too seriously.

Interesting for a different reason is *The Castle of the Carpathians*, in which Verne set out to write a gothic romance, albeit of a rationalized nature. Because of his association with science fiction and his use of scientific apparatus in assuring the verisimilitude of his early travelogues, Verne's interest in Romantic fiction of a more exotic character is often overlooked entirely, though he was a great admirer of Edgar Allan Poe and E. T. A. Hoffmann. In *An Antarctic Mystery*, Verne provided a continuation of Poe's classic *The Narrative of Arthur Gordon Pym* (1838), and the best of his own early works of short fiction—"Maître Zacharius: Ou, L'Horloger qui a perdu son âme" (1854; "Master Zacharius," 1874) and "Une Fantaisie du Docteur Ox" (1872; "Dr. Ox's Experiment," 1874)—are plainly a pastiche of Hoffmann. Both *The Castle of the Carpathians* and *An Antarctic Mystery*, however, show how difficult Verne found it to create any real sense of supernatural threat. Both stories are rationalized, but they are pedestrian and mundane even before the climactic "explanations." The fact that Verne could be interested in this kind of fantasy and yet be incapable of writing it is symptomatic of the fact that his work became steadily more detached from any real core of personal feeling; it became gradually more self-conscious and artificial, a product of intellectual craftsmanship, with no real roots in his own beliefs and feelings. By the 1880's, if not earlier, Verne seems to have made a decision that his writing was to be a commercial activity, a way of making a living, rather than a mode of self-expression. Only his works published before 1875—and not all of those—really show any measure of imaginative vigor. For all of its carefulness and frequent cleverness, all the later work is rather lifeless.

LATER WORKS

In the work of Verne's last years, a certain bleakness becomes gradually more evident. The misanthropy glimpsed in some of his earlier novels (in the character of Captain Nemo, for example) also gained rather freer expression. Members of the ape race in *The Village in the Treetops*, with their primitive caricature of religion, offer a challenge to human vanity, and a much more explicit condemnation of human traits is to be found in the criticisms of materialism that occur in several of the posthumous novels as satirizations of gold lust. This censure is most evident in *The Chase of the Golden Meteor*, which has a very moral ending in which the scientist-hero sinks the golden meteor rather than allow any of his greedy rivals in the pursuit to get their hands on it. It is perhaps more telling, however, in *The Survivors of the Jonathan*, in which the anarchist hero's attempts to found a utopian community are confounded by the discovery of a vicinity of gold. This novel is one of the few in which Verne's radical political sympathies are made unmistakably explicit. A rather different kind of bitterness is seen in *The Secret of Wilhelm Storitz*, in which a jilted lover uses unusual means in order to get back at the woman who rejected him. This downbeat streak in Verne's last period culminated in the short story "The Eternal Adam," a tale of historical cycles of decline and fall that gives voice to an almost Spenglerian pessimism. This is pure science fiction, but it is the work of a very different man from the young Verne who wrote *A Journey to the Centre of the Earth*.

It seems odd to write of a man whose work has been read by millions—a man who is possibly the most translated French writer of all time—that he kept very much to himself. Despite his involvement in a closely knit web of family relationships (which he seems to have regarded as a burdensome oppression), he was essentially a loner. His heroes are mostly independent and detached men who escape into situations in which they enjoy the undemanding companionship of tolerable acquaintances, but in which they have abundant opportunity to be by themselves, observing and meditating on the world around them. Verne's main appeal is to the reader's longing to "get away from it all," and the key to his great popularity as a writer is that it is precisely that impulse toward escape that drives many people to the activity of reading.

It is by no means surprising that a man with such a personality should have been so interested in science and technology, because it is very often men of such temperament who find contemplation of the abstract world of knowledge congenial. Painstaking research and attention to detail are the prerogatives of individuals willing and able to withdraw habitually from the routines of human intercourse. One may regret that Verne did not "put himself into" his works to any great extent, with the exception of *Twenty Thousand Leagues Under the Sea* and *The Mysterious Island*. One may also regret, especially if one values Verne primarily for his contribution to the emergent genre of scientific romance, that he kept such a disciplined rein on his imagination after the early extravagances of *A Journey to the Centre of the Earth* and *From the Earth to the Moon . . . and a Trip Around It*. These, however, are facets of the man's character, which undeniably has its puzzling aspects.

Verne was not a great writer, but he was a unique and interesting one. He is a literary phenomenon who remains even today something of an enigma despite the fact that his books are straightforward tales of adventure, mostly lacking in depth. Though his work was wide enough in its appeal to generate many imitations, there remains something inimitable about his best books—and not merely the naïveté that the passage of time has rendered impossible to duplicate. There is a Vernean esprit that remains his alone.

Brian Stableford

Other major works

SHORT FICTION: *Le Docteur Ox*, 1874 (*Dr. Ox's Experiment, and Other Stories*, 1874); *Hier et demain*, 1910 (*Yesterday and Tomorrow*, 1965).

PLAYS: *Les Pailles rompues*, pr. 1850; *Colin Maillard*, pb. 1853 (libretto); *Les Compagnons de la Marjolaine*, pr. 1855 (libretto).

NONFICTION: *Géographie illustrée de la France et de ses colonies*, 1867-1868 (with Théophile Lavellée); *Histoire des grandes voyages et grand voyageurs*, 1870-1873 (3 volumes; with Gabriel Marcel; *Celebrated Travels and Travellers*, 1879-1881).

Bibliography

Butcher, William. *Jules Verne: The Definitive Biography*. New York: Thunder's Mouth Press, 2006. Exhaustive examination of Verne is large in scope and reveals rich—and sometimes controversial—details of his life. Presents a portrait of Verne that is very different from the somewhat stodgy character depicted in Herbert Lottmann's biography (cited below).

_____. *Verne's Journey to the Centre of the Self: Space and Time in the Voyages Extraordinaires*. London: Macmillan, 1990. Presents a comprehensive discussion of Verne's science fiction, supplemented by detailed notes and a comprehensive bibliography.

Costello, Peter. *Jules Verne: Inventor of Science Fiction*. New York: Charles Scribner's

Sons, 1978. Readable biography places Verne's works of fiction within their historical context. Includes a bibliography.

Jules-Verne, Jean. *Jules Verne.* New York: Taplinger, 1976. Entertaining biography by Verne's grandson draws on material in the family archives to explore Verne's methods and the experiences that led to his novels and stories. Provides a good portrait of the times in which Verne lived and wrote. Includes detailed bibliography and index.

Lottmann, Herbert. *Jules Verne: An Exploratory Biography.* New York: St. Martin's Press, 1996. Graceful study by a veteran biographer of many French subjects. Describes the difficulties in Verne's life that made the writer a disillusioned man. Includes detailed notes that reflect extensive new research.

Lynch, Lawrence. *Jules Verne.* New York: Twayne, 1992. Reliable introductory study discusses Verne's early life, his early fiction, his period of masterpieces, and his final works of fiction. Includes an appendix listing film adaptations of Verne's works, detailed notes, a chronology, and an annotated bibliography.

Martin, Andrew. *The Mask of the Prophet: The Extraordinary Fictions of Jules Verne.* Oxford, England: Clarendon Press, 1990. Attempts to recapture Verne for modern readers, focusing on his fictions of subversion and law and disorder and on the prophetic nature of fiction itself.

Saint Bris, Gonzague. *The World of Jules Verne.* Translated by Helen Marx, illustrated by Stephane Heuet, with a preface by Arthur C. Clark. New York: Tuttle Point Press, 2006. Blends biographical material with anecdotes, extracts from Verne's novels, and illustrations in an attempt to re-create the settings and characters of Verne's visionary fiction.

Smyth, Edmund J., ed. *Jules Verne: Narratives of Modernity.* Liverpool, England: Liverpool University Press, 2000. Collection of essays by Verne scholars examines, among other topics, Verne's science fiction in relation to modernity and Verne's place in the French literary canon.

Unwin, Timothy. *Jules Verne: Journeys in Writing.* Liverpool, England: Liverpool University Press, 2005. Reexamines Verne's fiction, comparing his work with that of Gustave Flaubert and other nineteenth century French authors. Argues that Verne was a skillful creator of self-conscious, experimental novels.

VOLTAIRE
François-Marie Arouet

Born: Paris, France; November 21, 1694
Died: Paris, France; May 30, 1778
Also known as: François-Marie Arouet

PRINCIPAL LONG FICTION

Zadig: Ou, La Destinée, histoire orientale, 1748 (originally published as *Memnon: Histoire orientale*, 1747; *Zadig: Or, The Book of Fate*, 1749)
Le Micromégas, 1752 (*Micromegas*, 1753)
Histoire des voyages de Scarmentado, 1756 (*The History of the Voyages of Scarmentado*, 1757; also known as *History of Scarmentado's Travels*, 1961)
Candide: Ou, L'Optimisme, 1759 (*Candide: Or, All for the Best*, 1759; also known as *Candide: Or, The Optimist*, 1762; also known as *Candide: Or, Optimism*, 1947)
L'Ingénu, 1767 (*The Pupil of Nature*, 1771; also known as *Ingenuous*, 1961)
L'Homme aux quarante écus, 1768 (*The Man of Forty Crowns*, 1768)
La Princesse de Babylone, 1768 (*The Princess of Babylon*, 1769)

OTHER LITERARY FORMS

Voltaire (vohl-TAYR) is probably the most prolific and versatile writer of any age. He wrote in all the literary forms, and he wrote in them concurrently. His numerous plays fill 6 volumes, and his correspondence 102 volumes. He was especially active toward the end of his life; living at Ferney in his eighties, he wrote pamphlets, many plays, and one of his best philosophical poems, *Épître à Horace* (1772). He went to Paris at the age of eighty-three, shortly before he died, to see a production of his latest classical tragedy, *Irène* (pr. 1778). At the time of his death, he was at work on a new play and rewriting others.

In many ways, Voltaire wished to be considered as a defender of the classical tradition. His plays are mainly classical, embodying the unities and dealing with highborn heroes. *Œdipe* (pr. 1718; *Oedipus*, 1761) was widely acclaimed in Voltaire's day, as were *Zaïre* (pr. 1732; English translation, 1736) and *Mérope* (1743; English translation, 1744, 1749). He also, however, introduced devices and techniques that ultimately led to the demise of classical theater, including local color, such as red togas for members of the Senate in *Brutus* (pr. 1730; English translation, 1761) and real cannon fire in *Adélaïde du Guesclin* (pr. 1734). Voltaire's later plays include a certain amount of tearful sensibility that was a characteristic of Denis Diderot's bourgeois dramas.

Voltaire composed many kinds of poetry. As a young man, he achieved much acclaim with his epic poem *La Ligue* (1723) and *La Henriade* (1728, a rewriting of *La Ligue*; *Henriade*, 1732). *Henriade*, which narrates Henry IV's successful struggle against the

Voltaire
(Library of Congress)

Catholic League, was reprinted through the beginning of the nineteenth century. Today, these poems have no appeal. Voltaire also wrote satiric and philosophical poetry, including *Le Mondain* (1736; *The Man of the World*, 1764). This poem caused a scandal with its suggestion that a pleasurable life on earth is the only positive happiness one can grasp and that one should enjoy it rather than wait for a life after death. This element of audacious irreverence is a quality that spices all of Voltaire's work and was what his admirers appreciated. Voltaire's *Épître à Horace* is one of the best of Voltaire's philosophical epistles.

Voltaire has some renown as a historian. His *Le Siècle de Louis XIV* (1751; *The Age of Louis XIV*, 1752) reveals meticulous research and a journalistic bent. Voltaire praises the reign of Louis XIV in order to criticize the reign of Louis XV. *Essai sur les mœurs* (1756, 1763; *The General History and State of Europe*, 1754, 1759) presents a philosophical review of historic events. Other nonfiction works popularize the accomplishments of Sir Isaac Newton in science and of John Locke in philosophy (*Éléments de la philosophie de Newton*, 1738; *The Elements of Sir Isaac Newton's Philosophy*, 1738). In *Lettres philosophiques* (1734; originally published in English as *Letters Concerning the English Nation*, 1733; also known as *Philosophical Letters*, 1961), Voltaire, with his powerful satire, praises English customs and institutions as a method of criticizing French society of his day. Censorship, which outlawed much of Voltaire's work, not only added to the satirist's celebrity but also increased the prices charged for his books. The articles that Voltaire wrote for *Dictionnaire philosophique portatif* (1764, enlarged 1769; *A Philosophical Dictionary for the Pocket*, 1765; also known as *Philosophical Dictionary*, 1945, enlarged 1962) were also offensive to the establishment, full of his propaganda on the subject of fanaticism, judicial corruption, and social oppression.

Achievements

Voltaire's career spanned sixty years, and during that time he achieved great fame and even greater notoriety. Voltaire's literary ambitions were revealed when he chose *Œdipe* as the subject of his first tragedy. His ambition was to rival Pierre Corneille, and at the age of twenty-four he was already hailed as a worthy successor to both Jean Racine and Corneille. In the theater, Voltaire considerably delayed the demise of classical tragedy, and he remained an extremely popular dramatist of the age. Between 1745 and 1803, his plays were staged many more times than those of Corneille and Racine. Today, however, Voltaire's plays are no longer of interest to audiences.

Voltaire also enjoyed success in the field of poetry. *La Ligue* was so highly acclaimed that it put epic poetry back in fashion. Voltaire's love of the classical tradition stemmed, no doubt, from his Jesuit education at Louis-le-Grand. His poetry also brought him prestige at court and financial rewards. After the successful production of *La Princesse de Navarre* in 1745, performed at the wedding of Louis XV, Voltaire was given the post of royal historiographer and a pension of two thousand francs a year, and later was made a gentleman of the king's chamber. The following year, 1746, Voltaire achieved another ambition when he was finally elected to the Académie Française. He had been denied this privilege several times before because of the various scandals he had caused. Madame du Châtelet tried to protect him from his own indiscretion; she once locked up his outrageous *La Pucelle d'Orléans* (1755, 1762; *The Maid of Orleans*, 1758; also as *La Pucelle: Or, The Maid of Orleans*, 1785-1786), a scurrilous writing on the subject of Joan of Arc.

Voltaire's philosophical and satiric writings, such as his tales and pamphlets, not only brought him literary fame but also endangered his liberty. For this reason, Voltaire lived much of his life in exile or on the French-Swiss border.

One of the most astonishing aspects of Voltaire is his schizophrenic outlook. He dearly wished to have access to the noble classes (which accounts for his name change), while at the same time he despised the inequality inherent in the privilege of noble birth. A champion of the classical tradition, Voltaire inadvertently eroded its hold on his century by his innovations in drama and the novel. It is surprising that a champion of French classical tragedy and epic poetry should be the prime mover in introducing the latest developments in English literature, philosophy, and science into France. Voltaire's efforts to create a climate for liberty of thought and belief did eventually ameliorate conditions in France. The Encyclopedists, with Voltaire at their head, were ultimately responsible for producing a climate of critical thinking and a desire for reform that culminated in the French Revolution. Voltaire's *Philosophical Letters* were burned in public because they did not display the respect due "authority." Voltaire nevertheless would have been horrified to see the revolutionary tide sweep away this authority, even though it was corrupt. He enjoyed the cultivated nobility and the gracious support this class gave to the arts; he would have had no faith in the judgment of unrefined and poorly educated republicans. Still, the new ideas he had promulgated traveled through France and even to North America. Like John Locke, many of whose ideas are to be found in the American Bill of Rights and the Constitution, Voltaire contributed to political philosophy as it was developing in Europe and even in the United States.

It is through his satiric and philosophical writings that Voltaire exercised that influence. Whereas his effect on literature disappeared at the beginning of the nineteenth century, his emphasis on reason and critical thinking still dominates the French mind. The ideals of liberty of thought and justice are his legacy.

Biography

Voltaire was born François-Marie Arouet in Paris in 1694. His father was a highly placed official and belonged to the upper middle class. Voltaire received an excellent classical education at the Jesuit school of Louis-le-Grand in Paris, where he displayed a talent for writing poetry. He also probably acquired his taste for theater there.

The Abbé de Châteauneuf, Voltaire's godfather, introduced the twelve-year-old boy to the Society of the Temple, which was the domain of worldly libertines. Voltaire's taste for witty irreverence and for luxurious living was definitely encouraged by this company. In 1711, Voltaire became a law student. As early as 1716, his satiric writing, aimed at the king's regent and the poet Antoine Houdar de la Motte, caused Voltaire to be exiled twice to the provinces. In 1717, after writing a second time satirizing the regent, Voltaire was imprisoned (fairly comfortably) in the Bastille for eleven months. During this stay, he completed *Oedipus* and began to write *La Ligue*. Upon leaving prison, he changed his name to de Voltaire. He became famous with the success of *Oedipus* in 1718 and *La Ligue* in 1723, and as a result he was invited to the literary and social circles of the wealthy. He even became a habitué of the court and had three of his plays, *Oedipus, Mariamne* (pr. 1724; English translation, 1761), and *L'Indiscret* (pr., pb. 1725) performed as part of the celebrations for Louis XV's marriage in 1725.

Late in 1725, Voltaire had a dispute with the chevalier de Rohan, who ridiculed Voltaire's use of a false aristocratic name. Angered by a beating at the hands of Rohan's men, Voltaire challenged the noble to a duel. None of Voltaire's aristocratic friends supported him in the matter, which increased Voltaire's hatred of the unfairness of privilege. A *lettre de cachet* (a letter of arbitrary arrest issued by the king) sent him to the Bastille. Soon—in May, 1726—Voltaire was allowed to go into exile in England, where he spent three years frequenting the literary circles of the day. There he wrote his *Philosophical Letters*, prepared four tragedies, and published *Henriade*. Voltaire returned to France in 1729 and once again gained access to literary circles. In 1730, his play *Brutus* was produced. The influence of William Shakespeare, acquired in England, is obvious in Voltaire's drama. *Zaïre* was presented in 1732 and *Adélaïde du Guesclin* in 1734. In the same year, Voltaire also took a great risk when he published his highly critical *Philosophical Letters* for the first time in France.

From 1734 to 1744, Voltaire lived in the du Châtelet castle at Cirey, where Madame du Châtelet, Voltaire's mistress, restrained Voltaire's volatile literary indiscretions somewhat. This period proved to be a most productive one. Voltaire wrote several plays during this time, including *Alzire* (pr., pb. 1736; English translation, 1763) and *Mérope*. He also wrote his provocative *The Man of the World* while at Cirey. Both Madame du Châtelet and Voltaire took an interest in physics, chemistry, and astronomy; it is at Cirey that Voltaire wrote *The Elements of Sir Isaac Newton's Philosophy*.

For the three years following 1744, Voltaire was involved in life at court. His protectress, Madame de Pompadour, was, like him, of a humble background. The king and queen always distrusted Voltaire. After a thoughtless remark, Voltaire was obliged to flee the court and go to the summer home of the duchesse du Maine, the Château d'Anet at Sceaux. In *Zadig*, Voltaire satirizes life at court.

In 1747, Madame de Châtelet died in childbirth. Voltaire was extremely pained by this loss. There was no longer a reason to remain in France, and Voltaire spent the years from 1750 to 1753 at the court of Frederick the Great of Prussia. He published *The Age of Louis XIV* in Berlin in 1751. There he also wrote his satiric philosophical tale *Micromegas*. Although he had hoped to discover in Frederick his ideal of the "enlightened" monarch, Voltaire was as independent as Frederick was authoritarian, and the visit soon ended. These two men still respected each other greatly, however, and continued to correspond.

In 1755, Voltaire moved to Les Délices, an estate near the Swiss border. He lived there from 1755 to 1760, and it was there that, still in a depressed frame of mind, he wrote *Candide*.

From 1760 until his death, Voltaire resided in Ferney, on French soil, although situated very close to the Swiss border. Voltaire was extremely active during this period. He wrote some six thousand letters, as well as pamphlets, plays, and tales. In closing his letters, he usually wrote "Écrasez l'infâme" (crush the vile), by which he meant that superstition and intolerance must be eliminated. He wrote philosophical tales here, waging his battle against the usual targets; *Ingenuous* appeared at this time, as did many other philosophical tales. Voltaire championed the causes of the Calas and Sirven families and also of La Barre; all three were cases of the miscarriage of justice and of religious persecution.

Voltaire, taking his own advice at the end of *Candide*, did much to improve the region of Ferney. He built a church, installed a tannery, and established a watchmaking industry. He even had his area exempted from the salt tax. In 1778, at the age of eighty-three, Voltaire went to Paris in triumph to watch a production of *Irène*. His popularity was at its highest, and the accolades and honors he received during his sojourn proved too much for him; he died shortly thereafter.

ANALYSIS

Voltaire was the most influential writer in eighteenth century France. He epitomizes the philosopher of the *siècle des lumières*, the Age of Enlightenment; his curiosity embraces all the developments of his day, whether French or otherwise European, scientific or literary. His faith in human reason does not waver, although his optimism about human progress often does. His writings reflect the changing literary tastes of the century as he defends a waning classical tradition while himself introducing the most outrageous innovations. His theater particularly embodies both of these tendencies, whereas his tales tend to exploit traditional literary forms in order to introduce a unique type of satiric philosophical story.

Voltaire's long fiction includes many rather short stories, which have been called indiscriminately *romans philosophiques* (philosophical novels) or *contes philosophiques* (philosophical tales). According to Henri Coulet, Voltaire himself used the term *histoire* (story). Because satire such as Voltaire's depends on economy of style and the tales have no real development of plot or character, they are limited in length by the genre itself.

Candide is considered to be the most perfect example of the philosophical novel, revealing Voltaire's brilliant irony and vivacious wit. All the tales are humorous tragicomedies and include incidents that are by turns absurd, grotesque, poetic, romantic, and shocking. The unifying element is always the philosophical theme that Voltaire is stressing. Voltaire began writing his tales at the age of forty-five, when his ideas were firmly established; hence, the concerns and reforms he seeks to address remain fairly constant throughout the tales. Despite the fact that these stories are meant to appeal primarily to the intellect, they are eminently entertaining. Voltaire's writings are rooted firmly in the humanistic rationalism of the first half of his century rather than in the literature of pre-Romantic sensibility, which made its appearance in the late 1700's.

Henri Bénac's suggestion that the tales fall into four chronological groups related to the development of Voltaire's thought is widely accepted. Bénac proposes that the first two groups—of 1747 to 1752 and 1756 to 1759—reveal Voltaire's growing realization that war must be waged against evils such as intolerance, injustice, corruption, and ignorance. The first group includes such stories as *Le Monde comme il va* (1748; revised as *Babouc: Ou, Le Monde comme il va*, 1749; *Babouc: Or, The World as It Goes*, 1754; also known as *The World as It Is: Or, Babouc's Vision*, 1929), *Memnon: Or, Human Wisdom*, and *La Lettre d'un Turc* (1750); *Zadig* and *Micromegas* are the best known of the group. The second group includes *History of Scarmentado's Travels*, which is the outline of *Candide*. In the third group figure *Jeannot et Colin* (1764; *Jeannot and Colin*, 1929), *Le Blanc et le noir* (1764; *The Two Genies*, 1895), and, best known, *Ingenuous*, *The Man of Forty Crowns*, and *The Princess of Babylon*. According to Bénac, the tales in this third group are, like Voltaire's pamphlets, weapons in his war against oppression of all kinds. In the last group, Bénac sees Voltaire searching for a morality on which to base a humane and free society. Tales in this period include *L'Histoire de Jenni* (1775) and *Les Oreilles du Comte de Chesterfield* (1775; *The Ears of Lord Chesterfield and Parson Goodman*, 1826).

Zadig

The concerns of the early tales recur throughout all the stories, but Voltaire presents the different tales with a rich range of tones. *Zadig*, like other tales of this early group, is imbued with sunny humor and gaiety despite the sardonic irony that underscores the misfortunes of the hero. Voltaire sketches his hero Zadig with an unusually delicate touch, and some passages dazzle momentarily with rare poetry: "He marveled at these vast globes of light which to our eyes appear to be only feeble sparks.... His soul flew up into the infinite and, detached from his senses, contemplated the immutable order of the universe."

Memnon: Histoire orientale contained fifteen chapters that reappeared in *Zadig* in 1748. The story of Zadig is in the picaresque tradition, which is to say that the hero, on his travels, meets with many adventures. The plot of such a tale is of necessity episodic and highly imaginative. Zadig, a wealthy, virtuous, and handsome young Babylonian, is about to marry the beautiful young Semire, who loves him "passionately." When a jealous youth, Orcan, attempts to abduct Semire, Zadig bravely rescues his betrothed, receiving a wound that might mean the loss of an eye. Instead of expressing her gratitude, Semire protests that she hates one-eyed men, and she promptly marries Orcan. Zadig recovers quickly and marries another woman, Azora, whose faithfulness he puts to the test by pretending to have died. Unfortunately, Azora fails the test. Zadig encounters difficulties with the law when he makes scientific deductions from observing the tracks of the queen's dog and the king's horse, leading a huntsman to deduce that Zadig stole the animals. Zadig eventually becomes the king's prime minister.

His next misfortune arises through no fault of his own: Queen Astarté falls in love with him. The king, in jealousy, plots to kill them both, and Zadig has to flee. As he arrives in Egypt, he sees an Egyptian beating a woman, who asks Zadig to save her. In the ensuing fight, Zadig kills his adversary. Zadig is arrested and imprisoned for this act, then sold as a slave and taken to Arabia by his master, Sétoc, with whom he becomes close friends. Zadig dissuades a young widow from burning herself on her husband's funeral pyre, as is the religious custom. He also persuades an Egyptian, an Indian, a Chinese, a Greek, and a Celt to worship the same Supreme Being. Zadig is accused of impiety by Arabian priests and condemned to be burned. The young widow whom he saved now helps him escape.

Zadig next goes to the island of Serendib (Ceylon) on behalf of Sétoc. He makes a good impression on the king of the island and helps him to find an honest minister. On his travels, Zadig meets the brigand chief Arbogad and learns that King Moabdar has gone mad and been killed, and Astarté has disappeared. Zadig eventually discovers that Astarté is a captive of Ogul, who is sick with an imaginary illness. Zadig cures Ogul, and the two return to Babylon, where peace is restored. Zadig wins a tournament that is held to decide who shall be the new king of Babylon and marry Astarté. Zadig wins the tournament but is cheated, and his rival claims the victory. In the middle of his despair, Zadig meets a hermit who reveals to him the secret of happiness, and Zadig learns to accept the ways of Providence. Zadig guesses the correct answers to the riddles and finally marries Astarté.

Zadig the hero—whose name in Arabic means "just"—attempts to be happy in a world where goodness is frustrated by absurd and illogical interventions of fate. At one point, Zadig says: "I was sent to execution because I had written verses in praise of the King; I was on the point of being strangled because the Queen had yellow ribbons; and here I am a slave with you because a brute beat his mistress. Come, let's not lose heart; perhaps all this will end."

The absurdity of Zadig's world, which is out of control and beyond the powers of logical explanation, is not the horror evoked in Franz Kafka's fiction; unlike Kafka, Voltaire does not attempt to create a sense of dreamlike but undeniable reality in either setting or characterization. Voltaire's exotic Eastern novel is in the tradition of the fifteenth century *The Arabian Nights' Entertainments*, also known as *The Thousand and One Nights*, translated from the Arabic by Antoine Gallard and much in vogue after the success of Montesquieu's *Lettres persanes* (1721; *Persian Letters*, 1722). The events are as unreal as those of the fairy tale, and the sensibility of the reader is not touched by Zadig's dilemmas. Instead, Voltaire disturbs the comfort of the reader's reason, logic, and innate sense of order and justice; the irony of Voltaire is at work. The frustration of Zadig becomes that of his audience. The knight Itobad steals Zadig's white suit of armor during the night, leaving his green suit in its place so that Zadig cannot claim the hand of Astarté, and Zadig cannot prove that he is the victor of the tournament, because the combatants must conceal their identities until a victor is proclaimed. Zadig has often been punished unjustly for being good, and here he is once again cheated of a happiness that is almost within his grasp. The audience is robbed of an anticipated happy ending and is frustrated by this anticlimax.

Voltaire was a master of the art of satire, and he often made use of anticlimax as an effective satiric technique. Zadig, after bewailing a list of horrifying punishments he has narrowly escaped, says, "Come, let's not lose heart; perhaps all this will end." This anticlimactic statement satirizes both Zadig's naïve optimism and the ridiculous optimism of the philosophers Gottfried Wilhelm Leibniz and Friedrich August Wolf—that "this is the best of all possible worlds"—which was much in vogue in the eighteenth century.

This leitmotif, the attack on optimism, is one of the many minor satiric barbs that Voltaire uses to spice his tale. Other satiric attacks abound in *Zadig* and reappear throughout the tales. Eighteenth century readers, usually members of the nobility and upper middle class, took delight in synthesizing the apparent subject of Voltaire's narrative with the real and often audacious object of its satire. Voltaire makes a dangerous allusion to the court when the fisherman tells Zadig how archers "armed with a royal warrant were pillaging his house lawfully and in good order." The ironic effect is achieved by the surprising juxtaposition of "pillaging" and "lawfully." Voltaire's irony had its basis in reality: He had been forced to flee the court at Versailles after making disparaging remarks about the courtiers being cheats. In *Zadig*, Voltaire also frequently satirizes the judicial system and judges who are "abysses of knowledge," who "prove" Zadig looked out of a window even though Zadig has answered none of their questions.

Voltaire's anticlericalism and antireligious bent often figure in the satire of *Zadig*. Almona the Arab widow intends to burn herself on her husband's funeral pyre, as the Brahman religion demands. Zadig the philosopher reasons her out of this plan, convincing her that she is about to take a ridiculous course in order to satisfy her vanity and not her religious principles. Zadig also persuades Sétoc that it is ridiculous to worship shining lights (the stars), and he demonstrates his reasons by kneeling and appearing to worship lighted candles. The "bonzes," who represent the monks, "chanted beautiful prayers to music, and left the state a prey to the barbarians." Zadig's rationalism (and Voltaire's) is primarily concerned with people's practical problems in society.

Voltaire's primary philosophical theme, however, is people's concern with destiny. Zadig vacillates between hope and despair as fate deals him many adverse blows. Despite his ingenuity and virtue, which he displays when he acts as the prime minister of King Moabdar, Zadig is presented as the plaything of destiny. The fisherman's story and the hermit incident reinforce the supremacy of this philosophical question as the main theme. How do philosophers explain the sufferings of a good person in the hands of a malevolent destiny? Voltaire resolves this problem happily with a deus ex machina ending. The angel Jesrad, representing divine intervention, tells Zadig to stop his questioning and simply worship Providence. Most men, Jesrad explains, form opinions with limited knowledge. Zadig's virtue triumphs, and he wins his queen and rules with "justice and love. Men blessed Zadig and Zadig blessed heaven." The skies of Zadig remain free of the blackness of *Candide*.

MICROMEGAS

Micromegas, which appeared in 1752, is a philosophical tale in a more literal sense, being primarily a vehicle for ideas on relativity. It is a very short tale, with almost no action (in stark contrast to the episodic *Zadig*) and only two main protagonists. Micromegas (which is Greek for "little big one") is a very tall inhabitant of the planet Sirius who has been banned from court for writing a book about insects that the "Mufti" of his planet has found to be heretical. He goes on an interplanetary voyage, finally arriving on the planet Saturn, where he meets a dwarf. (Voltaire intended his readers to recognize in the dwarf a caricature of his own enemy, Bernard le Bovier de Fontenelle.) The two travelers arrive on Earth and finally discover minute humans in a boat. The travelers attend a banquet at which various forms of philosophical credos are represented, allowing Voltaire to launch a satiric attack on the theories of Aristotle, René Descartes, Nicolas Malebranche, and Leibniz. Voltaire approves of the philosophy of the follower of John Locke. A storm develops, and the philosophers fall into the pocket of Micromegas. Although the giant is angry that such small creatures have so much pride, he gives a book to the philosophers; its pages, however, are blank. Voltaire gives the closing line to the dwarf (his enemy, Fontenelle), who, upon receiving the blank book—supposedly a philosophical treatise revealing the final truth about things—says, "Ah . . . that's just what I suspected." This last line was extremely offensive to Fontenelle, because it implied that he agreed that all of his metaphysical speculations over the past years had been wasted effort—that such truths were impossible to discover and prove. This attack on metaphysics is the main thrust of Voltaire's satire in *Micromegas*. Voltaire ridicules the philosophers in the boat, implying that "our little pile of mud" is relatively unimportant when seen in relation to the rest of the cosmos and that the opinions of its inhabitants are hence practically worthless. The philosophers in the boat all talk at once and all have different opinions. Voltaire shows that this kind of truth is "relative" to the person uttering it, and unreliable.

Voltaire's *Micromegas* is in direct imitation of Jonathan Swift's *Gulliver's Travels* (1726), and Montesquieu had previously used this type of travel story in *Persian Letters*. Voltaire, then, used an established subgenre, the fictional travelogue, as a vehicle for social commentary: The traveler in a strange land, seeing things for the first time, has no prejudice and puts into a new perspective situations that have been seen in only a certain way for centuries. This fresh perspective opens the way for critical appraisal and reform.

In *Micromegas*, Voltaire makes little effort to convince the reader of the reality of his story; the tale must be accepted as fantasy. The satire is less complicated, less adroit, and less sparkling than it is in *Zadig*. The main purpose of the satire is to address subjects of great interest to Voltaire's contemporaries; little of the subject matter of *Micromegas* is of interest to the modern reader. These two early works, *Zadig* and *Micromegas*, do, however, share a lighthearted spirit of enjoyment as Voltaire ridicules general stupidity and personal enemies. In these works, too, Voltaire formulated what would become the constant subjects of his satiric attacks throughout his tales.

CANDIDE

Candide belongs to the second group of tales described by Bénac and is distinguished by its radical pessimism and bitter irony, in contrast to the sunny atmosphere of the previous two tales. *Candide* is considered the epitome of the philosophical tale, and it remains highly relevant today. Unlike Voltaire's other writings, *Candide* is still read everywhere. The tale's atmosphere is dark and often despairing. Voltaire was shocked by the horrors and atrocities of the Seven Years' War, which began in August, 1756, when Frederick the Great invaded Saxony. The Lisbon earthquake in 1755 also horrified Voltaire, causing him to reflect on what kind of Providence could inflict death on the innocent and guilty alike. The optimistic philosophy of Leibniz and Wolf seemed totally absurd in the midst of so much human suffering.

The satire in *Candide* is directed above all against this optimistic philosophy, epitomized in the character Pangloss. The characters in this tale are caricatures, deformed so that each represents only one characteristic or outlook. Candide, the hero, represents naïve, good, and reasonable humanity. The philosopher Martin symbolizes a cynical Manichaeanism that acknowledges the power of evil as well as of good in the world. James, who represents real human goodness and charity, is allowed to drown in stormy seas after rescuing a sailor who had attempted to murder him. Such is the bitter mood of the tale.

The form of this novel is basically picaresque, as in *Zadig*, but Voltaire also parodies the novel of adventure and the novel of sentiment. The characters continually die horrible deaths after suffering gruesome tortures in various lands, but they somehow miraculously (and ridiculously) reappear, having been saved or cured. Their tearful reunions are a parody of the sentimental literature that Samuel Richardson's *Pamela: Or, Virtue Rewarded* (1740-1741) introduced to France from England and that infiltrated the bourgeois dramas of Diderot, and indeed of Voltaire's own theater. These reappearances also reinforce the central unity of the novel. A finely orchestrated rhythm unifies the entire tale; it is not simply that the main aim of the satire holds the tale together, as in the other stories. The fates (and philosophies) of secondary characters affect the hero in a rhythmic ebb and flow of alternating hope and despair that echo across the desolate landscape of a sad humanity in the throes of war, persecution, and suffering.

A gloss of the incidents in the tale reveals that there is no development of character or plot as such, and it underlines the rapid and vertiginous pace of the tale's episodes. This brisk pace lightens the seriousness of the atrocities being described, preventing the reader from dwelling on them or taking them to heart. Hence, Voltaire employs a technique of diminution, undercutting the value and dignity of human life.

Candide lives happily in a château in Westphalia with the baron of Thunderten-tronckh. Pangloss, the disciple of the optimistic philosophy of Leibniz, also lives there as tutor, as does Cunegonde, the baron's beautiful daughter, whom Candide loves. Candide agrees with Pangloss that all works out for the best in this wonderful world at the château. The baron, however, discovering the two lovers embracing, chases Candide out of the château. He is carried off forcibly to join an army and fight. After deserting, he goes to Holland, where he meets Pangloss, who has become a beggar and is barely recognizable with the sores of a terrible disease. Candide learns that all the people of the château have been killed.

Candide takes Pangloss to his benefactor, James the Anabaptist, who restores the sick man. The three then set sail for Lisbon, where James has a business engagement. On the way to Lisbon, their ship is wrecked in a storm, and James is drowned, while a sailor who had tried to murder him is saved. In Lisbon, Pangloss and Candide live through an earthquake that kills thirty thousand people. As Candide and Pangloss wander through the destroyed city, Pangloss attempts to comfort the citizens with his philosophy that "all is for the best"—a philosophy that, as Voltaire makes clear in his juxtaposition of Pangloss's theories to the suffering about him, is ludicrous if not cruel. Overhearing Pangloss's remarks, an officer of the Inquisition questions Pangloss about his belief in Original Sin and Free Will. Pangloss, sputtering his rationalizations, is arrested along with Candide—"one for having spoken, the other for having listened with an air of approval." Pangloss is hanged, but Candide is saved by the timely arrival of Cunegonde, who has escaped from the massacre of her family.

As things are beginning to seem more hopeful, Candide is obliged to kill two people, and he has to flee to America. He takes refuge with some Jesuits in Paraguay, where he miraculously meets Cunegonde's brother, who has also escaped the massacre at the château and has become a priest. Although he embraces Candide as a brother, his mood suddenly shifts when Candide announces that he intends to marry Cunegonde, and in the ensuing fight, Candide kills the brother of his beloved. After similar incidents in Eldorado, Surinam, Venice, and Constantinople, Candide finally finds Cunegonde. After all of her suffering, she has become very ugly, but, true to his word, Candide marries her. He then takes the advice of a wise old Turk and installs himself and his companions in an estate. He refuses to ask any more philosophical questions about evil and suffering in favor of hard work and practical reality—thus the novel's famous closing line: "... we must cultivate our garden."

In 1759, the year that *Candide* was published, Voltaire bought Ferney, an estate on the French-Swiss border, which has led critics to surmise that Candide's conclusions about work and the happiness to be found in practical progress are those of Voltaire. Once Voltaire was installed at Ferney, he gained confidence and energy and bombarded his public and his enemies with pamphlets, essays, plays, and stories, waging numerous legal battles on behalf of those persecuted for religious reasons. *Ingenuous* was written during this last, very active period of Voltaire's life. Although Voltaire was seventy-three years old when he wrote this work, his incredible intellectual and creative vigor had not diminished.

INGENUOUS

Ingenuous is one of the weapons Voltaire used in his unremitting battle against intolerance and injustice and belongs to the third group of novels delineated by Bénac. Voltaire's confidence had returned, and he wrote with a sure hand; none of the tales that follow *Candide* can rival the grandeur of *Ingenuous*.

Ingenuous is the most romantic of Voltaire's stories, and its plot is narrative rather than episodic. The tone of the story is more naturalistic, as are the characters. The device of a voyage is used again; the religious and social systems of France in the time of Louis XIV are seen through the eyes of the Huron stranger, who, without prejudice and with candid reasoning, questions institutions and beliefs that have been taken for granted and must now be considered from a new perspective.

The character of the Huron is in the tradition of the "noble savage" popularized by a missionary, baron de Lahontan, who praised the uncorrupted American Indian. The unity of the tale lies in the unfolding of the story of two lovers: Hercules Kerkabon (as the Huron is later named) and Mademoiselle de St. Yves. The satire used here also unites with the central love theme, targeting the corrupt Catholic Church and its priests, monks, and practices, which are instrumental in separating the lovers and ruining their chance for happiness. Voltaire also satirizes the court officials and Jansenism.

Voltaire's wit has a somewhat subdued tone throughout *Ingenuous*; the satire resides in the calmly reasoned arguments of the Huron, who questions all the basic doctrines of Jesuit and Jansenist alike. Voltaire, using the Huron as his mouthpiece, explains very simply all of his objections to the two religions. At the time of writing this tale, Voltaire was involved in the trials of the Calas family, the Sirven family, and La Barre, and his hatred of religious persecution and his anger at the injustices meted out by a corrupt judicial system were therefore as intense as they had ever been.

The story reflects the century's taste for cosmopolitanism. The Huron has been reared by a Huron tribe in Canada and arrives on the Lower Brittany coast in 1689. It is "discovered" that he is the lost child of the Abbé Yerkabon and his sister. Their brother went to Canada as a soldier and was killed by the Iroquois. The Abbé claims Hercules as his nephew and baptizes him as a Catholic. The beautiful Mademoiselle de St. Yves acts as his godmother. Hercules later falls in love with Mademoiselle de St. Yves but cannot marry his godmother, because the Church forbids it. Mademoiselle de St. Yves is sent to a convent, and Hercules, who is by now a hero for helping to defend the French against an English attack, goes to Versailles to engage the king's help in his marriage scheme. At Versailles, he is arrested and imprisoned in the Bastille, where he meets Gordon, a Jansenist. After much study and discussion, he converts Gordon to Deism. Now Mademoiselle de St. Yves goes to Versailles to save Hercules, but she must submit to a government minister in order to obtain her lover's release. She never recovers from the shame and dies of her chagrin. Hercules is tempted to take his own life but recovers himself and becomes an excellent officer and philosopher. The tale does not end with the expected happy ending for the lovers, but Voltaire suggests that even if ambitions and ideals cannot be attained, there are compromises that can be made and one can be tolerably happy—a message similar to that of *Candide*.

The Man of Forty Crowns

The Man of Forty Crowns, published the year after *Ingenuous*, displays a strong contrast in style. The two tales have in common the underlying interest of Voltaire in practical things. In *Ingenuous*, Voltaire has Hercules recover from his loss and become a good soldier; in *The Man of Forty Crowns*, Voltaire has his protagonist discuss tax reform with a mathematician. There is a great difference, however, between these polemics and those of *Ingenuous*. In the later tale, Voltaire writes for a clever and agile mind able to follow the mathematical bent of his arguments. There is scarcely a plot or an appealing character to enliven the discussion. Voltaire, as usual, satirizes monks (who do not pay taxes), despotic monarchs, unfair judicial systems, and ignorant people who think they know more than they do. This highly polemical tale, amusing for Voltaire's eighteenth century circle, is of little interest today; not even the odd humorous remark, such as the suggestion that smiles and songs be taxed, can redeem the lack of relevance or interest of this story for a modern reader.

Voltaire's tales do suffer a slight impoverishment in translation. The musicality of the French language offsets the dryness of the succinct, economic prose and the laconic, pointed understatement. Polemical tales such as *The Man of Forty Crowns* particularly suffer in English translation.

Of Voltaire's many tales (some two dozen in all), *Candide* remains the most popular. Perhaps it has universal appeal because the evils it portrays persist in today's world. Wars are still waged in the name of religious causes, and political prisoners continue to be tortured and cast into jail without trial. Unfortunately, Voltaire is no longer here to provoke people's consciences and fire their minds with his energetic fury. Without him, the genre of the philosophical tale lies in disuse.

Avril S. Lewis

OTHER MAJOR WORKS

SHORT FICTION: *Le Monde comme il va*, 1748 (revised as *Babouc: Ou, Le Monde comme il va*, 1749; *Babouc: Or, The World as It Goes*, 1754; also known as *The World as It Is: Or, Babouc's Vision*, 1929); *Memnon: Ou, La Sagesse humaine*, 1749 (*Memnon: Or, Human Wisdom*, 1961); *La Lettre d'un Turc*, 1750; *Le Blanc et le noir*, 1764 (*The Two Genies*, 1895); *Jeannot et Colin*, 1764 (*Jeannot and Colin*, 1929); *L'Histoire de Jenni*, 1775; *Les Oreilles du Comte de Chesterfield*, 1775 (*The Ears of Lord Chesterfield and Parson Goodman*, 1826).

PLAYS: *Œdipe*, pr. 1718 (*Oedipus*, 1761); *Artémire*, pr. 1720; *Mariamne*, pr. 1724 (English translation, 1761); *L'Indiscret*, pr., pb. 1725 (verse play); *Brutus*, pr. 1730 (English translation, 1761); *Ériphyle*, pr. 1732; *Zaïre*, pr. 1732 (English translation, 1736); *La Mort de César*, pr. 1733; *Adélaïde du Guesclin*, pr. 1734; *L'Échange*, pr. 1734; *Alzire*, pr., pb. 1736 (English translation, 1763); *L'Enfant prodigue*, pr. 1736 (verse play; prose translation, *The Prodigal*, 1750?); *Zulime*, pr. 1740; *Mahomet*, pr., pb. 1742 (*Mahomet the Prophet*, 1744); *Mérope*, pr. 1743 (English translation, 1744, 1749); *La Princesse de Navarre*, pr., pb. 1745 (verse play; music by Jean-Philippe Rameau); *La Prude: Ou, La Grandeuse de Cassette*, pr., pb. 1747 (wr. 1740; verse play; adaptation of William Wycherley's play *The Plain Dealer*); *Sémiramis*, pr. 1748 (*Semiramis*, 1760); *Nanine*, pr., pb. 1749 (English translation, 1927); *Oreste*, pr., pb. 1750; *Rome sauvée*, pr., pb. 1752; *L'Orphelin de la Chine*, pr., pb. 1755 (*The Orphan of China*, 1756); *Socrate*, pb. 1759 (*Socrates*, 1760); *L'Écossaise*, pr., pb. 1760 (*The Highland Girl*, 1760); *Tancrède*, pr. 1760; *Olympie*, pb. 1763; *Le Triumvirat*, pr. 1764; *Les Scythes*, pr., pb. 1767; *Les Guèbres: Ou, La Tolérance*, pb. 1769; *Sophonisbe*, pb. 1770 (revision of Jean Mairet's play); *Les*

Pélopides: Ou, Atrée et Thyeste, pb. 1772; *Les Lois de Minos*, pb. 1773; *Don Pèdre*, pb. 1775 (wr. 1761); *Irène*, pr. 1778; *Agathocle*, pr. 1779.

POETRY: *Poème sur la religion naturelle*, 1722; *La Ligue*, 1723; *La Henriade*, 1728 (a revision of *La Ligue*; *Henriade*, 1732); *Le Mondain*, 1736 (*The Man of the World*, 1764); *Discours en vers sur l'homme*, 1738 (*Discourses in Verse on Man*, 1764); *Poème de Fontenoy*, 1745; *Poème sur la loi naturelle*, 1752 (*On Natural Law*, 1764); *La Pucelle d'Orléans*, 1755, 1762 (*The Maid of Orleans*, 1758; also known as *La Pucelle: Or, The Maid of Orleans*, 1785-1786); *Poème sur la désastre de Lisbonne*, 1756 (*Poem on the Lisbon Earthquake*, 1764); *Le Pauvre Diable*, 1758; *Épître à Horace*, 1772.

NONFICTION: *An Essay upon the Civil Wars of France . . . and Also upon the Epick Poetry of the European Nations from Homer Down to Milton*, 1727; *La Henriade*, 1728 (*Henriade*, 1732); *Histoire de Charles XII*, 1731 (*The History of Charles XII*, 1732); *Le Temple du goût*, 1733 (*The Temple of Taste*, 1734); *Lettres philosophiques*, 1734 (originally published in English as *Letters Concerning the English Nation*, 1733; also known as *Philosophical Letters*, 1961); *Discours de métaphysique*, 1736; *Éléments de la philosophie de Newton*, 1738 (*The Elements of Sir Isaac Newton's Philosophy*, 1738); *Discours en vers sur l'homme*, 1738-1752 (*Discourses in Verse on Man*, 1764); *Vie de Molière*, 1739; *Le Siècle de Louis XIV*, 1751 (*The Age of Louis XIV*, 1752); *Essai sur les mœurs et l'esprit des nations*, 1756, 1763 (*The General History and State of Europe*, 1754, 1759); *Traité sur la tolérance*, 1763 (*A Treatise on Religious Toleration*, 1764); *Commentaires sur le théâtre de Pierre Corneille*, 1764; *Dictionnaire philosophique portatif*, 1764 (enlarged 1769 as *La Raison par alphabet*; also known as *Dictionnaire philosophique*; *A Philosophical Dictionary for the Pocket*, 1765; also known as *Philosophical Dictionary*, 1945, enlarged 1962); *Avis au public sur les parracides imputés aux calas et aux Sirven*, 1775; *Correspondence*, 1953-1965 (102 volumes).

MISCELLANEOUS: *The Works of M. de Voltaire*, 1761-1765 (35 volumes), 1761-1781 (38 volumes); *Candide, and Other Writings*, 1945; *The Portable Voltaire*, 1949; *Candide, Zadig, and Selected Stories*, 1961; *The Complete Works of Voltaire*, 1968-1977 (135 volumes; in French).

BIBLIOGRAPHY

Aldridge, A. Owen. *Voltaire and the Century of Light*. Princeton, N.J.: Princeton University Press, 1975. Reexamines the life and career of Voltaire within the context of European intellectual and political history, providing many useful insights. Presents information in a pleasant style equally suited to specialists and general readers. Also offers stimulating readings of *Candide* and other selected works as well as a valuable bibliography.

Bird, Stephen. *Reinventing Voltaire: The Politics of Commemoration in Nineteenth Century France*. Oxford, England: Voltaire Foundation, 2000. Focuses on the critical response to Voltaire in nineteenth century France, where his legacy was both vilified and venerated. Includes bibliography and indexes.

Cronk, Nicholas, ed. *The Cambridge Companion to Voltaire.* New York: Cambridge University Press, 2009. Collection of essays examines Voltaire's life, philosophy, and works. Includes discussions of Voltaire as a storyteller, Voltaire and authorship, and Voltaire and the myth of England as well as an analysis of *Candide* by Philip Stewart.

Davidson, Ian. *Voltaire in Exile: The Last Years.* New York: Grove Press, 2004. Chronicles Voltaire's life during his exile from France, when he actively campaigned against censorship, war, torture, capital punishment, the alliance between church and state, and other perceived injustices. Includes an analysis of much of Voltaire's personal correspondence.

Gray, John. *Voltaire.* New York: Routledge, 1999. Volume in Routledge's Great Philosophers series provides a concise overview of Voltaire's philosophy. Includes bibliography.

Havens, George R. *The Age of Ideas.* New York: Henry Holt, 1955. Often reprinted and providing a model and inspiration for many writers, Havens's witty, informed overview of the Enlightenment and its precursors remains authoritative as a guide to trends and thinkers of the period. Contains groups of chapters devoted to Voltaire, Charles de Montesquieu, Denis Diderot, and Jean-Jacques Rousseau; the four chapters devoted to Voltaire provide an excellent introduction to the man and his work, with brief but perceptive readings of such texts as *Zadig* and *Candide.*

Knapp, Bettina Liebowitz. *Voltaire Revisited.* New York: Twayne, 2000. Good introductory study describes Voltaire's life and devotes separate chapters to all of the genres of his works, including *Candide* and other philosophical tales. Includes bibliography and index.

Mason, Haydn Trevor. *"Candide": Optimism Demolished.* New York: Twayne, 1992. Examination of Voltaire's novel is divided into two parts: The first addresses the work's literary and historical context, including its critical reception, and the second provides a reading of the book's view of history, philosophy, personality, structure, and form. Includes notes and annotated bibliography.

_____. *Voltaire.* New York: St. Martin's Press, 1975. Comprehensive monograph (not to be confused with the biography Mason published six years later, cited below) is intended for the interested undergraduate or general reader. Steers clear of the traditional chronological approach in order to present Voltaire's works by genre, treating first his drama and dramatic criticism and then proceeding to historiography, short fiction, poetry, and polemics. Supplemented by a useful if brief bibliography.

_____. *Voltaire: A Biography.* Baltimore: Johns Hopkins University Press, 1981. Presents a concise but lively survey of the subject's life, clearly relating the major works to their contexts, including their inspiration or—as is especially pertinent in the case of Voltaire—provocation. Closely documented, useful both as biography and as criticism, this volume is recommended to students and general readers alike.

Pearson, Roger. *Voltaire Almighty: A Life in Pursuit of Freedom.* London: Bloomsbury,

2005. Readable, compelling account of Voltaire's life focuses on his love of liberty and how that passion informed his life and work. Includes bibliography, index, and illustrations.

Vartanian, Aram. "*Zadig:* Theme and Countertheme." In *Dilemmas du roman*, edited by Catherine Lafarge. Saratoga, Calif.: Anima Libri, 1990. Analyzes Voltaire's novel and argues that its philosophical theme of impersonal fate is counterpoised against a background theme, creating a contrapuntal movement of the narrative structure. Asserts that the story is told in such a way that its overall meaning emerges from a network of tensions felt among its various elements.

BIBLIOGRAPHY

Every effort has been made to include studies published in 2000 and later. Most items in this bibliography contain a listing of secondary sources, making it easier to identify other critical commentary on novelists, movements, and themes.

THEORETICAL, THEMATIC, AND HISTORICAL STUDIES

Altman, Janet Gurkin. *Epistolarity: Approaches to a Form*. Columbus: Ohio State University Press, 1982. Examines the epistolary novel, explaining how novelists use the letter form to develop characterization, further their plots, and develop meaning.

Beaumont, Matthew, ed. *Adventures in Realism*. Malden, Mass.: Blackwell, 2007. Fifteen essays explore facets of realism, which was critical to the development of the novel. Provides a theoretical framework for understanding how novelists attempt to represent the real and the common in fiction.

Brink, André. *The Novel: Language and Narrative from Cervantes to Calvino*. New York: New York University Press, 1998. Uses contemporary theories of semiotics and narratology to establish a continuum between early novelists and those of the postmodern era in their conscious use of language to achieve certain effects. Ranges across national boundaries to illustrate the theory of the development of the novel since the seventeenth century.

Brownstein, Rachel. *Becoming a Heroine: Reading About Women in Novels*. New York: Viking Press, 1982. Feminist survey of novels from the eighteenth century through the latter half of the twentieth century. Examines how "becoming a heroine" defines for women a sense of value in their lives. Considers novels by both men and women, and discusses the importance of the traditional marriage plot.

Bruzelius, Margaret. *Romancing the Novel: Adventure from Scott to Sebald*. Lewisburg, Pa.: Bucknell University Press, 2007. Examines the development of the adventure novel, linking it with the medieval romance tradition and exploring readers' continuing fascination with the genre.

Cavallaro, Dani. *The Gothic Vision: Three Centuries of Horror, Terror, and Fear*. New York: Continuum, 2005. Study of the gothic novel from its earliest manifestations in the eighteenth century to the early twenty-first century. Through the lenses of contemporary cultural theories, examines readers' fascination with novels that invoke horror, terror, and fright.

Doody, Margaret Anne. *The True Story of the Novel*. New Brunswick, N.J.: Rutgers University Press, 1996. Traces the roots of the novel, traditionally thought to have been developed in the seventeenth century, to classical Greek and Latin texts that exhibit characteristics of modern fiction.

Hale, Dorothy J., ed. *The Novel: An Anthology of Criticism and Theory, 1900-2000*. Malden, Mass.: Blackwell, 2006. Collection of essays by theorists and novelists. Includes commentary on the novel form from the perspective of formalism, structuralism, poststructuralism, Marxism, and reader response theory. Essays also address the novel through the lenses of sociology, gender studies, and feminist theory.

_____. *Social Formalism: The Novel in Theory from Henry James to the Present.* Stanford, Calif.: Stanford University Press, 1998. Emphasizes the novel's special ability to define a social world for readers. Relies heavily on the works of contemporary literary and cultural theorists. Provides a summary of twentieth century efforts to identify a theory of fiction that encompasses novels of many kinds.

Hart, Stephen M., and Wen-chin Ouyang, eds. *A Companion to Magical Realism.* London: Tamesis, 2005. Essays outlining the development of Magical Realism, tracing its roots from Europe through Latin America to other regions of the world. Explores the political dimensions of the genre.

Hoffman, Michael J., and Patrick D. Murphy, eds. *Essentials of the Theory of Fiction.* 2d ed. Durham, N.C.: Duke University Press, 1996. Collection of essays by influential critics from the late nineteenth century through the twentieth century. Focuses on the essential elements of fiction and the novel's relationship to the world it depicts.

Lodge, David. *The Art of Fiction: Illustrated from Classic and Modern Texts.* New York: Viking Press, 1993. Short commentaries on the technical aspects of fiction. Examples from important and minor novelists illustrate literary principles and techniques such as point of view, suspense, character introduction, irony, motivation, and ending.

Lynch, Deirdre, and William B. Walker, eds. *Cultural Institutions of the Novel.* Durham, N.C.: Duke University Press, 1996. Fifteen essays examine aspects of long fiction produced around the world. Encourages a redefinition of the genre and argues for inclusion of texts not historically considered novels.

Moretti, Franco, ed. *The Novel.* 2 vols. Princeton, N.J.: Princeton University Press, 2006. Compendium exploring the novel from multiple perspectives, including as an anthropological, historical, and sociological document; a function of the national tradition from which it emerges; and a work of art subject to examination using various critical approaches.

Priestman, Martin, ed. *The Cambridge Companion to Crime Fiction.* New York: Cambridge University Press, 2003. Essays examine the nature and development of the genre, explore works by writers (including women and ethnic minorities) from several countries, and establish links between crime fiction and other literary genres. Includes a chronology.

Scaggs, John. *Crime Fiction.* New York: Routledge, 2005. Provides a history of crime fiction, explores key subgenres, and identifies recurring themes that suggest the wider social and historical context in which these works are written. Suggests critical approaches that open crime fiction to serious study.

Shiach, Morag, ed. *The Cambridge Companion to the Modernist Novel.* New York: Cambridge University Press, 2007. Essays explaining the concept of modernism and its influence on the novel. Detailed examination of works by writers from various countries, all influenced by the modernist movement. Includes a detailed chronology.

Vice, Sue. *Holocaust Fiction*. New York: Routledge, 2000. Examines controversies generated by novels about the Holocaust. Focuses on eight important works, but also offers observations on the polemics surrounding publication of books on this topic.

Zunshine, Lisa. *Why We Read Fiction: Theory of Mind and the Novel*. Columbus: Ohio State University Press, 2006. Applies theories of cognitive psychology to novel reading, explaining how experience and human nature lead readers to constrain their interpretations of a given text. Provides numerous examples from well-known novels to illustrate how and why readers find pleasure in fiction.

THE FRENCH NOVEL

Motte, Warren. *Fables of the Novel: French Fiction Since 1990*. Chicago: Dalkey Archive Press, 2003. Searches for common themes in French literature and elucidates techniques shared by late-twentieth-century novelists who are not necessarily part of mainstream French fiction.

Prince, Gerald. *Narrative as Theme: Studies in French Fiction*. Lincoln: University of Nebraska Press, 1992. Examines representative examples of French fiction of the eighteenth, nineteenth, and twentieth centuries, focusing on how writers use narrative to establish truths in their works.

Samuels, Maurice. *The Spectacular Past: Popular History and the Novel in Nineteenth-Century France*. Ithaca, N.Y.: Cornell University Press, 2004. Examines the relationship between history and literature during a period when realism dominated fiction writing. Considers work by major French novelists of the nineteenth century and the influence of Sir Walter Scott's historical novels on French fiction.

Unwin, Timothy. *The Cambridge Companion to the French Novel from 1800 to the Present*. New York: Cambridge University Press, 1997. Examines the evolution of the French novel from the early nineteenth century to the late twentieth century. Emphasizes major changes introduced by modernism, World Wars I and II, and the postcolonial period.

Laurence W. Mazzeno

Glossary of Literary Terms

absurdism: A philosophical attitude, pervading much of modern drama and fiction, that underlines the isolation and alienation that humans experience, having been thrown into what absurdists see as a godless universe devoid of religious, spiritual, or metaphysical meaning. Conspicuous in its lack of logic, consistency, coherence, intelligibility, and realism, the literature of the absurd depicts the anguish, forlornness, and despair inherent in the human condition. Counter to the rationalist assumptions of traditional humanism, absurdism denies the existence of universal truth or value.

allegory: A literary mode in which a second level of meaning, wherein characters, events, and settings represent abstractions, is encoded within the surface narrative. The allegorical mode may dominate an entire work, in which case the encoded message is the work's primary reason for being, or it may be an element in a work otherwise interesting and meaningful for its surface story alone. Elements of allegory may be found in Jonathan Swift's *Gulliver's Travels* (1726) and Thomas Mann's *Der Zauberberg* (1924; *The Magic Mountain*, 1927).

anatomy: Literally the term means the "cutting up" or "dissection" of a subject into its constituent parts for closer examination. Northrop Frye, in his *Anatomy of Criticism* (1957), uses the term to refer to a narrative that deals with mental attitudes rather than people. As opposed to the novel, the anatomy features stylized figures who are mouthpieces for the ideas they represent.

antagonist: The character in fiction who stands as a rival or opponent to the *protagonist*.

antihero: Defined by Seán O'Faoláin as a fictional figure who, deprived of social sanctions and definitions, is always trying to define himself and to establish his own codes. Ahab may be seen as the antihero of Herman Melville's *Moby Dick* (1851).

archetype: The term "archetype" entered literary criticism from the psychology of Carl Jung, who defined archetypes as "primordial images" from the "collective unconscious" of humankind. Jung believed that works of art derive much of their power from the unconscious appeal of these images to ancestral memories. In his extremely influential *Anatomy of Criticism* (1957), Northrop Frye gave another sense of the term wide currency, defining the archetype as "a symbol, usually an image, which recurs often enough in literature to be recognizable as an element of one's literary experience as a whole."

atmosphere: The general mood or tone of a work; atmosphere is often associated with setting but can also be established by action or dialogue. A classic example of atmosphere is the primitive, fatalistic tone created in the opening description of Egdon Heath in Thomas Hardy's *The Return of the Native* (1878).

bildungsroman: Sometimes called the "novel of education," the bildungsroman focuses on the growth of a young *protagonist* who is learning about the world and finding his or her place in life; typical examples are James Joyce's *A Portrait of the Artist as a*

Young Man (1914-1915, serial; 1916, book) and Thomas Wolfe's *Look Homeward, Angel* (1929).

biographical criticism: Criticism that attempts to determine how the events and experiences of an author's life influence his or her work.

bourgeois novel: A novel in which the values, preoccupations, and accoutrements of middle-class or bourgeois life are given particular prominence. The heyday of the bourgeois novel was the nineteenth century, when novelists as varied as Jane Austen, Honoré de Balzac, and Anthony Trollope both criticized and unreflectingly transmitted the assumptions of the rising middle class.

canon: An authorized or accepted list of books. In modern parlance, the literary canon comprehends the privileged texts, classics, or great books that are thought to belong permanently on university reading lists. Recent theory—especially feminist, Marxist, and poststructuralist—critically examines the process of canon formation and questions the hegemony of white male writers. Such theory sees canon formation as the ideological act of a dominant institution and seeks to undermine the notion of canonicity itself, thereby preventing the exclusion of works by women, minorities, and oppressed peoples.

character: Characters in fiction can be presented as if they were real people or as stylized functions of the plot. Usually characters are a combination of both factors.

classicism: A literary stance or value system consciously based on the example of classical Greek and Roman literature. While the term is applied to an enormous diversity of artists in many different periods and in many different national literatures, "classicism" generally denotes a cluster of values including formal discipline, restrained expression, reverence for tradition, and an objective rather than a subjective orientation. As a literary tendency, classicism is often opposed to *Romanticism*, although many writers combine classical and romantic elements.

climax/crisis: The term "climax" refers to the moment of the reader's highest emotional response, whereas "crisis" refers to a structural element of plot, a turning point at which a resolution must take place.

complication: The point in a novel when the *conflict* is developed or when the already existing conflict is further intensified.

conflict: The struggle that develops as a result of the opposition between the *protagonist* and another person, the natural world, society, or some force within the self.

contextualist criticism: A further extension of *formalist criticism*, which assumes that the language of art is constitutive. Rather than referring to preexistent values, the artwork creates values only inchoately realized before. The most important advocates of this position are Eliseo Vivas (*The Artistic Transaction*, 1963) and Murray Krieger (*The Play and Place of Criticism*, 1967).

conventions: All those devices of stylization, compression, and selection that constitute the necessary differences between art and life. According to the Russian Formalists, these conventions constitute the "literariness" of literature and are the only proper concern of the literary critic.

deconstruction: An extremely influential contemporary school of criticism based on the works of the French philosopher Jacques Derrida. Deconstruction treats literary works as unconscious reflections of the reigning myths of Western culture. The primary myth is that there is a meaningful world that language signifies or represents. The deconstructionist critic is most often concerned with showing how a literary text tacitly subverts the very assumptions or myths on which it ostensibly rests.

defamiliarization: Coined by Viktor Shklovsky in 1917, this term denotes a basic principle of Russian Formalism. Poetic language (by which the Formalists meant artful language, in prose as well as in poetry) defamiliarizes or "makes strange" familiar experiences. The technique of art, says Shklovsky, is to "make objects unfamiliar, to make forms difficult, to increase the difficulty and length of perception.... Art is a way of experiencing the artfulness of an object; the object is not important."

detective story: The so-called classic detective story (or mystery) is a highly formalized and logically structured mode of fiction in which the focus is on a crime solved by a detective through interpretation of evidence and ratiocination; the most famous detective in this mode is Arthur Conan Doyle's Sherlock Holmes. Many modern practitioners of the genre, however, such as Dashiell Hammett, Raymond Chandler, and Ross Macdonald, have de-emphasized the puzzlelike qualities of the detective story, stressing instead characterization, theme, and other elements of mainstream fiction.

determinism: The belief that an individual's actions are essentially determined by biological and environmental factors, with free will playing a negligible role. (See *naturalism*.)

dialogue: The similitude of conversation in fiction, dialogue serves to characterize, to further the *plot*, to establish *conflict*, and to express thematic ideas.

displacement: Popularized in criticism by Northrop Frye, this term refers to the author's attempt to make his or her story psychologically motivated and realistic, even as the latent structure of the mythical motivation moves relentlessly forward.

dominant: A term coined by Roman Jakobson to refer to that which "rules, determines, and transforms the remaining components in the work of a single artist, in a poetic canon, or in the work of an epoch." The shifting of the dominant in a *genre* accounts for the creation of new generic forms and new poetic epochs. For example, the rise of *realism* in the mid-nineteenth century indicates realistic conventions becoming dominant and *romance* or fantasy conventions becoming secondary.

doppelgänger: A double or counterpart of a person, sometimes endowed with ghostly qualities. A fictional character's doppelgänger often reflects a suppressed side of his or her personality. One of the classic examples of the doppelgänger motif is found in

Fyodor Dostoevski's novella *Dvoynik* (1846; *The Double*, 1917); Isaac Bashevis Singer and Jorge Luis Borges, among others, offer striking modern treatments of the doppelgänger.

epic: Although this term usually refers to a long narrative poem that presents the exploits of a central figure of high position, the term is also used to designate a long novel that has the style or structure usually associated with an epic. In this sense, for example, Herman Melville's *Moby Dick* (1851) and James Joyce's *Ulysses* (1922) may be called epics.

episodic narrative: A work that is held together primarily by a loose connection of self-sufficient episodes. *Picaresque novels* often have episodic structure.

epistolary novel: A novel made up of letters by one or more fictional characters. Samuel Richardson's *Pamela: Or, Virtue Rewarded* (1740-1741) is a well-known eighteenth century example. In the nineteenth century, Bram Stoker's *Dracula* (1897) is largely epistolary. The technique allows for several different points of view to be presented.

euphuism: A style of writing characterized by ornate language that is highly contrived, alliterative, and repetitious. Euphuism was developed by John Lyly in his *Euphues, the Anatomy of Wit* (1578) and was emulated frequently by writers of the Elizabethan Age.

existentialism: A philosophical, religious, and literary term, emerging from World War II, for a group of attitudes surrounding the pivotal notion that existence precedes essence. According to Jean-Paul Sartre, "Man is nothing else but what he makes himself." Forlornness arises from the death of God and the concomitant death of universal values, of any source of ultimate or a priori standards. Despair arises from the fact that an individual can reckon only with what depends on his or her will, and the sphere of that will is severely limited; the number of things on which he or she can have an impact is pathetically small. Existentialist literature is antideterministic in the extreme and rejects the idea that heredity and environment shape and determine human motivation and behavior.

exposition: The part or parts of a fiction that provide necessary background information. Exposition not only provides the time and place of the action but also introduces readers to the fictive world of the story, acquainting them with the ground rules of the work.

fantastic: In his study *The Fantastic* (1970), Tzvetan Todorov defines the fantastic as a *genre* that lies between the "uncanny" and the "marvelous." All three genres embody the familiar world but present an event that cannot be explained by the laws of the familiar world. Todorov says that the fantastic occupies a twilight zone between the uncanny (when the reader knows that the peculiar event is merely the result of an illusion) and the marvelous (when the reader understands that the event is supposed to take place in a realm controlled by laws unknown to humankind). The fantastic is thus essentially unsettling, provocative, even subversive.

feminist criticism: A criticism advocating equal rights for women in political, economic, social, psychological, personal, and aesthetic senses. On the thematic level, the feminist reader should identify with female characters and their concerns. The object is to provide a critique of phallocentric assumptions and an analysis of patriarchal ideologies inscribed in a literature that is male-centered and male-dominated. On the ideological level, feminist critics see gender, as well as the stereotypes that go along with it, as a cultural construct. They strive to define a particularly feminine content and to extend the *canon* so that it might include works by lesbians, feminists, and women writers in general.

flashback: A scene in a fiction that depicts an earlier event; it may be presented as a reminiscence by a character in the story or may simply be inserted into the narrative.

foreshadowing: A device to create suspense or dramatic irony in fiction by indicating through suggestion what will take place in the future.

formalist criticism: Two particularly influential formalist schools of criticism arose in the twentieth century: the Russian Formalists and the American New Critics. The Russian Formalists were concerned with the conventional devices used in literature to defamiliarize that which habit has made familiar. The New Critics believed that literary criticism is a description and evaluation of its object and that the primary concern of the critic is with the work's unity. Both schools of criticism, at their most extreme, treated literary works as artifacts or constructs divorced from their biographical and social contexts.

genre: In its most general sense, this term refers to a group of literary works defined by a common form, style, or purpose. In practice, the term is used in a wide variety of overlapping and, to a degree, contradictory senses. Tragedy and comedy are thus described as distinct genres; the novel (a form that includes both tragic and comic works) is a genre; and various subspecies of the novel, such as the *gothic* and the *picaresque*, are themselves frequently treated as distinct genres. Finally, the term "genre fiction" refers to forms of popular fiction in which the writer is bound by more or less rigid conventions. Indeed, all these diverse usages have in common an emphasis on the manner in which individual literary works are shaped by particular expectations and conventions; this is the subject of genre criticism.

genre fiction: Categories of popular fiction in which the writers are bound by more or less rigid conventions, such as in the *detective story*, the *romance*, and the *Western*. Although the term can be used in a neutral sense, it is often used dismissively.

gothic novel: A form of fiction developed in the eighteenth century that focuses on horror and the supernatural. In his preface to *The Castle of Otranto* (1765), the first gothic novel in English, Horace Walpole claimed that he was trying to combine two kinds of fiction, with events and story typical of the medieval romance and character delineation typical of the realistic novel. Other examples of the form are Matthew Gregory

Lewis's *The Monk: A Romance* (1796; also known as *Ambrosio: Or, The Monk*) and Mary Wollstonecraft Shelley's *Frankenstein: Or, The Modern Prometheus* (1818).

grotesque: According to Wolfgang Kayser (*The Grotesque in Art and Literature*, 1963), the grotesque is an embodiment in literature of the estranged world. Characterized by a breakup of the everyday world by mysterious forces, the form differs from fantasy in that the reader is not sure whether to react with humor or with horror and in that the exaggeration manifested exists in the familiar world rather than in a purely imaginative world.

Hebraic/Homeric styles: Terms coined by Erich Auerbach in *Mimesis: The Representation of Reality in Western Literature* (1953) to designate two basic fictional styles. The Hebraic style focuses only on the decisive points of narrative and leaves all else obscure, mysterious, and "fraught with background"; the Homeric style places the narrative in a definite time and place and externalizes everything in a perpetual foreground.

historical criticism: In contrast to *formalist criticism*, which treats literary works to a great extent as self-contained artifacts, historical criticism emphasizes the historical context of literature; the two approaches, however, need not be mutually exclusive. Ernst Robert Curtius's *European Literature and the Latin Middle Ages* (1940) is a prominent example of historical criticism.

historical novel: A novel that depicts past historical events, usually public in nature, and features real as well as fictional people. Sir Walter Scott's Waverley novels established the basic type, but the relationship between fiction and history in the form varies greatly depending on the practitioner.

implied author: According to Wayne Booth (*The Rhetoric of Fiction*, 1961), the novel often creates a kind of second self who tells the story—a self who is wiser, more sensitive, and more perceptive than any real person could be.

interior monologue: Defined by Édouard Dujardin as the speech of a character designed to introduce the reader directly to the character's internal life, the form differs from other kinds of monologue in that it attempts to reproduce thought before any logical organization is imposed on it. See, for example, Molly Bloom's long interior monologue at the conclusion of James Joyce's *Ulysses* (1922).

irrealism: A term often used to refer to modern or postmodern fiction that is presented self-consciously as a fiction or a fabulation rather than a mimesis of external reality. The best-known practitioners of irrealism are John Barth, Robert Coover, and Donald Barthelme.

local colorists: A loose movement of late nineteenth century American writers whose fiction emphasizes the distinctive folkways, landscapes, and dialects of various regions. Important local colorists include Bret Harte, Mark Twain, George Washington Cable, Kate Chopin, and Sarah Orne Jewett. (See *regional novel*.)

Marxist criticism: Based on the nineteenth century writings of Karl Marx and Friedrich Engels, Marxist criticism views literature as a product of ideological forces determined by the dominant class. However, many Marxists believe that literature operates according to its own autonomous standards of production and reception: It is both a product of ideology and able to determine ideology. As such, literature may overcome the dominant paradigms of its age and play a revolutionary role in society.

metafiction: This term refers to fiction that manifests a reflexive tendency, such as Vladimir Nabokov's *Pale Fire* (1962) and John Fowles's *The French Lieutenant's Woman* (1969). The emphasis is on the loosening of the work's illusion of reality to expose the reality of its illusion. Other terms used to refer to this type of fiction include "irrealism," "postmodernist fiction," "antifiction," and "surfiction."

modernism: An international movement in the arts that began in the early years of the twentieth century. Although the term is used to describe artists of widely varying persuasions, modernism in general was characterized by its international idiom, by its interest in cultures distant in space or time, by its emphasis on formal experimentation, and by its sense of dislocation and radical change.

motif: A conventional incident or situation in a fiction that may serve as the basis for the structure of the narrative itself. The Russian Formalist critic Boris Tomashevsky uses the term to refer to the smallest particle of thematic material in a work.

motivation: Although this term is usually used in reference to the convention of justifying the action of a character from his or her psychological makeup, the Russian Formalists use the term to refer to the network of devices that justify the introduction of individual *motifs* or groups of motifs in a work. For example, "compositional motivation" refers to the principle that every single property in a work contributes to its overall effect; "realistic motivation" refers to the realistic devices used to make a work plausible and lifelike.

multiculturalism: The tendency to recognize the perspectives of those traditionally excluded from the canon of Western art and literature. In order to promote multiculturalism, publishers and educators have revised textbooks and school curricula to incorporate material by and about women, members of minority groups, persons from non-Western cultures, and homosexuals.

myth: Anonymous traditional stories dealing with basic human concepts and antinomies. According to Claude Lévi-Strauss, myth is that part of language where the "formula *tradutore, tradittore* reaches its lowest truth value. . . . Its substance does not lie in its style, its original music, or its syntax, but in the story which it tells."

myth criticism: Northrop Frye says that in myth "we see the structural principles of literature isolated." Myth criticism is concerned with these basic principles of literature; it is not to be confused with mythological criticism, which is primarily concerned with finding mythological parallels in the surface action of the *narrative.*

narrative: Robert Scholes and Robert Kellogg, in *The Nature of Narrative* (1966), say that by "narrative" they mean literary works that include both a story and a storyteller. The term "narrative" usually implies a contrast to "enacted" fiction such as drama.

narratology: The study of the form and functioning of *narratives*; it attempts to examine what all narratives have in common and what makes individual narratives different from one another.

narrator: The *character* who recounts the *narrative*, or story. Wayne Booth describes various dramatized narrators in *The Rhetoric of Fiction* (1961): unacknowledged centers of consciousness, observers, narrator-agents, and self-conscious narrators. Booth suggests that the important elements to consider in narration are the relationships among the narrator, the author, the characters, and the reader.

naturalism: As developed by Émile Zola in the late nineteenth century, naturalism is the application of the principles of scientific *determinism* to fiction. Although it usually refers more to the choice of subject matter than to technical conventions, those conventions associated with the movement center on the author's attempt to be precise and scientifically objective in description and detail, regardless of whether the events described are sordid or shocking.

New Criticism: See *formalist criticism*.

novel: Perhaps the most difficult of all fictional forms to define because of its multiplicity of modes. Edouard, in André Gide's *Les Faux-monnayeurs* (1925; *The Counterfeiters*, 1927), says the novel is the freest and most lawless of all *genres*; he wonders if fear of that liberty is the reason the novel has so timidly clung to reality. Most critics seem to agree that the novel's primary area of concern is the social world. Ian Watt (*The Rise of the Novel*, 2001) says that the novel can be distinguished from other fictional forms by the attention it pays to individual characterization and detailed presentation of the environment. Moreover, says Watt, the novel, more than any other fictional form, is interested in the "development of its characters in the course of time."

novel of manners: The classic examples of this form might be the novels of Jane Austen, wherein the customs and conventions of a social group of a particular time and place are realistically, and often satirically, portrayed.

novella, novelle, nouvelle, novelette, novela: Although these terms often refer to the short European tale, especially the Renaissance form employed by Giovanni Boccaccio, the terms often refer to that form of fiction that is said to be longer than a short story and shorter than a novel. "Novelette" is the term usually preferred by the British, whereas "novella" is the term usually used to refer to American works in this *genre*. Henry James claimed that the main merit of the form is the "effort to do the complicated thing with a strong brevity and lucidity."

phenomenological criticism: Although best known as a European school of criticism practiced by Georges Poulet and others, this so-called criticism of consciousness is also propounded in the United States by such critics as J. Hillis Miller. The focus is less on individual works and *genres* than it is on literature as an act; the work is not seen as an object but rather as part of a strand of latent impulses in the work of a single author or an epoch.

picaresque novel: A form of fiction that centers on a central rogue figure, or picaro, who usually tells his or her own story. The plot structure is normally *episodic*, and the episodes usually focus on how the picaro lives by his or her wits. Classic examples of the mode are Henry Fielding's *The History of Tom Jones, a Foundling* (1749; commonly known as *Tom Jones*) and Mark Twain's *Adventures of Huckleberry Finn* (1884).

plot/story: "Story" refers to the full *narrative* of *character* and action, whereas "plot" generally refers to action with little reference to character. A more precise and helpful distinction is made by the Russian Formalists, who suggest that "plot" refers to the events of a narrative as they have been artfully arranged in the literary work, subject to chronological displacement, ellipses, and other devices, while "story" refers to the sum of the same events arranged in simple, causal-chronological order. Thus story is the raw material for plot. By comparing the two in a given work, the reader is encouraged to see the narrative as an artifact.

point of view: The means by which the story is presented to the reader, or, as Percy Lubbock says in *The Craft of Fiction* (1921), "the relation in which the narrator stands to the story"—a relation that Lubbock claims governs the craft of fiction. Some of the questions the critical reader should ask concerning point of view are the following: Who talks to the reader? From what position does the narrator tell the story? At what distance does he or she place the reader from the story? What kind of person is he or she? How fully is he or she characterized? How reliable is he or she? For further discussion, see Wayne Booth, *The Rhetoric of Fiction* (1961).

postcolonialism: Postcolonial literature emerged in the mid-twentieth century when colonies in Asia, Africa, and the Caribbean began gaining their independence from the European nations that had long controlled them. Postcolonial authors, such as Salman Rushdie and V. S. Naipaul, tend to focus on both the freedom and the conflict inherent in living in a postcolonial state.

postmodernism: A ubiquitous but elusive term in contemporary criticism, "postmodernism" is loosely applied to the various artistic movements that followed the era of so-called high modernism, represented by such giants as James Joyce and Pablo Picasso. In critical discussions of contemporary fiction, the term "postmodernism" is frequently applied to the works of writers such as Thomas Pynchon, John Barth, and Donald Barthelme, who exhibit a self-conscious awareness of their modernist predecessors as well as a reflexive treatment of fictional form.

protagonist: The central *character* in a fiction, the character whose fortunes most concern the reader.

psychological criticism: While much modern literary criticism reflects to some degree the impacts of Sigmund Freud, Carl Jung, Jacques Lacan, and other psychological theorists, the term "psychological criticism" suggests a strong emphasis on a causal relation between the writer's psychological state, variously interpreted, and his or her works. A notable example of psychological criticism is Norman Fruman's *Coleridge, the Damaged Archangel* (1971).

psychological novel: A form of fiction in which *character*, especially the inner lives of characters, is the primary focus. This form, which has been of primary importance at least since Henry James, characterizes much of the work of James Joyce, Virginia Woolf, and William Faulkner. For a detailed discussion, see *The Modern Psychological Novel* (1955) by Leon Edel.

realism: A literary technique in which the primary convention is to render an illusion of fidelity to external reality. Realism is often identified as the primary method of the novel form: It focuses on surface details, maintains a fidelity to the everyday experiences of middle-class society, and strives for a one-to-one relationship between the fiction and the action imitated. The realist movement in the late nineteenth century coincides with the full development of the novel form.

reception aesthetics: The best-known American practitioner of reception aesthetics is Stanley Fish. For the reception critic, meaning is an event or process; rather than being embedded in the work, it is created through particular acts of reading. The best-known European practitioner of this criticism, Wolfgang Iser, argues that indeterminacy is the basic characteristic of literary texts; the reader must "normalize" the text either by projecting his or her standards into it or by revising his or her standards to "fit" the text.

regional novel: Any novel in which the character of a given geographical region plays a decisive role. Although regional differences persist across the United States, a considerable leveling in speech and customs has taken place, so that the sharp regional distinctions evident in nineteenth century American fiction have all but disappeared. Only in the South has a strong regional tradition persisted to the present. (See *local colorists*.)

rhetorical criticism: The rhetorical critic is concerned with the literary work as a means of communicating ideas and the means by which the work affects or controls the reader. Such criticism seems best suited to didactic works such as satire.

roman à clef: A fiction wherein actual people, often celebrities of some sort, are thinly disguised.

romance: The romance usually differs from the novel form in that the focus is on symbolic events and representational characters rather than on "as-if-real" characters and events. Richard Chase says that in the romance, character is depicted as highly stylized, a function of the plot rather than as someone complexly related to society. The romancer is more likely to be concerned with dreamworlds than with the familiar world, believing that reality cannot be grasped by the traditional novel.

Romanticism: A widespread cultural movement in the late eighteenth and early nineteenth centuries, the influence of which is still felt. As a general literary tendency, Romanticism is frequently contrasted with *classicism*. Although many varieties of Romanticism are indigenous to various national literatures, the term generally suggests an assertion of the preeminence of the imagination. Other values associated with various schools of Romanticism include primitivism, an interest in folklore, a reverence for nature, and a fascination with the demoniac and the macabre.

scene: The central element of *narration*; specific actions are narrated or depicted that make the reader feel he or she is participating directly in the action.

science fiction: Fiction in which certain givens (physical laws, psychological principles, social conditions—any one or all of these) form the basis of an imaginative projection into the future or, less commonly, an extrapolation in the present or even into the past.

semiotics: The science of signs and sign systems in communication. According to Roman Jakobson, semiotics deals with the principles that underlie the structure of signs, their use in language of all kinds, and the specific nature of various sign systems.

sentimental novel: A form of fiction popular in the eighteenth century in which emotionalism and optimism are the primary characteristics. The best-known examples are Samuel Richardson's *Pamela: Or, Virtue Rewarded* (1740-1741) and Oliver Goldsmith's *The Vicar of Wakefield* (1766).

setting: The circumstances and environment, both temporal and spatial, of a *narrative*.

spatial form: An author's attempt to make the reader apprehend a work spatially in a moment of time rather than sequentially. To achieve this effect, the author breaks up the *narrative* into interspersed fragments. Beginning with James Joyce, Marcel Proust, and Djuna Barnes, the movement toward spatial form is concomitant with the *modernist* effort to supplant historical time in fiction with mythic time. For the seminal discussion of this technique, see Joseph Frank, *The Widening Gyre* (1963).

stream of consciousness: The depiction of the thought processes of a *character*, insofar as this is possible, without any mediating structures. The metaphor of consciousness as a "stream" suggests a rush of thoughts and images governed by free association rather than by strictly rational development. The term "stream of consciousness" is often used loosely as a synonym for *interior monologue*. The most celebrated example of stream of consciousness in fiction is the monologue of Molly Bloom in James Joyce's *Ulysses* (1922); other notable practitioners of the stream-of-consciousness technique include Dorothy Richardson, Virginia Woolf, and William Faulkner.

structuralism: As a movement of thought, structuralism is based on the idea of intrinsic, self-sufficient structures that do not require reference to external elements. A structure is a system of transformations that involves the interplay of laws inherent in the system itself. The study of language is the primary model for contemporary structuralism. The structuralist literary critic attempts to define structural principles that operate intertextually throughout the whole of literature as well as principles that operate in *genres* and in individual works. One of the most accessible surveys of structuralism and literature available is Jonathan Culler's *Structuralist Poetics* (1975).

summary: Those parts of a fiction that do not need to be detailed. In *Tom Jones* (1749), Henry Fielding says, "If whole years should pass without producing anything worthy of... notice... we shall hasten on to matters of consequence."

thematics: According to Northrop Frye, when a work of fiction is written or interpreted thematically, it becomes an illustrative fable. Murray Krieger defines thematics as "the study of the experiential tensions which, dramatically entangled in the literary work, become an existential reflection of that work's aesthetic complexity."

tone: The dominant mood of a work of fiction. (See *atmosphere*.)

unreliable narrator: A narrator whose account of the events of the story cannot be trusted, obliging readers to reconstruct—if possible—the true state of affairs themselves. Once an innovative technique, the use of the unreliable narrator has become commonplace among contemporary writers who wish to suggest the impossibility of a truly "reliable" account of any event. Notable examples of the unreliable narrator can be found in Ford Madox Ford's *The Good Soldier* (1915) and Vladimir Nabokov's *Lolita* (1955).

Victorian novel: Although the Victorian period extended from 1837 to 1901, the term "Victorian novel" does not include the later decades of Queen Victoria's reign. The term loosely refers to the sprawling works of novelists such as Charles Dickens and William Makepeace Thackeray—works that frequently appeared first in serial form and are characterized by a broad social canvas.

vraisemblance/verisimilitude: Tzvetan Todorov defines vraisemblance as "the mask which conceals the text's own laws, but which we are supposed to take for a relation to reality." Verisimilitude refers to a work's attempts to make the reader believe that it conforms to reality rather than to its own laws.

Western novel: Like all varieties of *genre fiction*, the Western novel—generally known simply as the Western—is defined by a relatively predictable combination of *conventions*, *motifs*, and recurring themes. These predictable elements, familiar from many Western films and television series, differentiate the Western from *historical novels* and idiosyncratic works such as Thomas Berger's *Little Big Man* (1964) that are also set in the Old West. Conversely, some novels set in the contemporary West are regarded as Westerns because they deal with modern cowboys and with the land itself in the manner characteristic of the *genre*.

Charles E. May

Guide to Online Resources

Web Sites
The following sites were visited by the editors of Salem Press in 2009. Because URLs frequently change, the accuracy of these addresses cannot be guaranteed; however, long-standing sites, such as those of colleges and universities, national organizations, and government agencies, generally maintain links when sites are moved or updated.

American Literature on the Web
http://www.nagasaki-gaigo.ac.jp/ishikawa/amlit

Among this site's features are several pages providing links to Web sites about specific genres and literary movements, southern and southwestern American literature, minority literature, literary theory, and women writers, as well as an extensive index of links to electronic text collections and archives. Users also can access information for five specific time periods: 1620-1820, 1820-1865, 1865-1914, 1914-1945, and since 1945. A range of information is available for each period, including alphabetical lists of authors that link to more specific information about each writer, time lines of historical and literary events, and links to related additional Web sites.

Books and Writers
http://www.kirjasto.sci.fi/indeksi.htm

This broad, comprehensive, and easy-to-use resource provides access to information about hundreds of authors throughout the world, extending from 70 B.C.E to the twenty-first century. Links take users from an alphabetical list of authors to pages featuring biographical material, lists of works, and recommendations for further reading about individual authors; each writer's page also includes links to related pages on the site. Although brief, the biographical essays provide solid overviews of the authors' careers, their contributions to literature, and their literary influences.

The Canadian Literature Archive
http://www.umanitoba.ca/canlit

Created and maintained by the English Department at the University of Manitoba, this site is a comprehensive collection of materials for and about Canadian writers. It includes an alphabetical listing of authors with links to additional Web-based information. Users also can retrieve electronic texts, announcements of literary events, and videocasts of author interviews and readings.

A Celebration of Women Writers
http://digital.library.upenn.edu/women
  This site presents an extensive compendium of information about the contributions of women writers throughout history. The "Local Editions by Authors" and "Local Editions by Category" pages include access to electronic texts of the works of numerous writers, including Louisa May Alcott, Djuna Barnes, Grazia Deledda, Edith Wharton, and Virginia Woolf. Users can also access biographical and bibliographical information by browsing lists arranged by writers' names, countries of origin, ethnicities, and the centuries in which they lived.

Contemporary Writers
http://www.contemporarywriters.com/authors
  Created by the British Council, this site offers "up-to-date profiles of some of the U.K. and Commonwealth's most important living writers (plus writers from the Republic of Ireland that we've worked with)." The available information includes biographies, bibliographies, critical reviews, news about literary prizes, and photographs. Users can search the site by author, genre, nationality, gender, publisher, book title, date of publication, and prize name and date.

Internet Public Library: Native American Authors
http://www.ipl.org/div/natam
  Internet Public Library, a Web-based collection of materials, includes this index to resources about writers of Native American heritage. An alphabetical list of authors enables users to link to biographies, lists of works, electronic texts, tribal Web sites, and other online resources. The majority of the writers covered are contemporary Indian authors, but some historical authors also are featured. Users also can retrieve information by browsing lists of titles and tribes. In addition, the site contains a bibliography of print and online materials about Native American literature.

LiteraryHistory.com
http://www.literaryhistory.com
  This site is an excellent source of academic, scholarly, and critical literature about eighteenth, nineteenth, and twentieth century American and English writers. It provides numerous pages about specific eras and genres, including individual pages for eighteenth, nineteenth, and twentieth century literature and for African American and postcolonial literature. These pages contain alphabetical lists of authors that link to articles, reviews, overviews, excerpts of works, teaching guides, podcast interviews, and other materials. The eighteenth century literature page also provides access to information about the eighteenth century novel.

Literary Resources on the Net
http.//andromeda.rutgers.edu/~jlynch/Lit

Jack Lynch of Rutgers University maintains this extensive collection of links to Internet sites that are useful to academics, including numerous Web sites about American and English literature. This collection is a good place to begin online research about the novel, as it links to hundreds of other sites with broad ranges of literary topics. The site is organized chronically, with separate pages for information about the Middle Ages, the Renaissance, the eighteenth century, the Romantic and Victorian eras, and twentieth century British and Irish literature. It also has separate pages providing links to Web sites about American literature and to women's literature and feminism.

LitWeb
http://litweb.net

LitWeb provides biographies of more than five hundred world authors throughout history that can be accessed through an alphabetical listing. The pages about each writer contain a list of his or her works, suggestions for further reading, and illustrations. The site also offers information about past and present winners of major literary prizes.

The Modern Word: Authors of the Libyrinth
http://www.themodernword.com/authors.html

The Modern Word site, although somewhat haphazard in its organization, provides a great deal of critical information about writers. The "Authors of the Libyrinth" page is very useful, linking author names to essays about them and other resources. The section of the page headed "The Scriptorium" presents "an index of pages featuring writers who have pushed the edges of their medium, combining literary talent with a sense of experimentation to produce some remarkable works of modern literature." The site also includes sections devoted to Samuel Beckett, Umberto Eco, Gabriel García Márquez, James Joyce, Franz Kafka, and Thomas Pynchon.

Novels
http://www.nvcc.edu/home/ataormina/novels/default.htm

This overview of American and English novels was prepared by Agatha Taormina, a professor at Northern Virginia Community College. It contains three sections: "History" provides a definition of the novel genre, a discussion of its origins in eighteenth century England, and separate pages with information about genres and authors of nineteenth century, twentieth century, and postmodern novels. "Approaches" suggests how to read a novel critically for greater appreciation, and "Resources" provides a list of books about the novel.

Outline of American Literature
http://www.america.gov/publications/books/outline-of-american-literature.html

This page of the America.gov site provides access to an electronic version of the ten-chapter volume *Outline of American Literature*, a historical overview of prose and poetry from colonial times to the present published by the U.S. Department of State. The work's author is Kathryn VanSpanckeren, professor of English at the University of Tampa. The site offers links to abbreviated versions of each chapter as well as access to the entire publication in PDF format.

Voice of the Shuttle
http://vos.ucsb.edu

One of the most complete and authoritative places for online information about literature, Voice of the Shuttle is maintained by professors and students in the English Department at the University of California, Santa Barbara. The site provides thousands of links to electronic books, academic journals, association Web sites, sites created by university professors, and many, many other resources about the humanities. Its "Literature in English" page provides links to separate pages about the literature of the Anglo-Saxon era, the Middle Ages, the Renaissance and seventeenth century, the Restoration and eighteenth century, the Romantic age, the Victorian age, and modern and contemporary periods in Britain and the United States, as well as a page focused on minority literature. Another page on the site, "Literatures Other than English," offers a gateway to information about the literature of numerous countries and world regions.

ELECTRONIC DATABASES

Electronic databases usually do not have their own URLs. Instead, public, college, and university libraries subscribe to these databases, provide links to them on their Web sites, and make them available to library card holders or other specified patrons. Readers can visit library Web sites or ask reference librarians to check on availability.

Canadian Literary Centre

Produced by EBSCO, the Canadian Literary Centre database contains full-text content from ECW Press, a Toronto-based publisher, including the titles in the publisher's Canadian fiction studies, Canadian biography, and Canadian writers and their works series, *ECW's Biographical Guide to Canadian Novelists*, and *George Woodcock's Introduction to Canadian Fiction*. Author biographies, essays and literary criticism, and book reviews are among the database's offerings.

Literary Reference Center

EBSCO's Literary Reference Center (LRC) is a comprehensive full-text database designed primarily to help high school and undergraduate students in English and the humanities with homework and research assignments about literature. The database contains massive amounts of information from reference works, books, literary journals, and other materials, including more than 31,000 plot summaries, synopses, and overviews of literary works; almost 100,000 essays and articles of literary criticism; about 140,000 author biographies; more than 605,000 book reviews; and more than 5,200 author interviews. It also contains the entire contents of Salem Press's MagillOnLiterature Plus. Users can retrieve information by browsing a list of authors' names or titles of literary works; they can also use an advanced search engine to access information by numerous categories, including author name, gender, cultural identity, national identity, and the years in which he or she lived, or by literary title, character, locale, genre, and publication date. The Literary Reference Center also features a literary-historical time line, an encyclopedia of literature, and a glossary of literary terms.

MagillOnLiterature Plus

MagillOnLiterature Plus is a comprehensive, integrated literature database produced by Salem Press and available on the EBSCO*host* platform. The database contains the full text of essays in Salem's many literature-related reference works, including *Masterplots, Cyclopedia of World Authors, Cyclopedia of Literary Characters, Cyclopedia of Literary Places, Critical Survey of Long Fiction, Critical Survey of Short Fiction, World Philosophers and Their Works, Magill's Literary Annual*, and *Magill's Book Reviews*. Among its contents are articles on more than 35,000 literary works and more than 8,500 writers, poets, dramatists, essays, and philosophers, more than 1,000 images, and a glossary of more than 1,300 literary terms. The biographical essays include lists of authors' works and secondary bibliographies, and almost four hundred overview essays offer information about literary genres, time periods, and national literatures.

NoveList

NoveList is a readers' advisory service produced by EBSCO. The database provides access to 155,000 titles of both adult and juvenile fiction as well information about literary awards, book discussion guides, feature articles about a range of literary genres, and "recommended reads." Users can search by author name, book title, or series title or can describe the plot to retrieve the name of a book, information about the author, and book reviews; another search engine enables users to find titles similar to books they have enjoyed reading.

Rebecca Kuzins

CATEGORY INDEX

ADVENTURE NOVEL
    Dumas, Alexandre, *père*, 104
    Verne, Jules, 228
ALLEGORICAL NOVEL
    Camus, Albert, 66

BILDUNGSROMAN
    Sand, George, 203

EPISTOLARY NOVEL
    Rousseau, Jean-Jacques, 194
EXISTENTIALISM
    Beauvoir, Simone de, 56
    Camus, Albert, 66
    Sartre, Jean-Paul, 217

FANTASY
    France, Anatole, 119
    Green, Julien, 131
FASCISM
    Sartre, Jean-Paul, 217
FEMINIST NOVEL
    Sand, George, 203

GAY AND LESBIAN NOVEL
    Green, Julien, 131
    Proust, Marcel, 157
    Sartre, Jean-Paul, 217
GOTHIC NOVEL
    Hugo, Victor, 142

HISTORICAL NOVEL
    Dumas, Alexandre, *père*, 104
    Sand, George, 203

IMPRESSIONISM
    Proust, Marcel, 157

MODERNISM
    Proust, Marcel, 157

NOBEL PRIZE WINNERS
    Camus, Albert, 66
    France, Anatole, 119
    Sartre, Jean-Paul, 217

PHILOSOPHICAL NOVEL
    Balzac, Honoré de, 41
    Beauvoir, Simone de, 56
    Cyrano de Bergerac, 92
    Voltaire, 242
PICARESQUE NOVEL
    Voltaire, 242
POLITICAL NOVEL
    Beauvoir, Simone de, 56
PSYCHOLOGICAL NOVEL
    Cocteau, Jean, 82
PSYCHOLOGICAL REALISM
    Green, Julien, 131
    Proust, Marcel, 157

REALISM
    Balzac, Honoré de, 41
RELIGIOUS NOVEL
    Green, Julien, 131
ROMANTIC NOVEL
    Dumas, Alexandre, *père*, 104
    Hugo, Victor, 142
    Sand, George, 203

SATIRE AND BLACK HUMOR
    Cyrano de Bergerac, 92
    France, Anatole, 119
    Rabelais, François, 185
    Voltaire, 242

SCIENCE FICTION
    Verne, Jules, 228
SOCIAL ACTIVISM
    Hugo, Victor, 142
SURREALISM
    Cocteau, Jean, 82

UTOPIAN NOVEL
    Cyrano de Bergerac, 92

WIT AND HUMOR
    France, Anatole, 119
WOMEN AUTHORS
    Beauvoir, Simone de, 56
    Sand, George, 203
WORLD WAR II
    Beauvoir, Simone de, 56

SUBJECT INDEX

Adventure novels, 10, 33
   Alexandre Dumas, *père*, 112
   Jules Verne, 235
Aestheticism, 160
Algren, Nelson, 58
All Men Are Mortal (Beauvoir), 60
Allegory
   Albert Camus, 66
   Jean Cocteau, 88
   Cyrano de Bergerac, 96
   George Sand, 209
Angot, Christine, 39
Apollinaire, Guillaume, 85
Archetypes
   Jean Cocteau, 84
   Victor Hugo, 149
   Marcel Proust, 164
Aristophanes, 97
Aristotle, 250
Arouet, François-Marie. *See* Voltaire
Astrea (Urfé), 5
Atmosphere, 132
Auerbach, Erich, 4
Augustine, Saint, 196

Bakhtin, Mikhail, 187
Bakunin, Mikhail, 205
Balzac, Honoré de, 17, 21, 41-55, 161, 204
Barthes, Roland, 231
Battle of Pharsalus, The (Simon), 37
Baudelaire, Charles, 217
Beat generation, 219
Beauvoir, Simone de, 56-65
Beckett, Samuel, 173
Begum's Fortune, The (Verne), 238
Belghoul, Farida, 39
Belle époque, 28

Bergson, Henri, 159
Bernanos, Georges, 132
Biblical themes, 214
Bildungsromans, 15
   Albert Camus, 72
   Jean-Jacques Rousseau, 200
   George Sand, 210
Blood of Others, The (Beauvoir), 59
Bouraoui, Nina, 39
Bourgeois novel, 2, 45
Butor, Michel, 37, 231

Camus, Albert, 33, 66-81, 219
Candide (Voltaire), 9, 251
Captive, The (Proust), 174
Catholic themes
   Honoré de Balzac, 49
   Denis Diderot, 6
   Julien Green, 139
   George Sand, 213
   Voltaire, 254
Censorship, 7, 244
Chateaubriand, François-René de, 207
Children of the Game (Cocteau), 87
Cities of the Plain (Proust), 172
Classicism
   Jean Cocteau, 89
   Victor Hugo, 145
Closed Garden, The (Green)), 135
Cocteau, Jean, 82-91, 136
Colette, 28, 32
Comédie humaine, La. See Human Comedy, The
Constant, Benjamin, 14
Consuelo (Sand), 212
Contemporary History (France), 126
Corinne (Staël), 15

Corneille, Pierre, 92, 244
Count of Monte-Cristo, The (Dumas), 114
Counterfeiters, The (Gide), 29
Cousin Bette (Balzac), 52
Crime of Sylvestre Bonnard, The (France), 123
Cyrano de Bergerac, 92-103

Dangerous Liaisons (Laclos), 12
Dark Journey, The (Green)), 136
Delphine (Staël), 15
Descartes, René, 250
Despentes, Virginie, 39
Devil's Pool, The (Sand), 213
Dickens, Charles, 163
Didactic novels
    Simone de Beauvoir, 59
    Cyrano de Bergerac, 97
Diderot, Denis, 11, 242
Dostoevski, Fyodor, 205
Dumas, Alexandre, *fils*, 108
Dumas, Alexandre, *père*, 104-118, 144, 210, 229
Dupin, Amandine-Aurore-Lucille. *See* Sand, George
Duras, Marguerite, 36

Eliot, George, 205
Epistolary novels, 13, 15, 194
Eugénie Grandet (Balzac), 50
Existentialism
    Albert Camus, 68
    Jean-Paul Sartre, 217

Fall, The (Camus), 77
Fantastic, 4
    Honoré de Balzac, 45
    Alexandre Dumas, *père*, 108
    François Rabelais, 191
Fatal Skin, The. See *Wild Ass's Skin*

Feminist fiction, 207
Fin du Potomak, La (Cocteau), 89
Flashbacks, 59
Flaubert, Gustave, 21, 48, 160, 205, 217
France, Anatole, 109, 119-130, 159
French novel
    mid-nineteenth century and earlier, 1-20
    mid-nineteenth century and later, 21-40
French Revolution, 12

Gao Xingjian, 38
Gargantua (Rabelais), 189
Gargantua and Pantagruel (Rabelais), 3, 189
Gay and lesbian novels
    Julien Green, 139
    Marcel Proust, 161
    Jean-Paul Sartre, 223
Genet, Jean, 217
Gide, André, 28, 85
Gil Blas (Lesage), 10
Gods Are Athirst, The (France), 126
Gothic novel
    Honoré de Balzac, 42
    Julien Green, 132
    Victor Hugo, 149
    George Sand, 212
    Jules Verne, 238
Green, Julien, 131-141
Greggio, Simonetta, 39
Grotesque
    Julien Green, 137
    Victor Hugo, 143
    Voltaire, 247
Guermantes Way, The (Proust), 169

Hadrian's Memoirs (Yourcenar), 37
Hans of Iceland (Hugo), 149
Happy Death, A (Camus), 72
Heptameron, The (Navarre), 3

Subject Index

Historical novels
   Honoré de Balzac, 44
   Alexandre Dumas, *père*, 109
   Marguerite Yourcenar, 37
Hoffmann, E. T. A., 238
Horror fiction, 237
Houellebecq, Michel, 39
Hugo, Victor, 16, 142-156, 205, 232
Human Comedy, The (Balzac), 17, 44
Hume, David, 197
Hunchback of Notre Dame, The (Hugo), 16, 150
Huysmans, Joris-Karl, 26

Immoralist, The (Gide), 29
Impressionism, 160
Ingenuous (Voltaire), 253

James, Henry, 205
Jealousy (Robbe-Grillet), 36
Jeanne (Sand), 208
Journey to the Centre of the Earth, A (Verne), 235
Joyce, James, 158
Justine (Sade), 13

Künstlerroman, 27, 31

Là-Bas (Huysmans), 26
Laclos, Pierre Choderlos de, 12
La Fayette, Madame de, 8
Lamartine, Alphonse de, 196
Le Clézio, J. M. G., 39
Leibniz, Gottfried Wilhelm, 249
Les Belles Images (Beauvoir), 62
Les Misérables (Hugo), 151
Lesage, Alain-René, 10
Liaisons dangereuses, Les. See *Dangerous Liaisons*
Libertinism, 11, 94

Local color
   Jean Cocteau, 89
   Voltaire, 242
Locke, John, 250
Lorris, Guillaume de, 2
Louis Lambert (Balzac), 49
Lélia (Sand), 208

Madame Bovary (Flaubert), 23
Magic Skin, The. See *Wild Ass's Skin, The*
Malebranche, Nicolas, 250
Malraux, André, 33
Man Who Laughs, The (Hugo), 153
Man of Forty Crowns, The (Voltaire), 254
Mandarins, The (Beauvoir), 61
Mann, Thomas, 158
Manon Lescaut (Prévost), 10
Mauprat (Sand), 210
Mauriac, François, 132, 224
Memoirs of Hadrian. See *Hadrian's Memoirs*
Meung, Jean de, 2
Micromegas (Voltaire), 250
Modernism, 10
Moira (Green)), 139
Molière, 92
Motifs
   Jean Cocteau, 88
   Cyrano de Bergerac, 97
   Marcel Proust, 163
   George Sand, 211
Mysterious Island, The (Verne), 236

Nabokov, Vladimir, 165
Naturalism
   France, 25
   Émile Zola, 24
Nausea (Sartre), 34, 219
Navarre, Marguerite de, 3
Nerval, Gérard de, 107
New Héloïse, The (Rousseau), 12, 198

New Novel, 36
Ninety-three (Hugo), 153

O'Hara, John, 136
120 Days of Sodom, The (Sade), 13
Orwell, George, 220
Other Worlds (Cyrano de Bergerac), 96

Pantagruel (Rabelais), 190
Passos, John Dos, 225
Père Goriot (Balzac), 51
Philosophes
    and Cyrano de Bergerac, 96
    and the French novel, 6
    and Jean-Jacques Rousseau, 195
    and the thesis novel, 9
Philosophical novels, 7, 34
    Honoré de Balzac, 47
    Simone de Beauvoir, 58
    Albert Camus, 72
    Cyrano de Bergerac, 96
    Voltaire, 247
Picaros, 190
Plague, The (Camus), 74
Point of view
    Simone de Beauvoir, 61
    Anatole France, 124
    Marcel Proust, 163
Political novels, 59
Prévost, Abbé, 10
Princess of Clèves, The (La Fayette), 8
Proust, Marcel, 28, 85, 157-184, 196, 205

Rabelais, François, 3, 97, 185-193
Racine, Jean, 165, 244
Realism, 16, 21
    Albert Camus, 74
    Alexandre Dumas, *père*, 108
    Marcel Proust, 158
    Jean-Jacques Rousseau, 198

Red Lily, The (France), 128
Remembrance of Things Past (Proust), 30, 160
Richardson, Samuel, 252
Rilke, Rainer Maria, 85
Roads to Freedom, The (Sartre), 223
Robbe-Grillet, Alain, 36
Rolland, Romain, 28
Romance novels, 2
Romance of the Rose, The (Lorris), 2
Romanticism, 12
    Victor Hugo, 143
    Marcel Proust, 161
    George Sand, 207
    Jules Verne, 237
Rostand, Edmond, 85, 93
Rousseau, Jean-Jacques, 11, 194-202, 208
Ruskin, John, 157

Sade, Marquis de, 13
Saint-Exupéry, Antoine de, 32
Salinger, J. D., 87
Sand, George, 18, 203-216
Sarraute, Nathalie, 33
Sartre, Jean-Paul, 33, 57, 68, 217-227
Satire
    Albert Camus, 77
    Cyrano de Bergerac, 101
    François Rabelais, 188
    Voltaire, 247
Science fiction, 229
Scott, Sir Walter, 44
Senancour, Étienne de, 14
She Came to Stay (Beauvoir), 58
Simon, Claude, 37
Soul Mountain (Gao), 39
Staël, Madame de, 15
Stendhal, 18
Strange River, The (Green)), 137
Stranger, The (Camus), 35, 73

Surrealism, 82
Swann's Way (Proust), 162
Sweet Cheat Gone, The (Proust), 177
Swift, Jonathan, 94, 251
Symbolism, 161

Thaïs (France), 124
Three Musketeers, The (Dumas), 112
Time Regained (Proust), 180
Toilers of the Sea, The (Hugo), 152
Troyes, Chrétien de, 2
Turgenev, Ivan, 204
Twenty Thousand Leagues Under the Sea (Verne), 235
Twenty Years After (Dumas), 113

Urfé, Honoré d', 5

Valentine (Sand), 207
Vergil, 191
Verne, Jules, 86, 228-241
Vicar of Tours, The (Balzac), 48
Vicomte de Bragelonne, The (Dumas), 113
Vigny, Alfred de, 119, 144
Voltaire, 94, 242-258

Wells, H. G., 229
Wild Ass's Skin, The (Balzac), 47
Wilson, Edmund, 157
Within a Budding Grove (Proust), 166
Wolf, Friedrich August, 249
Woolf, Virginia, 158

Yourcenar, Marguerite, 37

Zadig (Voltaire), 248
Zola, Émile, 24